Leisure in the Time of Coronavirus

As the world grapples with the coronavirus (COVID-19) pandemic, on almost every news website, across social media, as well as in its (many) absences, leisure has taken on new significance in both managing and negotiating a global crisis.

Leisure in the Time of Coronavirus: A Rapid Response, amidst the disruption, inconvenience, illness, fear, uncertainty, tragedy, and loss from COVID-19, generates discussions that enable leisure scholars to learn and to engage with wider debates about the crucial role of leisure in people's lives. The pandemic has brought tourism to a standstill with borders closed and travel restricted. From home (for those fortunate enough to have them), in physical isolation, and in attempts to socialize, at no time in recent memory has leisure seemed so vital, and yet also so hauntingly absent. Leisure, therefore, remains an important lens through which to view, question, and understand the world.

The chapters in this book were originally published as a special issue of the journal, *Leisure Sciences*.

Brett Lashua lectures in Cultural Sociology at the Institute of Education at University College London, UK. His scholarship is concerned with social inequalities read through youth leisure, popular music, critical cultural heritage, and urban geographies, underpinned by a commitment to participatory arts-based research methods.

Corey W. Johnson is Professor at the University of Waterloo, Canada. His theorizing and qualitative inquiry focuses on the power relations between dominant (white, male, heterosexual, etc.) and non-dominant populations in the cultural contexts of leisure, providing important insight into both the privileging and discriminatory practices in contemporary settings.

Diana C. Parry is Professor in Recreation and Leisure Studies and Associate Vice-President of Human Rights, Equity, and Inclusion at the University of Waterloo, Canada. Diana's research utilizes a variety of feminist theories to explore the personal and political links between women's leisure and women's health, broadly defined.

Leisure in the Time of Coronavirus

A Rapid Response

Edited by
**Brett Lashua, Corey W. Johnson
and Diana C. Parry**

LONDON AND NEW YORK

First published 2022
by Routledge
4 Park Square, Milton Park, Abingdon, Oxon, OX14 4RN

and by Routledge
605 Third Avenue, New York, NY 10158

Routledge is an imprint of the Taylor & Francis Group, an informa business

© 2022 Taylor & Francis

British Library Cataloguing-in-Publication Data
A catalogue record for this book is available from the British Library

ISBN13: 978-0-367-70260-1 (hbk)
ISBN13: 978-0-367-70261-8 (pbk)
ISBN13: 978-1-003-14530-1 (ebk)

DOI: 10.4324/9781003145301

Typeset in Minion Pro
by codeMantra

Publisher's Note
The publisher accepts responsibility for any inconsistencies that may have arisen during the conversion of this book from journal articles to book chapters, namely the inclusion of journal terminology.

Disclaimer
Every effort has been made to contact copyright holders for their permission to reprint material in this book. The publishers would be grateful to hear from any copyright holder who is not here acknowledged and will undertake to rectify any errors or omissions in future editions of this book.

Contents

Citation Information

The chapters in this book were originally published in *Leisure Sciences*, volume 43, issue 1–2 (2021). When citing this material, please use the original page numbering for each article, as follows:

For any permission-related enquiries please visit:
http://www.tandfonline.com/page/help/permissions

Notes on Contributors

Austin R. Anderson Department of Kinesiology, Health Promotion and Recreation; University of North Texas; Denton, USA.

Jack Black Academy of Sport and Physical Activity, Sheffield Hallam University, UK.

Alexander John Bond Centre for Social Justice in Sport & Society, Carnegie School of Sport, Leeds Beckett University, UK.

Shamaya Bowen School of Journalism & Media Studies, San Diego State University, USA.

Aishia Brown Department of Health Promotion & Behavioral Sciences, University of Louisville, USA.

Brooke N. Burk Recreation, Parks and Leisure Services; Minnesota State University, Mankato, USA.

David Cockayne Centre for Sport Business, University of Liverpool Management School, University of Liverpool, UK.

Bram Constandt Department of Movement and Sports Sciences, Ghent University, Belgium.

Matt Coward-Gibbs Department of Sociology, University of York, UK.

Karen Davies Tourism, Hospitality and Events, Welsh Centre for Tourism Research, Cardiff Metropolitan University, UK.

Frédéric Dimanche Ryerson University, Ted Rogers School of Hospitality and Tourism Management, Toronto, Canada.

Marko Djurdjić Department of Cinema and Media Arts, School of the Arts, Media, Performance & Design, York University, Toronto, Canada.

Daniel Dustin Department of Parks, Recreation, and Tourism; University of Utah, Salt Lake City, USA.

Gwyn Easterbrook-Smith School of English and Media Studies, Massey University, Wellington, New Zealand.

Karen M. Fox Faculty of Kinesiology, Sport, & Recreation, University of Alberta, Edmonton, Canada.

Simone Fullagar Department of Tourism, Sport and Hotel Management, Griffith University, Australia.

Myra Gayle Gabriel Independent Scholar, Atlanta, USA.

Sean Gammon Lancashire School of Business and Enterprise, University of Central Lancashire, Preston, UK.

Justin R. Garcia The Kinsey Institute, Indiana University, Bloomington, USA; Department of Gender Studies, Indiana University, Bloomington, USA.

Amanda N. Gesselman The Kinsey Institute, Indiana University, Bloomington, USA.

Audrey R. Giles School of Human Kinetics, University of Ottawa, Canada.

Troy D. Glover Recreation & Leisure Studies, University of Waterloo, Canada.

Jasmine Goodnow Department of Health and Human Development, Western Washington University, Bellingham, USA.

Mora Greer Arts for Incarcerated Youth Network, Los Angeles, USA.

Bryan S. R. Grimwood Department of Recreation and Leisure Studies, University of Waterloo, Canada.

Jack Harper Faculty of Kinesiology and Recreation Management, University of Manitoba, Winnipeg, Canada.

Mark Havitz University of Waterloo, Recreation and Leisure Studies, Southampton, Canada.

Shannon Hebblethwaite Department of Applied Human Sciences, Concordia University, Montreal, Canada.

Megan C. Janke Recreation Sciences, East Carolina University, Greenville, USA.

Corey W. Johnson Department of Recreation and Leisure Studies, University of Waterloo, Canada.

Eric Knee Department of Health & Sport Sciences, Adelphi University, USA.

Brian E. Kumm Recreation Management and Therapeutic Recreation, University of Wisconsin–La Crosse, USA.

Erik L. Lachance School of Human Kinetics, Faculty of Health Sciences, University of Ottawa, Canada.

Gene Lamke Emeritus, San Diego State University, USA.

Brett Lashua Department of Education, Practice and Society, University College London, UK.

Eric T. Lehman Department of Canadian Studies, Trent University, Peterborough, Canada.

Justin J. Lehmiller The Kinsey Institute, Indiana University, Bloomington, USA.

Maria León Department of Recreation, Park & Tourism Sciences; Texas A&M University, College Station, USA.

Toni Liechty Recreation, Sport & Tourism, University of Illinois at Urbana-Champaign, USA.

Shana MacDonald Communication Arts, University of Waterloo, Canada.

Susan Houge Mackenzie Department of Tourism, University of Otago, Dunedin, New Zealand.

Kristen P. Mark The Kinsey Institute, Indiana University, Bloomington, USA; Department of Kinesiology & Health Promotion, University of Kentucky, Lexington, USA.

Tristana Martin Rubio Department of Philosophy, Duquesne University, Pittsburgh, USA.

Rebecca Mayers School of Community and Regional Planning, University of British Columbia, Vancouver, Canada.

Lisa McDermott Faculty of Kinesiology, Sport, & Recreation, University of Alberta, Edmonton, Canada.

Cary McDonald Emeritus, University of Illinois, Champaign, USA.

Brad A. Meisner School of Kinesiology & Health Science, York University, Toronto, Canada.

Rasul A. Mowatt American Studies & Recreation, Park and Tourism Studies, Bloomington Indiana University, USA.

Utsa Mukherjee Department of Geography, Birkbeck University of London, UK.

James Murphy Emeritus, San Francisco State University, USA.

Jill J. Naar Hart School of Hospitality, Sport and Recreation Management, Appalachian State University, USA.

Galit Nimrod Communication Studies, Ben Gurion University of the Negev, Beer Sheva, Israel.

Linda Oakleaf Health, Physical Education, and Recreation; Missouri Western State University; Saint Joseph, USA.

Jacquelyn Oncescu Faculty of Kinesiology, University of New Brunswick, Fredericton, Canada.

Corliss Outley Department of Parks, Recreation and Tourism Management, Clemson University, USA.

Karen Paisley Parks, Recreation, and Tourism; University of Utah; Salt Lake City; USA.

Bonnie Pang Carnegie School of Sport, Leeds Beckett University, UK; School of Health Science, Institute for Culture and Society, Western Sydney University, Australia.

Daniel Parnell Centre for Sport Business, University of Liverpool Management School, University of Liverpool, UK.

Diana C. Parry Department of Recreation and Leisure Studies, University of Waterloo, Canada.

Joseph A. Pate Outdoor Leadership, Young Harris College, USA.

Adele Pavlidis Centre for Social and Cultural Research, Griffith University, Australia.

Anna Pechenik Mausolf Recreation, Park and Tourism Sciences; Texas A&M University, College Station, USA.

Matthew E. Perks Sociology & Legal Studies, University of Waterloo, Canada.

Jonathan Petrychyn Department of Recreation and Leisure Studies, University of Waterloo, Canada.

Harrison Pinckney Department of Parks, Recreation and Tourism Management, Clemson University, USA.

Mark P. Pritchard Central Washington University, College of Business, Ellensburg, USA.

Brandy N. Kelly Pryor Department of Health Promotion and Behavior Sciences, School of Public Health and Information Sciences, University of Louisville, USA.

Gregory Ramshaw Parks, Recreation and Tourism Management, Clemson University, USA.

Kyle Rich Department of Recreation and Leisure Studies, Brock University, St. Catharines, Canada.

Kevin Rodas Arts for Incarcerated Youth Network, Los Angeles, USA.

Jeff Rose Department of Parks, Recreation, and Tourism; University of Utah, Salt Lake City, USA.

Diane M. Samdahl Independent Researcher.

Callie S. Schultz Western Carolina University, Cullowhee, USA.

Brian Simpson Former Professor, School of Law, University of New England, Armidale, Australia.

Julie S. Son Movement Sciences, University of Idaho, Moscow, USA.

Terah J. Stewart School of Education, College of Human Sciences, Iowa State University, Ames, USA.

Monika Stodolska Department of Recreation, Sport and Tourism, University of Illinois, Champaign, USA.

Stephanie T. West James Madison University, Harrisonburg, USA.

Paul Widdop Manchester Metropolitan Institute of Sport, Manchester Metropolitan University, UK.

Annick Willem Department of Movement and Sports Sciences, Ghent University, Belgium.

D J Williams Center for Positive Sexuality (Los Angeles), USA; Department of Sociology, Idaho State University, Pocatello, USA.

Brett Wright Department of Parks, Recreation and Tourism Management, Clemson University, USA.

Laurel Young Creative Arts Therapies Department, Concordia University, Montreal, Canada.

Felice Yuen Concordia University, Montreal, Canada.

Introduction

Leisure in the Time of Coronavirus: A Rapid Response Special Issue

Brett Lashua, Corey W. Johnson, and Diana C. Parry

ABSTRACT

As the world grapples with the coronavirus (COVID-19) pandemic, on almost every news website, across social media, and also in its (many) absences, leisure has taken on new significance in both managing and negotiating a global crisis. Amidst the disruption, inconvenience, illness, fear, uncertainty, tragedy and loss from this disease, there are also opportunities for leisure scholars to generate discussions and to learn, to engage with wider debates about the crucial role of leisure in people's lives—during this pandemic, and beyond. This introduction lays out the foundations and scope of this special issue on leisure in the time of coronavirus.

As we write this introduction at the end of May 2020, the COVID-19 (severe acute respiratory syndrome coronavirus 2, or SARS-CoV-2) pandemic has claimed the lives of over 300,000 people and more than 5 million people have been infected worldwide. In attempts to contain the spread of COVID-19 and increase the safety of citizens, many countries have enforced lockdowns – although some have now begun to ease restrictions – requiring people "stay home" to "stay safe." As we have worked on this special issue, over half of the world has been living with some form of lockdown and "social" (physical) distancing: schools have been closed for most students, and where feasible, people have been asked to work from home; many workers have been furloughed, or have found themselves suddenly unemployed. At great risk to themselves and their families, many in health care have been working relentlessly to save lives, while legions have provided essential services, such as keeping public transport running, making deliveries, or ensuring there is food in supermarkets. In a matter of just a few months, COVID-19 has inescapably transformed the world.

Where lockdowns are in effect, almost all leisure spaces outside the home – restaurants, pubs, bars and nightclubs, leisure centers and gyms, arts venues, theaters, cinemas, museums and galleries – have been closed; most sports events have been canceled and the 2020 Olympic Games postponed for the first time in modern history. Parks, beaches and monuments have been closed, too (and others have re-opened too soon). Tourism is at a standstill, with borders closed and travel restricted. From home (for those fortunate enough to have them), in physical isolation, and in attempts to socialize, at no time in recent memory has leisure seemed so vital, and yet also so hauntingly absent.

"May you live in interesting times"?

Although it sounds like a blessing, the phrase "may you live in interesting times" is always used with irony: it is understood that uninteresting times are preferable to "interesting" ones, which are usually times of great hardships. These are, in every mordant sense of the phrase, *interesting times*. Unprecedented times. Challenging times. Scoundrel times, too, adapting a title from the playwright Lilian Hellman (1976), in view of the delays and failings of some governments during this pandemic (Glanz & Robertson, 2020; Scally et al., 2020).

These are also important times to pause, reflect, rethink, and learn – an "awakening of consciousness" (Bourdieu & Wacquant, 1992, p. 133) – to imagine a different world. We recognize, as the poet, novelist and psychologist Hala Alyan (2020) reminds us, that questions such as "what good can come of this?" are questions of the lucky, of the privileged. Yet, amidst the loss, grief and trauma of COVID-19, can the world be made anew? "What good?" Alyan repeats, again and again. Environmental activists such as Greta Thunberg, David Attenborough, and George Monbiot have called this "a time to rethink everything"; for Monbiot (2020) this could be a "a Great Reset. Let's use it to change the way we see ourselves and our place on Earth." Writing for the BBC, Syed (2020) noted one "upside to all this downtime" was the opportunity "to reimagine the world and one's place within it," using the pandemic as a kind of "reversal technique" to imagine new ideas and opportunities: was the leisure that many people had really what people wanted or needed? As many of the commentaries in this special issue convey, the pandemic has brought a re-appraisal of many leisure practices that were uncritically accepted, environmentally unsustainable, or systemically oppressive during "normal times." Contributors also highlight new, creative re-imaginings of leisure in response to the vicissitudes of physical distancing and enforced stay-at-home orders, and the innovative leisure affordances of online, virtual, digital spaces.

The pandemic has brought increased attention to many often-overlooked significances of leisure in everyday life, including those practices which may be referred to as a kind of slow leisure (Andrews, 2006). Examples abound, and some may have become familiar as "magnified moments" (Hochschild, 1994, p. 4) that are, perhaps, emblematic stories[1] of the lockdown: from children's hand-drawn rainbows displayed in windows with the phrase "everything will be alright" ("*andrà tutto bene*" in Italian; Otte, 2020), to balcony concerts (Clinch, 2020), shared TikTok dance videos (Awha, 2020), backyard marathons (Farzan, 2020), birthday parades (Picard, 2020), Teddy Bear hunts (New Zealand Bear Hunt, 2020), home workouts (Wicks, 2020), and widespread volunteering to help neighbors. The critical commentaries in this special issue also explore online get-togethers,

---

[1]Hochschild (1994, p. 4) explained: "Stories contain magnified moments, episodes of heightened importance, either epiphanies, moments of intense glee or unusual insight, or moments in which things go intensely but meaningfully wrong. In either case, the moment stands out; it is metaphorically rich, unusually elaborate and often echoes throughout" the story.

social media use, digital games and other forms of virtual play that have seen dramatically increased participation. At the same time, older pastimes such as board games and jigsaw puzzles (Butler, 2020), sewing (Smart, 2020) and home baking (Morton, 2020) have also seen renewed interest, too. These examples only begin to intone some of the immediate and often creative leisure adaptations and responses to the current moment.

The pandemic also has exposed persistent and vexing social problems that have been exacerbated during this crisis. These are also (often) manifest as questions of leisure, including matters of privilege and social inequalities (e.g., those escaping crowded cities to 2nd homes in rural areas; Ibraham, 2020); the absence of leisure for homeless people who cannot "stay home" to stay safe (Levin, 2020); the lack of spaces for children to play while confined in inadequate housing (Rosenthal et al., 2020), alarming increases of domestic violence during lockdown (Taub, 2020); the stark inequities of work and leisure at home especially for those who identify as women who are caregivers or are home-schooling their children (Fazackerley, 2020); the utter absence of leisure for those restricted to refugee camps or migrant detention centers (Strauss & Zander, 2020); and in view of public leisure spaces, there is also increased xenophobia and racist violence (e.g. toward members of east Asian communities; e.g., Tavernise & Oppel, 2020). For many, this moment is a double crisis, or worse, where coronavirus has compounded already difficult circumstances. Many of these issues are addressed by authors in this special issue, particularly in relation to identity politics, social inequalities and inequities.

Additionally, the pandemic has laid bare a number of difficult truths about leisure in contemporary, neoliberal societies. Neoliberalism is characterized by the marketization and commoditization of everyday life, the primacy of the individual, the accumulation of private capital and private property, in which the State protects markets and private property, but otherwise does not intervene, such as in the social welfare or healthcare of citizens (Harvey, 2005). The COVID-19 pandemic has demanded large-scale State (and supra-national) interventions, affordable public healthcare systems, far-reaching unemployment and welfare benefits (stimulus packages) and an economic shutdown. Neoliberal ideologies of the failed or "flawed" citizen (Bauman, 1998, p.1) as one who cannot consume unravels and frays when most commercial leisure spaces (shops and shopping centers, restaurants and bars, gyms and fitness clubs, professional sports venues, etc.) are closed. The COVID-19 crisis presents a moment to raise questions of shifting priorities toward greater collective social responsibilities, mutual interdependencies, shared resources, and collaborative approaches to social problems. Recent public polling has suggested that a majority of Britons (8 out of 10) want the government to prioritize health and wellbeing over economic measurements as indicators of quality of life (Harvey, 2020). Announcing the publication of the *World Happiness Report* (Helliwell et al., 2020), one of its authors exclaimed: "To get through this [COVID-19] we're going to have to develop a much higher level of social responsibility [and] move from an atomised society to a much more caring one" while adding: "Happiness is contagious too" (Moorhead, 2020).

Many of our contributing authors explore possible post-coronavirus leisure futures. Mair (2020) argued that an entirely "different mindset" in needed from neoliberalism: "Coronavirus, like climate change, is partly a problem of our economic structure. Although both appear to be 'environmental' or 'natural' problems, they are socially driven" and thus demand social solutions. Some solutions centralize leisure, such as shortening the working week, as well as some form of Universal Basic Income (Lashua, 2018). Some of our authors have written about the pandemic as a vital moment of leisure to pause, to stop, and to grieve. Amidst difficult lessons about "grief, empathy, and hope", for Alyan (2020, para. 14), "[t]his pandemic seems to have at its core a lesson of kinship. What do we owe each other? What do we owe strangers on the other side of the world? *Pull a thread here and you'll find it's attached to the rest of the world.*" We hope that this special issue represents such core lessons and plucks at such threads.

Leisure sciences in the time of coronavirus – and beyond

We remain acutely aware that these are complicated, disrupted, and difficult moments for scholars, too. We received some criticism, on social media and in personal correspondence, regarding the call for abstracts for this special issue. Is a "rapid response" special issue a form of hurried, smash-and-grab scholarship? We certainly do not think so, but we will let the commentaries speak for themselves. Some colleagues on Twitter raised concerns about "journalistic" outputs, and also questioned the abbreviated timelines for the special issue. In view of the former, we have invited scholarly short essays – "critical commentaries" – a standard academic format, that, once again, we will let speak for themselves. If journalistic in any sense, we sought only to invite commentaries that connect, highlight, or critique the relevance of leisure scholarship in the current moment; that is, to write with and through the pandemic as it is being discussed and debated on social media and in the news. Journalistic accusations aside, each commentary was peer-reviewed by two or more scholars.

A few were against a special issue in the midst of a pandemic; there will, no doubt, be volumes published about this crisis for years to come, and we will welcome those. However, at no other time in recent memory can we recall a moment when leisure has seemed both as utterly important, and yet so dramatically diminished. As Ken Roberts (2020) wrote in a recent blog for the Leisure Studies Association, the voices of leisure scholars are utterly vital at this moment, noting "this is a once in a lifetime moment when leisure's voice must speak loudly." We agree wholeheartedly, and add that "leisure's voice" is a diverse chorus, polyvocal and polyphonic – at times dissonant, too. This special issue is just one collection, in what we hope, like Roberts, is part of a loud and strong set of voices that will continue to speak of the importance of leisure.

We are grateful for the voices of all the authors, including those who submitted over 150 abstracts for initial consideration, and especially those who produced commentaries (all of whom agreed to review essays too). We owe particular thanks to the *Leisure Sciences* editorial assistant, Chris Hurst, a PhD student at the University of Waterloo, for her outstanding work and superlative organization in managing all phases of this special issue. We would also like to acknowledge Taylor and Francis for their continued support of our requests to do publishing differently, specifically Katie Gezi and Jacqueline Carrick. We have been humbled by the unwavering efforts and enthusiasm from everyone who has been involved, throughout.

We also have been heartened by the diversity of topics and contributors. Such diversity has been a core value for *Leisure Sciences* during Corey and Diana's tenure as Co-Editors. In this regard, we note that more than half (55%) of the contributing authors identify as women and 45% as men. We have had global participation, although highly Western representation, with scholars from Canada (37%), USA (39%), UK (13%), Australia (4.5%), New Zealand (4.5%), and Belgium (2%). The special issue includes voices from White, Black and Asian perspectives. It also transects academic ranks, with contributions from PhD students, post-doctoral fellows, lecturers and assistant professors, associate professors and senior lecturers, senior research fellows, professors and retired professors. Commentary topics also encompass much of the breadth of the leisure studies field, spotlighting recreation, sport, tourism, sociology, kinesiology, health, media, music, therapeutic recreation, youth development and higher education. Even with 46 essays, this special double issue offers just a snapshot of leisure in this moment. We acknowledge that there are gaps and omissions: Indigenous voices in particular are not present in this collection, amongst other important critical views. There is yet more work to do, for greater diversity, and toward internationalizing the journal.

Above all, we are reminded that leisure remains an important lens through which to view, question, debate and understand the world. There is no doubt that the COVID-19 pandemic has had immeasurable health and economic impacts; equally, there have been enormous social and political impacts too, with waves and ripples to resound for some time to come. As an interdisciplinary journal, *Leisure Sciences* provides a space for critical scholarship that spans these impacts, particularly during such unprecedented and distressingly *interesting* times.

References

Alyan, H. (2020). This in not a rehearsal. *Emergence Magazine*. https://emergencemagazine.org/story/this-is-not-a-rehearsal/

Andrews, C. (2006). Slow is beautiful: new visions of community, leisure, and joie de vivre. New Society Publishers.

Bourdieu, P., and Wacquant, L. J. (1992). An invitation to reflexive sociology. University of Chicago Press.

Awha, D. (2020, April 5). The best TikTok dances to learn during lockdown. *Viva Magazine*. https://www.viva.co.nz/article/stayhome/the-best-tiktok-dance-challenges-to-learn/

Bauman, Z. (1998). *Work, Consumerism and the New Poor*. Open University Press.

Butler, S. (2020, April 1). Sales of board games and jigsaws soar during coronavirus lockdown. *The Guardian*. https://www.theguardian.com/business/2020/apr/01/sales-of-board-games-and-jigsaws-soar-during-coronavirus-lockdown

Clinch, M. (2020, March 14). Italians are singing songs from their windows to boost morale during coronavirus lockdown. *CNBC*. https://www.cnbc.com/2020/03/14/coronavirus-lockdown-italians-are-singing-songs-from-balconies.html

Farzan, A. N. (2020, April 2). A British man ran a marathon in his 20-foot backyard during the coronavirus lockdown — and thousands tuned in. *The Washington Post*. https://www.washingtonpost.com/nation/2020/04/02/backyard-marathon-coronavirus/

Fazackerley, A. (2020, May 12) Women's research plummets during lockdown - but articles from men increase. *The Guardian*. https://www.theguardian.com/education/2020/may/12/womens-research-plummets-during-lockdown-but-articles-from-men-increase?CMP=Share_iOSApp_Other

Glanz, J., Robertson, C. (2020, May 20). Lockdown delays cost at least 36,000 lives, data show. *The New York Times*. https://www.nytimes.com/2020/05/20/us/coronavirus-distancing-deaths.html

Harvey, F. (2020, May 10). Britons want quality of life indicators to take priority over economy. *The Guardian*. https://www.theguardian.com/society/2020/may/10/britons-want-quality-of-life-indicators-priority-over-economy-coronavirus

Harvey, D. (2005). *A Brief History of Neoliberalism*. Oxford University Press.

Helliwell, J. F., Layard, R., Sachs, J. D. and De Neve, J. E. (Eds.). (2020). *World Happiness Report.* Sustainable Development Solutions Network

Hellman, L. (1976). *Scoundrel times.* Little Brown & Co.

Hochschild, A. R. (1994). The commercial spirit of intimate life and the abduction of feminism: Signs from women's advice books. *Theory, Culture & Society, 11*(2), 1–24. https://doi.org/10.1177/026327694011002001

Ibraham, H. (2020, April 5). 'There are risks" to going to rural areas and cottages, chief medical officer says. *CBC News.* https://www.cbc.ca/news/canada/new-brunswick/cottage-covid-19-summer-home-camp-grand-lake-kingston-peninsula-1.5522107

Lashua, B. D. (2018). The Time Machine: Leisure Science (Fiction) and Futurology. *Leisure Sciences, 40*(1-2), 85–94. https://doi.org/10.1080/01490400.2017.1376015

Levin, D. (2020, March 31). Las Vegas places homeless people in a parking lot, 6 feet apart. *The New York Times.* https://www.nytimes.com/2020/03/31/us/las-vegas-coronavirus-homeless-parking-lot.html

Mair, S. (2020, March 30). What will the world be like after coronavirus? Four possible futures. *The Conversation.* https://theconversation.com/what-will-the-world-be-like-after-coronavirus-four-possible-futures-134085

Monbiot, G. (2020, May 12). Coronavirus shows us it's time to rethink everything. Let's start with education. *The Guardian.* https://www.theguardian.com/commentisfree/2020/may/12/coronavirus-education-pandemic-natural-world-ecology

Moorhead, J. (2020, March 20). 'Happiness is contagious too': Caring for each other makes us feel better – experts. *The Guardian.* https://www.theguardian.com/society/2020/mar/20/happiness-is-contagious-too-caring-for-each-other-makes-us-feel-better-experts

Morton, B. (2020, April 9). Coronavirus: Flour mills working 'round the clock' to meet demand. *BBC News.* https://www.bbc.co.uk/news/uk-52212760

New Zealand Bear Hunt. (2020). New Zealand Bear Hunt. https://bearhunt.co.nz

Otte, J. (2020, March 12). 'Everything will be all right': message of hope spreads in Italy. *The Guardian.* https://www.theguardian.com/world/2020/mar/12/everything-will-be-alright-italians-share-slogan-of-hope-in-face-of-coronavirus-crisis

Picard, L. (2020, April 29). Why it's important to celebrate kids' birthdays during a pandemic — and how to do it. *The Washington Post.* https://www.washingtonpost.com/lifestyle/2020/04/29/why-its-important-celebrate-kids-birthdays-during-pandemic-how-do-it/

Roberts, K. (2020, April 27). Leisure and the Pandemic. *Leisure Studies Association.* http://leisurestudies.org/leisure-and-the-pandemic/

Rosenthal, D. M., Ucci, M., Heys, M., Hayward, A., Lakhanpaul, M. (2020). Impacts of COVID-19 on vulnerable children in temporary accommodation in the UK. *The Lancet, 5*(5), E241–E242. https://doi.org/10.1016/S2468-2667(20)30080-3

Scally, G., Jacobson, B., & Abbas, K. (2020). The UK's public health response to covid-19: Too little, too late, too flawed. *The BMJ, 369*, 1–3. https://doi.org/10.1136/bmj.m1932

Smart, A. (2020, March 13). Sewing in Times of Uncertainty. *Diary of a quilter.* https://www.diaryofaquilter.com/2020/03/sewing-in-times-of-uncertainty.html

Strauss, M., Zander, M. (2020, March 20). Coronavirus strands refugee children. *DW News.* https://p.dw.com/p/3ZoSI

Syed, M. (2020, 3 March). Coronavirus: The good that can come out of an upside-down world. *BBC News.* https://www.bbc.co.uk/news/world-us-canada-52094332

Tavernise, S., & Oppel, R. A. (2020, March 23) Spit on, yelled at, attacked: Chinese-Americans fear for their safety. *The New York Times.* https://www.nytimes.com/2020/03/23/us/chinese-coronavirus-racist-attacks.html

Taub, A. (2020, April 6). A new Covid-19 crisis: Domestic abuse rises worldwide. *The New York Times.* https://www.nytimes.com/2020/04/06/world/coronavirus-domestic-violence.html

Wicks, J. (2020, *The Body Coach* [video channel]. YouTube. https://www.youtube.com/channel/UCAxW1XT0iEJo0TYlRfn6rYQ

Color-Coded Activity Charts and Beachbody: "Momming" in COVID-19

Callie S. Schultz 🆔, Linda Oakleaf, and Karen Paisley

ABSTRACT
This piece is an invitation.
Our work consists of poetry by three moms, writing in the middle of a global pandemic about the realities of "momming" in these times. Why poems? We want the article to be short and digestible while also expressing the complexity and individuality of our lived experiences. Also, through poetry, we can invite you to bring your own story as you make meaning. In the poems, we struggle with ideas including discipline, "being enough," and the fact that things are fucked up. We are also left with the nagging question, "What leisure can we have on a regular day, much less in the midst of a pandemic?"

That time we had to mom in a pandemic...

Headlines read: "The virus doesn't discriminate"
Bullshit.

Juggling identities: Queer mom. Single mom. Het mom. We are bounded/unbounded by our place in this world.
Women's bodies sacrificed first. (And let's be honest, black and brown women and men and poor folks die in higher numbers.)
Nurses, bank tellers, supermarket checkers: predominantly women.
Inequities exacerbated. Pressure. Carry it.
Homeschool, craft projects, entertain, clean, cook, elder care, oh, and work full time (if you're lucky).

COVID-19; shit is going down. Shit's changing. My. Body. My. Mind. My. Labor. My. Leisure. Disciplined.

Shit's the same. The same shit. Surveillance, perfection. Driving self-discipline, disciplining me, power-over.

I am mom.

Facebook feed with color-coded schedules, picture perfect crafts, homeschool "tips." "You Should!" "Try This!" Perfect mom.

I am woman (mom).

Trapped inside? Beachbody! Buy it! I'm your mom friend. Watch me exercise; pushups with my kiddo. YOU can have it all, too! My before and after photo! [chili pepper emoji].
I am academic (mom).

Me: Scrolling on FB … while trying to write this paper.

Scroll … .stop! Colleague with no children: "Revised three manuscripts today. This slow-down was just what I needed to catch up on my research. #staypositiveandproductive"
4-year-old: "Mom!!!!!!! I dumped out all the paint we have to make tie-dye, but it is just making brown paint. Help me!!!"
3-year-old: "Mom!!!!!!!!!!! I pooped!!!"

Emotional labor. Supporting students. "Trauma-informed teaching?" "Pandemic pedagogy?" Do and be all for everyone. Now.

I am me (mom).
For my leisure I …?

That time that we were disciplined (like usual but more) …

"Discipline 'makes' individuals; it is the specific technique of a power that regards individuals both as objects and as instruments of its exercise. It is not a triumphant power … it is a modest, suspicious power, which functions as a calculated, but permanent economy." (Foucault, 1979/1995)

Global economies tanking.
The economy of disciplining women and "mom" to play a value-driven role? Thriving. Permanent.

We actively participate in this economy.
In our own subordination: Discipline our bodies, our emotions, our thoughts and souls.

In this pandemic pause, this discipline is magnified "in yo face" pressure;
It goes like this: "Oh no! There are no more rules. This feels super uncomfortable, unstable. We better enforce the old ones HARD or we risk a new normal with new rules .... and that's .... scary"
It looks like this:

> Dress up to take out the trash.
> Hair and make-up on point for those Zoom calls.
> Be a perfect mom: bake bread, teach children, follow AAP guidelines for screen-time.
> Get that fitness app; you'll emerge from COVID sexier!
> Fluff your space! House and yard projects are social distancing approved!

When we feel shaky, we try and stand on "solid ground:" stuff we know, the seductive comfort of old habits. Neoliberal capitalism ... Shopping Target app while I pee .... Ahhhh. We desire *normal.* Even if it means embracing the old, inequitable status quo.

Instead, let's ask ourselves @matisse.dupont's four questions.
They challenge us, *move* us, shake us and strip us bare.
These questions unveil our own embrace of the (gendered) discipline Foucault (1979/ 1995) aptly names.
Answers can break.make.strengthen.stop.*free* us:

SOME GENDER QUESTIONS
YOU COULD ASK YOURSELF

WHY ARE YOU PERFORMING
GENDERED HABITS WHILE STAYING
HOME AND SOCIAL DISTANCING?

WHICH GENDERED HABITS HAVE
YOU DROPPED NOW THAT SOCIETY
IS LESS PHYSICALLY OMNIPRESENT?

WHAT GENDERED HABITS HAVE YOU
TAKEN UP SINCE THE INCREASE OF
TIME SPENT IN VIRTUAL SPACES?

WHO ARE THESE CHANGES FOR?
HOW DO YOU KNOW?

The poems we share below are potions (healing, changing, thinking, making, laughing, breaking)
Questions (and some answers) we ask ourselves and you as we collectively make sense of and explore possibilities of *this* (time, space, place)

Mom Profiles:

All About [Callie]:	All About [Karen]:	All About [Linda]:

All About [Callie]:

Kids: 2, ages 3 & 4
Relationship status: Married to a man
Favorite "me" time activity: Pedicures, shopping, snowboarding
3 words to describe motherhood: Controlled-ish Chaos. Beautiful.

All About [Karen]:

Kids: 1, age 14
Relationship status: single
Favorite "me" time activity: I can't remember …
3 words to describe motherhood: Important. Intimidating. Shenanigans.

All About [Linda]:

Kids: One shark, one red panda. Twins. Age 7.
Relationship status: Married to a woman.
Favorite "me" time activity: Camping by myself (which I no longer get to do).
3 words to describe motherhood: Busy. Expensive. Fun.

That time I tried to Marie Kondo my closet during COVID-19 …
-Callie

"The coronavirus hasn't dimmed Marie Kondo's joy."
 – Ann Quito, *Quartz Magazine*, 2020

"Buy this, buy that, 'elevate' your McMansion" they say
No! "Tiny homes, Marie Kondo, minimalism's the way."
Renovate, repurpose, flip, make the old new,
Get that granite, quartz, and stainless steel too!
Move to a rural town in the south and then …
For $45,000, farmhouse perfect, JoJo, and Erin!

But why are we hooked on the "improvement" storyline?
Is it the "Merican dream picket fence" or "perfect couple" we pine?
For HGTV junkies like me,
"Fluff your nest—perfect life. You can do it! Believe!"

I'm stuck at home; obviously this is the time,
To Marie Kondo my closet; simplify my design.
Before I tell you the result of this feat, I've …
Gotta acknowledge my white privilege
Three piles of stuff: "Keep," "Donate," or "Sell"
The phrase "tidying up" seems trite as hell.
I mean, folks are dying, and I'm worried about my excess of stuff
Sick parallel: privilege decides who gets ventilators and who's sluffed

I google "Marie Kondo" and first thing comes up, I scream profane:
"Working from home? Five tips from Marie to stay productive and sane"
Create "joy at work." Organize. Makes me think, of insidehighered's #career advice:
Women: wash hair, hide piles of laundry; look put together no matter the price[1]!

It's 9:00, my kids are finally asleep.
"Me time;" 30 minutes before I pass out, exhausted heap.
I want to lie down, but my list is so long,
Maybe if I "organize myself" tomorrow won't go so wrong.
Happy cogs in the machine, aren't we?
Happiness exists in productivity.
So here I am glassy-eyed staring at my closet as I do hangry at my fridge.
I grab a shirt, ask, "Does this spark joy?" Maybe a smidge … ?

That time I made my son cry …
-Linda

I am an educator, right?
Explain why my 7-year-old is crying.
I don't make college students cry.
Much.
Unless that's just behind my back and not in my face.

At the back of my mind,
I think about the papers
I haven't graded.
We'll all be crying soon, if ever I get a moment
To do my job(s).
What's my job again? Educator, right?

That time I lost my shit on the Missionaries …
-Karen

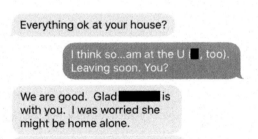

Salt Lake City.
Home of cultural Mormonism.
As an outsider
I see perfect
Women. Wives. Homes.
I know it's not fair
to them or me.
I am none of these.

---

[1] Isis the Scientist (2020)

Divorced. Working. Dusty shelves. Take-out.

I sense [imagine?] judgment.
Take the private school, stay-at-home, yoga pants, new SUV, tanned Alpha Mom
add Jesus
stir.

Text from Xena, Warrior Mom:

Is your precious, perfect, blameless, and reason for living child OK?

You thoughtlessly left her weeping at home alone after the earthquake this morning to
selfishly pursue your ego-driven career.

Might I rush in and bring her a care package of still-warm cookies, a soothing lavender-
scented candle tin, and a handwritten letter from my cherub to cheer and calm her
forgotten and lonely self? [worried emoji]

I think, Fuck. Off.
I write, I was home. She's fine. Thanks so much! [smiley emoji]
And I gag a bit as I tap send.
I worry I am not enough.

Said child actually is
joy of my life.
Struggling with boredom and busywork.
Missing friends who are, of course, teachers.
Worried that her father (my ex) has not been distancing
tries to protect her grandparents, my parents, by keeping her distance from him.
He retaliates by ignoring her 14th birthday.
Bastard.
I worry I am not enough.

Those parents huddle a short mile away.
Prone to darkness.
Healthy but aging.
A mile can be a chasm.
I worry I am not enough.

Rinse.
Repeat.

Hank The Fuzzy Dog barks as two young men in bike helmets and black ties approach
the house.
Checking in during the pandemic but
I feel pity.
The doorbell rings …

That time I thought I was Martha Stewart …
-Callie

The Covid mom started up Noom
Color-coded naps, school, and clean room
Then came week four …
Ain't Martha no more
Now I'm a hot mess on Zoom

That time you called me a superhero ...
-Linda

Heroes can take it.
They're superhuman, after all.
My kids think I have eyes at the back of my head
But I don't really have that superpower.
Where are my socks? Have you done your homework? When is that appointment? Did
you make it?

Moms. Nurses. Grocery store clerks.
We don't have special powers.
We're just doing work that you refuse to do.
Calling me a superhero doesn't mean that
I need to take your shit.

That time I got busted ogling the Caribbean on a Zoom call ...
-Karen

My first Zoom call of the day
coffee

daily news feed of five things to know.
Human interest story at the bottom

best part.
Wal-Mart tracks shopping patterns ...

Always. Duh.

In this pandemic, folks shop in waves.
Week One: sanitizing products.

Week Two: toilet paper.

> As if we missed that one.
> One more toilet paper
> meme, joke, song
> and I will fucking punch someone.

Week Three: Easter goods (candy, hams, yeast for bread).
Week Four: More of the same ...

> ... consumption in the name
> of Bunny-driven and/or religious hope.

Then a turn ...
Week Five: Hair color
people need a change, refresh.
Makes me pause, consider.
As working mom
more like Zoom-induced scrutiny.

> Go figure.
> I have seen and heard more of myself on camera than any other sentient being.
> I have dissected
> my complexion (sun damage?)
> my teeth (tissue test?)
> my neck (crepe-y?)
> my hair (greying?)
> my voice (baritone?)
> my ability to form a cogent thought, statement (   ).
> Performativity.
> Navel gazing cum self-loathing.
> Change doesn't cut it.
> Escape.
> Way better.
> Vacation.
> Somewhere warm.
> Jimmy Buffet.
> Umbrella drinks.
> Sand
> everywhere.

I'm sorry.
You were breaking up.
Garbled.
Can you repeat the question?

That time they fired 1/3 of the faculty ...
-Linda

A shout out to contingent labor everywhere
Disposable labor.
I study leisure, but losing my job
Did not mean I got a

Leisure experience.
I should know. I've got the references.

That time I looked on the bright side...
-Linda

I keep a somewhat depressing list:
Things I will teach differently now
Cruise ships. A field hospital in Central Park. Hotels and conference centers
Put to new uses.
The world has changed, and yet
Power still perpetuates itself. It is not coincidental who lives. Who dies.

I refuse to throw up my hands,
I can't fix everything, but I can (must?) resist.
Call you out when you're an asshole
Call it cisheteronormative patriarchy if I'm feeling fancy.
Resist by existing. Butch dyke. Feminist. Mom.
I eat fire, you know.

If they ever open the beach, then this pudgy butch body will be a
Beach body. Just watch.

We can rewrite the narrative, focus on the power of **and**. Seize the power, subvert
the discipline.
I teach and educate and, and, and...

Who decides what gets added?

> "We will not go back to normal. Normal
> never was. Our pre-corona existence was
> not normal other than we normalized greed,
> inequity, exhaustion, depletion, extraction,
> disconnection, confusion, rage, hoarding,
> hate and lack. We should not long to return,
> my friends. We are being given the
> oppurtunity to stitch a new garment. One
> that fits all of humanity and nature.
> SONYA RENEE TAYLOR

ORCID

Callie Schultz ⓘ http://orcid.org/0000-0002-6298-8881

References

Dupont, M. (2020, April 9). [@matisse.dupont] *Some gender questions you could ask yourself.* [Instagram photo]. https://www.instagram.com/p/B-w9i5sAxha/

Foucault, M. (1995). *Discipline and punish: The birth of the prison.* Random House. (Originally published 1975)

File: Cocktail Beach Africa [digital image]. *Wikimedia Commons, the free media repository.* https://commons.wikimedia.org/wiki/File:Cocktail_Beach_Africa.jpg

Isis the Scientist. (2020, April 17). Inside Higher Ed can fuck right off... How the academic insider publication is continuing its long trend of attacking women. *Skepckick.* https://skep-chick.org/2020/04/inside-higher-ed-can-fuck-right-off/?fbclid= IwAR28cF1Ve73R7sDca2URUu3f5NH0AO5ZHbfIsSsryKU-78v93VXvqBel03c

Taylor, S. R. (2020, April 2). [@sonyareneetaylor] *We will not go back to normal.* [Instagram photo]. https://www.instagram.com/p/B-fc3ejAlvd/

Quito, A. (2020, April 1). Marie Kondo's strategy for finding joy in coronavirus quarantine. *Quartz Magazine.* https://www.msn.com/en-my/lifestyle/smart-living/marie-kondos-strategy-for-finding-joy-in-coronavirus-quarantine/ar-BB122LUm?li=AAaD1A0&% 25252525252525252253Bocid=mailsignoutmd

Single Women's Leisure during the Coronavirus Pandemic

Audrey R. Giles and Jacquelyn Oncescu

ABSTRACT

The novel coronavirus has resulted in self-isolation and physical distancing for millions of people. In this critical commentary, we analyze the effects of these practices on our leisure as two single, professional, childless women who live alone. Women face societal expectations that they will play large roles in caregiving. We argue that in the current pandemic, women who are not responsible for the provision of care may face amplified resentment or belittlement for engaging in regular leisure activities. Further, many people have been limited in interacting with those outside of their household. For those who live alone, this is particularly isolating and has a huge effect on the types of leisure in which they can engage and removes them from their established networks of support and safety. We show that removal from our social and care networks can result in feelings of selfishness, shame, and fear during leisure participation.

The novel coronavirus that causes COVID-19 (hereafter "the coronavirus") has resulted in self-isolation and physical distancing for millions of people. In this critical commentary, we analyze the effects of these coronavirus-related practices on our leisure as two single, professional (in this case, academic) women who live alone. We argue that such experiences are interesting for two key reasons: First, women face societal expectations that they will play large roles in caregiving. Women who are not primarily responsible for the provision of care for children, parents, partners, etc. can already face resentment or belittlement for engaging in regular leisure activities. While this is not a new phenomenon (Henderson & Allen, 1991), it has been amplified during the current pandemic. Second, due to the coronavirus, many people have been limited in interacting with those outside of their household. A household often consists of a family unit but can also include housemates. For those who live alone, this is particularly isolating and has a huge effect on the types of leisure in which they can engage and removes them from their established networks of support and safety. While social isolation does offer time to focus on new activities or projects, including work, it also results in single women who live alone having to navigate tensions in leisure brought on by isolation.

Situating ourselves

We would like to begin by acknowledging the criticisms against scholarship in the time of a pandemic, some of which were directed to *Leisure Sciences'* call on Twitter for critical commentaries about leisure in the time of the coronavirus. Certainly, we recognize our privilege in being able to respond to this call. We are white, middle-class, cis-gender, heterosexual, able-bodied, professors in Canada, a country with universal healthcare. We have both maintained our jobs, incomes, and health in a time in which many have not. We do not have children, parents, or partners for whom we must provide direct care. It is not our intention to minimize the very real struggles of those who are providing such care at this time. In deciding to write this commentary, we follow British Sociological Association President Susan Halford (2020), who stated, "as the everyday practices of living in an unprecedented public health crisis evolve, we have the opportunity to learn more about social divisions, social cohesion and social change" (para. 3). Our interest in this commentary is in learning more about social expectations concerning what people like us – single, childless, professional women - should and should not be doing for leisure during the pandemic. While we acknowledge that several of our arguments can be extended to men, we nonetheless believe that the ways in which women are socialized concerning the ethic of care (Gilligan, 1982) and personal safety (Wesely & Gaardner, 2004) result in the need to discuss separately women's and men's leisure in the time of the coronavirus.

Selfishness and shame: Caring for oneself and others

Vignette 1 (Audrey):

   Scrolling through my Facebook feed, I notice a post that Laura, an old friend from Junior High, has made, referring to her work during coronavirus isolation and physical distancing measures: "Single teachers without children are deliberately trying to make me look bad by being productive!" My heart begins to beat quickly. My breathing rate increases. Not wanting to start a Facebook fight, I take the passive aggressive approach and go to Twitter to share my feelings. "Newsflash: Single people without kids aren't just staying home and being uber productive. We're lonely, trying to support others, and aren't just here trying to make people with kids look bad. We're in this together. Stop throwing folks like me under the bus." In the span of a few hours, 300 people "like" my tweet. A sense of calm settles over me. There are people who understand where I'm coming from as a single, childless, professional woman, I silently cheer. This feeling of calmness and vindication is short-lived. At my book club's online meeting the next day, my friend shouts over Zoom, "If one more person talks about how they've started taking online ukulele lessons, I'm going to lose it. Who has time for that?" Living alone and wanting to reengage in an activity I had previously enjoyed, I had just started taking online ukulele lessons. I had felt so proud of myself. I was making the best of this pandemic. But after this comment, I feel my stomach sink and my cheeks burn. My book club friends – women who are homeschooling their young kids while still working full-time – seem to hate people like me. I blink back tears. I could really use a hug. I haven't had one in over a month.

With a few notable exceptions (e.g., McKeown, 2015, McKeown & Parry, 2019), very few scholars have focused on the leisure lives of single, professional, childfree women who live alone. Instead, many studies that have focused on professional women's leisure have examined the ways in which women are/are not able to access leisure activities due to their childrearing responsibilities or the need to negotiate leisure time with a spouse. Given that the number of single women who live alone is rising (Sharp & Ganong, 2011), we believe that this group deserves scholarly attention, especially amongst the period of pandemic-induced social change that we are currently experiencing.

In her research with single Irish women, Byrne (2000) argued that there is a stereotype of single women being "independent, selfish … [and] having no ties or responsibilities" (p. 17). This stereotype stands in stark contrast to what Byrne identified as favored social identities for women that include "heterosexuality, marriage, and motherhood" (p. 16), all of which are dependent on women's relationships with others. It is important to note, however, that even women who do not fall into these categories have often followed developmental paths that have concentrated "on responsibility and commitment to others" and that encouraged them to "define themselves in relation to others" (Henderson & Allen, 1991, p. 99). As such, they may, contrary to Byrne's findings, in fact have ties and responsibilities due to what Gilligan (1982) referred to as the ethic of care and are engaged in rich webs of relations beyond the heteronormative family.

During the pandemic, many people's relationships have been disrupted; this disruption may be felt particularly acutely by single women who live alone. Indeed, even before the coronavirus' onset, some single women reported feeling socially isolated, often due to the tendency of couples to spend their leisure time with other couples (Byrne, 2000; Chasteen, 1994). These feeling have likely been heightened during this time of enhanced and enforced isolation. While in non-pandemic times single women may be engaged in networks of friends and their friends' families, even becoming "fictive kin" (Rae, 1992), the fiction of this kinship has been made apparent by the measures put in place due to the coronavirus. Though they may be "like family," by failing to be "true" family members, single women's physical distancing practices may result in the erosion of important relationships, and their failure to be able to continue to both provide and receive care in their networks.

As a result of isolation and physical distancing measures, there is the need for single women to find (even more) activities that they can do alone. Yet, our engagement in these activities has been met with derision from people in our lives: "It must be nice to have the time for that," or "I'd do anything for some time to myself" are common refrains that we have heard. Assumptions that inform such statements are that that single women do not have inhibitory constraints on their leisure and that they are not relational being. This is, of course, not the case. Single women's leisure constraints are amplified in societies that normalize partnership and childrearing as being more acceptable than being single and childless (Chasteen, 1994). Though being a single and childless woman is not as inappropriate or unacceptable as it once was (Park, 2002), this status can affect how we as single, childless women view ourselves, and the leisure activities in which we choose – or are able - to participate.

For example, after her book club member's remark about ukulele lessons, Audrey, who identifies as someone who actively resists discourses about what women "should do," found herself feeling guilty about engaging in certain leisure activities. As she had seen those around her engaged heavily in care activities (e.g., homeschooling, caring for elderly parents), she started feeling as though she was being perceived as being selfish. In hindsight, she sees her subsequent decisions to take in a foster dog from the local Humane Society, sew fifty face masks in exchange for donations to the local Food Bank or Humane Society, and taking her friend's children for physically distanced walks every morning so that their parents can do some uninterrupted work as responses to this perceived social disapproval. She has reflected that she finds these activities much easier to talk about to friends than her daily yoga challenge (at the time of writing, she had done a YouTube yoga video every day for five weeks), her online ukulele lessons, or continuing with her pre-pandemic running routine.

Research pertaining to women, leisure, and the ethic of care has typically focused on women as mothers. What we find interesting about Audrey's experiences is the way in which the ethic of care served as a constraint (Henderson & Allen, 1991) for her - a single woman who lives alone. Audrey felt selfish and ashamed for engaging in pleasurable leisure activities and not providing direct care for others - even though she has no one for whom she had the responsibility of direct care. As a result, she created her own other-centred, care-focused leisure activities to counteract her feelings of selfishness and shame.

Safety in numbers during a pandemic

Vignette 2 (Jackie):

I'm on my daily walk alone, making the most of my leisure while abiding by coronavirus physical distancing protocols. As I near the last house before the nearby vast, open fields, an older man in his sixties rides past me on a bike. He turns into the yard of this last house and walks toward the fence line and yells, "Happy Easter!" To be friendly, I respond, "It's a nice day to be on a bike." Clearly, he is eager to chat, as he wanders closer to the road. I cautiously stand away and keep the conversation polite but not inviting. Thirty seconds later, the conversation ends, and I walk away, feeling a sense of relief. Twenty minutes later, I see a black truck off in the distance. It is slowly making its way toward me, and I feel a sense of nervousness flood over my body. The hair stands up on the back of my neck. The truck stops. The window is rolled down, and the older man, the one I just walked away from, asks, "Would you like to ride bikes sometime?" Shocked, I respond, "I don't ride with people I don't know," and I quickly walk away. As my fear subsides, I can't help but think to myself, "now where the f*ck do I go?" The enjoyment of my walk is quickly lost.

Henderson and Bialeschki (1993) found that women have numerous safety concerns, including the fear of being physically harmed by another person, which affect their choices about the environments and leisure activities in which they engage. The challenge with coronavirus protocols is that they create a safety paradox for single women who want to pursue leisure activities. To stay safe from the virus, governments are requiring physical distancing. For leisure participation, in many places this has meant that one's activities are only to be done with people who live in one's household. Being active outside in nature - walking, hiking, and biking, while being physically distant from others has been promoted throughout communities as being "safe" activities; however, these leisure experiences become more dangerous for single women when they are required to do them alone.

Women's experiences in public settings and their perceptions of them are gendered (Massey, 1994). Many women have been socialized to be uncomfortable in outdoor and public spaces, and they have learned that private and domestic settings are their domain (Valentine, 1992). A woman in a public or outdoor setting can feel "vulnerable to unpredictable invasions of her 'physical self' with experiences ranging from objectification to a violent crime" (Wesely & Gaardner, 2004, p. 648). It is not uncommon for women to feel unsafe in public settings, that they are "targets" for predatory men who perceive women who are alone as being "sexually available" (Byrne, 2000, p. 20). Navigating leisure in outdoor settings can be similarly challenging for women, as they often feel more vulnerable to attacks in large, open, and deserted spaces such parks, woodlands, and the countryside (Valentine, 1989). In addition, women are socialized to fear being sexually assaulted by an unknown person, which significantly restricts the types of environment they see as appropriate spaces in which to engage in leisure (Chasteen, 1994). These processes of socialization act as forms of social control to maintain women's fear of engaging in leisure alone.

As evidenced by Jackie's account, the coronavirus pandemic has heightened both anticipation and experiences of risk in single women's everyday lives and when traveling to and from, and taking part in, leisure activities and using outdoor spaces for leisure. Physical distancing separates single women from their social support networks that were required for some forms of their leisure participation, particularly to mitigate fear of being alone in outdoor leisure settings. Women are expected to safeguard themselves through endless measures, including seeking safety in numbers (Bialeschki & Hicks, 1999; Coble et al., 2003; Hollander, 2001); however, for single women, the safety in numbers tactic is often impossible under coronavirus protocol. For example, Jackie is very active in a women's mountain biking community, but she does not feel that she can now mountain bike alone due to the risk of becoming injured while biking alone and the risks posed by unknown people. While many existing safety strategies for women serve as forms of social control, when combined with coronavirus protocols, they quite literally serve to keep single women in place in the home. The coronavirus has changed how leisure can be experienced by single women, but it has also enhanced fears and risks while participating. Though it can be argued that the coronavirus has taken away the freedom in leisure for all women, for single women – and particularly women of color, who experience higher levels of street harassment and sexual violence than white women (Kearl, 2010; Nielsen, 2009; Pain, 2001), there are limited options to safeguard themselves in what little leisure they have left.

Conclusions

Coronavirus-induced isolation and physical distancing protocols have enabled the perception that single, professional women who are childless and live alone have a plethora of new-found time in which to engage in leisure pursuits. While leisure is often thought of as an individualistic pursuit, it in fact profoundly relational. Current pandemic practices help to demonstrate the importance of social connection and the dangers of enforced isolation. Indeed, we have shown that women like us face a variety of leisure constraints that are far different from perceptions of us having endless options. Being removed from our social and care networks can result in feeling of selfishness, shame, and fear. Certainly, the psychological benefits that leisure participation can reap, such as personal control, freedom of choice, and autonomy (Coble et al., 2003), can be greatly diminished or even erased as we contend with objective or perceived threats of judgment or even violence for participating in leisure in the time of a pandemic.

As leisure is experienced differently for each individual, but it is informed by a person's positionality, future research needs to examine the impacts of the pandemic through an intersectional approach (Crenshaw, 1991) to account for the ways in which women with low incomes, those who receive care, women of color, Indigenous women, queer women, and older women experience leisure during a pandemic. As such, we encourage the development of richer public discourses on – and more compassion and understanding about – all women's engagement in leisure during this public health emergency.

References

Bialeschki, M. D., & Hicks, H. (1999). "I refuse to live in fear": The influence of fear of violence on women's outdoor recreation activities [Paper presentation]. Paper presented at the 1999 NRPA Leisure Research Symposium, Nashville, TN, October 20–24. http://www.unc.edu/depts/recreation/LSAfea

Byrne, A. (2000). Singular identities: Managing stigma, resisting voices. Women's Studies Review, 7, 13–24.

Chasteen, A. (1994). "The world around me": The environment and single women. Sex Roles, 31(5–6), 309–328. https://doi.org/10.1007/BF01544591

Coble, T., Selin, S., Erickson, W., & Beth, B. (2003). Hiking alone: Understanding fear, negotiation strategies and leisure experiences. Journal of Leisure Research, 35(1), 1–22. https://doi.org/10.18666/jlr-2003-v35-i1-608

Crenshaw, K. (1991). Mapping the margins: Intersectionality, identity politics, and violence against women of color. Stanford Law Review, 43(6), 1241. https://doi.org/10.2307/1229039

Gilligan, C. (1982). In a different voice. Harvard University Press.

Halford, S. (2020, March 25). Sociology and the social sciences in the COVID-19 crisis. British Sociological Association. https://es.britsoc.co.uk/sociology-and-the-social-sciences-in-the-covid-19-crisis/

Henderson, K. A., & Allen, K. R. (1991). The ethic of care: Leisure possibilities and constraints for women. Loisir et Société/Society and Leisure, 14(1), 97–113. https://doi.org/10.1080/07053436.1991.10715374

Henderson, K. A., & Bialeschki, M. D. (1993). Exploring an expanded model of women's leisure constraints. Journal of Applied Recreation Research, 18(4), 229–252.

Hollander, J. (2001). Vulnerability and dangerousness: The construction of gender through conversations about violence. Gender & Society, 15(1), 83–109. https://doi.org/10.1177/089124301015001005

Kearl, H. (2010). Stop street harassment: Making public places safe and welcoming for women. Praeger.

Massey, D. (1994). Space, place and gender. University of Minneapolis.

McKeown, J. (2015). I will not be wearing heels tonight! Journal of Leisure Research, 47(4), 485–500. https://doi.org/10.1080/00222216.2015.11950372

McKeown, J., & Parry, C. (2019). First comes love, then comes marriage, then comes baby in the baby carriage? Exploring how women can use leisure as resistance to gendered ideologies. *Leisure Studies, 38*(2), 191–203. https://doi.org/10.1080/02614367.2018.1553995

Nielsen, L. (2009). *License to harass: Law, hierarchy, and offensive public speech.* Princeton University Press.

Pain, R. (2001). Gender, race, age and fear in the city. *Urban Studies, 38*(5–6), 899–913. https://doi.org/10.1080/00420980120046590

Park, K. (2002). Stigma management among the voluntarily childless. *Sociological Perspectives, 45*(1), 21–45. https://doi.org/10.1525/sop.2002.45.1.21

Rae, H. M. (1992). Fictive kin as a component of the social networks of older people. *Research on Aging, 14*(2), 226–247. https://doi.org/10.1177/0164027592142004

Sharp, E., & Ganong, L. (2011). "I'm a loser, I'm not married, let's just all look at me": Ever-single women's perceptions of their social environment. *Journal of Family Issues, 32*(7), 956–980. https://doi.org/10.1177/0192513X10392537

Valentine, G. (1989). The geography of women's fear. *Area, 21,* 385–390.

Valentine, G. (1992). Images of danger: Women's sources of information about the spatial distribution of male violence. *Area, 24,* 22–29.

Wesely, J., & Gaardner, E. (2004). The gendered "nature" of the urban outdoors: Women negotiating fear of violence. *Gender & Society, 18*(5), 645–663. https://doi.org/10.1177/0891243204268127

Pandemic Motherhood and the Academy: A Critical Examination of the Leisure-Work Dichotomy

Brooke N. Burk, Anna Pechenik Mausolf, and Linda Oakleaf

ABSTRACT

In late 2017, a critical investigation of the impact of motherhood on perceptions of success in academia, specific to leisure scholars in the United States, was undertaken by the authors of this critical review. Results from this study indicated that leisure scholars who are also mothers experience a great deal of pressure to be productive educators and researchers. This stems from unrealistic work expectations, unsupportive colleagues, and workplace policies that are difficult to navigate. The impacts of these are exacerbated by the pandemic conditions caused by COVID-19 due to existing patriarchal structures in academia. Community mitigation efforts result in working mothers balancing multiple full-time responsibilities, including providing childcare and education for their children while struggling to complete their paid work. We asked our previous research participants to share how their work and family experiences have been affected by the COVID-19 pandemic conditions, specifically as it relates to performing simultaneously as both primary childcare providers and faculty members at their institutions. While necessary to address a global health emergency, transitioning to remote work has increased employment expectations for mothers employed in higher education. Leisure scientists reported that telecommuting has led to an unideal merger of their personal and professional spaces, disrupting any harmony that these mothers were working so tirelessly to achieve. Leaders in higher education must address this misguided "hurry up model" and lack of concern for their employees as both scholars and human beings that need leisure to ensure quality of life and wellbeing.

Introduction

When the novel coronavirus began rapidly infecting Americans in early 2020, concerns about the spread of the virus altered the working experience of many employed in higher education. Colleges and universities first suggested, and eventually mandated, policies that all employees who could work from home do so. Institutions also swiftly altered the delivery of academic courses, resulting in students completing their semester fully online. For many educators teaching in the traditional classroom, these changes required substantial overhauls of course planning and design. The time commitment required to rewrite syllabi, reformat assignments, and develop online lectures was significant for instructors. This unideal and unfortunate necessity was increasingly challenging for faculty forced to swiftly adjust to distance learning technologies that were new and unfamiliar to them.

Higher education administrators and policymakers explained that this rapid, mid-semester transition of course delivery originated due to an unforeseen and unprecedented social situation, so therefore systems that had yet to be fully explored and vetted were compulsory for crisis response. With this transition, faculty were asked to be patient, caring, and compassionate with students (e.g. Minnesota State University, Mankato, 2020). In many higher education institutions, little attention was given to the impact these changes would have on faculty's work/life balance, especially for those employees whose children were also suddenly home and therefore would need care and attention. At some institutions, faculty members were not provided the same space for modifications, processing, and patience that was requested these same faculty provided to their students. For example, one academic mother's recent social media post, in a group designed to support educators in higher education, states:

> A big mistake that universities are making right now is assuming that their faculty are OK. Besides the assumption is [sic] that faculty are curriculum delivery machines and equally yoked pedagogically, many administrators are turning a blind eye to the emotional distress of faculty. (Evans-Winters, 2020)

This sentiment is one of numerous indications of the profound disconnect between the support that faculty desperately needed from their employer during the COVID-19 pandemic, and the support that institutions of higher education readily provided enrolled students.

The research we shared in 2019 (Oakleaf et al.) suggests that academia has transformed into a business (Bunds & Giardina, 2017; Vostal, 2015; Ylijoki, 2003) leaving women, particularly mothers, in situations where they have to do more, be more, and struggle to feel "enough" in any of their roles. The COVID-19 pandemic has exacerbated these feelings with the spread of telecommuting policies, demands on time and workload management, and the general stress of providing care to loved ones. When the health crisis began, and educational institutions across the United States began shutting their physical doors and offering education in distance learning formats, the landscape of home and work for academic mothers changed in uneasy ways. In 2019, we reported that mothers worked desperately hard to separate work from home so that each could have its own place for moms to "be". Now that we are experiencing a serious pandemic, mothers are caught, tethered among a myriad of roles, constantly wondering if they are spending "enough" time "being" any of these.

As we report in this critical commentary, during the COVID-19 pandemic, academic mothers (and fathers who serve as primary childcare providers) find themselves simultaneously creating curriculum, reviewing assignments, collecting data, developing reports, answering emails, mentoring students, printing coloring pages, explaining third-grade science, preparing meals, rocking babies, caring for aging parents, attending virtual meetings, and trying to protect their families from a deadly virus which causes life-altering sickness.

Furthermore, these mothers describe feelings of failure, guilt, unhappiness, and being overwhelmed by employment. Refusal of leaders in higher education to heed multiple warnings of its underpreparedness for the current health crisis has directly impacted its workforce (Ekmekci & Bergstrand, 2010; Schwartz & Bayles, 2012). We conclude this commentary with calls to action: For fellow leisure scholars to reflect on the purpose of our work, for institutions of higher education to enact policies that demonstrate care for their employees' wellbeing, and for all of academia to seriously plan ahead when considering potential threats to its relevance.

Literature review

Prior to the current pandemic working and living conditions in the US, mothers in academia experienced their employment in ways that have profound impacts on their work outputs, leisure opportunity, and family availability. Most notably are workplace policies, feelings of inadequacy, and figuring out how to find balance among multiple roles (Oakleaf et al., 2019). For example, a common cultural practice is to provide mothers with temporal flexibility in scheduling and completing work-related tasks, yet some are not provided any alternative options to complete tasks. Workplace flexibility practices tend to benefit the employer more than the employee because the policies allow (perhaps unintentionally) for increases in expectations of productivity as people will work longer hours to finish their duties (Wattis et al., 2013). When mothers do request or negotiate for flexible working hours, they report increased pressure because of the compulsion to complete tasks amidst constant negotiation of work and family (Sallee et al., 2016; Wattis et al., 2013). This stress accumulates and manifests as the greatest concern for mothers in academia who are also navigating a global health crisis.

Work-life balance is clearly about more than just work and family. There are three major responsibilities to consider: work, family, and personal life (Wattis et al., 2013). In either setting, whether during a pandemic or in a typical working environment, work happens at the expense of leisure and personal time, as work provides necessary benefits to the employee. Mothers frequently compensate for long work hours by spending more time caring for their children (Sallee et al., 2016; Ward & Wolf-Wendel, 2004). As is well understood in our academic discipline, however, caring for children is certainly not a leisure pursuit. However, Trussell (2015) argues that leisure can help women "transition" into motherhood (p. 171) underscoring the importance of leisure for mothers as they navigate a new identity in ways that are positive and beneficial. There are times in the lives of academic mothers when leisure is limited or nearly absent because childcare becomes a necessary priority, particularly among mothers of younger children. The responsibilities tied to childcare are often invisible or ignored while a mother is at work (Wattis et al., 2013), tucked away as though motherhood should be hidden for life at work. During this current pandemic, though, American mothers in academia whose campuses are closed suddenly and no longer have access to spaces and others to care for their children. As a result, motherhood can no longer be invisible in academia, making academic motherhood less about balancing and more about establishing arbitrary, yet desired, boundaries in their homes and lives. Boundaries between work and life, real or perceived, help people feel as though they have balance and explore various roles more fruitfully (Kreiner et al., 2009).

This crisis in academic parenting comes as little surprise to those knowledgeable in public health. Pandemic influenzas are not a question of if, but when, and of what magnitude. Public health researchers have been repeatedly encouraging public preparedness; the literature strongly sounds the alarm for decades that higher education is ill-prepared to effectively continue operation during a flu pandemic. For one relevant example of a community-level intervention, school and daycare closures are a common policy to mitigate the effects of a severe influenza outbreak (Blendon et al., 2008; Logan, 2008). These mandatory dismissals from school and daycare settings create an immediate childcare coverage need for working parents, which are estimated to be nearly one-third of the workforce in education (Sadique et al., 2008). Therefore, experts in multiple fields have expressed concern about inadequate planning and preparedness for a pandemic's economic and social impacts, especially on working families with school-aged children (Blendon et al., 2008; Bruce-Barrett et al., 2007; Sadique et al., 2008).

It would be wise to use this historical event as a catalyst for positive change whenever possible. We strive to show that academia can, and should, change to meet the needs of female parents (Acker & Armenti, 2004). Prior to a pandemic, women have been forced to cope with high stress, little sleep, and exhaustion on a continual basis (Acker & Armenti, 2004). As leisure scholars and social scientists, we investigate, ask questions, and create knowledge to move society forward on a more informed and enlightened trajectory, as opposed to returning to any previous, unideal "normal." Therefore, we conducted the following critical investigation to examine ways the COVID-19 pandemic conditions exacerbate existing patriarchal structures in academia, especially for mothers of school-age and younger children.

Methods

To gather and examine current experiences, we contacted ten of the seventeen participants from our earlier study of self-identified mothers who had taught in leisure studies or a related field (Oakleaf et al., 2019). This subset of ten participants from the previous study was chosen because they still had school-aged and younger children living in their homes. Participants were sent a list of questions by email. Of the ten participants we contacted, eight responded. The respondents' feedback was incorporated into this critical investigation.

Academic motherhood during a global pandemic

While the coronavirus has created a new set of social and working conditions, these changes are happening within a familiar context. Preexisting structures increase the workload for academic moms at work and at home. Structural inequity was a concern of the mothers we reconnected with as well as a primary concern of the authors. The idea that faculty have the same work expectations in the midst of a global health crisis was alarming and appalling. As indicated by Monique, "The actual work being done is more fast-paced as we workto make temporary policy changes, deal with fallout related to bringing study abroad students home, plan for summer schedules, etc."

According to Naomi, "I feel like I need to be more available for meeting requests, as it seems like our college's administration feels like they need to hold multiple meetings a week." Although quarantine requirements eliminated any available childcare for her two young children, Anna echoed Naomi's thoughts, reporting, "The immediate expectation from the faculty senate was that we keep the exact same lecture schedule, but instead have all the students meet digitally." Despite the expectations of "business as usual," making adjustments to cope was often a personal choice. Brooke explained it this way:

> I need to change my expectations of the day and acknowledge that caring for my children, ensuring they are happy and enriched are also accomplishments that cannot be taken for granted but I feel like I need to be told from leadership at work that that is okay.

For many faculty, expectations of productivity have not changed during the current crisis. Research, teaching, and service expectations have not changed in spite of the fact that the conditions under which faculty are working have changed dramatically. Although some universities have put in place a mechanism to extend the tenure clock, accessing that option has the effect of extending the time during which mothers are more vulnerable to job loss. Journal editors are also noticing the impact of the pandemic on mothers' workload, specifically noting a significant gender gap in scholarly productivity, with men outperforming women by 25%-50% since the start of pandemic campus closures (Flaherty, 2020; Kitchener, 2020). This is especially problematic at a time when state budgets are sure to be reduced in the face of contracting tax receipts. Brooke shared the following related to policies:

> I got an example 'working from home etiquette' from a male colleague that he thought I would like to share and use. It included language about keeping kids quiet and out of the room during meetings. Setting up a clean workspace and that the same workday should be followed. There is absolutely no way that is possible. My kids are two and five. They need and want me all day. I need to supervise their activities. Luckily, I have a fenced-in yard for short bursts of unsupervised play, but that cannot last for a 60-90 minute meeting.

For parents, especially mothers of young children, the responsibility of caring for their children has landed squarely on their shoulders. Single mothers may have no other adults in their household with whom to share this responsibility. Academic mothers with partners who are continuing to work outside the home also are left home alone with their kids while their partner is at work. Anna described her experience like this, "I absolutely cannot keep my teaching up to par, my research going, my service emails answered, my house clean, my marriage alive, my kids happy, and not have a mental breakdown from the world chaos right now." Linda described similar feelings:

> I've been struggling to get my work done, honestly. My wife and I split up the day so that we could educate and care for our kids. Since she has to be at the computer during specific hours, and I'm 'flexible,' I kind of get the short end of the stick.

She later went on to connect this to her leisure experiences:

> To be honest, I didn't have much leisure before COVID 19. This hasn't helped. It takes a lot to parent two seven-year-olds. Parenting them AND educating them only reinforces my belief that we don't pay teachers enough. And there's never a break.

Conclusion

Although challenges related to motherhood in academia were pervasive prior to the 2020 health pandemic, work, life, family, and leisure have all become increasingly difficult to navigate during it. In the midst of COVID-19, where a quick review of social media would suggest increased amounts of leisure time for all to binge-watch a television series or explore a new hobby, we find that this is absolutely not the case for academic mothers. Instead, additional responsibilities have been added to an already full day with little feeling of accomplishment or perceptions of success. We must promote the work of valuable leisure scholars by communicating important and relevant research from leisure studies and encouraging our colleagues to consider leadership positions.

One way to ensure women's stories are heard in the policy-development discussions is to eliminate the underrepresentation of mothers in leadership and not allowing the "problem" to be invisible. More leisure scholars are needed in leadership and administrative roles across the United States. Mothers need to be at the table for their voices to be heard and their quality of life should be considered. If there is little to no time for mothers to experience leisure when work and family are competing for prioritization, mothers will be left feeling ridden with guilt and fears of inadequacy.

It is of great concern, especially during this pandemic, that the repeated suggestions from experts go unheeded. Higher education administration cannot claim that the COVID-19 pandemic has created unforeseen and extreme circumstances; we were forewarned by experts who urged preparedness and even made specific suggestions for change in higher education structures (Ekmekci & Bergstrand, 2010; Logan, 2008; Schwartz & Bayles, 2012). There has similarly been a constant clamor of forewarning of inadequate workplace policies, most notably the powerful argument for paid family leave in the United States (Connelly & Ghodsee, 2011; Teti et al., 2017). Moreover, childcare: on-campus, during academic events, and assistance in securing it during new hire onboarding, substantially reinforces an institution's claims of family-friendliness. Checks and balances regarding workload assignments, even during a global crisis; *especially* during a global crisis, foster clear and equitable expectations in employment.

It is during times like this that we wonder, what is our role as leisure scholars? When do we decide to find an audience ready to digest our work and humanize academia for academics? What is the purpose of leisure scholarship if nobody – not even ourselves – is listening? The COVID-19 pandemic is highlighting what is most important to the world, leaving leisure scholars wondering why leisure experts who are mothers are not more strongly showing their support for family bonding, physical health, and mental stability.

References

Acker, S., & Armenti, C. (2004). Sleepless in academia. *Gender and Education, 16*(1), 3–24. https://doi.org/10.1080/0954025032000170309

Blendon, R. J., Koonin, L. M., Benson, J. M., Cetron, M. S., Pollard, W. E., Mitchell, E. W., Weldon, K. J., & Herrmann, M. J. (2008). Public response to community mitigation measures for pandemic influenza. *Emerging Infectious Diseases, 14*(5), 778–786. https://doi.org/10.3201/eid1405.071437

Bruce-Barrett, C., Matlow, A., Rafman, S., & Samson, L. (2007). Pandemic influenza planning for children and youth: Who's looking out for our kids? *Healthcare Management Forum, 20*(1), 20–24. https://doi.org/10.1016/S0840-4704(10)60254-2

Bunds, K. S., & Giardina, M. D. (2017). Navigating the corporate university: Reflections on the politics of research in neoliberal times. *Cultural Studies↔Critical Methodologies, 17*(3), 227–235.

Connelly, R., & Ghodsee, K. (2011). *Professor mommy: Finding work-family balance in academia.* Rowman & Littlefield Publishers.

Ekmekci, O., & Bergstrand, J. (2010). Agility in higher education: Planning for business continuity in the face of an H1N1 pandemic. *SAM Advanced Management Journal, 75*(4), 20.

Evans-Winters, V. (2020). A big mistake that universities are making right now is assuming that their faculty are OK. Besides the assumption is [*sic*] that faculty are curriculum delivery machines and equally yoked pedagogically, many administrators are turning a blind eye to the emotional. [Twitter]. https://twitter.com/drvevanswinters?lang=en

Flaherty, C. (2020, April). No room of one's own. *Inside Higher Ed.* https://www.insidehighered.com/news/2020/04/21/early-journal-submission-data-suggest-covid-19-tanking-womens-research-productivity?fbclid=IwAR2fOaF7vgPNKGZRyGf6qGY4bLj_ikuyJLTtjFz10aUoHiDi1HRyFsHCMt0

Kitchener, C. (2020, April). Women academics seem to be submitting fewer papers during coronavirus. 'Never seen anything like it,' says one editor. *The Lily.* https://www.thelily.com/women-academics-seem-to-be-submitting-fewer-papers-during-coronavirus-never-seen-anything-like-it-says-one-editor/

Kreiner, G. E., Hollensbe, E. C., & Sheep, M. L. (2009). Balancing borders and bridges: Negotiating the work-home interface via boundary work tactics. *Academy of Management Journal, 52*(4), 704–730. https://doi.org/10.5465/amj.2009.43669916

Logan, C. (2008). Pandemic preparedness in the states: An assessment of progress and opportunity. *NGA Center for Best Practices*, 1–18.

Minnesota State University, Mankato. (2020). *Keep teaching: Resources and tools for teaching online.* https://mankato.mnsu.edu/faculty-and-staff/center-for-excellence-in-teaching- and-learning/teaching-continuity/getting-started-teaching-online-quickly/

Oakleaf, L., Burk, B. N., & Pechenik Mausolf, A. (2019). Shouldn't leisure scholars know better? How the work/leisure dichotomy affects policy and culture for academic mothers. *SCHOLE: A Journal of Leisure Studies and Recreation Education, 34*(2), 96–108. https://doi.org/10.1080/1937156X.2019.1622947

Sadique, M. Z., Adams, E. J., & Edmunds, W. J. (2008). Estimating the costs of school closure for mitigating an influenza pandemic. *BMC Public Health, 8*(1), 135. https://doi.org/10.1186/1471-2458-8-135

Sallee, M., Ward, K., & Wolf-Wendel, L. (2016). Can anyone have it all? Gendered views on parenting and academic careers. *Innovative Higher Education, 41*(3), 187–202. https://doi.org/10.1007/s10755-015-9345-4

Schwartz, R. D., & Bayles, B. R. (2012). US university response to H1N1: A study of access to online preparedness and response information. *American Journal of Infection Control, 40*(2), 170–174. https://doi.org/10.1016/j.ajic.2011.02.021

Teti, D. M., Cole, P. M., Cabrera, N., Goodman, S. H., & McLoyd, V. C. (2017). Supporting parents: How six decades of parenting research can inform policy and best practice. *Social Policy Report, 30*(5), 1–34. https://doi.org/10.1002/j.2379-3988.2017.tb00090.x

Trussell, D. E. (2015). Pinstripes and breast pumps: Navigating the tenure-motherhood-track. *Leisure Sciences, 37*(2), 160–175. https://doi.org/10.1080/01490400.2014.980590

Vostal, F. (2015). Academic life in the fast lane: The experience of time and speed in British academia. *Time & Society, 24*(1), 71–95. https://doi.org/10.1177/0961463X13517537

Ward, K., & Wolf-Wendel, L. (2004). Academic motherhood: Managing complex roles in research universities. *The Review of Higher Education, 27*(2), 233–257. https://doi.org/10.1353/rhe.2003.0079

Wattis, L., Standing, K., & Yerkes, M. A. (2013). Mothers and work-life balance: exploring the contradictions and complexities involved in work-family negotiation. *Community, Work & Family, 16*(1), 1–19.

Ylijoki, O. H. (2003). Entangled in academic capitalism? A case-study on changing ideals and practices of university research. *Higher education, 45*(3), 307–335.

Laughing While Black: Resistance, Coping and the Use of Humor as a Pandemic Pastime among Blacks

Corliss Outley ⓘ, Shamaya Bowen, and Harrison Pinckney ⓘ

ABSTRACT

For centuries Africans were captured and brought to America in bondage and forced to forge a new culture. The development of a Black culture gave rise to humor as a coping mechanism against the oppressive state they found themselves in. For centuries, humor became a way to protest their conditions by creating various humorous styles that infused social political commentary on oppression as a sign of defiance, while also providing hope for the hopeless. This commentary seeks to introduce leisure scholars to how Black Twitter (Sharma, 2013) users' expressions of humor during the COVID-19 pandemic serve as a form of resistance to injustices and inequalities, while simultaneously adopting coping strategies to reclaim power and control in order to speak their truth all while cultivating individual and collective identity in/through leisure.

Black culture has been the impetus behind the internet's funniest moments and has become synonymous with propelling social media use across the globe. From Thanksgiving songs to fashion styles to crying Jordan, Black culture has influenced American society through social media (Brock, 2012). Yet, despite all the laughs, the cultural group's history with oppression – slavery, Jim Crow laws, segregation and legalized systemic racism – the role of using humor to deal with extensive trauma has rarely been examined. This commentary explores how Black Twitter users' expressions of humor serve as a form of resistance to injustices and inequalities during the COVID-19 pandemic, while simultaneously adopting coping strategies to reclaim power and control in order to speak their truth all while continuing to thrive during this difficult time.

Humor, leisure and trauma

The use of humor has been found in all social settings throughout history and has resulted in researcher's attempts to explain its philosophical underpinnings, the various types, what elements make it successful and why humans are motivated to consume. Humor has often been attributed to the work of Plato, Aristotle and Hobbes, in that it is the production of laughter that results from the observed misfortune and suffering of others and viewed as the ultimate soul cleansing. The word *humor* is linked to the philosophical underpinnings of leisure through its formal and casual link to various leisure concepts such as ludicrous (from *ludere, L.,* to play), funny, word play, horseplay, trick, and joke. McGhee (1999) has argued that humor is a sub-variant of play and serves as the basis for humor - a play on ideas. Conversely, the idea of playfulness and humor is also related to our understanding of the role of humor during lifespan development. Barnett (2007, p. 955) states that playfulness is "[...] the predisposition to frame (or reframe) a situation in such a way as to provide oneself (and possibly others) with amusement, humor, and/or entertainment." The strong association with humor and humorous behavior is evident here in its relation to playfulness and leisure in its ability to frame or reframe situations or experiences in ways perceived as being more interesting for the individual. Humor as part of the human condition has been shown to reduce stress, instill hope, impact group solidarity, as well as, divisiveness through the sharing of jokes (Vinton, 1989), and even serves as a fundamental structure in child development.

As James Baldwin (p. 205) noted, throughout US history, "[t]o be a Negro in this country and to be relatively conscious, is to be in a rage almost all the time. So that the first problem is how to control that rage so that it won't destroy you." This rage produces humor in everyday leisure experiences that is directed toward individuals, events and institutions that create and maintain oppressive structures. *Boal (2007), author of Theater of the Oppressed,* asserts that, "perhaps the theater is not revolutionary in itself, but it is surely a rehearsal for the revolution." Blacks have rehearsed this rage through oral and written words as early as the 18th century when oratorical speech practices like storytelling, singing and signifying became a dominant discourse hidden from white members in the dominant group. Each was forged as a mode of resistance and enabled Blacks to critique the racial caste system, and its subsequent oppression, as well as instill kinship ties and strengthen cultural identity. The mere act of resistance often includes the performative acts of reappropriating language tools with double meanings, wordplay and misdirection (Florini, 2014). But it was the everyday forms of resistance within various leisure based performative acts that played a prominent role in Black lives and community. These small acts included short term flight and feigning illness (Camp, 2006), jumping the broomstick (an act symbolizing a marital union) (Raboteau, 2004), staring directly into a camera to humanize themselves (Campt, 2017), singing songs (Levine, 1977), shucking and jiving (Gates, 1984), and signifying and playing the dozens (Levine, 1977) in the 18th and 19th century. Humor joins these acts as a deliberate form of resistance that is used to guide collective action and "the need to laugh at our enemies, our situation, ourselves is a common one but exists more urgently in those who exert the least power over their immediate environment" (Levine, 1977, p. 300).

Blacks historically used humor to challenge political discourse surrounding oppression that shape racism in American life (Boskin, 1997) and is a powerful strategy to defy dominant narratives by illuminating conflicting issues and confronting them through critical socio-political commentary. Following the tradition of parrhesia

(Foucault & Pearson, 2001), in which a person from an inferior position challenges a more powerful person or institution through truth telling, the use of humor in the online Black public sphere provides a viable space to be authentic, preserve Black culture and challenge the dominant culture (Pinckney et al., 2018) . In contrast, White supremacists and white patriarchal systems utilize these digital leisure spaces to continually police the ways in which marginalized bodies engage. This is evident in the increase of racist engagement on YouTube, Reddit, Twitter and now TikTok. For example, 'digital Blackface' has become more pervasive and though it may be less overt than Blackface, it similarly reduces Blacks to stereotypes and allows whites to use them for their own white gaze through Gifs, memes, etc., This digital Blackface reinforces the dehumanization of Black people through visual content and becomes a form of leisure.

Covid-19 and pandemic pastimes

The use of humor is both significant and purposeful in how Black people attempt to deal with not only their traumatic past but also their present. The next section introduces several categories where examples of everyday humorous expressions are used to illustrate this sentiment within digital leisure spaces.

Resistance to white supremacy

Many Blacks use digital leisure spaces to deliberately confront the systems of power by inciting radical thought and critical discourse through laughter and discomfort. Humor in this sense strives to entertain and persuade by infiltrating the mind subtly in comparison to face-to-face discourse that may raise defenses. Resistance comedy is unique in its "deployment of humor and creation of space where marginalized groups can speak outside of oppressive discourse" (Billingsley, 2013, p. 20).

Early on in the COVID-19 crisis, it became obvious that Gen Z-ers (ages 5-23) had taken claim to social video platform TikTok to pass the time they would now be spending at home instead of school and extracurricular activities. This led to a number of viral trends for them to partake in, good and bad. Of the bad, few things came close to the depravity of an antiblack video uploaded by a high school aged couple (see Villarreal, 2020). The video, as stated by its creators, detailed how to make "Niggers" as they added the ingredients such as 'don't have a dad,' 'go to jail,' and 'rob people' among others. Once reposted to Twitter by a white ally, the video went viral as users tracked down the TikTok's creators and contacted their high school, extracurricular programs and prospective colleges.

Despite the depravity in the posting, reactions from Black and White viewers ranged from wonderment, appreciation of white allies to sarcastic memes and gifs all in humorous form were circulated in response. The young man and woman were quickly dropped from their sports teams, criticized by classmates and local leaders and expelled from school which also led to comedic responses (Garcon, 2020; Figure 1).

Figure 1. Response to Stephanie Freeman being expelled as a result of her TikTok video.

Reclaiming black power

Blacks have been represented as negative stereotypic portrayals throughout American history. Ironically, humor has been used to reinforce these stereotypes and are reproduced in the production and reproduction of repressive ideology. Humor is also used to reclaim power by challenging these stereotypical images and dismantling discourses that surrounds it. Evidence of Black disruption discourse, particularly signification– "verbal art of insult" between individuals used to communicate a message through wordplay, provides communal commentary based on shared experiences. Without knowledge and understanding of Black American pop culture, audiences won't be able to decode the joke tweeted (Figure 2) by Zellie (2020) –a great example of how these jokes and conversations remain within the community; for us, by us!

The next two examples represent further communal commentary on how our parents/grandparents recalled their experiences in conversation with us – especially those which are traumatic and have had a lasting impact, and recognizes how we will likely do the same in recalling the current COVID-19 experience in conversation with our own children/grandchildren (K*rens give me heebie jeebie, 2020; Figures 3 and 4).

Traditionally referred to as "The Dozens" game and played between two people in Black communities in front of an audience, the practice has moved into broader linguistic discourses including social media platforms. In the Twitter realm despite the absence of a physical audience, a public performance of Black identity and activism emerges that collectively challenges and ridicules dominant racial narratives (Brock, 2012).

Figure 2. A meme in response to whites violating the shelter in place policies.

Making the invisible, visible

Black people are not often granted the opportunity to disengage from assumed or apparent identities and don't hold the privilege of disidentifying with our Blackness. Identity is both embraced and forced upon through humor by challenging expectations of race by demanding space for themselves.

In the midst of COVID-19, Black entertainers found ways to do what they do best – entertain. What started as a head-to-head battle of hits between producers Timbaland and Swizz Beats on Instagram Live grew into brackets of other hitmakers Black audiences wanted to see battle it out for 12 rounds by introducing their best songs and having the audience declare the winner. The battle most in-demand, however, was a hit-for-hit battle between legendary producers Babyface Edmonds and Teddy Riley scheduled April 18th. The original 3-hour battle date had to be postponed after only an hour due to technical difficulties with Riley's equipment and as a result sparked conversation, jokes and a social media storm. The highly anticipated rematch had upwards of 3.7 M users, according to Instagram, trying to access the rescheduled battle (For the playlist, see Rated R&B, n.d.). Unfortunately, the juxtaposition of Babyface's cool demeanor and smooth voice to Teddy's confused, frustrating and downright laughable technical difficulties (again) made for a Black cultural moment. dear.HER (2020) and Powell's (2020) tweets illustrate how the final battle allowed the world to not only see us, but to *laugh with us* and *not at us* (Figures 5).

Figure 3. A speculative future conversation between Black parent and child regarding COVID-19.

Figure 4. Tweet on a future history lesson regarding COVID-19 between a Black father and son.

dear.HER
@basiK_PHenomena

This battle is starting to look real senior citizen-ish with this technology 🙂. Y'all don't have no grandkids or something that can help right quick
?#TeddyRileyvBabyface #VERZUZ

GIF

5:12 PM · Apr. 20, 2020 · Twitter for iPhone

22 Retweets   **98** Likes

Figure 5. One of many tweets posted during the battle teasing the battling artists for not knowing how to use Instagram.

Flick
@Frediculous

My wife: how arent you more nervous about the
Coronavirus?

Me: first of all, its The Rona now, and twitter said we
were fine because we're black. Where have you been
getting your news from?

7:17 PM · Mar 11, 2020 · Twitter for Android

Figure 7. A humorous conversation between a husband and wife in which the husband explained why they were immune to COVID-19.

Through humor Blacks denounce their oppression in conversation with their oppressors. In doing so they become visible to those who are the cause of their marginalization. Through this process, in making themselves visible, the Black community serves as a mirror that challenges their oppressors to not only see themselves, but to reconcile their discomfort with the ongoing inequities.

Knowledge production

Collins (2002) suggests that subversive discourse has been instrumental to the production of knowledge in marginalized communities. The authors assert that these everyday behaviors include humor as an alternative site for Black consciousness and knowledge production within and outside the culture. Flick (2020) illustrates this with dialogue played out in the dynamics between a Black husband and wife regarding who is most susceptible to COVID-19 when there were very few known cases of Blacks contracting the virus (Figure 7).

Educating those outside the Black community has also led to pure comedy as Whites seek to learn about various cultural artifacts during the quarantine. I SELL BUNDLES (2020) illustrates comedic 'cultural outreach' activities as she, a Black woman, explains to a White man how to style a weave on Black hair on Instagram Live.

Conclusion

The richness of Black leisure should be examined not only within its historical context but as complex moments that mark our ability to push back dominant narratives and make visible our humanity. As presented in this essay, humor has played a prominent role in the Black community and its performative acts of reappropriating language (Florini, 2014) has led to acts of resistance to white supremacy. Similar to previous research (Boskin, 1997; Boal, 2007), humor as an everyday form of resistance allows Blacks to utilize leisure realms and its rhetorical discourses in an attempt to not only destroy oppressive structures but to expose the privileges of oppressors while simultaneously dismantling societal hierarchies and standards of superiority held by these oppressors. Thus humor can lead to increased levels of awareness of self and Black identity along with the production of knowledge by illustrating the value of a Black worldview in order to reaffirm our experiences in America (Collins, 2002).

Finally, beyond the health impact of COVID-19, this pandemic has contributed to the loss of jobs, economic downturn, and separation from public life – all conditions that are familiar to the Black experience. Therefore, while people find the unknown future surrounding the pandemic stressful, seek to adjust to new routines and establish new leisure patterns; Blacks find themselves facing conditions that they've overcome in previous generations. Blacks turn to a familiar practice that is intimate to their history—humor, and has carried them through slavery, Jim Crow, Segregation, the battle for Civil Rights and now modern day microaggressions and systemic racism. It is this humor that has and will continue to provide Black people with the distraction, reassurance and strength needed to face these uncertain times.

Ultimately, we believe Sherronda Brown (2020) conveys our sentiment, "I'm just so goddamn glad for Black laughter."

ORCID

Corliss Outley ⓘ http://orcid.org/0000-0001-7698-9749
Harrison Pinckney ⓘ http://orcid.org/0000-0002-1700-5938

References

Baldwin, J., Capouya, E., Hansberry, L., Hentoff, N., Hughes, L., & Kazin, A. (1961). The Negro in American culture. *CrossCurrents, 11*(3), 205–224.

Barnett, L. (2007). The nature of playfulness in young adults. *Personality and Individual Differences, 43*(4), 949–958. https://doi.org/10.1016/j.paid.2007.02.018

Billingsley, A. (2013). *Laughing against patriarchy: humor, silence, and feminist resistance.* Philosophy Matters Prize Winning Essays, University of Oregon. Retrieved July 24, 2017, from URL: pages.uoregon.edu

Boal, A. (2007). *Theater of the oppressed.* London: Pluto Press.

Boskin, J. (1997). African American humor: Resistance and retaliation. In J. Boskin (Ed.), *The Humor Prism in Twentieth-Century America* (pp. 145–158). Detroit, MI: Wayne State University Press.

Brock, A. (2012). From the Blackhand side: Twitter as a cultural conversation. *Journal of Broadcasting & Electronic Media, 56*(4), 529–549. https://doi.org/10.1080/08838151.2012.732147

Brown, S. J. (2020, January 10). *"Laughing barrels" and the defiant spirit of Black laughter.* http://blackyouthproject.com/laughing-barrels-and-the-defiant-spirit-of-black-laughter/

Camp, S. M. H. (2006). *Closer to freedom: Enslaved women and everyday resistance in the plantation South.* University of North Carolina Press.

Campt, T. M. (2017). *Listening to images.* Durham, NC: Duke University Press.

Collins, P. H. (2002). *Black feminist thought: knowledge, consciousness, and the politics of empowerment.* New York, NY: Routledge.

dear.HER [@basik_Phenomena]. (2020, April 20). *This battle is starting to look real senior citizenish with this technology* ☺ *Y'all don't have no grandkids or something* [Tweet]. Twitter. https://twitter.com/basiK_PHenomena/status/1252389593829138434

Flick [@Frediculous]. (2020, March 11). *My wife: how arent you more nervous about the Coronavirus? Me: first of all, its The Rona now, and twitter said we were fine because we're black.* [Tweet]. Twitter. https://twitter.com/Frediculous/status/1237895500247920641

Florini, S. (2014). Tweets, tweeps, and signifyin. *Television & New Media, 15*(3), 223–237. https://doi.org/10.1177/1527476413480247

Foucault, M., & Pearson, J. (2001). *Fearless speech* (p. 12). Los Angeles, CA: Semiotext.

Garcon, D. [@ALLSTARGarcon]. (2020, April 17). *HOW YOU GET EXPELLED ON YO OFF DAY?!* 😂😂😂 [Tweet]. Twitter. https://twitter.com/ALLSTARGarcon/status/1251278013926379520

Gates, H. L., Jr. (1984). The Blackness of Blackness: A critique of the sign and the signifying monkey. In H. L. Gates, Jr. (Ed.), *Black Literature and Literary Theory* (pp. 285–321). New York: Methuen.

I SELL BUNDLES [@Nayz100]. (2020, April 18). Meet my new friend Geezerman 😊😊😊 follow my insta @nayz100 for more live tutorials [Tweet; IG Live Video https://www.instagram.com/p/B_IaQ4IADe_/] Twitter. https://twitter.com/Nayz100/status/1251540489154834439

K*rens give me heebie jeebies [@Mt_Everett1]. (2020, April 18). *I can already hear the Black parenting lines we bout to use. "I ain't survive the Rona to bring you* [Tweet]. Twitter. https://twitter.com/Mt_Everett1/status/1251567895445987328

K*rens give me heebie jeebies [@Mt_Everett1]. (2020, April 18). *Me telling my kids about #TheRonin20s "... and then the govt handed us these funky ass 1200 dollar checks that* [Tweet]. Twitter. https://twitter.com/Mt_Everett1/status/1251571988918865920

Levine, L. W. (1977). *Black culture and black consciousness: Afro-American folk thought from slavery to freedom.* New York, NY: Oxford University Press. https://doi.org/10.1086/ahr/83.1.281

McGhee, P. E. (1999). *Health, healing and the Amuse System: humor as survival training.* Dubuque, IA: Kendall/Hunt.

Pinckney, H. P., Mowatt, R. A., Outley, C., Brown, A., Floyd, M. F., & Black, K. L. (2018). Black spaces/White spaces: Black lives, leisure, and life politics. *Leisure Sciences, 40*(4), 267–287. https://doi.org/10.1080/01490400.2018.1454361

Powell, K. [@theKPexperience]. (2020, April 18). 500k people: We can't hear you, Teddy! Teddy Riley: [Tweet]. Twitter. https://twitter.com/theKPexperience/status/1251726971177857024

Raboteau, A. J. (2004). *Slave religion: The "invisible institution" in the antebellum south.* Oxford: Oxford University Press.

Sharma, S. (2013). Black Twitter? Racial Hashtags, Networks and Contagion. *New Formations, 78*(78), 46–64. https://doi.org/10.3898/NewF.78.02.2013

Villarreal, D. (2020, April 18). *High schoolers expelled over racist viral video showing 'recipe' for African Americans.* https://www.newsweek.com/high-schoolers-expelled-over-racist-viral-video-showing-recipe-african-americans-1498683

Vinton, K. L. (1989). Humor in the workplace: It is more than telling jokes. *Small Group Behavior, 20*(2), 151–166. https://doi.org/10.1177/104649648902000202

Zellie [@zellieimani]. (2020, April 22). How fast could you translate this? [Tweet]. Twitter. https://twitter.com/zellieimani/status/1252964513093242881

Beyond Hypervisibility and Fear: British Chinese Communities' Leisure and Health-Related Experiences in the Time of Coronavirus

Bonnie Pang

ABSTRACT

This paper examines British Chinese communities' lived experiences of leisure in response to the COVID-19 pandemic. The data that inform this paper are based on my ongoing ethnographic research with British Chinese students in two supplementary schools in the United Kingdom (UK) about their leisure and health-related experiences (supported by Marie Skłodowska-Curie Fellowship 2019–2020). The current findings are discussed in relation to my field notes, interviews with the students and their significant others from the schools, and social media sites that report on Chineseness and COVID-19. Results include the participants' change of lifestyles; fear and the pandemic; experiences of racism in relation to their leisure; and leisure and solidarity among Chinese communities. As a Hong Kong Chinese Australian researcher situated in the UK, I have an "insider and outsider" positionality which has an impact on data collection with the participants amidst the pandemic.

Researching with British Chinese students and leisure

Boy (12-year-old): You can't just blame the Chinese, only because they're the ones that started the virus in China. (15-2-2020, face-to-face interview)

Parent (mother): The media needs to educate ALL people not to relate the virus only with the Chinese. Just like would you say all Blacks have Ebola, or AIDS? Of course not. This is the same racial mentality. This is how the society has constructed fear towards the Chinese. (19-4-2020, telephone interview)

There are many lessons to be learned, losses to grieve, and uncertainties to bear during the COVID-19 pandemic. But one thing is clear: there is not just one pandemic but two concurrent pandemics. One is the virus, but the second one that is closely tied to the first, is a pandemic of Othering of Chineseness. There is an uncanny parallel between the discourses of the "Yellow Peril" at the end of the 19th century and the current coronavirus where the Chinese/East Asians are positioned as a threat to the

Western world, bringing to light racial inequalities that have long taken root in society (Pang, 2020). For example, a recent survey about the pandemic showed that one in seven people in the United Kingdom (UK) would avoid contact with people of Chinese origin/appearance (Beaver, 2020). The British Chinese student participants in this study attend Chinese language and cultural activities classes at weekend Chinese supplementary schools. These schools have traditionally been regarded as an important social, cultural and political context for British Chinese students and families to accumulate social and cultural capital and provide a safe space for them to escape from everyday racism (Archer & Francis, 2006). With the closure of the schools amidst the pandemic, the British Chinese communities are arguably deprived of their established social networks. This deprivation is coupled with a historical backdrop of living within an intersection of isolation and otherness associated with limited visibility and is underpinned by a lack of cultural representations and academic discussions (Pang, 2020).

Research on the Chinese diaspora's leisure is predominantly based on quantitative/survey or once-off interview methods; for example, in Canada (Walker et al., 2011) and America (Huang et al., 2015). These studies offer a limited analytical understanding of the younger Chinese students' leisure-related *experiences* which this paper will examine. This research focuses on two Chinese supplementary schools in Leeds and Manchester (UK) where I am conducting my ongoing ethnographic research with the British Chinese students (11–15 years old) and their significant others regarding their leisure and health-related experiences.[1] The content analysis is based on my field notes, ongoing interviews[2] with the students and their significant others from the schools, and social media sites that report on Chineseness and COVID-19.

How does fear of the pandemic influence British Chinese communities' leisure?

A discourse of fear is a common thread amongst the data. The fear is coupled with boredom as the students are not allowed to go to the Chinese schooling during the lockdown, whilst at the same time, being overwhelmed by constant news reports on social media, and worrying about their vulnerable relatives in China, Hong Kong and Malaysia. As a School Principal said:

> The Chinese community has become more nervous, some has lessened their contacts, and it affects the community lifestyle. We seem to be living alone and get really nervous even when a person just sneezes. Our Tuesday's opera has stopped for 3 weeks because they don't want to see each other, they've stopped yum cha[3] too. (15-2-2020, face-to-face interview)

---

[1] The students vary in their home locations within the Yorkshire and Lancashire regions; birthplace (England, Mainland China, Hong Kong Special Administrative Region (HKSAR)); language use patterns at home (from English only to a mixture of English, Malaysian, Mandarin, Cantonese); parents' birthplace (Malaysia, HKSAR, Mainland China), and day school attendance. Ethical clearance for the research was gained through the university and from the gatekeepers, students and adults.

[2] The interviews before the lockdown were completed face-to-face at the field sites. During the lockdown, interviews are conducted online or over the telephone by snowball sampling method, and an online ethnographic platform was used to collect a third phase of visual, audio and text data with three students.

[3] A style of traditional Cantonese cuisine involving Chinese tea and dim sum, a small bite-sized portion of food.

Despite the ongoing worries, overall, they acknowledge being content and safe at home with their families, with some parents and children appreciating this quarantine as a down time to rejuvenate and to catch up on lost sleep. The families are acutely aware of the social and political happenings surrounding the pandemic and at times feel quite helpless about the situation, particularly when they perceive the government is not enforcing high-level preventive and protective measures. This crisis situation has created an impetus for one Chinese parent to contemplate about her life and rethink where her "home" is:

> Mother: I'm seriously thinking of going back to China for good. Here they don't even have enough resources to cure their own British people, how will they have the resources to cure us, the second-class citizen? (19-4-2020, telephone interview)

Leisure, families and Chinese schooling

Research about leisure scholarship has highlighted that parental leisure time spent with children is crucial for their wellbeing and development (Shaw & Dawson, 2001). Since the schools had partially closed down in mid-February, the students' weekly schedule had changed, compared to the research interviews conducted in 2019. During April's Easter break and lockdown time, some of their leisure has become more homogenized as they are spending more time playing video games. This "home-based digital leisure" (López-Sintas et al., 2017) not only helps them to "kill time" but also plays a part in essential online grocery shopping for their parents.

Some families are spending more quality time together doing backyard football or squash and trying out new recipes and preparing for meals. One family whose mother is a dancing teacher consciously provides a creative and active environment for her three children such as decorating/painting the walls so that they do not indulge in video games or become sedentary. Her child said she enjoys doing "PE Joe"[4] in the morning and kick-boxing classes online and making creative family videos using TikTok.[5] Several mothers highlight they are pleased that their husbands and children are offering to "help" with the housework which was taken-for-granted as a "mom's" job before the lockdown. In these families, there is an increase in leisure sharing experiences and family bonding during this time of the pandemic (Craig & Mullan, 2012). These newly found leisure times and spaces seem to be a safe haven from the two concurrent pandemics, and have rearranged how housework, groceries and childcare responsibilities are shared at home.

About one month before the social distancing rules were enforced in England, many students and parents had resisted attending the Chinese schools, and class numbers were significantly reduced. They thought it was the Chinese people who started the virus, and with some families traveling overseas during the Chinese New Year in February, that they could return carrying the virus. Arguably, the Chinese supplementary schools can be seen as akin to the students' "weekend families" providing them with the space to socialize, take up cultural activities and develop Chinese cultural identity. The pandemic has shifted this "weekend parenting" responsibility from the schools to the parents. In order to avoid the burden of ongoing negotiations about daily

---

[4]A live series which Joe Wicks, a fitness coach runs online fitness routines.
[5]TikTok is a Chinese video-sharing social networking service founded in China in 2012.

activities, a few families set up strict timetable schedules in order to help their children develop a routine during the lockdown. One parent was worried that his son might gain too much weight without the weekly swimming class, and therefore his timetable included a daily 3 km run on a treadmill, a fruit and vegetables only diet for snack time, and no iPad time before homework and exercise. The timetable is an important "discipline technique" (Foucault, 2012) to manage their children's behavior at home. This regulation of space and time is enforced with parental surveillance regarding the son's leisure behavior and tied to a "body at risk" discourse (Pang, 2020). Another family, however, gave up following the timetable after three days as they struggled to wake up early for "work" as usual. Despite the challenges of being "normal" in a pandemic, the families feel privileged in that they have sufficient spaces at home and an income to carry out a variety of activities that help to maintain sense of stability. While in the current data it is difficult to ascertain how social class impacts on Chinese families' leisure, their narratives about financial security allude to the support from their families overseas and long-term investment and saving (which some said was a value lacking in White British culture) and the government furlough scheme.

When fear becomes racism and its impact on students' leisure

The coronavirus seems to act as a catalyst for these families to more openly discuss racism, and specifically that aims at Chinese people, something previously silenced. There seems to be a shift to the normalized Chinese docility[6] when some parents consciously taught their children to speak up against racial inequalities using an example of Chinese people wearing masks in London and being attacked on the street. A few students have personally experienced racist jokes, such as being called, "you're the virus," from their peers at school. The students are aware that the current heightened racism has deep roots in the UK, and that this coronavirus has provided a fertile breeding ground for its further, more overt, manifestation in society:

> Boy (12-year-old): I think now people, those who are not Chinese, they see the coronavirus as a further chance to racially abuse the Chinese. It's like there's an increase to racial abuse now. They have another weapon to like aim at you. The previous one is like the standard small eyes. (15-2-2020, face-to-face interview)

The families do not seem to be deterred individually by this overt racism and media-induced moral racial panics from outdoor activities; nevertheless, they expressed worries about racism toward the Chinese community more generally. As a result of social distancing, the students' friendship networks and leisure spaces have changed, and new virtual friendship impacted by racialization in online networking platforms.

> Girl (11-year-old): The Chinese school has a WeChat group where parents talk about things. There was this person whom I know, and her White Dad said don't be friends with this Chinese girl as he doesn't want his daughter to get the coronavirus. I feel sad and I'm not friends with this person anymore. (15-2-2020, face-to-face interview)

---

[6]When compared to other ethnic groups in the UK, the Chinese have been perceived as the "minority among minorities", "quiet" or "reserved" (Pang, 2020).

The topic of face masks sparks interesting discussion; the students question the controversies around its protection from coronavirus, and issues related to maska-phobia and racial gaze (Fanon, 1967). They critically address the cultural differences regarding the adherence to mask-wearing and their subjectivities in being in a public space:

> Boy (12-year-old): Apparently when you wear a mask, it sends a signal to the White people, it's like you've got the virus. Because the Chinese wear masks in order to prevent from spreading it, as you don't really know if you've got it or not which is different to the White people. (15-2-2020, face-to-face interview)

One of the students extends this cultural difference to the work ethics and governance between China and England:

> Girl (11-year-old): In China, people will follow the lockdown rules but in England they will protest against it. China has such a strong government and they can control everyone. In England, people are slow in setting up things, like they can't build as fast as in China. It took three years to build a library here while it took four days to build a hospital in China. (15-2-2020, face-to-face interview)

Solidarity and leisure in Chinese communities

Being a Hong Kong Chinese Australian researcher and residing in England, my position in this research field, since COVID-19, has become somewhat precarious. For example, I learned that one of the schools has been bombarded with media press invitations to talk about the impact of the pandemic on their students which they had turned down. I, too, might be positioned as an outsider akin to those journalists about whom they have concerns that the facts may be twisted. On the other hand, being an "insider" has allowed the ongoing research to be enriched by my everyday connections with my Chinese communities locally and globally. Despite a growing tide of anti-Chinese sentiment in the UK and across the globe, the Chinese communities are resilient in fighting the two concurrent pandemics. I am touched by their solidarity, enacted through speaking up against injustice in academic (University of Westminster, 2020) and online forums (Lai, 2020); donating resources to care homes and the NHS; and sharing Chinese Complementary doctor contacts available for online consultations related to COVID-19.

> Mother: My friend's husband got the virus. He couldn't get help from the NHS as he's not feeling that ill. He got better as he's got help from a group of Chinese medical doctors in treating the virus on this WeChat group we shared in the school. The UK government can't help us, but we've got Chinese medicine which can help. (19-4-2020, online interview)

While there is hope for a vaccine that could limit the virus in the near future, what some have called "the second pandemic of racism," exacerbated by the media (Campbell, 2020; Day, 2020), will involve a lot of rethinking and education to lift its impact. The longer-term impact on students' leisure and health-related experiences is summarized by a School Principal's note:

> The biggest issue is not the actual virus, but the exclusion, bullying, abuse, and racism. Once you've got it, you'll become scared and lose confidence and hope which will have a longer-term impact on these students' health and leisure experiences. (17-4-2020, telephone interview)

Conclusion

The crisis situation sparks an "awakening of consciousness" (Bourdieu & Wacquant, 1992, p. 133) about the racialization of British Chineseness that has long been invisible in leisure scholarship and the UK society. This consciousness evokes anxiety and triggers an array of reimagination related to the participants' senses of belongingness and the return to their ancestral homeland; and resistance against racism (physical, verbal and symbolic) that was once silenced in their habitus and entrenched in the pre-COVID-19 structure. Their senses of time and space have reframed the rhythms of everyday life for familial leisure that is underpinned by their socio-material culture (the intersection of resources, technology, and work). As solidarity forges worldwide beyond local contexts, the needs to alleviate the fears and bridge the chasm between the "European reality" (Kinnvall, 2016) and Chinese reality are ever more important. Spivak (1988) reminds us that representation is not only a matter of speaking about but also speaking for. As Gilroy (2005) notes, the "postcolonial melancholia"[7] (Gilroy, 2005) has enabled the residual colonial desire, such as China as the "backward other" to continue to color perceptions of Chineseness. This short paper speaks for British Chinese communities' leisure and health-related experiences that are silenced and/or misrepresented by a resurgence of fear and hypervisibility amidst the pandemic.

Acknowledgment

The author would like to thank Emeritus Professor Anne Flintoff, Dr Beccy Watson and the editors and reviewers for their comments which helped to improve an earlier version of this short paper.

Funding

This work was supported by H2020 Marie Skłodowska-Curie Actions.

References

Archer, L., & Francis, B. (2006). Challenging classes? Exploring the role of social class within the identities and achievement of British Chinese pupils. *Sociology*, *40*(1), 29–49. https://doi.org/10.1177/0038038506058434

Beaver, K. (2020, February 14). COVID-19 - One in seven people would avoid people of Chinese origin or appearance. *Ipsos MORI*. https://www.ipsos.com/ipsos-mori/en-uk/covid-19-one-seven-people-would-avoid-people-chinese-origin-or-appearance

Bourdieu, P., & Wacquant, L. J. (1992). *An invitation to reflexive sociology*. University of Chicago Press.

Campbell, L. (2020, February 9). Chinese in UK report 'shocking' levels of racism after coronavirus outbreak. *The Guardian*. https://www.theguardian.com/uk-news/2020/feb/09/chinese-in-uk-report-shocking-levels-of-racism-after-coronavirus-outbreak

---

[7]The denial of the violence of the colonial past provides the fertile ground for racism that penetrates everyday cultural practices. "A mass lamentation of the loss of colonial power, played out through alternating bouts of racist hostility and collective guilt" (in Kinnvall, 2016, p. 158)

Craig, L., & Mullan, K. (2012). Shared parent–child leisure time in four countries. *Leisure Studies, 31*(2), 211–229. https://doi.org/10.1080/02614367.2011.573570

Day, R. (2020, February 6). 'Keep away, they are all poisoned': Manchester's Chinese community hit out at racism after coronavirus spread. *Manchester Evening News.* https://www.manchestere-veningnews.co.uk/news/greater-manchester-news/keep-away-poisoned-manchesters-chinese-17701894

Fanon, F. (1967). *Black skin white masks.* Grove Press.

Foucault, M. (2012). *Discipline and punish: The birth of the prison.* Vintage.

Gilroy, P. (2005). *Postcolonial Melancholia.* Columbia University Press.

Huang, W. J., Norman, W. C., Ramshaw, G. P., & Haller, W. J. (2015). Transnational leisure experience of second-generation immigrants: The case of Chinese-Americans. *Journal of Leisure Research, 47*(1), 102–124. https://doi.org/10.1080/00222216.2015.11950353

Kinnvall, C. (2016). The postcolonial has moved into Europe: Bordering, security and ethno-cultural belonging. *JCMS: Journal of Common Market Studies, 54*(1), 152–168. https://doi.org/10.1111/jcms.12326

Lai, A. (2020, April 12). The hypervisibility of Chinese bodies in times of COVID-19 and what it says about being British. *Discover Society.* https://discoversociety.org/2020/04/12/the-hypervisi-bility-of-chinese-bodies-in-times-of-covid-19-and-what-it-says-about-being-british/

López-Sintas, J., Rojas-DeFrancisco, L., & García-Álvarez, E. (2017). Home-based digital leisure: Doing the same leisure activities, but digital. *Cogent Social Sciences, 3*(1), 1309741. https://doi.org/10.1080/23311886.2017.1309741

Pang, B. (2020). Problematising the (in)visibility of racialized and gendered British Chineseness in youth health and physical cultures. *Sport, Education and Society,* 1–11. https://doi.org/10.1080/13573322.2020.1732338.

Shaw, S. M., & Dawson, D. (2001). Purposive leisure: Examining parental discourses on family activities. *Leisure Sciences, 23*(4), 217–231. https://doi.org/10.1080/01490400152809098

Spivak, G. C. (1988). Can the subaltern speak? In C. Nelson & L. Grossberg (Eds.), *Marxism and the interpretation of culture,* 24–28. University of Illinois Press.

University of Westminster. (2020, April 30). Racism and orientalism: An online roundtable on racialised discourse on COVID-19. *Contemporary China Centre.* https://www.eventbrite.co.uk/e/racism-and-orientalism-a-roundtable-on-racialised-discourse-on-covid-19-tickets-102094158376

Walker, G. J., Halpenny, E., Spiers, A., & Deng, J. (2011). A prospective panel study of Chinese-Canadian immigrants' leisure participation and leisure satisfaction. *Leisure Sciences, 33*(5), 349–365. https://doi.org/10.1080/01490400.2011.606776

Capitalism and the (il)Logics of Higher Education's COVID-19 Response: A Black Feminist Critique

Terah J. Stewart ⓘD

ABSTRACT

In keeping with a recent wave of leisure studies focusing on race, racism, power, and oppression broadly and using a Black feminist lens, I will examine higher education's response to COVID-19 and illustrate how the illogic of capitalism robs us of our ability to recognize that we are in crisis. Despite the lip-service of our prepared statements in the midst of this chaos our responses were actually about organizational continuity, capitalism, and reducing our value to what we were able to sustain and what our bodies were able to produce.

Capitalism and labor are inextricably tied, they have a symbiotic relationship as one cannot exist without the other. I recall once answering a question on social media about my "dream" job, and it was interesting to witness various reactions to my pushback that I do not have one because I do not dream of work. I do not desire to labor, as labor robs from us our ability and opportunity to truly engage in leisure. I arrived at this perspective after the difficult experience of my mother dying. My mother, who alone raised my siblings and me, worked hard to provide for us. She worked herself to an early grave – with the help of oppression broadly – and her untimely passing forced me to contend with the violence of labor and all the ways it robs us of the things that matter most in life. COVID-19 places us squarely in a tumultuous and unprecedented time of crisis, and while we should be focusing on how to survive the pandemic, the (il)logics of capitalism yet march on.

Power & dominance

To begin, it is important that I articulate my personal and political worldview which colors how I perceive this particular moment that higher education finds itself. As Black feminists have instructed for decades, the impact of oppression on minoritized people is violent, magnified depending on the number of minoritized identities you have, and informs the contexts that you exist in (Bauer, 2000; Richie, 2012). This concept has been explained through the use of terms such as the matrix of dominance, intersectionality, and white supremacist capitalist patriarchy imperialism (Collins, 2002; Crenshaw, 1991; Hooks, 2015). I prefer the latter term because I believe that specificity is critical when engaging these topics. Also, bell hooks articulated that her creation and use of that terminology was to illustrate that the system of oppression - dominance in the world - was happening altogether at the same time; and that minoritized people are always already at the mercy of this system in some way. Further, her use of the term was a way to avoid elevating one piece of the oppression "pie" as the most important issue.

While each term connects in profound ways to how higher education operates, structures itself, and organizes its politics, I focus on the idea of capitalism specifically because many of the behaviors of our organizational leaders and institutions can be explained, understood, and analyzed through capitalism. There are many definitions for capitalism, for the purposes of this commentary I turn to Carruthers (2018) who offered,

> **Capitalism:** an economic system in which the means of production, access to goods, and the value of goods are controlled by private individuals and corporations. *Racial capitalism,* as theorized by Cedric Robinson, argues that this system was built and flourished through the exploitation of people through slavery, imperialism, and genocide. *Neoliberalism* is a model of capitalism that operates through the privatization of public goods, deregulation of trade, diminishment of social services, and emphasis on individual freedoms (p. x)

In addition to this, the will and ability of the people to work tirelessly, aimlessly, and perpetually – and to believe there is no other way – is necessary for capitalism to flourish. Further leisure is intrinsically bound with capitalism as it is also bound to work. The degree that we need to work as a means of survival is proportional to our (in)ability to engage in leisure.

Try as we may, higher education must operate within this violent system which often means we reproduce these values and ethics in many overt and covert ways; and Black women writers, academics, feminists, and scholars have highlighted and critiqued higher educations' reproductions (such as the violence they produce for minoritized people and the capitalistic logics they abide by) for many years (Hooks, 1994; McMillan Cottom, 2017; Porter, 2019). Said differently, there were critiques of higher education long before COVID-19; however, I argue those critiques now ring more forcefully because the failings that previously existed were exacerbated by the spread of coronavirus. Furthermore, in many ways the pandemic revealed *and* violated higher education's capitalistic and neoliberal sensibilities.

Higher education and COVID-19

By March 6th, 2020 the University of Washington was the first major U.S. institution of higher education to cancel in person classes as a result of the novel coronavirus (COVID-19) (Thomason, 2020). Their decision came on the heels of a university staff member testing positive for the virus which was unsurprising given that Seattle, Washington – and the state broadly – had become a hotspot by March 2nd 2020 (Soucheray, 2020).

What followed in the subsequent weeks were rolling campus closures in the U.S. - while institutions around the world were already dealing with the devastation - and moves to online instruction as a way to mitigate the spread of COVID-19. While I am in full agreement of our collective decisions to move to online instruction, *how* we moved to online instruction and the resultant expectations around moving online were troubling to say the least, and downright violent at worst. For example, I observed students – rightfully – complaining about unreasonable expectations placed up on them by their professors. Students commented that some faculty refused to let go of synchronous meetings and expected them to maintain face-to-face supervision, pandemic, or not. Students shared that they were expected to keep every assignment as is, (even if the conditions of social distancing, and quarantine preclude meaningful completion of many assignments).

Additionally, students complain that some professors actually *increased* engagement expectations, given that some faculty likely desire to ensure they demonstrate that they are being productive (what capitalism instructs us to do), and that the quality of class instruction did not diminish. There are instructors of asynchronous classes who expect students to log-on daily to complete tasks and engage discussion posts, while we are actively in crisis. Faculty have tried to reason with students that our current realities are our "new normal" when nothing is normal about this moment.

Faculty have also experienced incredibly difficult expectations, as well as unclear or confusing communication from university leadership, including in their home units and departments. Faculty in various online groups have shared how their institutions forbade asynchronous classes and asked faculty to deliver synchronous lectures. Other universities had no plan or strategy to support students who did not have access to high-speed Internet, computers, other necessary devices/resources, and safe space to meet the expectations of their faculty. This left some faculty to determine how to support students and to find a pedagogical way through this crisis, on their own. Further when institutions did take inaugural steps in the right direction (for example tenure clock extensions) they often did not account for the most marginalized among faculty who hold contingent appointments (Gonzales & Griffin, 2020). Contingent faculty whom are largely underpaid (Nica, 2018) were expected to spend considerable time to make the shift to online instruction without the necessary time and resources to do so. I believe it is key to note here that the shift from face-to-face to online instruction was initiated as a result of capitalistic concerns and not pedagogical or curricular ones. How different might our shift have been if we meditated on our options with these critical considerations in mind?

I recognize the difficult position our institutional leaders find themselves, there will be devastating consequences as a result of COVID-19, some so challenging that they may preclude some institutions of being able to continue to operate. Institutions are bracing for impact and meanwhile they want us to do the best we can to stay the course, to keep it all together, and to keep it all going to help mitigate the potential crash to come. Some institutions have begun to announce hiring freezes, furlough days for faculty and staff, and sadly layoffs and terminations.

As coronavirus sweeps across the globe along with the corresponding measures to mitigate its spread, higher education was uniquely positioned to model how to put people first, how to center people in the margins, how to care for students, and how to demonstrate our mission to be a public good, yet, we failed. The violation of our logics - to produce, to survive, to financially thrive - are mired in capitalistic violence. With an ever-rising death toll, millions of people continue to face incredibly challenging home lives, financial hardships, and both mental and physical health issues; higher education does not know what it means to stop or pause. Higher education struggles to put humanity above our ability to produce. The illogic of capitalism robs us of our capacity to recognize that we are in crisis and despite the lip-service of our prepared sentiments/ statements about how we are all "in this together"; in the midst of this chaos our responses have actually been about organizational continuity, capitalism, and reducing our value to what we are able to sustain and what our bodies are able to produce.

Inherent in all of this confusion was the perplexing conversations about how great it would be to "work from home". Sentiments that people in the academy and beyond would be thrilled to do their work from the comfort of their home abounded. This assumption presumed that everyone lived in comfortable homes and also erased those who could not work from home. Further, there was an assumption that leisure might then be centered or central to the lives of the newly physically distant and quarantined. Given these are conditions no one asked for, leisure has been rendered impossible or improbable for many. This reinforces the notion of leisure as a political project (Watson and Scraton, 2013), and our (in)ability to take care of ourselves, a political imposition.

A black feminist critique

There are a few different ways to articulate the core foundations of Black feminism, for example Richie (2012) outlined five elements, including: interlocking oppressions which I have discussed briefly, standpoint epistemology, everyday knowledge, dialectical images and finally social justice praxis. While each of these complement and fuze with each other and their assumptions/truths flow in and out each other, I focus on social justice praxis to frame my critique. The work of the academy *should* be "accomplished through challenging hierarchies of power, transforming academic institutions, advancing a new kind of organizational leadership and reinvigorating grassroots mobilization efforts for social change" (p. 131). Black feminism at its core is a liberation framework, an emancipatory ethic and as such instructs that we should all strive to change the material conditions of the marginalized – especially the hyper marginalized – both in the academy and beyond (Bauer, 2000; Collins, 2002; Hooks, 1994).

The terms liberation and emancipation are deliberate in that they oppose bondage and restriction, and the ultimate goal is to liberate people from structural violence (Van dernoot Lipsky & Burk, 2009). Structural violence is particularly insidious because it is,

> a form of violence which corresponds with systematic ways in which a given social structure or social institution kills people slowly by preventing them from meeting their basic needs ... Life spans are reduced when people are socially dominated, politically oppressed, or economically exploited (Galtung n.d., as cited in Van dernoot Lipsky & Burk, 2009 p. 29).

Said differently, liberation theory/ethics and emancipatory politics will always have a critique for institutions and institutional behavior that perpetually privilege production and capital gain or survival, over people. During this pandemic we needed and deserved to witness higher education worry less about the institution (including how to continue instruction) in favor of providing the necessary concessions for faculty, staff and students; and to ensure that collectively we are as well as we can be. Our institutions should have given until it hurt, and while some may have – many have not. Further, systems, structures and organizations – including colleges and universities – are harmful because they are not rooted in an ethic of care, or people.

If within our collective imagination we understood and believed the organization to be the *people*, then there is no way that the loss of infrastructure (either temporarily or permanently) would trump our ability to center that ethic in this moment; deliberately and unapologetically. To be clear, many university missions and purpose statements allude to similar ethics, but the praxis of those ethics are routinely not realized. We, the people, are the organization. I do not believe higher education broadly is capable of a radical justice-oriented response because I do not believe we accept our organizations to be, the people. A Black feminist response would have unapologetically centered the people – including and especially those in the margins. A Black feminist ethic would have battened down the hatches for people even if doing so was at the expense of the buildings and the name on the letterhead. Universities sit on billion-dollar endowments, and yet, the people are bearing the brunt of this wave of loss, of disease, unemployment, and inequitable work. Colleges and universities are risk averse (when it comes to sacrificing and taking bold action for the people), therefore responses have been focused on how to save institutions, even if the people who make it up are unwell, are tired, are sick, are dying.

Institutions are bureaucratic and care is not the ethic of institutions; the ethic of the institution is productivity and preservation. Even if we could not collectively stop, pause, or shut down our operations to focus on the people, a Black feminist ethic requires honesty. We owe each other the honesty of naming who has been and will be harmed as a result of the actions of our collective responses and lack of response – and how we would/will try to reconcile that harm. For example, many institutions have faculty and staff who are being furloughed, laid-off; there are hiring freezes and job offers are being rescinded. Institutional leaders often use the phrase "we are in this together" as a way to foster unity during a difficult time, but we are not all "in it" equally. The impact of salary reduction on an administrator in a top pay-band is not the same as a junior level faculty member being forced to take furlough days and completing work during them anyway; is not the same as that post-doc that no longer has a post-doc; is not the same as the staff member who is working tirelessly through hectic home life and screen burnout; is not the same as that undergrad now homeless, stressed, and dealing with violence of all kinds. To pretend there is no harm that institutions are facilitating, or that the harm is marginal, is to be dishonest and to perpetuate the harm with no reconciliation.

Black feminism would instruct us to not only reduce but to eliminate any harm that might exist for the people. The Combahee River Collective (1983), asserted that if Black women were free it would necessitate the destruction of all systems of oppression. Black women in particular almost always bear the brunt of trauma when there are crises of any kind because of their positioning along the lines of race, class, and gender. As it relates to higher education and COVID-19, it is Black women specifically I worry about: faculty, staff and students, who often have more difficult times in the academy, are paid less, have higher expectations and labor loads, and who have marginal presence in the ranks across the board.

Conclusion

No one knows what the future holds for our individual work or leisure lives, and the life of the institutions that we serve. Higher education has the potential to be a space of radical openness and transformational change that is rooted in justice. However, we may not ever realize our greatest potential if we do not work more diligently to recognize and disrupt when our actions and praxis mirrors the violence of oppressions that exists broadly in society. By failing to interrogate how and why we operate as we do, we allow oppression to flourish and further diminish the ability for people to live balanced, rested lives; to leisure in meaningful and material ways.

At the time of this writing I have witnessed several academic calls for manuscripts, chapters, and proposals all seeking to examine the impact of COVID-19 in numerous contexts. While timely information and analysis is important, at what point are we once again falling to a neoliberal and capitalistic ethic in doing this work (and sacrificing leisure in the process)? How are we to know what the impact is or will be while we are still in it? Are these calls about the knowledge in hopes that we might improve or do better next time? Or are these actions actually about wanting to be the first to talk about COVID-19 in any given context?

Now is our opportunity to live the values of a Black feminist ethic, which requires radical action that disrupts the very foundations of the social order. Black feminism asks that we work to transform material conditions that help foster social change. Black feminism would require us to name and recognize that we are in a crisis, and our action to manage should first, foremost, and always be about the people, particularly in the margins; people like my late-mother. We are in a crisis; many of us are not okay. If there were ever a time to stop, to pause, to breathe, and to do better, it is now.

Disclosure statement

The author has no conflict of interests to disclose.

ORCID

Terah J. Stewart ⓘ http://orcid.org/0000-0001-5205-0999

References

Bauer, M. (2000). An essay review: Implementing a liberatory feminist pedagogy: Bell Hooks's strategies for transforming the classroom. *Melus: Multi-Ethnic Literature of the United States, 25*(3-4), 265–274. https://doi.org/10.2307/468246

Carruthers, C. (2018). *Unapologetic: A black, queer, and feminist mandate for radical movements.*

Collins, P. H. (2002). Black feminist epistemology. In *Black feminist thought: Knowledge, consciousness, and politics of empowerment* (pp. 252–271). Unwin Hyman.

Combahee River Collective. (1983). The combahee river collective statement. In B. Smith (Ed.), *Home girls: A Black feminist anthology* (pp. 272–282). Rutgers University Press.

Crenshaw, K. (1991). Mapping the margins: Intersectionality, identity politics, and violence against women of color. *Stanford Law Review, 43*(6), 1241–1299. https://doi.org/10.2307/1229039

Gonzales, L. D., & Griffin, K. A. (2020). Supporting faculty during & after COVID-19: Don't let go of equity. *Aspire Alliance.* 1–7.

Hooks, B. (1994). *Teaching to transgress: Education as the practice of freedom.* Routledge.

Hooks, B. (2015). *Yearning: Race, gender, and cultural politics.*

Lipsky, L., & Burk, C. (2009). *Trauma stewardship an everyday guide to caring for self while caring for others.*

McMillan Cottom, T. (2017). *Lower Ed: The troubling rise of for-profits.* The New Press.

Nica, E. (2018). Has the shift to overworked and underpaid adjunct faculty helped education outcomes? *Educational Philosophy and Theory, 50*(3), 213–216. https://doi.org/10.1080/00131857.2017.1300026

Porter, C. J. (2019). Metaphorically speaking: Being a Black woman in the academy is like .... In D. J. Mitchell, Jr., J. Marie, & T. Steele (Eds.), *Intersectionality & higher education: Theory, research, and praxis.* (2nd ed., pp. 99–109). Peter Lang

Richie, B. (2012). *Arrested justice: Black women, violence, and America's prison nation.*

Soucheray, S. (2020, March 2). Seattle is hot spot for COVID-19 as US cases hit 100. https://www.cidrap.umn.edu/news-perspective/2020/03/seattle-hot-spot-covid-19-us-cases-hit-100

Thomason, A. (2020, March 6). U. of Washington cancels in-person classes, becoming First Major U.S. institution to do so amid coronavirus fears. https://www.chronicle.com/article/U-of-Washington-Cancels/248198

Watson, B., & Scraton, S. J. (2013). Leisure studies and intersectionality. *Leisure Studies, 32*(1), 35–47. https://doi.org/10.1080/02614367.2012.707677

"If We're Lost, we Are Lost Together": Leisure and Relationality

Felice Yuen

ABSTRACT
The COVID-19 pandemic has brought on a sense of freedoms lost with the emergence of regulatory practices aimed at reducing the spread of the virus. This loss has likely impacted experiences of leisure, particularly in western societies where the perception of freedom is a significant indicator of leisure. The article explores the significance of relationality and leisure from a decolonizing perspective. Building upon observations of the author's experiences during the pandemic, the article will drawn upon relational ontology, the centrality of relationship, and connection with self, family, and other entities of life.

> *Strange and beautiful are the stars tonight*
> *That dance around your head*
> *In your eyes I see that perfect world*
> *I hope that doesn't sound too weird*
> —Blue Rodeo (1992)[1]

With the onset of the COVID-19 pandemic, the world we know has changed. In a matter of days, our sense of freedom was lost with the emergence of regulatory practices aimed at reducing the spread of the virus. For example, ongoing pleas for people to stay at home, the closure of libraries, arenas, and playgrounds, fines imposed for gathering in a park, and canceled international flights became facts of life—a necessity for survival. Leisure experiences undoubtedly changed. The setting in which they occur is now at home, and, if we are lucky, outside for a walk, run, or bike ride, while maintaining a 2 m (6 feet) distance from individuals who are not from the same household. Our sense of time is blurred as we work, play, recreate, cook, eat, and clean in the same setting, alone, or with the same people day after day. As described by Giurge and Bohns (2020), "the lines between work and non-work are blurring in new and unusual ways" (2nd para.). Psychologists emphasize the importance of structure and routine (Leung, 2020), but this is easier said than done.

---

[1]All headings in this article are lyrics from the song Lost Together, written by Greg Keelor and Jim Cuddy from the band Blue Rodeo (1992).

While setting and time are examples of how leisure has changed, this paper focuses on how the meaning of leisure may be evolving during this pandemic. In western societies, such as North America and Europe, where the perception of freedom is generally understood to be the most important criteria for leisure experiences (Kleiber et al., 2011), it is highly likely that the sudden loss of freedom has impacted leisure experiences. Briefly, relatedness is "feeling connected to significant individuals" (Sheldon, 2002, p. 48). As defined by Saulteaux and Nêhiýaw (Saskatchewan, Canada) scholar Kovach and her colleagues (2013), relationality has the potential to further non-Indigenous understandings of relatedness as it acknowledges connection *and* obligation to *all* our relations of place, elders, self, friends, and family. This change might be temporary or it may be the beginning of a paradigm shift (Kuhn, 1970). Nonetheless, as the song Lost Together (Blue Rodeo, 1992) reminds us, the world (with COVID-19) is strange (and perhaps scary), but beauty can be found in the connections that are created, unearthed, and/or strengthened.

Notably, the intent of this article is not to generalize, nor is it meant to impose an experience. Rather, it is a reflection based on my own experiences and observations as a Chinese, Canadian-born mother, woman, and researcher who had the privilege of learning from and working with Indigenous communities for nearly two decades and subsequently, whose worldview was sharpened by a *decolonizing* lens. That is, a perspective that deliberately counters "Eurocentric assumption (error) that some human beings have the power to 'know' others … but would rather acknowledge and focus on the complexities of our … conditions(s)" (Cannella & Manuelito, 2008, p. 49[2]). As argued by Rojek (2013), different paradigms fundamentally lead to different conceptualizations of leisure. This reflection is simply another perspective to add to our understandings of leisure.

And I wonder why I bother … Stumbling from one disaster to another

My COVID-19 lockdown began with building a Star Wars Lego set with my six-year-old son. The Lego set was one of many, broken up by my son, and thrown into an old suitcase with thousands of other pieces. Over the course of the week, this activity became an agonizing experience because we could not find Anakin Skywalker's head. My life was suddenly centered around building Anakin's fighter jet and finding his head. My husband even joked, "when I think back to our experience of COVID-19, I'm going to think of Anakin's lost head." Before COVID-19 became a common term in our home, building Lego was one of my favorite leisure activities to do with my children, but this no longer felt like leisure. Tempers rose and patience waned. Moreover, we never found Anakin's head. This experience is not what I expected, nor what I was hoping for.

In western societies, optimal leisure experiences have been equated with concepts such as flow (Cohen, 2013; Csikszentmihalyi & LeFevre, 1989) and self-actualization (Cohen; Murdock, 1994). That is, concepts where personal growth and development are at the core of the experience. Flow is experienced when challenge meets the individual's

---

[2]Manuelito is Dine (Southwestern USA).

skills (Csikzentmihalyi, 1997), while self-actualization emphasizes an individual's development and fulfillment of potential (Maslow, 1943). As Cohen contends, such conceptualizations of this ideal leisure experience dominate western perspectives of leisure. He further emphasizes that individual growth and development are grounded in a sense of freedom to learn for its own sake. Moreover, Ryan and Deci (2017) emphasize how autonomy (personal choice and control) and competence (mastery of task and skill) are significant motivators for participation.

As noted by Hunnicutt (2006), western perspectives of leisure (and work) stem from ancient Greece (e.g., Plato and Aristotle), and the Industrial Revolution. Given the profoundly male perspectives that shaped our field, there is no surprise that dominant western leisure perspectives continue to be male[3]. From this perspective, it is understandable that my Lego experience led to feelings of dissatisfaction and frustration. There was no fulfillment of one's potential in this scenario—Anakin's head was gone, likely sucked up by the vacuum cleaner long ago. If learning patience and anger management were personal skills to be developed, the activity was also a failure. In fact, I would argue it added to feelings of incompetence brought on by my diminished capacity to be as efficient and productive as I used to be at work and to keep up with the dust-bunnies that seem to have multiplied exponentially at home, just to name a few. While there may have been opportunities for flow, it was nearly impossible due to the mounting stress of work and household obligations, and living with a sense of freedoms lost. In other words, experiences of flow, which are characterized by absorption, timelessness, creativity, and inner clarity (Csikzentmihalyi, 1997), may have been possible under "normal" circumstances but were either quickly disrupted or too difficult to achieve with the impact of COVID-19.

As Rojek (2001) acknowledges, numerous critics challenge the classical definition of leisure as freedom, choice, and self-determination. Specifically, he emphasizes Veblen's (2005) idea of conspicuous consumption, which underscores using leisure as a representation of class (i.e., a demonstration of who has wealth and power) and feminist leisure scholars such as Shaw (1985) and Wearing (1998), who bring forth the relationship between patriarchy and leisure. While counter narratives of leisure date back centuries, disruptions to the ideology of "good" leisure are imperative as they are reflections of their own values and are an enactment of power against colonial values, attitudes, and structures (Fox & Lashua, 2010). The following section explores what may happen when relationality becomes a central focus our lives and, more specifically, becomes a main indicator of "good" leisure.

And if we're lost, we are lost together

According to Tewa (New Mexico, USA) scholar Cajete (2015), the production of knowledge in western societies "suffer[s] a kind of sensory and emotional starvation" and that "matter, life, mind, soul, and spirit … must be unified if the field of human knowledge and meaning are to move beyond the current mono-dimensional view" (p. 123).

---

[3]While dominant western perspectives of leisure are inherently male, several feminist leisure scholars have challenged these perspectives and put forth alternative conceptualizations (see Henderson & Shaw, 2006; Parry, 2018; Parry & Fullagar, 2013).

Importantly, he contends logic and rational empiricism continue to be necessary, as do "sensation, perception, imagination, emotion, symbols, and spirit" (p. 122). As suggested by Springgay (2011), privileging other forms of knowledge creates the capacity for extending boundaries of normalized and dominant perspectives. Certain theories of affect contend impingements felt in the body, or visceral reactions, are reality—they are *affective facts* (Massumi, 2010). For example, the bodily sensations informing us of fear or sadness is the felt reality of what cannot be seen. Affect is also used as a method of knowing (e.g., Hickey-Moody, 2013; Yuen et al., 2019) by focusing on sensations such as rhythm, movement, force, and intensity, as opposed to cognition, reason, and distance. Focusing on sensations and emotions requires an awareness and connection with self and others. This awareness and connection includes people, as well as all things present in nature (Cajete). As such, centering our worldviews around relationality may be an approach to seeing and experiencing diverse realities and understandings.

Noonuccal (Queensland, Australia) scholar Martin and Mirraboopa (2003) states, a relational ontology focuses on interrelatedness, interdependence, and coming to know our responsibilities related to self and others. Specifically, she articulates:

> All things are recognised and respected for their place in the overall system. Whilst they are differentiated, these relations are not oppositional, nor binaric, but are inclusive and accepting of diversity. These relations serve to define and unite, not to oppose or alienate … You no longer know yourself as a 'person', you've become an Entity amongst other Entities. Through a relational ontology, the connections are restored relatedness reciprocated and maintained.

When relationality becomes central, individual growth and development become less important, relations of mutuality become more prevalent, and empathy becomes more accessible. Over the course the second week of my COVID-19 lockdown, a shift in my perception of leisure occurred: I began to focus on the connections with my son, daughter, husband, myself, and the world around me. In other words, freedom (e.g., freedom from obligation, freedom of choice, freedom to learn and experience personal growth and development) became less important and patience and kindness become more accessible. Anakin's head will never be found, and that is okay. Dozens of Lego sets are mixed together and it takes countless hours to sift through, organize, find, and that is okay. What I have is an opportunity to be with my son, (re)connect with him, my six-year old self, our imaginations, and nourish these relationships. Occasionally, our Lego building became a family affair: Big sister joined and amazed us with her ability to find the pieces we were looking for and together we celebrated. Other times, she sat with us and read her book. Dad would also join, sort, find, and build. These were 'good' leisure moments. Now, I look forward to the mornings when my son wakes me up with "Mommy, L-E-G-O, Lego time!"

And in that second of a shooting star it all makes sense … your love's all I need

Perhaps the shift in my expectations and defining criteria of leisure emerged from the culmination of cognitive dissonance (i.e., a sense of freedom is not possible, so I will value it less), the integration of numerous Indigenous teachings (e.g., concepts of

Image 1. Writing, snuggling, reading, and making bracelets … together Photo: Jonathan Driver.

relationality), and a stronger desire to honor my connection to my Chinese heritage and value systems (based upon collectivism) with the one year anniversary of the passing of my maternal grandmother (see Iyengar & Lepper, 1999). Furthermore, as we all might feel during moments of immense and intense change, transformation is/was filled with tension and internal conflict. Akin to Anakin, we might feel like we lost our heads. Given the focus of this article, analyzing motivations for and experiences of change are better left for another day. Regardless of the reasons why and how change occurs, the intent of this paper was to contemplate the centrality of relationality in leisure experiences. Observations of my own leisure experiences during the COVID-19 pandemic suggest that they became more enjoyable, meaningful, and satisfactory when they were centered upon relationality. Building Lego is one example detailed in this paper, but there were others: listening to my mother tell Asian legends and my father share eastern philosophies over Skype with my children; baking cookies for neighbors under a 14-day quarantine; making Jello in memory of my grandmother; cooking meals with my husband for the health-care-workers we know; eating more take-out than ever from the locally-owned and operated Mexican restaurant in our neighborhood; going for family walks simply to notice the rebirth of spring; and witnessing our children saying hello to all the squirrels they have named in our backyard.

Notably, affect is paramount in relationality. That is, relationality and its existence is felt. For example, the kinship I feel with my maternal grandmother is not physically tangible as she is not physically present, but she is there and I feel closer and more connected to her than ever. Recognizing that relationality occurs through experience reminds me of the legend of how the tiger got his stripes, a story I heard when I was a child. Incidentally, my mom recently shared this legend with my children over Skype. The moral of the story, which originated from Vietnam, is that wisdom cannot be given or taken. Rather, it emerges through experience. In short, the intangible realities of wisdom and relationality are felt and cannot be scene.

Since COVID-19, relationality has became a grounding force. Structuring and compartmentalizing aspects of life (e.g., work-leisure space and time) is representative of a colonized perspective (Bear, 2000[4]). Rather, adopting a relational ontology is about inter-connection and interdependence of all things. In this way, relationality is not contextually about being central to leisure, but central to a way of life. Hard as one might try, structure and routine are hard to re-produce during this pandemic. Perhaps it is not about maintaining the boundaries, but breaking them down and (re)connecting with each other, ourselves, our ancestors, nature, spirits, energies, and entities that surround us. During the COVID-19 lockdown, some of my most meaningful moments were grounded in relationality—when my children were with me as I wrote this article (see Image 1, and yes, we are in my bedroom, it is after noon, and my son is still in his pyjamas), sitting on my lap, and typing these letters you see, one-by-one with their little index fingers. Productivity, efficiency, self-development and growth went out the window, but there was no frustration. Nowhere to go and nothing to do but savor in this moment of connection.

Acknowledgments

A special thank you to the reviewer for your insightful, supportive, and encouraging feedback. Immense and heartfelt gratitude to Maxine and Clearlight, for your infinite wisdom and the gentle impact you've had on my life and subsequently, this article.

References

Bear, L. L. (2000). Jagged worldviews colliding. In M. Battiste (Ed.), *Reclaiming indigenous voice and vision* (pp. 77–85). UBC Press.

Blue Rodeo. (1992). Lost Together [Song]. On Lost Together [Album]. Warner Music Canada.

Cajete, G. A. (2015). Where there is no name for science. In S. Grande (Ed.), *Red pedagogy: Native American social and political thought* (2nd ed.). Rowman & Littlefield.

Cannella, G. S., & Manuelito, K. D. (2008). Feminisms from unthought locations. In N. Denzin, Y. S. Lincoln, & L. Tuhiwai Smith (Eds.), *Handbook of critical and indigenous methodologies* (pp. 45–59). Sage Publications Inc.

Cohen, S. A. (2013). Leisure, identities and personal growth. In S. Elkington, & S. Gammon (Eds.), *Contemporary perspectives in leisure: Meanings, motives and lifelong learning* (pp. 197–206). Routledge.

Csikzentmihalyi, M. (1997). *Finding flow*. Ziff-Davis Publishing Company.

Csikszentmihalyi, M., & LeFevre, J. (1989). Optimal experience in work and leisure. *Journal of Personality and Social Psychology, 56*(5), 815–822. https://doi.org/10.1037/0022-3514.56.5.815

Fox, K. M., & Lashua, B. D. (2010). Hold gently people who create space on the margins: Urban Aboriginal-Canadian young people and hip hop rhythms of "leisures. In H. Mair, S. M. Arai, & D. G. Reid (Eds.), *Decentring work: Critical perspectives on leisure, social policy and human development* (pp. 229–250). University of Calgary Press.

Giurge, L. M., & Bohns, V. K. (2020). 3 Tips to Avoid WFH Burnout. Havard Business Review. https://hbr.org/2020/04/3-tips-to-avoid-wfh-burnout

Henderson, K. A., & Shaw, S. M. (2006). Leisure and gender: Challenges and opportunities for feminist research. In C. Rojek, S. Shaw, & A. J. Veal (Eds.), *A handbook of leisure studies* (pp. 216–230). Palgrave Macmillan.

---

[4]Bear is Blackfoot (Alberta, Canada).

Hickey-Moody, A. (2013). Affect as method: Feelings, aesthetics and affective pedagogy. In R. Coleman, & J. Ringrose (Eds.), *Deleuze and research methodologies* (pp. 79–95). Edinburg University Press.

Hunnicutt, B. K. (2006). The history of western leisure. In C. Rojek, S. Shaw, & A. J. Veal (Eds.), *A handbook of leisure studies* (pp. 55–74). Palgrave Macmillan.

Iyengar, S. S., & Lepper, M. R. (1999). Rethinking the value of choice: a cultural perspective on intrinsic motivation. *Journal of Personality and Social Psychology*, 76(3), 349–366. https://doi.org/10.1037/0022-3514.76.3.349

Kleiber, D. A., Walker, G. J., & Mannell, R. C. (2011). *A social psychology of leisure* (2nd ed.). Venture.

Kovach, M., Carriere, J., Barrett, M. J., Montgomery, H., & Gillies, C. (2013). Stories of diverse identity locations in indigenous research. *International Review of Qualitative Research*, 6(4), 487–509. https://doi.org/10.1525/irqr.2013.6.4.487

Kuhn, T. S. (1970). *The structure of scientific revolutions* (2nd ed.). University of Chicago Press.

Leung, W. (2020, March 16). Tips for managing anxiety during the COVID-19 pandemic. *The Globe and Mail*. https://www.theglobeandmail.com/canada/article-tips-for-managing-anxiety-during-the-covid-19-pandemic/

Martin, K., & Mirraboopa, B. (2003). Ways of knowing, being and doing: A theoretical framework and methods for indigenous and indigenist re-search. *Journal of Australian Studies*, 27(76), 203–214. https://doi.org/10.1080/14443050309387838

Maslow, A. H. (1943). Conflict, frustration, and the theory of threat. *The Journal of Abnormal and Social Psychology*, 38(1), 81–86. https://doi.org/10.1037/h0054634

Massumi, B. (2010). The political ontology of threat. In M. Gregg, G. J. Seigworth, & S. Ahmed (Eds.), *The affect theory reader* (pp. 52–70). Duke University Press.

Murdock, G. (1994). New times/hard times: Leisure, participation and the common good. *Leisure Studies*, 13(4), 239–248.

Parry, D. C. (2018). *Feminisms in leisure studies*. Routledge.

Parry, D. C., & Fullagar, S. (2013). Feminist leisure research in the contemporary era: Introduction to the special issue. *Journal of Leisure Research*, 45(5), 571–582. https://doi.org/10.18666/jlr-2013-v45-i5-4363

Rojek, C. (2001). Leisure and life politics. *Leisure Sciences*, 23(2), 115–125. https://doi.org/10.1080/014904001300181701

Rojek, C. (2013). *Capitalism and leisure theory* (Routledge Revivals). Routledge.

Ryan, R. M., & Deci, E. L. (2017). *Self-determination theory: Basic psychological needs in motivation, development, and wellness*. Guilford Publications.

Shaw, S. (1985). Gender, leisure and constraint: Towards a framework for the analysis of women's leisure. *Journal of Leisure Research*, 17(4), 266–282. https://doi.org/10.1080/00222216.1985.11969637

Sheldon, K. M. (2002). The self-concordance model of healthy goal striving: When personal goals correctly represent the person. In E. L. Deci, & R. M. Ryan (Eds.), *Handbook of self-determination research*. University Rochester Press.

Springgay, S. (2011). The ethico-aesthetics of affect and a sensational pedagogy. *Journal of the Canadian Association for Curriculum Studies*, 9(1), 66–82.

Veblen, T. (2005). *The theory of the leisure class: An economic study of institutions*. Aakar Books.

Wearing, B. (1998). *Leisure and feminist theory*. Sage.

Yuen, F., Ranahan, P., Linds, W., & Goulet, L. (2019). Leisure, cultural continuity, and life promotion. *Annals of Leisure Research*, 1–22. https://doi.org/10.1080/11745398.2019.1653778

Power and Social Control of Youth during the COVID-19 Pandemic

Myra Gayle Gabriel ⓘ, Aishia Brown, Maria León ⓘ, and Corliss Outley

ABSTRACT

While people across the globe adapt to the COVID-19 pandemic, young people have been the center of many news stories. Millions of young people are required to stay home due to school closures, and adults are forced to consider alternative structures to support youths' needs. The COVID-19 pandemic has exposed multiple injustices and forms of oppression experienced by the most vulnerable in our country, which includes young people experiencing poverty, incarceration, foster care, homelessness, and those with marginalized identities. This article will discuss the role of power and social control in the lives of youth during the COVID-19 pandemic and present strategies leisure researchers and practitioners can adopt to overcome the loss of critical support structures and mitigate exponential effects of COVID-19 on our most vulnerable youth.

Introduction

The COVID-19 pandemic has exposed multiple injustices and forms of oppression experienced by the most vulnerable in the United States, including *vulnerable youth*. Here the authors define "vulnerable youth" as those *between the ages of 10 and 24 years old who are racialized, experiencing poverty, incarceration, mental health issues, food scarcity, abuse, foster care, homelessness, and/or youth who have marginalized identities* (Emig, 2020; Hager, 2020; Sawyer et al., 2018; United Nations Population Fund, 2014; World Health Organization [WHO], 2020). Their vulnerability is further exacerbated by the youths' lack of power and control due to sociopolitical systems, structures, and policies that are produced based on adult-centric biases rooted in Eurocentric colonialism, particularly oppression and power. Injustices and oppression are results of power, with roots in global colonialism and conquests and reflected in centuries of violent conflict, cultural and spatial displacement, and social, economic, and political oppression that continue to produce inclusionary/exclusionary practices today (Palmer et al., 2019).

Unfortunately, many adults serve as agents of oppression who deny the occurrence of injustices and believe control is needed to monitor perceived problematic behaviors and actions of youth. As a result, these youth become subjects of increased surveillance and control measures. However, research has shown that providing vulnerable youth opportunities for voice and to exercise their own agency greatly contributes to positive developmental pathways toward adulthood (Caldwell, 2018; Outley et al., 2018). This article will discuss the role of power and social control in the lives of youth during the COVID-19 pandemic and present strategies leisure researchers and practitioners can adopt to address the loss of critical support structures and mitigate exponential effects of COVID-19 on our most vulnerable youth.

Current status of COVID-19

It may seem that youth populations are at lower risk for COVID-19 fatality; however, all youth, especially vulnerable youth, are suffering the abrupt end to employment, educational programs, and community and social services due to closures and social distancing measures intended to minimize the spread of COVID-19.

While social distancing and other guidelines to protect the public health of the U.S. population at-large are implemented, COVID-19's impact on youth goes beyond staying home from school. Rates of poverty, abuse, neglect, and unemployment have risen during this pandemic, and millions of youth are not receiving the necessary support (Bartlett & Vivrette, 2020). If anything, COVID-19 has exacerbated day-to-day challenges for our most vulnerable youth, mainly youth of color who are trapped in generational poverty, associated with the juvenile justice system, in foster care, with disabilities, homeless or housing insecure, and youth who are undocumented. Furthermore, the sudden losses of health and educational services continue to marginalize vulnerable youth by removing avenues to use their voice, thus introducing greater instability and insecurity.

Leisure behavior, youth, and COVID-19

Leisure activities are important for youth because they support healthy growth and development, improve mental health, assist in building social skills, and reduce disease later in life. However, during times of stress, youth with the most access to support, opportunities, programs, and services (SOPS) in leisure settings are more likely to succeed in maintaining a healthy future (Caldwell, 2018). In contrast, vulnerable youth do not have the same opportunities for leisure as youth who have greater access to SOPS. Even the temporary loss of SOPS greatly impacts the health and wellbeing of marginalized and vulnerable youth, who might rely on such community organizations for food, clothing, safe spaces, or employment.

Without SOPS even temporarily, vulnerable youth have limited structured options for leisure and recreation outside of using the internet and social media platforms. Historically, the unstructured leisure time of vulnerable youth has often come under scrutiny and has been viewed with skepticism and assumptions of wrongdoing or vagrancy (Maimon & Browning, 2010). Unfortunately, COVID-19 has exacerbated the policing and controlling of vulnerable and marginalized youth bodies as youth cope with the loss of structured and group activities (Davis, 2020; Human Rights Watch, 2020; Leon, 2020; Robinson, 2020).

Power and social control of youth during COVID-19

During these unprecedented times, we must place a critical lens on the power dynamics and forms of social control experienced by our most vulnerable youth. Power exerted through policy enactment is often used to practice social control on marginalized youth and their communities (Hirschi, 1969). Social control theory suggests that youth who engage in what is often deemed "negative" behavior lack protective factors, such as strong familial bonds, high academic achievement, and so on. The public health and other fields hold a long history of adopting social control theory in youth prevention and intervention efforts by advocating for policy change within social systems (Hirschi, 1969; Huebner & Betts, 2002). However, unless such policies are critically examined, the systems will maintain and reinforce disparities at a macro level. Given that adults hold control of decision-making processes at the local, state, and federal levels, there is an implicit bias that favors adults, particularly white men who have been at the helm of decision-making groups for centuries. The exclusion of youth and people of color from decision making maintains the engrained thought processes rooted in racist and adultist ideology (Bell, 1995; Feagin, 2013). Policies that exert social control in this manner disproportionately impact vulnerable youth by placing them into social systems like juvenile justice or foster care, where their likelihood of experiencing trauma significantly increases. These effects could be exacerbated during pandemics like COVID-19 where social distancing policies and shelter-in-place orders are enacted. This is especially the case in how the current discourse on reopening many localities has played out. Furthermore, Freire (2003) asserts that when the interests of the oppressors are foremost, the oppressor is able to maintain and embody oppressive acts through the dehumanization of the oppressed.

How adults use social control to exert power over vulnerable youth is clear in the early April 2020 incident where a white man attempted to strangle a black teenage girl who was lounging with her friends on a picnic blanket (Fieldstadt, 2020). Despite the man breaking the social distancing guidelines himself by coming within six feet of the group of girls, the most violent actions were reserved for the nlack teenage girl and not anyone else involved in the situation. Through the COVID-19 pandemic, the social control of youth is acted out by adults and takes place in a number of ways, including how media cover the activities of black youth during the pandemic, and parallels the racism experienced by black youth in the phenomena of "playing while black" (Martinez, 2020; Pinckney et al., 2018).

The leisure of Asian American youth has also suffered in light of the COVID-19 pandemic and the president's politicizing of the virus. If not the outward discrimination faced in public spaces, Asian American youth face increased online bullying as well. Following social distancing guidelines, a young Asian American girl turned to the chat site Omegle in search of new friends. Instead, she found a cesspool of xenophobic users who barraged her with racist verbal comments and pantomimed slanted eyelids meant to represent Asian people (Nguyen, 2020). Whether in physical spaces or over the internet, the scrutiny and xenophobia meted out to Asian Americans during COVID-19 has greatly reduced their power of choice in leisure activities and instead produced a heightened anxiety surrounding their emotional and physical safety. Consequently, Asian American youth are pushed even further to the margins by xenophobia and the "model minority" myth (Chou & Feagin, 2015; Margolin, 2020). As leisure researchers, we must employ strategies that promote, advocate, and practice equity and social justice for groups experiencing racism and discrimination, and for those subject to policies that exert power and social control in ways that exacerbate inequities.

Strategies to address issues of power and social control

Efforts to flatten the curve during the COVID-19 pandemic often fail to consider how social distancing and shelter-in-place orders may affect vulnerable youth. Social support systems vital to physical, mental, and emotional health of youth, such as schools, public parks, community centers, and recreational youth programs, are experiencing strains on their ability to provide services. Many of these support systems are losing federal funds due to closures and are having to furlough or terminate staff who serve as caring adults in the lives of vulnerable youth. These social support systems also serve as safe spaces for vulnerable youth and those with marginalized identities (LGBTQIA+, homeless, disconnected, and justice-involved youth). Economic strain of these social support systems also influences factors like youth employment, causing many youth who work out of necessity to lose their only source of income. We note that the experiences of youth in group homes, detention centers, and on the streets were not considered when decision making took place at the federal, state, and local levels in response to the COVID-19 pandemic.

Current strategies to address the pandemic have been actions like school closures and shelter-in-place orders for nonessential work and activities. However, these strategies have exposed vulnerable youth to the lack of resources and disparities in communities across the country. This, we contend, amounts to a form of power and social control where only those who are nonvulnerable are centered. So how do we begin to change the current discourse? As leisure researchers and practitioners, we must use the history of systemic racism and oppression in the United States to inform our strategies to address issues experienced by youth during this pandemic.

Adopting social justice youth development as a strategy

Historically, the voices of the most vulnerable in our society have been censored or not taken seriously when it comes to informing both policy and practice decisions. With young people under the age of 18 not having the right to vote, we must reexamine the ways we value youth civic engagement and its importance. Outley et al. (2018) defines this as "an approach focused on the development of equitable access and opportunities for all youth by actively reducing or eliminating disparities in education, health, employment, justice, and any other system that hinders the development of young people" (p. 486).

In practice, social justice youth development requires intentional support from caring adults focused on ending injustices and obstacles that harm vulnerable youth in our society. A focus on inequalities brings to light the deficit and cultural pathological colonial views that keep youth and the communities they live in powerless. This strategy not only ensures that youth voice is transformative but also allows youth to challenge systemic inequalities by raising their critical consciousness to analyze their lived experience through a broader sociopolitical systemic lens along with their connected histories (Cammarota & Fine, 2010; Outley et al., 2018).

Cultivating sociopolitical development through culturally responsive programming

There is a long history of marginalized communities adopting culturally responsive programing to serve the needs of children and youth. For example, the Black Panther Party for Self-Defense Free Breakfast Program provided more than just free food to black children and youth living in Oakland, Calif., in the 1970s. This group also focused on promoting positive collective identity and political self-efficacy development while youth attended the breakfast program. Events leading up to the student walkouts of 1968 organized by East Los Angeles youth from the Chicano Student Movement were also heavily influenced by similar approaches where out-of-school time was used as a tool to cultivate sociopolitical development among vulnerable youth. Sociopolitical development or the process where youth build awareness of how culture and politics shape their status in society and engage in action in social and political systems is shown to be vital to the developmental process for vulnerable youth (Watts et al., 2003; Ginwright, 2010; Outley et al., 2018). To be culturally responsive to oppressed and vulnerable youth experiences, youth programs should adopt sociopolitical development as a key indicator in all culturally responsive programing.

Adopting youth impact analysis as a methodology

We should also adopt new research methodologies that amplify the voices and lived experiences of youth, especially those who were experiencing inequities before the pandemic. One strategy is to conduct what we refer to as a *youth impact analysis* to inform emergency and contingency plans and policies to prepare for pandemics like COVID-19 (Bogenschneider et al., 2012; National Center for Environmental Health, Centers for Disease Control & Prevention, 2016). Adopted from public health and family studies, this strategy integrates youth voice in the decision-making process and involves them in analyzing policies and programs to calculate and predict their impact on youth and their communities prior to implementation (León, 2020). Through a youth impact analysis, youth can force many decision makers to consider the effects policies such as closing public parks, community centers, and schools have on their wellbeing. This crucial step will increase accountability among decision makers as they are presented with a full scope of potential consequences for all youth, especially those considered vulnerable.

Conclusion

Scholars and practitioners must begin to challenge the colonial systems rooted in whiteness that have created the current inequitable experiences for vulnerable youth. As more researchers begin to examine the connection between power and vulnerable youth, the importance of examining how adults use adultism, the white racial frame, and its associated control mechanisms to maintain inequality and dehumanize the most vulnerable among us will allow us to more fully critique the social, historical, economic, and political implications for the field of youth development and leisure. It is our hope that the strategies above will lead to empowering vulnerable youth to take the lead to activate change in their community rather than be oppressed by the current inequitable systems, policies, and practices.

Disclosure statement

We have no known conflicts of interest to disclose.

ORCID

Myra Gayle Gabriel ⓘ http://orcid.org/0000-0002-5138-7810
Maria León ⓘ http://orcid.org/0000-0002-6055-6372

References

Bartlett, J. D., & Vivrette, R. (2020). *Ways to promote children's resilience to the COVID-19 pandemic.* https://www.childtrends.org/publications/ways-to-promote-childrens-resilience-to-the-covid-19-pandemic

Bell, J. (1995). Understanding adultism. A major obstacle to developing positive youth-adult relationships. *Hrsg. von.* YouthBuild USA. http://actioncivics.scoe.net/pdf/Understanding_Adultism.pdf

Bogenschneider, K., Little, O., Ooms, T., Benning, S., & Cadigan, K. (2012). *The family impact rationale: An evidence base for the family impact lens.* Madison, WI: Family Impact Institute.

Caldwell, L. (2018). The big picture: Youth today and tomorrow. In P. Witt & L. Caldwell (Eds.), *Youth development principles and practices in out-of-school- time settings* (pp. 27–56). Champaign, IL: Sagamore Venture.

Cammarota, J., & Fine, M. (Eds.). (2010). *Revolutionizing education: Youth participatory action research in motion.* Routledge.

Chou, R. S., & Feagin, J. R. (2015). *Myth of the model minority: Asian Americans facing racism.* Routledge.

Davis, J. (2020, April 29). The COVID-19 pandemic didn't stop this California cop from getting physical during a teen smoking arrest. *Reason.* https://reason.com/2020/04/29/the-covid-19-pandemic-didnt-stop-this-california-cop-from-getting-physical-during-a-teen-smoking-arrest/

Emig, C. (2020, March 30). COVID-19's forgotten children. Child Trends. https://www.child-trends.org/covid-19s-forgotten-children

Feagin, J. R. (2013). *The white racial frame: Centuries of racial framing and counter-framing.* Routledge.

Fieldstadt, E. (2020, April 8). Doctor arrested for attacking teen girls, choking one, apparently for not social distancing. *NBC News.* https://www.nbcnews.com/news/us-news/doctor-arrested-attacking-teen-girls-choking-one-apparently-not-social-n1179251

Freire, P. (2003). *Pedagogy of the oppressed* (30th anniv. ed.). London, UK: Continuum.

Ginwright, S. A. (2010). Peace out to revolution! Activism among African American youth: An argument for radical healing. *Young, 18*(1), 77–96. https://doi.org/10.1177/110330880901800106

Hager, H. (2020, March 24). Coronavirus Leaves Foster Children with Nowhere to Go: New placements, family visits and child-abuse investigations falter across the country. The Marshall Project. https://www.themarshallproject.org/2020/03/24/coronavirus-leaves-foster-children-with-nowhere-to-go

Hirschi, T. (1969). A control theory of delinquency. *Criminology Theory: Selected Classic Readings, 1969,* 289–305.

Huebner, A. J., & Betts, S. C. (2002). Exploring the utility of social control theory for youth development: Issues of attachment, involvement, and gender. *Youth & Society, 34*(2), 123–145. https://doi.org/10.1177/004411802237860

Human Rights Watch. (2020). *Human rights dimensions of COVID-19 response.* https://www.hrw.org/news/2020/03/19/human-rights-dimensions-covid-19-response#

Leon, J. (2020, April 18). Coronavirus: City fills skatepark with 37 tons of sand to deter skaters. *Kiro7 News.* https://www.kiro7.com/news/trending/coronavirus-city-fills-skatepark-with-37-tons-sand-deter-skaters/P36K2J3RLBBCZB3RVJC3G2X5HY/

León, M. (2020). Addressing the school to prison pipeline through youth impact analysis [Unpublished manuscript]. Texas A&M University, College Station, TX.

Maimon, D., & Browning, C. R. (2010). Unstructured socializing, collective efficacy, and violent behavior among urban youth. *Criminology, 48*(2), 443–474. https://doi.org/10.1111/j.1745-9125.2010.00192.x

Margolin, J. (2020, March 27). FBI warns of potential surge in hate crimes against Asian Americans amid coronavirus. *ABCNews.* https://abcnews.go.com/US/fbi-warns-potential-surge-hate-crimes-asian-americans/story?id=69831920

Martinez, A. (2020, March 26). *Videos show large groups of teens fighting in Louisville during coronavirus crisis.* https://www.wave3.com/2020/03/27/videos-show-large-groups-teens-fighting-louisville-during-coronavirus-crisis/

National Center for Environmental Health, Centers for Disease Control and Prevention. (2016). *Health impact analysis.* https://www.cdc.gov/healthyplaces/hia.htm

Nguyen, K. (2020, April 22). Woman records racists she's met on omegle during the pandemic. *NextShark.* https://nextshark.com/sophie-wang-omegle-racists/

Outley, C., Brown, A., Gabriel, M. G., & Sullins, A. (2018). The role of culture in youth development. In P. Witt & L. Caldwell (Eds.), *Youth development principles and practices in out-of-school- time settings* (pp. 463–492). Champaign, IL: Sagamore Venture.

Palmer, G., Fernández, J. S., Gordon, L., Masud, H., Hilson, S., Tang, C., … Bernal, I. (2019). Oppression and power. In L. A. Jason, O. Glantsman, J. O'Brien, & K. Ramian (Ed.), *Introduction to community psychology: Becoming an agent of change* (Chapter 9). Redbus Press.

Pinckney, H. P., IV, Outley, C., Brown, A., & Theriault, D. (2018). Playing while black. *Leisure Sciences, 40*(7), 675–685. https://doi.org/10.1080/01490400.2018.1534627

Robinson, I. (2020, May 3). Chicago mayor tells black teens on playground to go home, gets roasted in response on camera. *The Root.* https://www.theroot.com/chicago-mayor-tells-black-teens-on-playground-to-go-hom-1843225595

Sawyer, S. M., Azzopardi, P. S., Wickremarathne, D., & Patton, G. C. (2018). The age of adolescence. *The Lancet. Child & Adolescent Health, 2*(3), 223–228. https://doi.org/10.1016/S2352-4642(18)30022-1

United Nations Population Fund. (2014). *The state of world population 2014.* https://www.unfpa.org/sites/default/files/pub-pdf/EN-SWOP14-Report_FINAL-web.pdf

Watts, R. J., Williams, N. C., & Jagers, R. J. (2003). Sociopolitical development. *American Journal of Community Psychology, 31*(1–2), 185–194. https://doi.org/10.1023/A:1023091024140

World Health Organization (WHO). (2020). *Adolescent health.* https://www.who.int/southeastasia/health-topics/adolescent-health

Leisure Behind Bars: The Realities of COVID-19 for Youth Connected to the Justice System

Maria León, Kevin Rodas, and Mora Greer

ABSTRACT

The introduction of the coronavirus in any community is detrimental, however for correctional institutions the effects can be especially devastating. In an effort to reduce the impact of the virus, many locales have begun releasing youth back home. However, for young people experiencing the highest degree of constraint, the ability to choose how to spend their leisure has become even more restrained in light of COVID-19 due to increased restrictions and decreased resources. This essay exposes the reality of leisure during the corona pandemic for youth with justice system involvement through first-hand interviews with and by youth involved with Arts for Incarcerated Youth in Los Angeles. These personal narratives are contextualized with a comprehensive policy evaluation of leisure and recreation programming for juvenile justice facilities and theoretical implications according to Social Justice Youth Development (Ginwright & Cammarota, 2002; León et al., 2019).

Introduction

COVID-19 has transformed leisure behaviors and spurred innovation among advocates to promote wellness in the midst of a pandemic. While no population is free of challenges, youth in detention are at the intersection of invisibility and vulnerability given the impact of the virus on older populations and the unwavering dismissal of incarcerated kids. As young people are being released to their communities during this pandemic, leisure advocates and scholars should be engaged in the promotion of leisure programs for youth in the justice system particularly because "returning youth to communities as "better functioning individuals" includes "knowledge and (the) ability to properly use free time" (Robertson, 2001, p. 23). Including the voices of those dealing with the realities of leisure and COVID-19 while incarcerated is necessary in order to have an accurate conversation that is inclusive of all perspectives, seen and unseen.

While steps are taken to release men, women and children to their homes, each day there are new reports of outbreaks in jails and prisons that failed to take the necessary precautions to keep those currently detained safe. At the time of writing, 150 youth and 253 staff are known to have tested positive for COVID-19, however it is fair to assume this number has increased by time of publication due to the transmissibility of the virus, increased testing and improved reporting measures (Rovner, 2020). Establishing an idea of the unique context of a prison environment during a pandemic is necessary to have a more meaningful conversation surrounding leisure in correctional institutions, this paper will aim to achieve both. In addition to reviewing data and publications in popular press articles that speak to the realities of juvenile justice facilities, the authors of this paper interviewed youth involved in the Arts for Incarcerated Youth Network (AIYN). The authors, some of whom are youth themselves, developed questions and collected responses through online questionnaires and personal phone interviews. The responses were then coded by the authors to identify emergent themes and are woven throughout this paper as support of the larger discussion. To protect the identities of the individuals who participated, names of individuals and facilities have been changed and/or removed.

The remainder of this paper will include an overview of the current status of COVID-19 in juvenile justice facilities including the provision of leisure before exploring the legal precedent for leisure programing in U.S. juvenile justice facilities. A brief discussion on the integration of Social Justice Youth Development in working with young people in marginalized communities is included prior to the conclusion.

COVID-19 in juvenile justice facilities

Over the past few weeks, individual states and counties have taken action to reduce the population of incarcerated individuals in justice facilities, although initiatives specifically for juvenile facilities have been slower. On March 30th, the National Governors Association issued a memo addressing strategies to mitigate the negative impact of COVID-19 in the juvenile justice system (McBride, 2020). The primary emphasis of the letter urges states to release young people to their communities to minimize the risk of infecting large numbers of detained youth (McBride, 2020). The task to safely release youth is further complicated by the fact that black and brown communities are disproportionately affected by COVID-19 and have fewer resources to test and provide treatment; let alone that black and brown youth are overrepresented in the juvenile justice system (NAACOP, 2020; Noe-Payne, 2020). In conversations regarding COVID-19 and leisure in juvenile justice with those currently involved in some capacity, two primary themes emerged: communication and isolation. It became clear throughout the conversations that health and safety was the priority for those currently incarcerated and their families.

Communication

The first theme that arose from the interviews was communication. For family members on the outside there is a lack of communication, causing concern for loved ones that are incarcerated. Given the disparities of rates of incarceration, entire communities are plagued with compounded stress during this pandemic (NAACP, 2020). When asked what some of her concerns are for incarcerated friends and family she has not been able to communicate with, one young woman shared several unanswered questions, including: *"Are they sharing bunks or are they separated? Are they getting the right care they need? Are they eating the right things to help their immune system? Is visitation canceled? If so for how long? Are the people that are scheduled to get out getting out on the date they are supposed to? Are there clothes being washed properly?"* (Kayla, personal communication, April 9, 2020).

Phone correspondence for youth in some facilities has been limited to ten minute phone calls on a semi-regular basis (Green, 2020). At the time of her interview in the second week of April, over one month after a state of emergency had been declared in her state, Kayla raised the issue that what is known about the prison population and pre-COVID-19 conditions of confinement needs to be addressed in the current pandemic. She says, *"I read in an article that people that are in prison/jails are more at risk then the general public because they are filled up with people who have high rates of serious health problems. In a full jail or prison it is hard to self-quarantine because they are full so how are they handling it?"* (Kayla, personal communication, April 9, 2020).

One young man reflects on his recent incarceration in a juvenile facility and worries about the health and safety of his friends still inside. He reports that he is *"afraid that they might contract the virus (and) might not see them for a long time. And also not knowing what resources they need or how to help them out."* (Shaun, personal communication, April 9, 2020). Depending on the facility and state policy, soap must be bought with personal money through the commissary, making it difficult to comply with the recommendations to wash hands frequently. Shaun reiterated the lack of communication as a particular challenge during the pandemic because *"they are in strict lockdown and cannot get visits and are most likely not getting money deposited because of the unemployment due to the virus."* Youth who have largely been stripped of their ability to protect themselves are now further stratified according to their access to income. This exact situation is a clear demonstration that the health of those entrusted to the state is secondary to the economic status of the justice system. The emphasis on maintaining a profitable system combined with the resistance to close facilities and release youth raises the question of whether or not it is profitable to have a smaller juvenile justice population.

As Kayla mentioned, incarcerated populations have always been at increased risk during public health crises because of the "petri dish" conditions (Green, 2020, para. 11; Wetsman, 2020). In addition to overcrowding, sanitizer and many cleaning agents are considered contraband, thereby limiting the ability to ward off exposure and contracting the virus. While incarcerated individuals are theoretically separated from the outside world, staff and vendors break that barrier by going in and out of the facility on a daily basis. The impact of this has already been actualized in at least Texas, Georgia, Connecticut, Virginia, New York and Washington D.C. where a staff member at a juvenile justice facility recently died of COVID-19 (Green, 2020; Kingkade, 2020; Noe-Payne, 2020).

The daily, sometimes hourly changes in facility protocol creates challenges for the staff who plan and facilitate programing. As a result of the rapid spread of the disease, changes are made on a daily basis, making it difficult for staff to communicate within and across facilities and establish best practices per reports from staff and advocates across the nation.

Isolation

The second theme discovered was isolation, which is exacerbated due to the lack of communication as previously discussed. One young man told a staff member in Louisiana, "if you die, nobody is coming," (Kingkade, 2020, para. 5). because as the staff member said, "They're worried about being left behind" (Kingkade, 2020, para. 7). One of the concerns of advocates across the nation is the overuse of solitary confinement as a strategy to reduce the spread of COVID-19. For young people, this means that they spend 23 h locked in a cell and are allocated one hour to spend outside their cell. This does not necessarily mean that time will be spent outdoors or in any type of organized activity (COVID-19 Response, 2020). Prolonged isolation is detrimental to the mental health and neurological development youth, particularly those with a history of trauma, that is 80% of youth in the justice system (Dierkhising et al., 2013). Recognizing the severity of isolation reveals that in effect, the changes to curb COVID-19 create extreme conditions that disincentivize youth to report symptoms. There are states that are offering additional phone time for youth at free or reduced cost as a result of visitations being canceled (COVID-19 Response, 2020). However, it is naive to believe that the extra time on the phone is sufficient to compensate for the reduced human interaction. Outside of schools and therapy sessions that have been altered to promote social distancing, leisure and recreation has been an opportunity for healthy interaction among youth and staff in facilities.

Leisure programming

Among the recommendations from the National Governors Association is for facilities to "Replace any activities or programs typically run by outside volunteers or service providers to ensure days are filled with positive activities" and "Provide mental and physical health resources to youth in custody" (McBride, 2020, para. 5). While leisure and recreation programing is not explicitly identified in these statements, such services do promote positive outcomes that include mental and physical health (Caldwell & Faulk, 2013).

Leisure and recreation programing in juvenile justice facilities is heavily dependent on volunteers. However, in an effort to minimize the risk of exposing incarcerated populations to COVID-19, the majority of volunteers are no longer allowed, or have chosen not to, enter facilities. To mitigate some of the impact, volunteers and staff have worked together in order to provide activities and support youth through sending holiday cards in lieu of hosting a program or using technology to hold virtual music classes.

Further implications for providing recreation and leisure services is the reality that many facilities are operating with a skeleton staff to limit the number of people on a campus. In order to keep with legal ratios, the time allocated for recreation has been reduced to 30 minutes per day in one facility (Green, 2020). When youth do have opportunity for leisure and recreation, access to resources and equipment is also restricted. Due to the design and operations of facilities, equipment is shared either in a gym, dorm or pod, and multiple youth use the same equipment, so without proper cleaning procedures between uses the risk of spreading COVID-19 is heightened.

State by state leisure guidelines

A basic understanding of the U.S. juvenile justice system is necessary in order to understand the challenges to simultaneously combat a pandemic and evaluate the quality of leisure and recreation programing for incarcerated youth. There is no federal juvenile justice system that regulates programs and services at a national level. Each state has its own juvenile justice system, housed in different departments. Each department has a written authority that includes rules, regulations, administrative codes, guidelines, etc. Additionally, depending on the state, each written authority has a different legal weight, meaning that the provision of leisure and recreation services in juvenile justice facilities is not necessarily legally protected.

On a national scale, there are no mandates outlining the provision of recreation and leisure services in juvenile justice facilities as a result of the independent systems. Given the historical and intentional design of the justice system in the United States, many of the challenges facing incarcerated individuals and correctional recreation staff are not new. A comprehensive state by state analysis of the minimum guidelines of recreation within U.S. juvenile correctional facilities was conducted and documents were evaluated on 17 items including the type, frequency, amount of time, purpose, restrictions, etc. (León et al., 2020). The results show that only 60% of states have a purpose statement in their written authorities, 38% of states describe physical and active activities, while 30% of states describe passive and leisure activities to be provided to youth (León et al., 2020). Pre-COVID-19, only 70% of states outlined daily mandatory minimum requirements for recreation in juvenile justice facilities (León et al., 2020). Only 44% of written authorities include that youth have access to spend time outdoors during the day (León et al., 2020).

Regardless of the current pandemic, these guidelines are inappropriate for young people and should be cause for concern among leisure scholars and advocates. Given the developmental benefits for participation in leisure and recreation programs, additional support for the use of leisure in correctional institutions is supported by the data on juvenile offending (Caldwell & Faulk, 2013; Robertson, 2001). Juvenile crime has consistently peaked in the afterschool hours and justified the creation of after school extra-curricular programs for youth. Robertson (2001) emphasizes the responsibility of correctional institutions to promote healthy leisure behaviors to support the rehabilitation and reintegration process (OJJDP, 2018). As increasing numbers of youth are being released to their communities as a result of COVID-19, it is in the interest of young people and the community to ensure that equitable and accessible leisure activities are available to youth. Shaun reflects that being a part of program like AIYN has *"been a way for me to express myself and be involved in positive things & focus on my community and ways to make it better ... it has been a way for me to stay away from trouble and be on a path to a new beginning."* Armed with the knowledge of the significant, positive impact that leisure can have for individuals, leisure scholars have a duty to engage and advocate for leisure and recreation services for youth in corrections.

Social justice youth development

The simple act of asking young people to comment on the justice system in which they are intertwined is promoting a critical consciousness and expanding their social awareness. In turn, the discussion regarding the leisure of incarcerated young people is more complete with their voices. In line with Social Justice Youth Development, in order to challenge the oppressive systems surrounding youth in social, economic and political contexts, young people must have the opportunity to contribute meaningfully to create equitable solutions (Ginwright & Cammarota, 2002). If we are to pause and consider the critiques and ideas of youth who have direct experience with the juvenile justice system, the response of the academic community concerned with leisure will have more relevance.

Conclusion

The challenges that have been raised in wake of COVID-19 presents an opportunity for leisure scholars to pivot toward a more equitable, fair, appropriate, and humane approach, particularly in the juvenile justice system. Teams of youth, staff, and scholars are needed in order to provide relevant and accurate critiques of the justice system that fails to afford appropriate opportunities for leisure. Unless the education and preparation for leisure time is addressed simultaneously in correctional institutions and communities, all segments of the population will suffer as young people are being released home to communities that are not designed to promote success. Now is the time to challenge the traditional delivery of youth services to promote the well-being of young people in a pandemic. The responsibility for ensuring the protection of leisure for incarcerated youth falls on the shoulders of those who believe it to be an essential facet of life, anything less is hypocrisy.

Disclosure statement

The authors have known conflict of interest to disclose.

References

Caldwell, L. L., & Faulk, M. (2013). Adolescent leisure from a developmental and prevention perspective. In *Positive leisure science* (pp. 41–60). Springer.

COVID-19 Statement. (2020, March 19). https://yclj.org/covid19statement

COVID-19 Response. (2020). http://www.tjjd.texas.gov/index.php/covid19

Dierkhising, C. B., Ko, S. J., Woods-Jaeger, B., Briggs, E. C., Lee, R., & Pynoos, R. S. (2013). Trauma histories among justice-involved youth: Findings from the National Child Traumatic Stress Network. *European Journal of Psychotraumatology*, 4(1), 20274.

Ginwright, S., & Cammarota, J. (2002). New terrain in youth development: The promise of a social justice approach. *Social Justice*, 29(4), 82–95.

Green, E. L. (2020, April 14). 'Pacing and praying': Jailed youths seek release as virus spreads. https://www.nytimes.com/2020/04/14/us/politics/coronavirus-juvenile-detention.html

Kingkade, T. (2020, March 27). Coronavirus in juvenile detention is a 'nightmare scenario,' doctors and advocates say. https://www.nbcnews.com/news/us-news/coronavirus-juvenile-detention-nightmare-scenario-doctors-advocates-say-n1170256

León, M., Outley, C., Marchbanks, M., & Kelly Pryor, B. (2020). A review of recreation requirements in U.S. juvenile justice facilities. *Criminal Justice Policy Review*, 31(5), 763–782.

McBride, B. (2020). *Memorandum: COVID-19 responses in the juvenile justice system*. National Governors Association.

National Association for the Advancement of Colored People (NAACP). (2020). *Ten equity implications of the coronavirus COVID-19 outbreak in the United States.* https://naacp.org/wp-content/uploads/2020/03/Ten-Equity-Considerations-of-the-Coronavirus-COVID-19-Outbreak-in-the-United-States_Version-2.pdf

Noe-Payne, M. (2020, April 20). Virginia Juvenile Correctional Facility Overwhelmed By Coronavirus. Retrieved from https://www.npr.org/sections/coronavirus-live-updates/2020/04/20/838790229/virginia-juvenile-correctional-facility-overwhelmed-by-coronavirus

OJJDP. (2018). Statistical Briefing Book. Online. https://www.ojjdp.gov/ojstatbb/offenders/qa03301.asp?qaDate=2016.

Robertson, B. J. (2001). The leisure education of incarcerated youth. *World Leisure Journal, 43*(1), 20–29.

Rovner, J. (2020, May 4). COVID-19 in juvenile facilities. https://www.sentencingproject.org/publications/covid-19-in-juvenile-facilities/?eType=EmailBlastContent&eId=5710e096-3e6c-427f-adf3-f648cd23eed1

Wetsman, N. (2020, March 7). Prisons and jails are vulnerable to COVID-19 outbreaks. https://www.theverge.com/2020/3/7/21167807/coronavirus-prison-jail-health-outbreak-covid-19-flu-soap

Rainbows, Teddy Bears and 'Others': The Cultural Politics of Children's Leisure Amidst the COVID-19 Pandemic

Utsa Mukherjee (iD)

ABSTRACT
In countries currently under lockdown, schools and leisure facilities have closed their gates to the vast majority of children. Having to stay indoors for most of the day, children's leisurescapes have been radically transformed. In these circumstances, instances have emerged from across the globe of children adapting to the lockdown in creative ways and constructing leisurescapes within the limits of the home, by putting up rainbows and teddy bears on windows and porches. Drawing upon media reports about children's rainbow drawings and teddy bear hunts, in this paper, I deploy a sociological lens to demonstrate how children are using these leisure narratives as tools for participating in the wider conversation around the pandemic. At the same time, however, in pinning romanticized notions of hope and 'national spirit' upon the normative image of the child at play, media narratives are obfuscating the inequalities that fracture lived childhoods in the developed world.

Introduction: children's leisure in the time of COVID-19

The COVID-19 pandemic has resulted in more than half of the world's population being asked by governments to stay at home and practice 'social distancing' measures in an effort to curb the spread of the pestilence. These so-called social distancing measures signify acts of *physical* distancing which in turn have reconfigured the *social* in fundamental ways. With lockdowns underway, schools, leisure centers and recreation facilities have closed their doors to the vast majority of children. These emergency measures have reassembled children's everyday geographies – reshaping the social institutions, processes, and relationships in which their daily lives are embedded. However, amidst these disruptions and uncertainties, instances have emerged from across the globe of children adapting to the lockdown in creative ways and crafting their narratives of leisure within the limits of the home, using resources available to them. Italy, which is amongst the worst affected countries, has seen children make drawings of rainbows inscribed with the slogan 'andrà tutto bene' (everything will be all right) and display them on windowpanes since the pandemic forced the country into lockdown at the beginning of March (Otte, 2020). In the United Kingdom too, children have been drawing rainbows – often featuring thank you notes for the National Health Service (NHS) – and putting them up on street-facing windows and outside their homes (Freshwater, 2020). In a similar veins, lockdown 'teddy bear hunts' have become extremely popular in New Zealand (NZ) wherein children are displaying teddy bears on their front windows and pinning their location onto the 'NZ Bear Hunt' website – enabling other children to 'hunt' the bears from afar as they go out for their government mandated daily exercise in the local area with their parents (Roy, 2020). This window 'bear hunt' has since spread to the United States (Alexander, 2020), Canada (Desai, 2020), Australia (Alba, 2020), the Netherlands (Salm, 2020) and Belgium (Johnston, 2020) among other countries. Whilst familiar leisure spaces are out of bounds, these emergent leisure narratives produced by children can offer us a fresh ingress into the conceptualization of children's leisure cultures and illustrate how they have been reshaped by the COVID-19 outbreak. Pulling together media reports on the construction of lockdown leisurescapes by children, in this critical commentary I deploy the sociological lens of children's participation to unpack the implications of these emergent leisure narratives and to reflect upon the ways in which they have been framed by the media. In particular, I will draw upon reports about children's drawings in the UK and children's teddy bear hunts in New Zealand to unravel the cultural politics of children's leisure under the current lockdown. I further demonstrate that the frames news-media outlets have brought to bear on these leisure activities of children offer important insights into how ideals of childhood and that of children's leisure are being socially constructed and circulated amidst the pandemic. I will begin by sketching the theoretical framework for understanding children's participation before looking into the UK and New Zealand cases in further details.

Children's everyday participation: a sociological lens

In unpacking and analyzing these leisure narratives of children, I embrace the critical framework offered by the 'new' sociology of childhood which departs significantly from developmental psychology. Whilst the psy-sciences conceive of childhood as a universal biological category that undergoes a linear development across fixed stages, the 'new' sociology of childhood draws upon historical and across-cultural accounts to argue that ideas as well as lived experiences of childhood vary across time and place (James et al., 1998). This sociological framework understands childhood as an unequal space where generational divides intersect with classed, gendered and racial inequalities to produce a multiplicity of lived childhood within any given time-space (Wells, 2017). Children, in this view, are agentic social actors in the here and now who are shaped by and who in turn contribute to the social milieu they inhabit (Mayall, 2002). Issues of power are therefore central to this sociological understanding of children's lives in terms of how structural inequalities shape children's life chances, how children's subjectivities are produced and how children from their historically constituted social location engage with social institutions and processes.

The theoretical lens of children's participation, anchored within this broader socio-logical framework of childhood studies, can put into perspective the leisure narratives of children outlined above. This idea of children's participation, which is closely linked to children's agency, has been framed in two main ways. One set of scholars have looked into institutionalized and normative modes of children's participation which take as its point of departure formal provisions made by adults that involve children in decision-making processes. This encompasses instances such as student councils in schools, which largely maintain status-quo while incorporating the voices of some children (Savyasaachi Butler, 2014; Thomas, 2009). In contrast, there is another body of scholar-ship which takes a more holistic view of participation by unmooring it from the narrow emphasis on institutional mechanisms and grounding it instead in children's everyday life, social-material encounters and relationships (Wyness, 2018). This view directs our attention to *children's spaces* where childhoods are lived out and which are environ-ments of many possibilities shaped by children's encounters with adults and other chil-dren (Moss & Petrie, 2002). These 'children's spaces' mark the realm for the construction of non-predictable futures. In this sense, children's participation offers a window into understanding children as political actors either in terms of the issues and structures they engage with or in terms of the micropolitics of their inter-generational (child-adult) and intra-generational (child-child) relations.

Rainbows, teddy bears and leisure

In countries currently under lockdown, schools have closed their gates to the vast majority of children and other facilities that school-age children attend are closed too. Confined largely to their homes with no access to peer groups and leisure centers, children's physical leisurescapes have been transformed. At home, children's education, family time and leisure are intertwined like never before with digital leisure assuming greater importance. However, amidst these changes, children in several countries are co-creating leisure narratives that are responding directly to this lockdown.

News media outlets in the UK have widely reported the growing phenomenon of children's hand-drawn rainbows which are appearing on windowpanes across the coun-try. This trend started in Italy – the first country in Europe to go into lockdown – where children drew rainbows often inscribed with the message 'andrà tutto bene' (everything will be all right) and put them on windows and balconies for others to see (Otte, 2020). UK children are writing 'Thank You NHS' on their rainbow drawings – expressing gratitude for the tireless work being done by healthcare workers of the National Health Service (NHS) which is a publicly-funded healthcare system that is free to people at the point of use. These leisure narratives that children are crafting through their acts of drawing and displaying their rainbows on front windows are not only vis-ible to people on the street, it has attracted significant media attention with TV chan-nels and newspapers actively asking children to send in pictures and videos of their rainbows (BBC, 2020). On Twitter, these pictures and videos are being tagged with the hashtag #chasetherainbow - indicating both the illusionary chase after the rainbow as well as turning the trend itself into a virtual adventure under lockdown. The 'thank you' messages for the NHS and the bright colors of the rainbow are increasingly being portrayed in the media as harbingers of "hope" and "positivity" (Freshwater, 2020; Doherty, 2020) that are helping to "raise spirits of passers-by" (Dracott, 2020). Amidst this lockdown, Queen Elizabeth II delivered a rare televised broadcast where she reflected on how Britons have expressed their gratitude to key workers:

> The moments when the United Kingdom has come together to applaud its care and essential workers will be remembered as an expression of our national spirit; and its symbol will be the rainbows drawn by children. (HM The Queen, 2020, para. 5)

Here the notions of childhood and nation are closely entangled, with the representation of the purported 'national spirit' being built upon ideals of childhood. Indeed, the consolidation of the modern nation-state in the West in the 19th century coincided within the construction of the modern ideal of childhood that quarantined children from the adult-world, confining children to the realm of the family and the school and severing their erstwhile role as economic actors (Hendrick, 1997). Children located outside this ideal were seen as 'out of place' and therefore needed 'rescuing' by state agencies and philanthropists. These historical processes produced the frames within which romanticized notions of domesticated and scholarized childhood became ideal vehicles in whose name the nation came to act and craft policies. At the same time, children in many respects are 'not citizens', being bereft of such privileges such as voting rights and obligations such as financial responsibility (Cockburn, 2013).

The deficit model of children's citizenship – which can be exploited as the basis of the nation – has no room for understanding the lives of actual children and their participation in wider debates. Aspects of children's leisure encapsulated by the rainbow drawings take us beyond this individualized model of children-as-future-citizens to their *lived citizenship* in the here and now (Baraldi & Cockburn, 2018). These drawings straddle the new divisions erected by the lockdown, acting as the bridge between the home and the street, the private and the public, the lockdown and its future. Rather than framing children's leisure narratives during this lockdown as replicable acts upon which notions of futurity can be projected, the materiality of these drawings constitute one of the many ways through which children are engaging with the wider social issue of this pandemic and symbolically participating in national conversations. These leisurescapes of children are embedded in an assemblage of humans and materials implicating parents, family members, drawing paraphernalia and the internet.

In New Zealand (NZ), Deb Hoffman founded the 'teddy bear hunt' on a Facebook page where she invited children to place a teddy bear on their windows and mark their location by dropping a 'pin' on the NZ Bear Hunt website. This enabled children to spot bears in windows when they go out in their local areas with parents for their daily exercises – which is allowed under current lockdown rules. Although it was started by an adult, the bear hunt has not only gathered pace across the globe, it has been appropriated by children themselves. It has been reported that many children are changing the attire of their teddies every day and creating elaborate displays on their porches and gardens of bears fishing and playing in different formations (Roy, 2020). Inspired by the children's book *We're Going on a Bear Hunt* by Michael Rosen, this lockdown leisure phenomenon brings home the significance of internet-enabled global flows of ideas, affect and materials. Meanwhile two sisters in the US, aged 8 and 12, have started a Facebook group with the help of their parents through which others are sharing pictures of 'bear hunts' from across the country and further field (Fortin, 2020). The two sisters are putting pushpins on maps in their room to keep track of all the bear sightings reported on their group. The teddy bear which has been emblematic of American consumer culture has traveled places and its significance as a companion object within children's emotional geographies is well known. In the time of COVID-19, however, this teddy bear hunt has become a vehicle for children's participation and lived citizenship. Through these leisure narratives, children are making their presence felt and symbolically engaging in the public debate on the lockdown and its future.

Popular framing of children's COVID-19 leisurescapes as harbingers of hope and symbols of 'national spirit' conspicuously leaves out – and thereby *otherizes* – the leisure narratives and modes of participation of marginalized children who often lack material resources at their disposal. Their lived citizenship and agency might assume forms that are different from those of middle-class children, whose life experiences often get projected as ideal norms of childhood (Wells, 2017). In fact, within high-income countries, one child in five lives in poverty (UNICEF, 2017) with limited access to permanent accommodation or the internet. Their leisure narratives during the lockdown is absent from available media accounts. With this lockdown adversely affecting the marginalized sections of society and unraveling the reaches of health inequalities, future leisure scholars should look carefully into children's participation through leisure across multiple social contexts. Indeed, critically unpacking the inequalities of childhood and that of children's leisure can help us re-assess the state of the nation and re-assemble an inclusive and socially just 'national spirit'.

Conclusion

The leisure narratives children are constructing through rainbow drawings and teddy bears represent a small portion of their everyday lives and these are indeed geographically limited examples that I have discussed above. Nonetheless, they matter – to the children themselves and to their communities – and they offer a range of crucial insights into the cultural politics of children's leisure amidst this COVID-19 pandemic. The rainbow and the teddy bear are both readily available cultural texts that children and their parents are harnessing during this lockdown. The leisure spaces thus created are connected to the wider conversation around the pandemic while being embedded within a range of generational and material relations involving the child, their family members, their drawing kits, and other paraphernalia. These leisure narratives demonstrate that children's leisure cultures are never insulated from the adult world but are embedded in a range of social relationships of inter-dependence through which children (co)construct leisure and make it meaningful.

The distinction I made earlier between *physical* and *social* distancing bears repeating here for although children are keeping physical distance by staying at home, they are weaving social intimacies through the material production and display of their rainbows and bear hunts. As evidenced by the media reports above, the conversation around these leisure activities have become vehicles for solidarity and social communication for many. However, in pinning romanticized notions of hope and 'national spirit' upon the normative image of the child at play, media narratives are obfuscating the extent of childhood poverty and inequality that inflect the lives – and leisure opportunities – of millions of children in the developed world.

ORCID

Utsa Mukherjee ⓘ http://orcid.org/0000-0002-1073-6367

References

Alba, B. (2020, March 31). People are putting bears in their front windows to bring children joy. *SBS.* https://www.sbs.com.au/topics/voices/culture/article/2020/03/30/how-teddy-bear-hunts-are-giving-children-some-simple-joy

Alexander, B. (2020, April 10). 'Teddy Bear Hunt': Stuffed animal scavenger hunts are making life bearable for bored kids. *USA Today.* https://www.usatoday.com/story/life/2020/03/30/coronavirus-teddy-bear-hunts-challenges-children-safe-walking-activities/2937592001/

Baraldi, C., & Cockburn, T. (2018). Introduction: Lived citizenship, rights and participation in contemporary. In C. Baraldi & T. Cockburn (Eds.), *Theorising childhood* (pp. 1–27). Palgrave Macmillan.

Cockburn, T. (2013). *Rethinking children's citizenship.* Palgrave Macmillan.

Desai, D. (2020, April 2). 'We're going on a bear hunt': Canadians place teddy bears in windows to distract children from COVID-19. *National Post.* https://nationalpost.com/news/were-going-on-a-bear-hunt-canadians-place-teddy-bears-in-window-to-distract-children-from-covid-19

Doherty, R. (2020, March 24). Children's handmade rainbows are popping up in windows all over the UK – here's why. *CountryLiving.* https://www.countryliving.com/uk/news/a31894717/rainbows-in-windows-coronavirus/

Dracott, E. (2020, March 23). Children put rainbows in windows to raise spirits of passers-by. *Belfast Telegraph Digital.* https://www.belfasttelegraph.co.uk/news/uk/children-put-rainbows-in-windows-to-raise-spirits-of-passers-by-39067017.html

Europe BBC. (2020, March 26). Coronavirus rainbow window pictures and videos - we want them! https://www.bbc.co.uk/newsround/52034134

Fortin, J. (2020, April 3). Children are hunting teddy bears during the coronavirus outbreak. *The New York Times.* https://www.nytimes.com/2020/04/03/style/teddy-bear-scavenger-hunt.html

Freshwater, P. (2020, April 4). 30 pictures of your children's drawings to thank NHS workers and show hope amid coronavirus pandemic. *GrimsbyLive.* https://www.grimsbytelegraph.co.uk/news/grimsby-news/gallery/30-pictures-your-childrens-drawings-4012467

Hendrick, H. (1997). *Children, childhood and English society, 1880–1990.* Cambridge University Press.

HM The Queen. (2020, April 5). *The Queen's broadcast to the UK and Commonwealth.* https://www.royal.uk/queens-broadcast-uk-and-commonwealth

James, A., Jenks, C., & Prout, A. (1998). *Theorizing childhood.* Polity.

Johnston, J. (2020, March 31). Coronavirus: Belgian children go on a (teddy) bear hunt. *The Brussels Times.* https://www.brusselstimes.com/belgium/103775/coronavirus-belgian-children-go-on-a-teddy-bear-hunt/

Mayall, B. (2002). *Towards a sociology for childhood: Thinking from children's lives.* Open University Press.

Moss, P., & Petrie, P. (2002). *From children's services to children's spaces: Public policy, children and childhood.* RoutledgeFalmer.

Otte, J. (2020, March 12). 'Everything will be all right': message of hope spreads in Italy. *The Guardian.* https://www.theguardian.com/world/2020/mar/12/everything-will-be-alright-italians-share-slogan-of-hope-in-face-of-coronavirus-crisis

Roy, E. A. (2020, March 31). 'Bear hunt' helps banish coronavirus boredom for New Zealand children. *The Guardian.* https://www.theguardian.com/world/2020/mar/31/bear-hunt-helps-banish-coronavirus-boredom-for-new-zealand-children

Salm, H. (2020, March 26). Een knuffelbeer achter elk raam maakt het dagelijkse luchtje scheppen tot een ware berenjacht. *Trouw*. https://www.trouw.nl/binnenland/een-knuffelbeer-achter-elk-raam-maakt-het-dagelijkse-luchtje-scheppen-tot-een-ware-berenjacht~b24dfc35/

Savyasaachi Butler, U. M. (2014). Decolonizing the notion of participation of children and young people. In E. K. M. Tisdall, A. M. Gadda, & U. M. Butler (Eds.), *Children and young people's participation and its transformative potential* (pp. 44–60). Palgrave Macmillan.

Thomas, N. (2009). Introduction: children, politics and communication. In N. Thomas (Ed.), *Children, politics and communication* (pp 1–6). Policy Press.

UNICEF. (2017). *Building the future: Children and the sustainable development goals in rich countries* (Innocenti Report Card 14).

Wells, K. (2017). *Childhood studies: Making young subjects*. Polity.

Wyness, M. (2018). Children's participation: Definitions, narratives and disputes. In C. Baraldi & T. Cockburn (Eds.), *Theorising childhood* (pp. 53–72). Palgrave Macmillan.

Are You OK, Boomer? Intensification of Ageism and Intergenerational Tensions on Social Media Amid COVID-19

Brad A. Meisner

ABSTRACT
Social media is a useful tool for connecting with family, friends and others while physically distancing and self-isolating due to COVID-19. Simultaneously, it is being used for purposes of expressing antagonistic stereotypes, prejudice, and discrimination against older adults. This commentary draws on social media trending topics (e.g., "OK, Boomer," "Boomer Remover") to demonstrate how generalizations regarding chronological age and COVID-19 age-related biomedical risks have: (a) exacerbated ageism on social media, and (b) further exposed ongoing tensions between so-called "Millennial" and "Baby Boomer" generations in ways that are targeted against the older generation and serve in favor of younger ones. The implications of this ageist discourse in and on society are discussed. Anti-ageism efforts by social media users and organizations are highlighted. In this state of emergency, we must bring awareness to and resist ageism that depersonalizes and dehumanizes older adults and undervalues later life during and following the COVID-19 pandemic.

The rapid and radical changes that COVID-19 brought to our daily lives have shifted how we engage with one another in society. Due to physical distancing and self-isolation recommendations, we are in pursuit of alternative ways to connect personally and socially during this pandemic. Some people are turning to social media to communicate with each other virtually, but apart from each other physically. Despite the contributions that social media can make to our lives in this time of crisis, it also comes with some significant limitations. For instance, it can be used as a platform for hurtful messages, such as online bullying, which can result in psychological and social harms. These messages can be targeted at specific social media users or be about members of a social group on social media and/or in society, including older adults and the "older generation." Unfortunately, the wake of COVID-19 has brought a resurgence of hostile messages on social media, even classifying as hate speech, that exhibit ageism against older adults (Ayalon, in press).

Ageism was first exposed by Butler in 1969 (Butler, 1969) and described as, "the subjective experience implied in the popular notion of the generation gap ... a deep seated uneasiness on the part of the young and middle-aged—a personal revulsion to and distaste for growing old, disease, and disability" (p. 243). Since then, the definition of ageism evolved to encompass cognitive (i.e., age stereotypes, beliefs), emotional (i.e., age prejudice, attitudes) and behavioral (i.e., age discrimination, actions) components (Ayalon & Tesch-Römer, 2017). These components manifest at individual, interpersonal, as well as institutional and cultural levels that result in older people being perceived and treated differently due to chronological age (Iversen et al., 2009).

The expression of ageism on social media is not new. For example, in 2019, before the COVID-19 pandemic, the catchphrase "OK, Boomer" went viral around the world on TikTok and other social media platforms. It became a slogan for "Millennials" who felt "Baby Boomers" were out-of-touch with modern realities because of outdated and conservative beliefs, and were delaying progress on important societal issues, such as domestic economic inequities and global climate change. The expression even managed to find its way into government affairs. In November 2019, 25-year-old New Zealand politician Chlöe Swarbrick was presenting the Zero Carbon Bill that was challenged by an older Parliament member (Elliott, 2019). Her reply was "OK, Boomer" which dismissed the challenge and aimed to discredit her colleague. This Millennial motto sparked debate of what constitutes free speech versus hate speech between generations (Iannone, 2020).

But now COVID-19 is going viral around the world—in terms of actual transmission and in discussions on social media. A similarity between "OK, Boomer" and COVID-19 is that both disproportionately implicate older people. Symptoms of COVID-19 are typically mild for children, youth and adults. However, older adults and individuals with preexisting medical conditions (e.g., cardiovascular and pulmonary diseases, cancers, diabetes) are typically more likely to develop serious illness, require hospitalization and intensive care, as well as die from the virus or acquire chronic conditions with survival (World Health Organization, 2020a). To counteract these negative outcomes, chronological age and compromised health status are included as major risk factors within local and global public health COVID-19 campaigns. For example, the New Zealand Government (2020) COVID-19 strategy includes being kind and supportive to friends, neighbors and extended family, especially the "elderly and vulnerable." The Government of Canada (2020) identifies those most likely to experience severe COVID-19 illness and encourages all Canadians to limit contact with people at higher risk such as "older adults and those in poor health." The World Health Organization (2020b) states people who are "60+ and those with underlying health conditions" should avoid areas where they may interact with people who are sick to protect themselves against COVID-19. These campaigns aim to prevent or reduce virus transmission—across and within countries, communities, families and generations of people—based on early biomedical evidence of the risk factors associated with how the virus *generally* expresses in hosts of different ages and states of health. However, these campaign messages depict an oversimplification of both "age" and the risks of COVID-19 associated with "age", which represents and reinforces ageism.

More specifically, the "elderly" or "older adult" group is categorized arbitrarily using chronological age cutoff points, which falsely homogenizes the many individual differences and personal diversities observed in later life (Ayalon et al., in press; Gullette, 2017). Then this heterogeneous group is uniformly labeled as "vulnerable" and "at risk"—inextricably intertwined with assumptions of poor health and underlying health conditions—indicating a conflation of age and disease. These representations go against more recent evidence that shows other more robust risk factors of COVID-19 exist, such as certain underlying health conditions, irrespective of age (Garg et al., 2020; Montero-Odasso et al., 2020). Unfortunately, this oversimplified age and age-related risk messaging characterizes generalized negative beliefs and attitudes about aging and older adulthood (i.e., age stereotypes and prejudice, respectively), which can, and do, result in the differential treatment of older adults based on age (i.e., age discrimination) as well as a multitude of negative biopsychosocial health outcomes in later life (Levy, 2009; Meisner, 2012a; Meisner & Levy, 2016). Even more unfortunately, the wide-spread correlation of aging and poor health status with COVID-19 risk has caused the repopularization and intensification of ageism and intergenerational tensions in public discourse far worse than "OK, Boomer."

On social media, COVID-19 has many names, several of which pertain to older adults. The virus is referred to as the "Boomer Doomer," "Senior Deleter" and "Elder Repeller." However, one name that is arguably the most viral is "Boomer Remover" which was a trending topic and hashtag on Twitter in March 2020. According to some opinions shared online, the "purpose" of COVID-19 as the "Boomer Remover" is to: efficiently address global and domestic overpopulation by targeting older adults and sparing the lives of children, youth, and younger adults; decrease the demand and burden that older adults put on health care and tax systems; remove older adults from society so that more jobs, opportunities, and resources can be provided to younger and healthier people; and reduce the number of right-wing conservative voters.

Within these tweets there exist clear themes of population cleansing across generations. Population cleansing signifies, "a planned, deliberate removal from a certain territory of an undesirable population distinguished by one or more characteristics such as ethnicity, religion, race, class, or sexual preference" (Bell-Fialkoff, 1996, p. 3). Regarding "Boomer Remover," it is implied online that the COVID-19 virus was "designed" to remove older adults from society. Further, the political nature of population cleansing is observed in these views as well—that is to endorse or permit the elimination of one social group for the benefit of another group (Bell-Fialkoff, 1996). COVID-19 acts *against* older adults and serves in *favor* of younger adults. Younger age groups are "the desirables" while the older age group portrays "the undesirables"—not only are older adults undesirable, they are viewed as an expendable nuisance to younger generations.

There is considerable gerontological literature that has, for years, documented these issues. For example, Gee (2000) described the "apocalyptic demography" ideology to represent popular concerns that the growing proportion of older adults in the population would have catastrophic consequences on society (e.g., the "grey tsunami"). The notion that social resources, "get funnelled to the sick, the old, and the retired at the expense of the healthy, the young and the working" (Gee, 2000, p. 5). These similarly oversimplified beliefs and attitudes problematize aging and homogenize, objectify, and blame older people (Gee, 2000; Longino, 2005). Such views are also used to justify or rationalize actions that prevent or counteract perceived intergenerational injustices through social policy (Gee, 2000; Gee & Gutman, 2000).

Therefore, we should be concerned that apocalyptic demography and COVID-19 "Boomer Remover" ideologies are finding their way into government matters, just as

"OK, Boomer" did. For example, United States Texas Lieutenant Governor Dan Patrick stated on Fox News in March and April 2020 that grandparents should be willing to take their chances and accept the risk of death to prevent lockdowns and protect the economy for their children and grandchildren (Knodel, 2020), and that saving his country for his children and grandchildren is, and should be, more important to him than living (Madani, 2020). We need to be hypervigilant and responsive when ageist ideas and actions are endorsed by officials who have the authority to inform or make decisions that affect the lives of others—particularly in the context of COVID-19 health care policies. The detrimental influence of ageism was present in health care before COVID-19 (Levy et al., 2020; Meisner, 2012b), so the increased attention to these issues is even more vital now that medical decision-making directives are being created in terms of who does and does not receive the limited resources and life-saving equipment in hospital and long-term care settings. It should be clear that not only are these ageist ideas and actions blatantly discriminatory, but that taking away the rights, privileges, and lives of one social group to benefit another is a human rights violation and characterizes genocide based on age (Bell-Fialkoff, 1996; Government of Canada, 1982).

This is not to say that age is not a factor related to COVID-19. However, it should not be *the* factor that determines how older adults are treated—socially or medically (Ayalon, 2020; Levy, 2009; Meisner & Levy, 2016; Montero-Odasso et al., 2020). Unfortunately, some clinical ethics recommendations for the provision of COVID-19 medical intervention in exceptionally resource-limited situations indicate that, "it might be needed to set an age limit for the admission to intensive care" (Cesari & Proietti, 2020, p. 576). Again, we must recognize that chronological age is not an inherently robust predictor of health and functioning, which is particularly true in later life (Montero-Odasso et al., 2020). There are reports of 100-year-olds recovering (and 20-year-olds dying) from COVID-19. So, rather than relying on chronological age as *the* indicator of COVID-19 discussions, debates, and decisions, we should identify and use valid, reliable, and objective measures, which are quick and easy to obtain for rapid medical decision making, that operate independently of age (Cesari & Proietti, 2020; Montero-Odasso et al., 2020).

The use of "Boomer Remover" and other similar terms to refer to COVID-19 should be criticized for being ageist against older people. Optimistically, the problematic nature of COVID-19 ageism is recognized by dissenting voices on social media and beyond. In opposition of the term "Boomer Remover," anti-ageism advocates on Twitter note that: unlike people, COVID-19 does not discriminate based on age; if younger people think COVID-19 will not negatively affect them, then they may not take precautionary measures, unintentionally become infected, and transmit the virus to their family members; how serious it would be if a younger person's grandparent or someone else they love was sick; and that it is just a matter of time until younger people will become older and then ageism (and possibly COVID-19) will affect them too. Additionally, in statements pertaining to COVID-19, national and international associations are resolutely condemning ageism and reminding us that: "people of all ages are privileged with the same rights" (British Society of Gerontology, 2020); that we, "need to tackle ageism and stigma against older persons head-on" (United Nations, 2020, p. 4); and that:

It is essential that policies, programmes and communications provide a differentiated, undistorted picture of the impact of the pandemic on older persons and their contribution to the response to ensure they are not being stigmatized. Broader community engagement can help to promote intergenerational solidarity, combat ageism and monitor and address violence, abuse and neglect against older persons (United Nations, 2020, p. 9).

These messages emphasize that *we are all people*—within families and communities and across age groups, generations, and time. People who are valued *individuals* with meaningful lives, no matter what our age. These messages also emphasize that the "us vs. them" and "Millennial vs. Baby Boomer" framing works against us, despite being socially constructed and maintained by us (Ayalon, 2020; Gullette, 2004). Until there is an effective vaccine, we must consider how COVID-19 will impact the aging experiences of our current, and future, older generations. In the meantime, although we cannot control the year we were born, we can control how we think about, treat, respect, and empathize with each other—across generations, in solidarity—especially in a time of crisis.

Declaration of interest statement

No potential conflict of interest was reported by the author.

References

Ayalon, L. (in press). There is nothing new under the sun: Ageism and intergenerational tension in the age of the COVID-19 outbreak. *International Psychogeriatrics, Online*, 1–4.

Ayalon, L., & Tesch-Römer, C. (2017). Taking a closer look at ageism: Self- and other-directed ageist attitudes and discrimination. *European Journal of Ageing, 14*(1), 1–4.

Ayalon, L., Chasteen, A., Diehl, M., Levy, B., Neupert, S. D., Rothermund, K., Tesch-Römer, C., & Wahl, H. W. (in press). Aging in times of the COVID-19 pandemic: Avoiding ageism and fostering intergenerational solidarity. *The Journals of Gerontology Series B: Psychological Sciences and Social Sciences*.

Bell-Fialkoff, A. (1996). *Ethnic cleansing*. St. Martin's Press.

British Society of Gerontology. (2020). BSG statement on COVID-19: 20 March 2020. https://www.britishgerontology.org/publications/bsg-statements-on-covid-19/statement-one

Butler, R. N. (1969). Ageism: Another form of bigotry. *The Gerontologist, 9*(4), 243–246.

Cesari, M., & Proietti, M. (2020). COVID-19 in Italy: Ageism and decision making in a pandemic. *Journal of the American Medical Directors Association, 21*(5), 576–577.

Elliott, J. (2019, November 6). 'OK boomer': Millennial MP shuts down heckler with viral comeback in New Zealand. *Global News*. https://globalnews.ca/news/6133526/ok-boomer-meaning-chloe-swarbrick

Garg, S., Kim, L., Whitaker, M., O'Halloran, A., Cummings, C., Holstein, R., Prill, M., Chai, S. J., Kirley, P. D., Alden, N. B., Kawasaki, B., Yousey-Hindes, K., Niccolai, L., Anderson, E. J., Openo, K. P., Weigel, A., Monroe, M. L., Ryan, P., Henderson, J., … Fry, A. (2020). Hospitalization rates and characteristics of patients hospitalized with laboratory-confirmed coronavirus disease 2019 - COVID-NET, 14 States, March 1-30, 2020. *MMWR Morbidity and Mortality Weekly Report, 69*(15), 458–464.

Gee, E. (2000). Voodoo demography, population ageing, and Canadian social policy. In E. Gee & G. Gutman (Eds.), *The overselling of population ageing: Apocalyptic demography, intergenerational challenges and social policy* (Chapter 1, pp. 5–25). Oxford University Press.

Gee, E. M., & Gutman, G. M. (2000). *The overselling of population ageing: Apocalyptic demography, intergenerational challenges and social policy*. Oxford University Press.

Government of Canada. (1982). Canadian Charter of Rights and Freedoms (Equality Rights, Section 15.1). https://laws-lois.justice.gc.ca/eng/Const/Const_index.html

Government of Canada. (2020). Coronavirus disease (COVID-19): Outbreak update. https://www.canada.ca/en/public-health/services/diseases/2019-novel-coronavirus-infection.html

Gullette, M. M. (2004). *Aged by culture*. University of Chicago Press.

Gullette, M. M. (2017). *Ending ageism, or how not to shoot old people*. Rutgers University Press.

Iannone, C. (2020). Don't "OK, Boomer" us. *Academic Questions, 33*(1), 9–16.

Iversen, T. N., Larsen, L., & Solem, P. E. (2009). A conceptual analysis of ageism. *Nordic Psychology, 61*(3), 4–22.

Knodel, J. (2020). March 24. Coronavirus: Texas Lt. Gov. Dan Patrick suggests he, other seniors willing to die to get economy going again. *NBC News*. https://www.nbcnews.com/news/us-news/texas-lt-gov-dan-patrick-suggests-he-other-seniors-willing-n1167341

Levy, B. R. (2009). Stereotype embodiment: A psychosocial approach to aging. *Current Directions in Psychological Science, 18*(6), 332–336.

Levy, B. R., Slade, M. D., Chang, E. S., Kannoth, S., & Wang, S. Y. (2020). Ageism amplifies cost and prevalence of health conditions. *The Gerontologist, 60*(1), 174–181. https://doi.org/10.1093/geront/gny131

Longino, C. F. (2005). The future of ageism: Baby boomers at the doorstep. *Generations, 29*(3), 79–83.

Madani, D. (2020, April 21). Dan Patrick on coronavirus: 'More important things than living'. *NBC News*. https://www.nbcnews.com/news/us-news/texas-lt-gov-dan-patrick-reopening-economy-more-important-things-n1188911

Meisner, B. A. (2012a). A meta-analysis of positive and negative age stereotype priming effects on behavior among older adults. *The Journals of Gerontology Series B, Psychological Sciences and Social Sciences, 67*(1), 13–17.

Meisner, B. A. (2012b). Physicians' attitudes toward aging, the aged, and the provision of geriatric care: A systematic narrative review. *Critical Public Health, 22*(1), 61–72.

Meisner, B. A., & Levy, B. R. (2016). Age stereotypes' influence on health: Stereotype Embodiment Theory. In V. Bengtson & R. Settersten (Eds.), *Handbook of theories of aging*. (3rd ed., Chapter 14, pp. 259–276). Springer Publishing Company.

Montero-Odasso, M., Hogan, D. B., Lam, R., Madden, K., MacKnight, C., Molnar, F., & Rockwood, K. (2020). Age alone is not adequate to determine health-care resource allocation during the COVID-19 Pandemic. *Canadian Geriatrics Journal, 23*(1), 152–154.

New Zealand Government. (2020). Ways we're uniting against COVID-19. https://covid19.govt.nz/

United Nations. (2020). Secretary-General's policy brief: The impact of COVID-19 on older persons. http://www.un.org/development/desa/ageing/wp-content/uploads/sites/24/2020/05/COVID-Older-persons.pdf

World Health Organization. (2020a). Global research on coronavirus disease (COVID-19). https://www.who.int/emergencies/diseases/novel-coronavirus-2019/global-research-on-novel-coronavirus-2019-ncov

World Health Organization. (2020b). Coronavirus disease (COVID-19) advice for the public. https://www.who.int/emergencies/diseases/novel-coronavirus-2019/advice-for-public

Promoting Older Adults' Physical Activity and Social Well-Being during COVID-19

Julie S. Son ⓘ, Galit Nimrod, Stephanie T. West ⓘ, Megan C. Janke,
Toni Liechty, and Jill J. Naar

ABSTRACT

Staying healthy while following social distancing protocols is of great importance to older adults due to increased risk of serious complications from COVID-19. Mild to moderate physical activity improves immune system responses to viral respiratory infections. Additionally, social engagement has cumulative health protective benefits across the lifespan. At present, active and social recreation opportunities have been drastically reduced or disbanded due to group size limitations, stay-at-home orders, and reductions in services and facilities. As a result, community dwelling older adults are homebound and need alternative exercise and social opportunities to maintain their health during this time. Leisure professionals can promote physical activity and social well-being among older adults by increasing home-based opportunities, including offering additional online leisure services, opportunities for volunteerism, and social interactions.

Introduction

Staying healthy during the COVID-19 pandemic is particularly important for older adults due to increased concerns of contracting the disease and greater risks of it leading to serious complications, such as pneumonia or cytokine storm (Centers for Disease Control and Prevention [CDC], 2020). Although mortality rates are still being determined, preliminary COVID-19 data suggests that the likelihood of death increases exponentially with age (CDC, 2020; Onder et al., 2020). Researchers have found that moderate physical activity increases immune response to viral respiratory infections (Nieman, 2011; Nieman & Wentz, 2019), and social engagement provides protective health benefits across the lifespan (Umberson & Montez, 2010). During the shelter-in-place mandates established during COVID-19, physical activity and sporting events have been shuttered, residential communities' activities and clubs have been suspended, and municipal facilities have ceased on-site operations. Older adults sheltering in place need alternative options for physical activity and social interaction to promote health and well-being. The current pandemic offers an opportunity to learn how municipalities and recreation professionals can offer more online recreation information and opportunities targeting older adults. In this commentary, we will briefly review the benefits of leisure-based physical activity and social recreation opportunities for older adults' health and well-being, and then discuss key issues and recommendations for action during the pandemic.

Supporting older adults' health and well-being through leisure

Physical activity is recognized as a central contributor to physical health and mental well-being generally (Haskell et al., 2009) and, more specifically, as a protective factor against viral infections (Zhu, 2020). In their review of evidence on immunological responses to physical activity, Nieman and Wentz (2019) found that moderate exercise enhanced immunosurveillance and reduced systemic inflammation. Of note, they found support for an association between moderate exercise and a decrease in Upper Respiratory Tract Infections (URTI). These findings are particularly relevant to older adults who have increased risks of serious health complications and death from COVID-19 (Onder et al., 2020). Although physician approval should be sought prior to starting a new exercise regime, particularly for older adults with chronic conditions or health concerns (Elsawy & Higgins, 2010), research indicates that even frail older adults obtain physical benefits from exercise (e.g., McPhee et al., 2016). The American Heart Association (2018) recommends that adults participate in 150 minutes per week of moderate exercise, such as brisk walking or gardening, physical activities which older adults tend to favor (Amireault et al., 2019). Given the older population's increased risk of health complications from COVID-19, and the potential of exercise to enhance immunological protection from viral respiratory illnesses, it is crucial for recreation professionals to facilitate older adults' physical activity.

In addition to physical activity, social activities are associated with older adults' health and well-being. There are protective effects of social engagement and these benefits continue into later life (Umberson et al., 2010; Umberson & Montez, 2010). Older adults' social activities are associated with reduced mortality rates above and beyond other leisure activities (Maier & Klumb, 2005). Social activities provide a stress buffering effect, and social integration promotes positive psychological states that, in turn, enhance positive physiological responses (Cohen, 2004). These findings indicate the importance of maintaining social connections and ties during COVID-19. Moreover, social connections and social support increase exercise adherence in older adults (Smith et al., 2017). In this way, the interconnections between social and physical leisure can be reinforcing and provide "value added" benefits.

Having relevant expertise and resources, leisure scientists and practitioners are uniquely positioned to support older adults' physical and social well-being during the COVID-19 pandemic. Municipal parks and recreation departments have provided physical activity classes and social opportunities for older adults for decades (Roth, 2017). Additionally, leisure scholars have examined individual- and community-based health promotion programs targeting older adults and individuals with chronic conditions (Hutchinson & Lauckner, 2020; Skalko et al., 2016). As such, practitioners and scholars have the capacity to adapt existing site-based programs to home-based opportunities. A central question is how best to provide home-based leisure resources to older adults during the COVID-19 pandemic. Below are key issues and recommendations that we believe are timely during the pandemic.

Issue 1: Building capacity for inclusive online recreational services

Increased home-based activity is the new reality for the foreseeable future. Given the possibility of a second wave of COVID-19, this shift will be especially important for older adults who, with higher risks, may need to self-sequester for months beyond official stay requirements (American Medical Association, 2020). Despite misconceptions, many older adults are online and want to be online. Recent research indicates that, in advanced economies, such as the U.S., Canada, and Western Europe, more than sixty percent of older adults use the Internet (Schumacher & Kent, 2020). Those who are online use the Internet for information, communication, task performance, and leisure. Of these four principle online functions, however, only leisure is significantly associated with well-being in later life (Lifshitz et al., 2018).

Recommendation

Parks and recreation professionals should be at the forefront of both referring older adults to existing online resources as well as providing recreational services online. After vetting resources, they should provide users with information that is easy to follow (e.g., an email with a list of options including links and simple instructions). Free online physical activity videos and exercise resources that are designed for older adults and/or individuals with functional limitations are already available (e.g., National Institute on Aging's "Go4Life"; AARP's "Exercising at Home Just Got Easier"). There are also free or free-option meditation and mindfulness-based stress reduction applications (e.g., Insight Timer, UCLA Mindful). Local recreation classes might also be transitioned to an online format to capitalize on existing social connections between participants and instructors, or among participants. Classes can be prerecorded and then placed on an organization's website or conducted live using a platform like Skype or Zoom, which is particularly useful when instructor feedback maximizes activity benefits and/or minimizes potential risks. The city of Calabasa, California serves as a good case in point. Currently, they offer more than fifty synchronous online classes for adults aged 50 and older, including Acrylic Painting, American Life through Broadway, Gentle Yoga for Seniors, Current Events, and Meditation and Mindfulness.

One possible benefit of moving some recreation programing online could be inter-district and inter-provincial collaboration. Sharing resources and content can be done more readily in an online setting and may facilitate adjustment to staff cuts and budget challenges that municipalities are facing. To assist with the development of such resources, parks and recreation agencies might seek or build on relationships with those who teach in leisure studies and aligned disciplines who are familiar with online platforms. Likewise, academics with expertise should offer to assist parks and recreation professionals. Land-grant state universities are already positioned to incorporate service to local communities through cooperative extension programs. Municipalities may find that converting some programs to an online format or option provides increased accessibility, capacity, and scheduling flexibility. Online options might help with pre-pandemic issues like lack of facility space in general and limited ADA accessible space more specifically.

Issue 2: Older adults' internet access and technology skills

As outlined above, many but not all older adults are online. One challenge is reaching the most vulnerable older adults who do not have access to online resources. For instance, the oldest, lower income, and lower educational attainment older adults may not have access to digital technologies (Schumacher & Kent, 2020). Even those who have access differ in their digital knowledge and skills. Although some have excellent digital literacy, others hold only basic skills (Nimrod, 2016; Schumacher & Kent, 2020). Such gaps in access and use of technology reflect the so-called "grey digital divide." The literature describes numerous factors explaining this digital divide, including technical issues (e.g., costs), physical constraints, cognitive impairments, environmental conditions, and psychological constraints (Friemel, 2016). This divide also has a geographical aspect, as persons residing in rural, periphery, or small-sized localities have both poorer Internet infrastructure and lower levels of education (Hodge et al., 2017). Combined with fewer leisure services offered in such localities (Edwards & Matarrita-Cascante, 2011), this spatial digital inequality makes these older residents the most vulnerable to the pandemic's negative effects on leisure.

Recommendation

In addition to providing free or low-cost online leisure services as outlined above, professionals should connect older adults to government and nonprofit agencies that provide computer equipment and Internet subsidies in accordance with distancing protocols. Professionals also might consider offering technology education classes and/or facilitate connections to government and nonprofit agencies who provide these services. Leisure providers might partner with community organizations that serve older adults (e.g., Meals on Wheels, Paratransit) to distribute information regarding online physical activity resources. Additionally, they could work with local libraries or continuing education programs (e.g., Osher Lifelong Learning Institutes) to provide online discussion groups. This partnership building transcends the current pandemic and may facilitate improved leisure services for older adults in the future.

Issue 3: Creating new opportunities for older adults' volunteerism

As a result of COVID-19 and social distancing orders, older volunteers can no longer volunteer in-person. This situation makes it nearly impossible to maintain volunteerism with local youth centers, schools, park planning committees, community centers, etc. Finding ways to support volunteerism is important, as volunteerism has been found to provide a sense of purpose and meaningful social connections (Hood et al., 2018). Volunteerism also improves self-esteem and self-efficacy (Brown et al., 2012). In addition, continuing to support older volunteers' social engagement may not only promote their well-being but it might put them in position to support other older adults and individuals in the community as well.

Recommendation

Identify and provide alternative volunteer opportunities for older adults. For example, they can make telephone calls to provide emotional support to the most vulnerable housebound individuals or conduct a leisure class online. Older adults also can volunteer by writing for a local newspaper or posting a blog for a charitable organization. Even those who do not use the Internet, or who have limited digital skills, should be considered as potential volunteers. Such individuals can be recruited for community projects that could make use of lifelong acquired skills (e.g., sewing, carpentry). Parks and recreation departments can facilitate these efforts by compiling a list of volunteer options and distributing it to existing volunteers. They also might consider dedicating a section of their website to COVID-19-related volunteer opportunities. Additionally, they can create a mutual aid group using organizational platforms, such as the AARP's "Community Connections," which allows users to organize and find local volunteer groups to help pick up groceries, provide financial assistance, or lend emotional support to others.

Issue 4: Providing a sense of community while sheltering-in-place

Due to concerns about COVID-19, older adults may choose to shelter in place past government stay-at-home requirements. Isolation puts older adults at greater risk for loneliness and depression (Huang, 2020), and this risk increases dramatically among those residing alone, who make up about 30% of the community dwelling older population (Stahl et al., 2017). Personal stories of the authors' older parents – who, four weeks into the stay-at-home order, were feeling isolated and/or who continued to socialize with others despite recommendations – indicate the need for options. Social digital leisure can be one way to combat this isolation by building a sense of community (Lizzo & Liechty, 2020; Nimrod, 2019). Operated via various platforms (e.g., SNSs, forums, email lists), online communities enable the exchange of information and emotional support for older adults (Nimrod, 2016). Practical information helps community members better manage their health and finances, and leisure-related information exchanges (e.g., book recommendations, recipes) promote offline leisure. Intellectual discussions and online social games provide users with enjoyable online pastimes, and sharing personal experiences and emotions help older adults cope with events and transitions. Through a sense of personal connection, online communities can combat feelings of isolation and help older adults self-manage their physical and social well-being (Nimrod, 2016).

Recommendation

Build community online. Parks and recreation professionals can create a sense of community in a variety of ways, including hosting online social games, book clubs, and social hours. Professionals can direct older adults to existing online opportunities that already have a strong sense of community or they can create new ones where leisure gaps exist. As examples, older adults could gather online to discuss a book, share creative writing efforts, discuss woodworking or home improvement projects, or even participate synchronously in shared hobbies, such as cooking, playing music, or quilting. Some in-person events have been replaced with online versions. For example, parks and recreation can provide "virtual races" in which participants walk or run individually (e.g., in a neighborhood or on a treadmill) and receive medals in the mail. Another option is a home-based 30-day exercise challenge that can be hosted by municipal parks and recreation or university recreation programs. These programs can be designed to engender social opportunities and social support; for instance, by providing a weekly online check-in with participants leading up to or during the event. Additionally, leisure scholars have developed leisure-based health promotion programs for in-person formats (e.g., Hutchinson & Lauckner, 2020; Janke et al., in press). Some of these programs could be converted to an online format.

Conclusion

Parks and recreation organizations fulfill a vital role in ensuring all community residents have the means and the opportunity to lead the healthiest lives they can. With growing evidence that older adults are disproportionately experiencing negative effects of COVID-19, leisure professionals should support older adults' physical health and social well-being during and after the pandemic. Professionals can provide support, resources, and routine while older adults self-sequester. We advocate a repositioning of parks and recreation to provide more home-based resources that will extend beyond COVID-19. As a result, the profession will be more robust and more accessible to older adults in the longer term. One unintended benefit could be that the profession serves more of the most vulnerable older adults, individuals with disabilities, and others in our society to provide enhanced physical and socioemotional quality of life. Even once this pandemic has passed, it is imperative that municipalities and other leisure service providers increase capacity for online and other home-based opportunities benefitting older adults and others in need.

ORCID

Julie S. Son ⓘ http://orcid.org/0000-0002-3939-7370
Stephanie T. West ⓘ http://orcid.org/0000-0002-7740-0040

References

American Association of Retired Persons (AARP). (2020, April 1). *Exercising at home just got easier*. https://www.aarp.org/health/healthy-living/info-2020/exercising-at-home.html

American Heart Association. (2018). *American Heart Association recommendations for physical activity in adults and kids*. https://www.heart.org/en/healthy-living/fitness/fitness-basics/aha-recs-for-physical-activity-in-adults

American Medical Association. (2020, April 6). *What's ahead on COVID-19? Expert offers forecast for summer, fall*. https://www.ama-assn.org/delivering-care/public-health/what-s-ahead-covid-19-expert-offers-forecast-summer-fall

Amireault, S., Baier, J. M., & Spencer, J. R. (2019). Physical activity preferences among older adults: A systematic review. *Journal of Aging and Physical Activity, 27*(1), 128–139. https://doi.org/10.1123/japa.2017-0234

Brown, K. M., Hoye, R., & Nicholson, M. (2012). Self-esteem, self-efficacy, and social connectedness as mediators of the relationship between volunteering and well-being. *Journal of Social Service Research, 38*(4), 468–483. https://doi.org/10.1080/01488376.2012.687706

Centers for Disease Control and Prevention (CDC). (2020, March 31). *Coronavirus disease 2019: People who are at higher risk for severe illness*. https://www.cdc.gov/coronavirus/2019-ncov/need-extra-precautions/people-at-higher-risk.html

Cohen, S. (2004). Social relationships and health. *The American Psychologist, 59*(8), 676–684. https://doi.org/10.1037/0003-066X.59.8.676

Edwards, M. B., & Matarrita-Cascante, D. (2011). Rurality in leisure research: A review of four major journals. *Journal of Leisure Research, 43*(4), 447–474. https://doi.org/10.1080/00222216.2011.11950245

Elsawy, B., & Higgins, K. E. (2010). Physical activity guidelines for older adults. *American Family Physician, 81*(1), 55–59.

Friemel, T. N. (2016). The digital divide has grown old: Determinants of a digital divide among seniors. *New Media & Society, 18*(2), 313–331. https://doi.org/10.1177/1461444814538648

Haskell, W. L., Blair, S. N., & Hill, S. N. (2009). Physical activity: Health outcomes and importance for public health policy. *Preventive Medicine, 49*(4), 280–282. https://doi.org/10.1016/j.ypmed.2009.05.002

Hodge, H., Carson, D., Carson, D., Newman, L., & Garrett, J. (2017). Using Internet technologies in rural communities to access services: The views of older people and service providers. *Journal of Rural Studies, 54*, 469–478. https://doi.org10.1016/j.jrurstud.2016.06.016

Hood, S., Lu, Y. Y. F., Jenkins, K., Brown, E. R., Beaven, J., Brown, S. A., Hendrie, H. C., & Austrom, M. G. (2018). Exploration of perceived psychosocial benefits of senior companion program participation among urban-dwelling, low-income older adult women volunteers. *Innovation in Aging, 2*(2), igy018–12. https://doi.org/10.1093/geroni/igy018

Huang, K. (2020, April, 3). How to help older adults fight loneliness during COVID-19: Social isolation can be dangerous for older adults. Here's how to help. *Psychology Today*. https://www.psychologytoday.com/us/blog/hope-resilience/202004/how-help-older-adults-fight-loneliness-during-covid-19

Hutchinson, S. L., & Lauckner, H. (2020). Recreation and collaboration within the expanded chronic care model: Working towards social transformation. *Health Promotion International*. https://doi.org/10.1093/heapro/daz134

Insight Timer. [Online or mobile app]. https://insighttimer.com/meditation-playlists/

Janke, M. C., Payne, L. L., & Son, J. S. (in press). Leisure education in chronic disease management: A case study and lessons learned. *Leisure/Loisir*.

Lifshitz, R., Nimrod, G., & Bachner, Y. (2018). Internet use and well-being in later life: A functional approach. *Aging & Mental Health, 22*(1), 85–91. https://doi.org/10.1080/13607863.2016.1232370

Lizzo, R., & Liechty, T. (2020). The Hogwarts Running Club and sense of community: A netnography of a virtual community. *Leisure Sciences*. https://doi.org/10.1080/01490400.2020.1755751

Maier, H., & Klumb, P. L. (2005). Social participation and survival at older ages: Is the effect driven by activity content or context? *European Journal of Ageing*, *2*(1), 31–39. https://doi.org/10.1007/s10433-005-0018-5

McPhee, J. S., French, D. P., Jackson, D., Nazroo, J., Pendleton, N., & Degens, H. (2016). Physical activity in older age: Perspectives for healthy ageing and frailty. *Biogerontology*, *17*(3), 567–580. https://doi.org/10.1007/s10522-016-9641-0

National Institute on Aging. (n.d.). *Go4Life*. https://www.youtube.com/playlist?list=PLmk21KJuZUM7kDgg7EOsXqPKAoOnD5QN

Nieman, D. C. (2011). Moderate exercise improves immunity and decreases illness rates. *American Journal of Lifestyle Medicine*, *5*(4), 338–345. https://doi.org/10.1177/1559827610392876

Nieman, D. C., & Wentz, L. M. (2019). The compelling link between physical activity and the body's defense system. *Journal of Sport and Health Science*, *8*(3), 201–217. https://doi.org/10.1016/j.jshs.2018.09.009

Nimrod, G. (2016). Online self-management of well-being in later life. *Interdisciplinary Studies on the Family*, *28*, 247–262.

Nimrod, G. (2019). Aging well in the digital age: Technology in processes of selective optimization with compensation. *The Journals of Gerontology: Series B*. https://doi.org/10.1093/geronb/gbz111

Onder, G., Rezza, G., Brusaferro, S. (2020). Case-fatality rate and characteristics of patients dying in relation to COVID-19 in Italy. *JAMA*. https://jamanetwork.com/journals/jama/article-abstract/2763667

Roth, K. (2017). *Parks and recreation: Serving a growing, older population*. https://www.nrpa.org/parks-recreation-magazine/2017/july/parks-and-recreation-serving-a-growing-older-population/

Schumacher, S., & Kent, N. (2020). *Eight charts on internet use around the world as countries grapple with COVID-19*. Pew Research Center. https://www.pewresearch.org/fact-tank/2020/04/02/8-charts-on-internet-use-around-the-world-as-countries-grapple-with-covid-19/

Skalko, T. K., Burgess, L. A., & Janke, M. C. (2016). A comparative study of the effects of Tai Chi and Matter of Balance on measures of balance and fall efficacy in older adults. *American Journal of Recreational Therapy*, *15*(3), 29–39. https://doi.org/10.5055/ajrt.2016.0109

Smith, L. G., Banting, L., Eime, R., O'Sullivan, G., & van Uffelen, J. G. Z. (2017). The association between social support and physical activity in older adults: A systematic review. *International Journal of Behavioral Nutrition and Physical Activity*, *14*, 56. https://doi.org/10.1186/s12966-017-0509-8

Stahl, S. T., Beach, S. R., Musa, D., & Schulz, R. (2017). Living alone and depression: The modifying role of the perceived neighborhood environment. *Aging & Mental Health*, *21*(10), 1065–1071. https://doi.org/10.1080/13607863.2016.1191060

UCLA Mindful [Mobile app]. https://www.uclahealth.org/ucla-mindful

Umberson, D., Crosnoe, R., & Reczek, C. (2010). Social relationships and health behavior across life course. *Annual Review of Sociology*, *36*, 139–157. https://doi.org/10.1146/annurev-soc-070308-120011

Umberson, D., & Montez, J. K. (2010). Social relationships and health. *Journal of Health and Social Behavior*, *51*(1_suppl), S54–S66. https://doi.org/10.1177/0022146510383501

Zhu, W. (2020). Should, and how can, exercise be done during a coronavirus outbreak? An interview with Dr. Jeffrey A. Woods. *Journal of Sport and Health Science*, *9*(2), 105–107. https://doi.org/10.1016/j.jshs.2020.01.005

Prosumption, Networks and Value during a Global Pandemic: Lockdown Leisure and COVID-19

Alexander John Bond ⓘ, Paul Widdop ⓘ, David Cockayne ⓘ, and Daniel Parnell ⓘ

ABSTRACT

Following advances in information technology and the rise of social media, prosumption – a model of simultaneous production and consumption of the commodity – has become a significant focus in many industries and for academic study. Prosumption represents a new message creation and delivery paradigm, where anyone can seamlessly shift from consumer to contributor, to creator. Central to this is the idea of creating 'use-value' and re-orientating 'exchange value'. Perhaps an overlooked facet, but one deeply engrained in its manifestation is that prosumption is inherently relational, involving micro-interaction between consumer and producer. The recent global COVID-19 pandemic, it too being relational in its transmission, has had a paralysing effect on global leisure activities with households and sports organisations experiencing some form of state-enforced residential lockdown. Using social network analysis, this commentary examines the network structure of a prosumed leisure activity during societal lockdown and its implications for the leisure industries.

Introduction

COVID-19 is a highly infectious severe acute respiratory syndrome, transmissible through human (and animal) interaction, formally known as SARS-CoV-2 (WHO, 2020a). Initially reported in Wuhan, China early-December 2019, in a matter of months, the virus spread to all corners of the globe demonstrating our structured networked society (WHO, 2020b). While reportedly less deadly than other recent epidemics and pandemics, such as SARS (severe acute respiratory syndrome), MERS (Middle East respiratory syndrome) and Ebola virus, COVID-19 seems to spread much easier with a basic reproduction number (R_0) of 2 – 2.5, making it more contagious than seasonal flu (Callaway et al., 2020). At the time of writing, according to WHO (2020c) approximately 5.4 million cases of COVID-19 have been confirmed with 343,514 reported deaths globally, inferring a death-rate of ∼6%. However, actual cases are expected to be higher amid testing and protocol issues and the WHO (2020d) estimate a mortality rate of 3.4%. Notwithstanding these infection and mortality rates, this virus will have lasting impacts on global society and economies, laying bare the fragility of neoliberalist markets. Indeed, at the time of writing the price of oil had dipped to an 18-year low, with forecasts of deep recessions following.

Often, depending upon national cultures, societies react in different ways to trauma. In Western Europe, Australia, North America, among other nations, a population's initial reaction to the pandemic was to stockpile food and supplies, especially toilet roll; in anticipation of governmental social distancing procedures (Jankowicz, 2020; Taylor, 2020). The global response from governments (with some exceptions) has been national (or regional) lockdowns, border closures, restricting people's movements, or even confining them solely to the household (Kaplan et al., 2020). Consequently, sport and leisure opportunities have become vastly limited and confined to more individual constrained forms (i.e., exercises such as walking, running and cycling limited to once per day and not beyond the household). Therefore, any form of leisure that brings people in close contact, from theme parks to museums, have closed in physical form to the public. Even professional and recreational sports have been postponed, or even completely canceled in some cases (i.e. The Football Association in England has canceled all grassroots adult and youth recreational football for the 2019/2020 season; Parnell et al., 2020).

The increase in leisure time and a reduction in leisure opportunities has forced people into alternative means of consumption (and production), generating make-shift leisure opportunities. For example, the stockpiling of toilet roll provided an opportunity for what became the #ToiletRollChallenge. This developed into a leisure form accessed on the social media platform Twitter, whereby people filmed themselves trying to do 'keepy-ups' with a toilet roll (i.e. the skills of keeping up the toilet roll off the ground using parts of your body). Indeed, this challenge became one of many social media-driven leisure opportunities developed during the lockdown. Taken in isolation, this challenge appears somewhat frivolous, amongst the backdrop of mortality rates and a depressed economy; yet it nevertheless offers insight into consumption and production patterns of leisure in a constrained but networked society. To that end, this commentary discusses how this lockdown leisure is reliant on Toffler's (1980) notions of prosumption, which also fragments the notion of value, but is only accessible through prosumer networks. By analyzing the recent "ToiletRoleChallange", we add to the theoretical understanding of prosumption, by uncovering how the concept is fundamentally relational, involving micro-interactions, generating a structure that facilitates this lockdown leisure; however, this structure also generates opportunities for corporate leisure and sports organizations to exploit.

Prosumption and value

Since Toffler (1980, p. 265) anticipated "the rise of the prosumer", much has been written on the field of prosumption – mainly since the global recession in 2007 (Ritzer &

Jurgenson, 2010). Overlooked for decades, prosumption depicts the interlinked processes of production and consumption, identifying mutual interdependence which cannot be separated (Andrews & Ritzer, 2018). Ritzer (2015a, 2015b) offers development phases of prosumption, leading to the *new world*, depicting the shift from the 'material' to the 'digital' world, which is now normal reality. This entanglement of digital technologies within people's daily lives has brought Toffler's (1980) prosumption work to the fore of cultural, societal and consumption debate.

Examples of prosumption can be found in all industries, yet sport and to a lesser degree, leisure has gone relatively unexplored in comparison to other industries (Andrews & Ritzer, 2018). The lack of attention may pertain to most leisure (and sport) opportunities requiring a mix of the material (theatres, parks, stadia) and digital world (marketing, ticket purchases, content engagement) and are not necessarily seen as 'products'. Nevertheless, the COVID-19 lockdown made the material world and associated leisure opportunities inaccessible. Thus, people are only able to access most opportunities within the digital world, mainly through the rise of Web 2.0 (Ritzer & Jurgenson, 2010). The different Web 2.0 platforms are nuanced and fit different categories (see Orenga-Roglá & Chalmeta, 2016; Zajc, 2015). Yet, they all share the 'user-generated' model as users become 'active contributors' (Lai & To, 2015). Ultimately, these applications are modern-day digital prosumption systems, meaning the user-generated content becomes the commodity which is consumed and demanded.

As these prosumption systems blur the lines between consumer and producer, conceptualizing value becomes equally blurred. The notion of 'prosumers' represents a fundamental change in economic organization and how we understand market actors (Humphreys & Grayson, 2008). Traditionally, the relationship between consumers and producers is an exchange relationship where each party trades one kind of value for another (Bagozzi, 1975). In sport, for example, the 'product' (event) is 'consumed' by the end-user (fan). Importantly, however, both the organization and the end-user have worked to create value in the live event. Thus, the creation of value does not adequately distinguish the roles of 'producer' and 'consumer'. What does differentiate the two roles is whether the value-creation activity produces what Marx (1867/2001) referred to as 'exchange-value' or 'use-value'.

The exchange-value of an object is its relative worth "when placed in a value or exchange relation with another commodity of a different kind" (Marx, 1867/2001, p. 88). However, commodities, and experiences, have value beyond their market valuation (Cockayne, 2019), as they have an intrinsic utility to whoever owns or purchases them, or 'use-value'. Traditionally, exchange-value is realized only at the point of sale; however, use-value is only realized through consumption; implying an order – exchange-value occurs before use-value (Cockayne, 2019). However, within Web 2.0 prosumption applications, often producers first need to consume, inversing the traditional ordering of value conception. That is, user-generated content is often produced through a process of consumption (sharing a video, news article, other items consumed elsewhere), which is consumed by sharing, liking or commenting, producing content for others to consume, and so on. In this instance, use-value comes before exchange-value, in that, users first consume content, placing a value on the usefulness. If the use-value is sufficient to attract further social interest, users will reproduce the content for others to consume, in essence, creating an exchange-value. For the purposes here, we term this prosumption value. We argue, however, that this value only exists relationally, between prosumers. It is the networked nature of prosumption that enables value to be generated and exchanged, only existing in an ongoing social network.

Prosumer networks

We argue that prosumption is inherently relationally bound in networks of people interacting. Accordingly, we reject neoclassical principles of leisure being consumed independently by atomistic actors governed by rules of methodological individualism. Instead, we follow Granovetter's (2017) lead in arguing that purposive action is embedded in ongoing systems of social relations. These social relations, according to Crossley (2015) form a networked social world of numerous interactions and ties between actors who are themselves formed in those interactions. To that end, we believe leisure and co-production of it, to be fundamentally relational, being contained and facilitated through overlapping networks, which are impacted by micro-interactions, but the structure impacts back upon these interactions, that is to say, leisure networks are always in flux.

Therefore the notions of digital prosumption systems, and prosumption value, rely on connections within the digital world; hence we term these systems prosumer networks. Integral to these prosumer networks is economic sociology which emphasizes the (social) structure of economic action (Burt, 1992; Granovetter, 1985, 2005). Therefore, to understand these prosumer networks further, we must adopt a network perspective which is engrained within economic sociology. Granovetter's (1985) theory of embeddedness stipulates that economic behavior is embedded structurally and relationally in relationships throughout society, especially sports and leisure (Bond et al., 2018, 2019; Parnell et al., 2018). Hence, economic behavior, such as producing and consuming user-generated content concerning #ToiletRollChallange, is structured and influenced by social (media) world.

Moreover, Granovetter (2017) identified four underpinning theoretical frameworks forming embeddedness. Firstly, density and cohesion, relate to norms and conventions, meaning shared ideas and behavior are impacted by the size, density and cohesion of the network structure. Therefore, the larger the prosumer networks become, the more use- and exchange-value is created for the content. Thus the content's ideas or messages becomes more conventional. Secondly, the strength of weak ties suggests new information and innovation comes from weak ties, whereas strong ties reinforce trust and bonding. Therefore, within prosumer networks, there is potentially more value (especially utility) in content from weak ties within the structure.

Thirdly, Burt's (1992, 2004) structural holes theory, notes the importance of individual actor position in the network structure. For Burt, individuals (or organizations) who connect multiple, otherwise unconnected networks, enjoy some strategic advantage. Therefore, within prosumer networks, these actors can extract prosumption value by brokering content throughout networks (Burt, 2004). Finally, temporal embeddedness, positing transactions or interactions have a past, meaning all micro-interactions create a global structure, which, if persistent for long enough, form an institution. While,

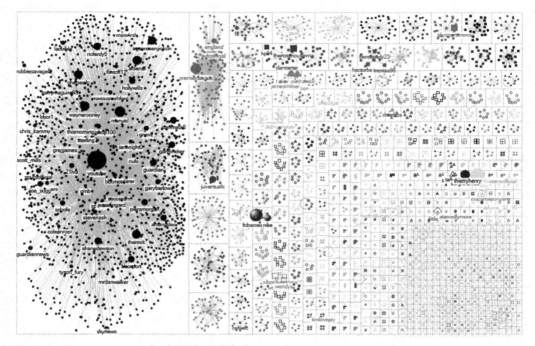

Figure 1. Prosumer network of #ToiletRollChallange.

prosumer networks such as #ToiletRollChallange may be temporal in nature, the history of the connections made will then influence the structure of other initiatives. That is, a network has history and can be quickly mobilized again; with the previous structure impacting future prosumption leisure.

A prosumer network example

Using the idea of a prosumer network, we can identify how people used #ToiletRollChallange as a sport and leisure opportunity during the COVID-19 lock-down. Using, NodeXL software (Smith et al., 2010) to collect Twitter data following the #ToiletRollChallange hashtag, we applied Social Network Analysis (SNA; see, Borgatti et al., 2018; Wasserman & Faust, 2009); for a brief notation on the methods please see the Supplemental Online Material. Figure 1 provides an example of the #ToiletRollChallange prosumer network, during the COVID-19 pandemic.

Figure 1 illustrates visualization of the network formed around the leisure pursuit of #ToiletRollChallange, while Table 1 shows the graph metrics. The visualized network demonstrated a patterned structure of value creation through prosumed leisure. Indeed, our sample includes 4,138 twitter identities (individuals or organizations) connected by 6,123 ties (tweeting, retweeting or mentions). However, this is quite a sparse network (density = 0.0003) identifying almost all potential ties are not realized, suggesting there are more value creation opportunities. Yet, the average shortest path length (average geodesic distance) connecting two individuals is 7.67, suggesting that information, thus value, can flow through the network relatively quickly. Finally, the clustering coefficient,

Table 1. Graph metrics for #ToiletRollChallange prosumer network.

Metric	#ToiletRollChallange
Actors	4138
Edges (ties)	6123
Density	0.0003
Average geodesic distance	7.67
Average degree	1.38
Clustering coefficient	0.07
Modularity	0.77

measuring the clustering tendency of nodes, is relatively low (0.07 on a scale of $0 =$ low $- 1 =$ high), indicating a network comprised predominately of weak ties. This would align to the low density and may suggest user-generated content from weak ties has more prosumption value within prosumer networks because it is more novel than content from strong ties.

Interestingly, this prosumer network also includes different sub-communities, illustrated by the different grids of Figure 1 These communities demonstrate smaller value creation groups. Importantly, these sub-communities have what we may call key influencers, or value-creators. For example, the largest community (see left grid in Figure 1) includes; YouTube (another prosumption site), BBCSport, Arsenal FC, Manchester United, The Guardian, Gary Neville, Gary Lineker, Gary Barlow, Wayne Rooney, and even Piers Morgan (a prominent British Journalist). Additionally, there are multiple smaller communities, such as; English Football – with the likes of Premier League and Aston Villa FC; Italian football driven by Juventus FC; and smaller communities driven by individuals; such as Thierry Henry and Stan Collymore. This entanglement of organizations and personalities demonstrates how they can drive value creation, but by doing so also extract their own value, also known as prosumption capital (Andrews & Ritzer, 2018; Ritzer, 2015a, 2015b; Ritzer & Jurgenson, 2010).

Conclusion

The pursuit of leisure is very rarely an isolated act, even when it appears to be so. An act of an individual improvising football skill with an inanimate object, during a period of state-imposed isolation, for all intents and purposes is very much that. However, we have shown that this leisure pursuit is relational and prosumed leisure. Indeed, behind these leisure acts are complex network structures, that places this act into a wider social structure. Furthermore, when a social structure has certain structural configurations, such as being dominated by weak ties, isolated leisure acts become part of a social movement, it becomes relational. This also distorts our conceptualisations of value in the traditional sense. Especially as individuals (celebrities) and large multi-national corporations can exploit this network to promote their brand and organizations, extracting their own prosumption value.

This commentary raises the question on the neo-liberalism of leisure during the confinement of freedom. If we are all now prosumers, are we as consumers being exploited two-fold by capitalists under the guise of leisure? First, by generating content for social media platforms and secondly through enhancing the value of network influencers and international corporations. Arguably, therefore, this becomes leisure for other people's sake.

ORCID

Alexander John Bond ⓘ http://orcid.org/0000-0002-9667-4143
Paul Widdop ⓘ http://orcid.org/0000-0003-0334-7053
David Cockayne ⓘ http://orcid.org/0000-0002-5473-6967
Daniel Parnell ⓘ http://orcid.org/0000-0001-5593-0633

References

Andrews, D. L., & Ritzer, G. (2018). Sport and prosumption. *Journal of Consumer Culture, 18*(2), 356–373. https://doi.org/10.1177/1469540517747093

Bagozzi, R. P. (1975). Marketing as exchange. *Journal of Marketing, 39*(4), 32–39. https://doi.org/10.1177/002224297503900405

Bond, A. J., Widdop, P., & Chadwick, S. (2018). Football's emerging market trade network: Ego network approach to world systems theory. *Managing Sport and Leisure, 23*(1–2), 70–91. https://doi.org/10.1080/23750472.2018.1481765

Bond, A. J., Widdop, P., & Parnell, D. (2019). Topological network properties of the European football loan system. *European Sport Management Quarterly*, Advance online publication. https://doi.org/10.1080/16184742.2019.1673460

Borgatti, S. P., Everett, M. G., & Johnson, J. C. (2018). *Analyzing social networks* (2nd ed.). SAGE Publications Ltd.

Burt, R. S. (1992). *Structural holes: The social structure of competition.* Harvard University Press.

Burt, R. S. (2004). Structural holes and good ideas. *American Journal of Sociology, 110*(2), 349–399. https://doi.org/10.1086/421787

Callaway, E., Cyranoski, D., Mallapaty, S., Stoye, E., & Tollefson, J. (2020). The coronavirus pandemic in five powerful charts. *Nature, 579*(7800), 482–483. https://doi.org/10.1038/d41586-020-00758-2

Cockayne, D. (2019). Whose side are we on? Balancing economic interests with social concerns through a service-thinking approach. *European Sport Management Quarterly*, Advance online publication . https://doi.org/10.1080/16184742.2019.1674354

Crossley, N. (2015). Relational sociology and culture: A preliminary framework. *International Review of Sociology, 25*(1), 65–85. https://doi.org/10.1080/03906701.2014.997965

Granovetter, M. (1985). Economic action and social structure: The problem of embeddedness. *American Journal of Sociology, 91*(3), 481–510. https://doi.org/10.1086/228311

Granovetter, M. (2005). The impact of social structure on economic outcomes. *Journal of Economic Perspectives, 19*(1), 33–50. https://doi.org/10.1257/0895330053147958

Granovetter, M. (2017). *Society and economy: Framework and principles.* The Belknap Press of Harvard University Press.

Humphreys, A., & Grayson, K. (2008). The intersecting roles of consumer and producer: A critical perspective on co-production, co-creation and prosumption. *Sociology Compass, 2*(3), 963–980. https://doi.org/10.1111/j.1751-9020.2008.00112.x

Jankowicz, M. (2020, March 10). The coronavirus outbreak has prompted people around the world to panic buy toilet paper. Here's why. *Business Insider* [Online]. https://www.businessinsider.com/coronavirus-panic-buying-toilet-paper-stockpiling-photos-2020-3?r=US&IR=T

Kaplan, J., Frias, L., & McFall-Johnsen, M. (2020). A third of the global population is on coronavirus lockdown — Here's our constantly updated list of countries and restrictions. *Business Insider* [Online]. https://www.businessinsider.com/countries-on-lockdown-coronavirus-italy-2020-3?r=US&IR=T

Lai, L. S., & To, W. M. (2015). Content analysis of social media: A grounded theory approach. *Journal of Electronic Commerce Research, 16*(2), 138–152.

Marx, K. (2001). *Capital: A critique of political economy.* Penguin Books. (Original work published 1867).

Orenga-Roglá, S., & Chalmeta, R. (2016). Social customer relationship management: Taking advantage of Web 2.0 and Big Data technologies. *SpringerPlus, 5*(1), 1462. https://doi.org/10.1186/s40064-016-3128-y

Parnell, D., Widdop, P., Bond, A., & Wilson, R. (2020). COVID-19, networks and sport. *Managing Sport and Leisure,* Advance online publication. https://doi.org/10.1080/23750472.2020.1750100

Parnell, D., Widdop, P., Groom, R., & Bond, A. (2018). The emergence of the sporting director role in football and the potential of social network theory in future research. *Managing Sport and Leisure, 23*(4–6), 242–254. https://doi.org/10.1080/23750472.2018.1577587

Ritzer, G. (2015a). The "new" world of prosumption: Evolution, "return of the same," or revolution? *Sociological Forum, 30*(1), 1–17. https://doi.org/10.1111/socf.12142

Ritzer, G. (2015b). Prosumer capitalism. *The Sociological Quarterly, 56*(3), 413–445. https://doi.org/10.1111/tsq.12105

Ritzer, G., & Jurgenson, N. (2010). Production, consumption, prosumption: The nature of capitalism in the age of the digital 'prosumer'. *Journal of Consumer Culture, 10*(1), 13–36. https://doi.org/10.1177/1469540509354673

Smith, M., Ceni, A., Milic-Frayling, N., Shneiderman, B., Mendes Rodrigues, E., Leskovec, J., & Dunne, C. (2010). NodeXL: A free and open network overview, discovery and exploration add-in for Excel 2007/2010/2013/2016. From the Social Media Research Foundation: https://www.smrfoundation.org

Taylor, C. (2020). Here's why people are panic buying and stockpiling toilet paper to cope with coronavirus fears, *CNBC* [Online]. https://www.cnbc.com/2020/03/11/heres-why-people-are-panic-buying-and-stockpiling-toilet-paper.html

Toffler, A. (1980). *The third wave* (Vol. 484). Bantam books.

Wasserman, S., & Faust, K. (2009). *Social network analysis: Methods and applications* (9th ed.). Cambridge University Press.

World Health Organisation. (2020a). *WHO Coronavirus disease (COVID-19) outbreak.* https://www.who.int/emergencies/diseases/novel-coronavirus-2019

World Health Organisation. (2020b). *WHO announces COVID-19 outbreak a pandemic.* http://www.euro.who.int/en/health-topics/health-emergencies/coronavirus-covid-19/news/news/2020/3/who-announces-covid-19-outbreak-a-pandemic

World Health Organisation. (2020c). *Coronavirus disease 2019 (COVID-19) Situation Report – 127. World Health Organisation.* https://www.who.int/docs/default-source/coronaviruse/situation-reports/20200526-covid-19-sitrep-127.pdf?sfvrsn=7b6655ab_8

World Health Organisation. (2020d). *WHO Director-General's opening remarks at the media briefing on COVID-19 - 3 March 2020.* https://www.who.int/dg/speeches/detail/who-director-general-s-opening-remarks-at-the-media-briefing-on-covid-19—3-march-2020

Zajc, M. (2015). Social media, prosumption, and dispositives: New mechanisms of the construction of subjectivity. *Journal of Consumer Culture, 15*(1), 28–47. https://doi.org/10.1177/1469540513493201

"Last Night a DJ Saved My Life" @Dnice #ClubQuarantine: Digitally Mediating Ritualistic Leisure Spaces during Isolation

Brandy N. Kelly Pryor and Corliss Outley

ABSTRACT
Drawing on the DJ's divination as hope purveyor and healer, this commentary examines the trendiest club scene during the COVID-19 and worldwide social distancing—#ClubQuarantine. It explores how DJ and producer Derrick "D-Nice" Jones uses Instagram Live to reproduce and perform hope through dual components of his musical sets: (1) participatory/performative healing and (2) cultural preservation. Situating this DJ within the Black aesthetic, these two elements are explored in conversation with Kelly's (2013) performance of hope theory. This commentary provides understanding for leisure scholars about the flow of Black visual and aesthetic culture and how the house party or the club can be a space of healing and cultural preservation—even in the face of a global health and economic crisis.

Prelude

For many, the spread of the novel coronavirus (COVID-19) and 2020 shelter-in-place orders represent a crisis moment. The mind, body, and soul seek to make sense of crises by creating archetypes, and today, through this particular crisis, heroes are the essential personnel—health care, food workers, and transit operators. Among the growing list, another lifesaving hero has surfaced—the DJ. One of those heroes depicted in _imagery_ throughout social media is DJ D-Nice and #ClubQuarantine on Instagram Live is his superpower.

#ClubQuarantine [Kelly Pryor]

> *It was the first full week of shelter-in-place across the United States. Incessantly scrolling through social media sites, the need/want for information felt inseparable from my work in communities; and I was utterly consumed.*
>
> *Then came the feeling of hopeful enthusiasm, the kind when I would see tweet after tweet about grief and isolation interrupted by a baby announcement; but this tweet was different—an invitation to "the best party in the world." Entering the [online] party, I heard the soul songs of my birth—Shalamar, the S.O.S. Band, D Train—and DJ D-Nice masterfully spun. With virtual hearts filling the screen, he called out new people as they entered the Instagram Live room. In that moment, as if he saw me, he played to heal my grief. As he narrated the culture, my body and soul moved in ways I had not felt in weeks and I was transported. Musically*

traveling through the Diaspora, from the year of my birth to my coming of age, to years and times I had not known—I worked up a sweat and swayed in my living room—and my soul exhaled—"thank you D-Nice."

For many days after the historic party my check-in conversations began with...

"How are you? Were you at the party?"

#ClubQuarantine [Outley]

It was Summer of 1983 as we walked down Grape Street in Watts, California and heard the music from the sidewalk. The house party was in full swing as my sister Shamell, her friend Nina and big cousin Stephanie and myself entered by the front door. The 4-room house was packed wall to wall with young Black people, smoke filled the air and the floor trembled from the bass in the music. As we inched over to the far wall trying to avoid being touched by older boys, I was in awe experiencing my 'first' unsupervised house party under the strobing blue light as Fantastic Voyage blasted from the speakers. This was the memory that captured my mood during ClubQuarantine as DJ D-Nice mastered the turntables rotating hits from the 70s through today. I was hit with wave after wave of memories—family, youthfulness and even Black pride, each engulfing my spirit and enriching my heart.

"...Girl, yes I was at the party! It was amazing!"

Introduction

For the first time in history, the world is witnessing—simultaneously—a pandemic that is causing a global economic crisis, and digitally mediated moments of grief and healing. Through social media, the flow of visual global culture takes on new meanings and viewers' experiences in perception and reality, exemplified by Pratt (2020), and provides new spaces for leisure and cultural analysis.

Building off the political-ethnocultural premise of the Black Arts Movement, this commentary explores how DJ and producer Derrick "D-Nice" Jones uses one social media space—Instagram Live—and the aesthetic of the house party to create #ClubQuarantine. We examine two key components of D-Nice's digitally mediated sets which re(create) and perform hope: (1) participatory/performative healing and (2) cultural preservation. Using Kelly's (2013) analysis of *hope theory*, we use this historical moment to understand intersections of culture, leisure, and hope—even when digitally mediated.

Spaces of Hope

The ubiquity of social media has enhanced a sense of helplessness and hopelessness about this viral and racial pandemic (Kendi, 2020). Recognizing the deleterious health implications of low hope (Snyder et al., 2005) and association between depressive symptoms and Instagram use (Lup et al., 2015), we ground this commentary at the intersection of these two spaces. Departing from hope as mere emotion, Snyder et al. (1991) define hope cognitively: derived from a sense of successful agency (goal/will) and pathways (way). Using a Black feminist/womanist framework, Kelly's (2013) phenomenological study extends the definition to include five key spaces of hope—personal agency, creativity and playfulness, advocacy and social justice, divine, and intimate relation. These spaces involve communal elements critical to survival, thus acting as the catalyst for "will" and "way." Examining performative locations/spaces where hope flourishes or constricts is important for understanding one's lived experience, and decreasing the harmful aspects of hopelessness within entire communities. In this commentary we contend Twitter, Instagram, and specifically, Instagram Live serve as performative spaces, with insight into culture and leisure during COVID-19.

Context

By March 2020, the United States led the world in reported infections of COVID-19 (Cornwall et al., 2020). Particularly, but not solely, in the United States, COVID-19 illuminates that beyond the natural impact of epidemics, there is a complex socio-political influence by the actions of the state on life and death of a population (Foucault, 2003). Black and brown communities, despite narratives of a post-racial society, are experiencing disproportionate mortality rates due to the virus (Farley et al., 2020). Although structural and systemic oppressions are the cause of a multitude of health inequities, paternalistic narratives of personal responsibility guide political rhetoric (Kendi, 2020). Returning to the performance of hope (Kelly, 2013), contextualizing COVID-19 within the United States is important for understanding the healing that comes from #ClubQuarantine.

Startling statistics, stay-at-home orders, and the lack of political responsiveness can be debilitating and deteriorating hope. As noted on numerous exchanges on social media, a sense of fear and stillness abound, perhaps from the impact of 24-hour reporting of new cases in epicenters around the world, reflections on isolation, firsthand accounts of the virus's toll on the body, heartfelt obituaries, or even government (in)action. However, in spite of fear, people explicitly mention finding a space of hope in #ClubQuarantine and as some suggest, regaining hope when it was most needed. Our commentary's title, in part, borrows from Indeep's 1982 hit song, to suggest the role D-Nice plays in curating culture for his followers, and in some cases, saving lives. These descriptions by followers around the lifesaving aspects of #ClubQuarantine further elucidate "hope" is cognitively in motion with emotions, while uniquely performing community with others (Kelly, 2013).

#ClubQuarantine as Participatory and Performative Healing

Oprah Winfrey, Michelle Obama, Quincy Jones, elected officials, childhood friends, and both authors—the world—show up at DJ D-Nice's #ClubQuarantine. In an Apple TV video tweeted on March 25, Winfrey (2020) called #ClubQuarantine "the most hopeful, healing experience… in a collective virtual community in the United States." Through his Instagram Live platform—@dnice and using the virtual language—#ClubQuarantine/#CQ/#C-QAD—participants, no matter their social identity or status, engage in the intimacy of Derrick "D-Nice" Jones' house party. More than an invitation to passively consume the music, viewers engage in the ritual of (re)creating community and participatory healing, and the leisure experience of everyone is enlivened as others grow the community.

With 43% of Instagram users being Black, and 67% between 18 and 29 years old, understanding the intersections of race and age in digital leisure spaces is important (Perrin & Anderson, 2019). Through online connections, Black Americans expand what Parry et al. (2013, p. 26) call the "sphere of sociability" by utilizing digital leisure spaces for equity and justice. Digital space is a place for healing and transformation, where a communal language is created.

D-Nice began #ClubQuarantine on March 17th with 200 of his friends (Winfrey, 2020). Using Instagram Live to perform his craft, he also participates in his own healing, reinforcing Hickey-Moody and Willcox's (2019) notion that "the process of being together re-makes us" (p. 4). As a DJ/artist, D-Nice is adept at musically engaging crowds; however, this unique isolation went beyond "re-making" a club scene. During global isolation D-Nice subsumed the task, through virtual space, of "re-making" the part of the human spirit that feels in communion with others. By March 21, D-Nice played a nine-hour music set, getting global attention. To date, D-Nice engages viewers in the space through music, open dialogue, and authentic participation. D-Nice re-makes the digital space taking it from gazing to healing.

In commenting on iconic renderings of his unprecedented digital moment, the party that "broke the internet," Jones (2020) demonstrates that while a performer, he is living in communion with and re-made alongside the global community. Although not the first DJ or artist to use Instagram Live to create community, D-Nice's musical sets utilize a unique dialogue with viewers to create togetherness. As some of his favorite artists enter, he openly welcomes them and appreciates that they came to the party. If he is playing a record, and a musical icon virtually enters, he mixes the record to show homage to the artist with one of their popular tunes. Musical legends such as George Clinton, Stevie Wonder, Queen Latifa, and others participate in the global community while D-Nice performs his healing and our collective cultural music histories.

Cultural Curation and Artifact Preservation

By the middle of March 2020, D-Nice's nightly sets touched a diverse audience, with a wide array of celebrity figures (i.e., Oprah, Rihanna, Joe Biden) and corporate accounts (i.e., Forbes, Instagram, Taco Bell) that joined. Viewers appreciated and recognized the multicultural and multigenerational nature of the space. In Figure 1, Victoria (2020) praises D-Nice's ability to bridge generational divides, equating this musical gathering to a family, and D-Nice as the curator, keeping the Black cultural legacy alive.

D-Nice follows in the footsteps of past DJs by using music to blend varying cultural dimensions, within a singular space of the house party. Hope is aroused in places that have particular history and meaning (Kelly, 2013) and for centuries, Black music has been the sound of hope, "the heart and soul of American culture" (Hannah-Jones, 2019). The DJ can curate a space of affirmation, survival, and empowerment, or in contrast a space of subjugation and domination. With a playlist of largely Black musical artists and genres largely influenced by these artists, D-Nice creates a space of affirmation, survival, and empowerment for viewers (Langlois, 1992). Through blending different

I love that #ClubQuarantine is multigenerational! That's Black life at the family cook out /reunion you gotta get the young folks something contemporary to dance to, classics for the old heads, and some slow jams and throwbacks for everybody. That's how you keep the legacy alive!

1:30 AM · Apr 19, 2020 · Twitter Web App

12 Retweets   67 Likes

Figure 1   *#ClubQuarantine multigenerational family reunion @CrownVictoria22 discusses the multigenerational aspects of #ClubQuarantine.*

SOURCE: Victoria, S. [@CrownVictoria22]. (2020, April 19). *I love that #ClubQuarantine is multigenerational! That's Black life at the family cook out /reunion you gotta get the young folks something* [Tweet]. Twitter. https://twitter.com/CrownVictoria22/status/1251744979720028166

time frames and cultures in the musical selections, DJs have the ability to suspend time, while teaching history and preserving culture through the soundscape. Fellow rapper Ludacris (Bridges, 2020) praised D-Nice for his seemingly "effortless" ability to blend and preserve the culture, creating a sense of agency and pathways through the music and through history.

DJing is cultural curation through music. When a DJ plays music at a house party, the party becomes a space of homage to ancestors, survival, and affirmation (Langlois, 1992; Smith, 2003) that is admired, celebrated, and revered as a spiritual healing (St John, 2006). DJing has a long history; since 1905 DJs have used technical and social skills to evoke a sense of emotion or "vibe" required of a cultural curator (Smith, 2003). DJs guide their listeners on a transformative and transcendental journey through a *common experience* (St John, 2006). In this sense, D-Nice's house party is reminiscent of house parties which have occurred within the Black community for centuries. "Frolics" of the 1800s in Southern rural homes, the 1920s Harlem Renaissance "rent parties," urban "shin digs" in the 1970s, and the 1990s backyard parties in L.A. (Library of Congress, 2020); all served as primary social events for creating, maintaining, and reaffirming culturally based social structures and informal personal interactions. Rietveld (2019) emphasized this communal experiences, comparing club scenes as a leisure spaces similar to "night time church" (p. 129) where DJs ministeri to congregants as they explore, test, and reaffirm their individual and collective identities (Langlois, 1992). For Hill (2020) D-Nice's #ClubQuarantine is in service to the people and deserving of the Nobel Peace Prize or what she calls "doing the Lord's work." It is in this way that D-Nice creates "just spaces" (Kelly Pryor & Outley, 2014) filled with liberation from the structural and systemic oppression "outside," and restores peace, camaraderie, and hope "inside."

Ms Cris Wmsn @Crissypoo492 · Mar 23
Replying to @CharlesMBlow
I thought my lasting memory of the covid19 quarantine would be the empty store shelves. It made me anxious and depressed. Then I went to #ClubQuarantine. It was so cool!!! I hope I can get a t-shirt as a positive and happy memory of this time in **history**.

Figure 2   Wishing for a T-shirt. @Crissypoo492 discusses what she believed would be lasting memory of COVID-19 until she experiences #ClubQuarantine.
SOURCE: Wmsn, C. [@Crissypoo492]. (2020, March 23). I thought my lasting memory of the covid19 quarantine would be the empty store shelves. It made me anxious [Tweet]. Twitter. https://twitter.com/Crissypoo492/status/1242081320525795329

Lashua and Fox (2006) discussed the tension in the role music plays in youth recreation, yet even greater attention needs to be given to the role house parties play as cultural pedagogy and the creation and maintenance of individual and group identity. As Wmsn (2020) discusses (see Figure 2), she believed her lasting memories of COVID-19 would be different; then she experienced #ClubQuarantine and now wishes for an artifact as cultural commemoration. Recognizing that Instagram is largely dominated by Generation Z (born between 1995 and 2015), these nightly sets are broadcast to a population in transition from adolescence to adulthood, and developing its wider cultural education. This generation, as well as Millennials (born between 1980 and 1994), finds hope in online spaces of creativity, activism, and community (Kelly, 2013). Mixing cultural artifacts with philanthropy, D-Nice taps into viewers' desire for activism (i.e. relief funding), rites of passage, and commemoration of #ClubQuarantine by collaborating with other artist like Will Smith to donate to the CDC Foundation. In creating a t-shirt for relief there are multiple meanings for those in experiencing the relief funds and those experiencing the relief of #ClubQuarantine.

As memorialized convergence of Kelly's (2013) five spaces, artifacts provide connections to individual and group identities. Thus, not only is #ClubQuarantine a place to learn about the culture as Kaye (2020) elucidates in Figure 3, in socializing her children to R&B music, but also a place to consume and identify oneself with the cultural artifacts created, e.g., Tweets, or T-shirts (Cornwell, 1990).

T-shirts, limited in their material value, serve as an "illustrative example of our search for meaning" and particularly with music, provide an artifact of belonging to/or coming of age at a particular time (Cornwell, 1990, p. 375). During COVID-19, D-Nice and #ClubQuarantine helped create a sense of belonging and ease our transitions.

Outro

During a crisis, hope is critical to well-being and survival. As this commentary discusses, *hope* is not only individual will and way, but is belief and action, influenced by performance of/in collective spaces—even during the required physical distancing due to COVID-19. For communities experiencing perpetual crises of structural oppressions and inequalities, COVID-19 amplifies a greater need—and opportunity—for collective healing spaces. The

Figure 3. *T-shirt as Artifact* @Brandyka22 and her children display t-shirts as they bond as family with the global community.

SOURCE: Kaye, B. [@Brandyka22]. (2020, May 6). Thanks to @djdnice creating Club Quarantine on Insta love, my girls now appreciate my of 70s–90s R&B. He's partnered with a lot of great orgs to raise $ for COVID relief and built a positive online community for the past 6 weeks through #CQ #music #community [Tweet]. Twitter. https://twitter.com/Brandyka22/status/1258067601139412992

popularity of Instagram Live for D-Nice's #ClubQuarantine creates a turning point for understanding culture, social justice, and future digitally mediated leisure spaces. D-Nice leverages #ClubQuaranitne to resist hopelessness, bridge divides, and pave the way for future artists. Using the Black aesthetic, primarily the sounds of Black music, he sustains a space of hope, liberation, and virtual healing. D-Nice also walks in the pathway of artists before him, to curate culture and create new artifacts. Examining #ClubQuarantine and other virtual spaces developed during COVID-19, particularly those influenced by the Black aesthetic, can help situate emerging studies of isolation, belonging, and social media, during the pandemic and beyond. For us, D-Nice is a hero…. *and for that our souls exhale—"thank you D-Nice."*

References

Bridges, C. [@Ludacris]. (2020, March 22). *This is how @djdnice had me last night. Effortlessly Blending Timeless Music from different genres, decades & cultures* [Tweet]. Twitter. https://twitter.com/Ludacris/status/1241749165639528449

Cornwall, W., Kaiser, J., Kupferschmidt, K., Malakoff, D. & Servick, K. (2020). *The United States leads in coronavirus cases, but not pandemic response.* Science. https://www.sciencemag.org/news/2020/04/united-states-leads-coronavirus-cases-not-pandemic-response

Cornwell, T. B. (1990). T-Shirts as wearable diary: An examination of artifact consumption and garnering related to life events. *Advances in Consumer Research, 17*(1), 375–379.

Farley, J. H., Hines, J. F., Lee, N. K., Brooks, S. E., Nair, N., & Chapman-Davis, E. (2020, May 2). *Promoting health equity in the COVID-19 era.* Society of Gynecologic Oncology. https://www.sgo.org/clinical-practice/management/covid-19-resources-for-health-care-practitioners/promoting-health-equity-in-the-covid-19-era/

Foucault, M. (2003). *Society must be defended*. Lectures at the Collège de France 1975–76. Picador.

Hannah-Jones, N. (Host). (2019, September 6). The Birth of American Music (Episode 3) [podcast]. 1619/ The New York Times. https://www.nytimes.com/2019/09/06/podcasts/1619-black-american-music-appropriation.html?action=click&module=audio-series-bar&region=header&pgtype=Article

Hickey-Moody, A., & Willcox, M. (2019). Entanglements of difference as community togetherness: Faith, art and feminism. *Social Sciences, 8*(9), 264.

Hill, J. [@jemelehill]. (2020, March 21). *Somebody needs to nominate @DJ_DNICE for a Nobel Peace Prize when this pandemic ends. He is doing the Lord's* [Tweet]. Twitter. https://twitter.com/jemelehill/status/1241538515357167618

Jones, D. [@dnice]. (2020, March 23). *I had a tearful moment this morning after realizing that we all came together as a global community and danced* [Text and Photo]. Instagram. https://www.instagram.com/p/B-EJerzg4xV/?utm_source=ig_web_copy_link

Kaye, B. [@Brandyka22]. (2020, May 6). *Thanks to @djdnice creating Club Quarantine on Insta love, my girls now appreciate my of 70s-90s R&B. He's partnered* [Tweet]. Twitter. https://twitter.com/Brandyka22/status/1258067601139412992

Kelly, B. N. (2013). *Ripples of hope: Women of African descent emerging into adulthood and the performance of hope* [Unpublished doctoral dissertation]. Texas A&M University.

Kelly Pryor, B. N., & Outley, C. W. (2014). Just spaces: Urban recreation centers as sites for social justice youth development. *Journal of Leisure Research, 46*(3), 272–290.

Kendi, I. X. (2020, April 6) *What the racial data show*. The Atlantic. https://www.theatlantic.com/ideas/archive/2020/04/coronavirus-exposing-our-racial-divides/609526/

Langlois, T. (1992). Can you feel it? DJs and House Music culture in the UK. *Popular Music, 11*(2), 229–238.

Lashua, B., & Fox, K. (2006). Rec needs a new rhythm cuz rap is where we're livin'. *Leisure Sciences, 28*(3), 267–283.

Library of Congress. (2020, May 5). *Harlem rent parties*. https://www.loc.gov/teachers/classroom-materials/presentationsandactivities/presentations/timeline/progress/prohib/rent.html

Lup, K., Trub, L., & Rosenthal, L. (2015). Instagram #Instasad?: Exploring associations among Instagram use, depressive symptoms, negative social comparison, and strangers followed. *Cyberpsychology, Behavior, and Social Networking, 18*(5), 247–252.

Parry, D. C., Glover, T. D., & Mulcahy, C. M. (2013). From "Stroller-Stalker" to "Momancer": Courting friends through a social networking site for mothers. *Journal of Leisure Research, 45*(1), 23–46.

Perrin, A., & Anderson, M. (2019). *Share of US adults using social media, including Facebook, is mostly unchanged since 2018*. Pew Research Center. https://www.pewresearch.org/fact-tank/2019/04/10/share-of-u-s-adults-using-social-media-including-facebook-is-mostly-unchanged-since-2018/

Pratt, T. [@TrentonxPratt] (2020, March 22). ♪♪ *This is black superhero music right here baby..."* ♪♪ *– HOV "Roc Boys" (2007). Got inspired* [Tweet]. Twitter. https://twitter.com/TrentonxPratt/status/1241756523317116929

Rietveld, H. C. (2019). *This is our house: House music, cultural spaces and technologies*. Routledge.

Smith, W. E. (2003). *Hip Hop as performance and ritual: A biographical and ethnomusicological construction of a Washington D.C. Hip Hop artist named Priest Da Nomad* [Unpublished doctoral dissertation]. University of Maryland.

Snyder, C. R., Cheavens, J. S., & Michael, S. T. (2005). Hope theory: History and elaborated model. In J. A. Eliott (Ed.), *Interdisciplinary perspectives of hope* (pp. 101–118). Nova Science Publishers, Inc.

Snyder, C. R., Harris, C., Anderson, J. R., Holleran, S. A., Irving, L. M., Sigmon, S. T., Yoshinobu, L., Gibb, J., Langelle, C., & Harney, P. (1991). The will and the ways: Development and validation of an individual-differences measure of hope. *Journal of Personality and Social Psychology, 60*(4), 570–585.

St John, G. (2006). Electronic dance music culture and religion: An overview. *Culture and Religion, 7(1)*, 1–25. https://doi.org/10.1080/01438300600625259

T. P. [@Sofia_Charrua]. (2020, March 22). *I had barely moved or smiled all week. Started watching/ listening yesterday - it was exactly what I needed, got me* [Tweet]. Twitter. https://twitter.com/ Sofia_Charrua/status/1241717936718520321

Victoria, S. [@CrownVictoria22]. (2020, April 19). *I love that #ClubQuarantine is multigenerational! That's Black life at the family cook out /reunion you gotta get the young* [Tweet]. Twitter. https:// twitter.com/CrownVictoria22/status/1251744979720028166

Winfrey, O. [@Oprah]. (2020, March 25). *Ya'll missed a PARTY on Saturday if you weren't tuned into D-Nice's #QuarantineParty on IG.* [Tweet]. Twitter. https://twitter.com/Oprah/ status/1242932426747326466

Wmsn, C. [@Crissypoo492]. (2020, March 23). *I thought my lasting memory of the covid19 quarantine would be the empty store shelves. It made me anxious* [Tweet]. Twitter. https://twitter.com/ Crissypoo492/status/1242081320525795329

COVID-19 and its Impact on Volunteering: Moving Towards Virtual Volunteering

Erik L. Lachance (iD)

ABSTRACT

These unprecedented times due to the COVID-19 pandemic have impacted the everyday lives of individuals. A particular activity impacted by this pandemic is leisure. Within leisure, an important activity to enhance social outcomes (e.g., civic participation) and the survival of organizations and events is volunteering. However, and given social distancing measures and the combination of postponements or cancelations of organizational or event operations, the traditional form of in-person volunteering is threatened. The purpose of this essay is to discuss opportunities and challenges for organizations and events to apply virtual volunteering as a strategy during the pandemic and beyond. Both opportunities (i.e., creating accessibility) and challenges (i.e., management process) are discussed according to pertinent literature. From this, an understanding of virtual volunteering's value to create leisure opportunities during the COVID-19 pandemic and beyond is presented to advance its implementation in organization and events by leisure practitioners.

Given these unprecedented times, countries in North America, Europe, and Asia have imposed measures for social distancing to limit COVID-19's spread. These social distancing measures have created negative impacts on leisure activities including: recreation, sport, parks, travel, and tourism. Beyond these leisure activities, one particular activity inherently linked with other leisure-based activities that has also been negatively impacted by COVID-19 is traditional volunteering.

Understood as a freely chosen leisure activity, volunteering is an integral activity for civic participation and the operations of organizations and events (Hoye et al., 2020). Given the societal conditions of COVID-19, the traditional form of volunteering is threatened as this typically occurs with individuals fulfilling their activities in-person. This threat is the result of two factors: government legislations and social distancing, and postponement or cancelation of organizational and event operations.

The impact of this public policy and these leisure opportunities are entangled and linked together. On one hand, events of various levels have been postponed (e.g., 2020 Tokyo Summer Olympics) or canceled (e.g., Toronto Pride Parade) before government action was taken to constrict leisure opportunities. On the other hand, non-essential businesses (e.g., sport and recreation organizations) have been mandated to suspend all in-person operations and services (Government of Ontario, n.d.). This forces organizations to transition operations (e.g., meetings) to virtual spaces (e.g., Zoom), restructure through layoffs, or temporarily suspend operations.

The postponement and cancelation of organizational and event operations has restricted individuals from practicing their freely chosen leisure activity in-person. For example, more than 80 000 individuals will be unable to volunteer this year at the 2020 Tokyo Summer Olympics (Callos, 2020). This negative impact on volunteering is relevant for organizations and events given the unpredictability of COVID-19 and the breadth of social distancing measures. However, and while individuals may not be able to fulfill their volunteering activities in-person, this threat creates an opportunity for virtual volunteering (VV).

Since the inception of the world wide web, VV has emerged as a variation to traditional in-person volunteering (Liu et al., 2016). Unlike traditional in-person volunteering, VV (synonymous with online volunteering) is a leisure activity where individuals complete all tasks off-site through virtual spaces (Volunteer Canada, 2020). While some volunteers combine both traditional in-person volunteering and VV to complete their tasks, the type of VV discussed in this essay is pure online volunteering. Pure online volunteering is selected for this essay to bound the following discussion on volunteering that occurs uniquely in virtual spaces and away from others, yet in formal association with an organization or event (Liu et al., 2016).

To date, VV is practiced more by males than females, and is participated by a variety of groups (e.g., youth, older adults), education levels, and employment status (Liu et al., 2016). Despite this, research has shown that VV is more popular among youth in their 20s and 30s, people who are educated (e.g., post-secondary), but also unemployed (Murray & Harrison, 2005). This is compared to traditional in-person volunteering where the majority of the volunteer workforce is comprised of individuals over 35 years old that are educated and employed (McGregor-Lowndes et al., 2017). VV have also been discussed as having less work experience and skills as opposed to traditional in-person volunteers (Liu et al., 2016), and this can be explained by its practice being more popular among youth.

The relevance of VV is ever-present within this intersection of the COVID-19 pandemic, and the prominence of technology in our contemporary times (Liu et al., 2016). For instance: "[s]ocial distancing is the recommended course for containing virus spread. This may mean looking for volunteer opportunities that can be done virtually or remotely from your home" (Volunteer Canada, 2020, p. 1). Given societal circumstances caused by COVID-19, it is important to discuss VV – its opportunities and challenges – as this form of volunteering is the only viable option for this leisure activity.

Thus, the purpose of this essay is to critically discuss opportunities and challenges for organizations and events (hereafter referred to as leisure practitioners; LP), to harness VV during the COVID-19 pandemic, and beyond. The essay is structured as followed. Opportunities VV provides LP will be presented, followed by challenges, and a brief conclusion.

Discussion

Opportunities

For LP, VV provides the ability to (re)create accessible leisure opportunities for individuals. These opportunities will be discussed according to current and new volunteers.

Current volunteers

Social distancing makes it impossible for current volunteers to complete their activities in-person. However, VV enables current volunteers to transition their activities online, and still be engaged in their leisure activity during COVID-19. For instance, Board members who regularly meet in-person are now forced to complete their volunteering through virtual spaces. However, and while fulfilling current duties, these Board members could also seek to complete other, and often over-looked, tasks, such as strategic planning, performance evaluations, and maintaining external relationships with stakeholders. This same situation applies to current volunteers (e.g., presidents, executive directors, coaches) as roles and responsibilities can be completed through virtual spaces during COVID-19. Thus, VV makes the leisure activity of current volunteers accessible through technology despite current circumstances.

The current situation with COVID-19 may also provide the opportunity for LP to transition certain roles to virtual spaces after the pandemic. While considering the prominence of technology in contemporary times, COVID-19 could lead to a greater implementation and sustainment of VV. As opposed to simply using VV for short-term roles or projects, LP could look to transition specific roles online and leverage technology on a long-term strategic basis.

The flexibility of VV is also a worthy point of discussion for current volunteers. For instance, current volunteers who may only be marginally involved in organizational or event operations, and state time and additional commitments (e.g., family, work) as factors limiting their accessibility, have the liberty of volunteering autonomously and from the comfort of their own homes during COVID-19. The accessibility of VV allows these individuals to be meaningfully involved and enjoy leisure opportunities despite current circumstances.

New volunteers

As individuals practice social distancing, LP have an opportunity to provide an accessible leisure opportunity for new volunteers through VV. As geographical boundaries are broken with virtual spaces, VV allows LP to broaden the involvement of individuals from different regions and/or countries (Volunteer Canada, 2019). Without VV, LP may be unable to capitalize on a vast population of individuals that were not would not be able to volunteer through traditional in-person means due to geographical restrictions. Thus, the current situation with the COVID-19 pandemic and social distancing measures allows LP to extend the boundary of their organization or event through VV opportunities and be engaged with a wide variety of individuals. Considering that these individuals would not otherwise be involved in volunteering, LP can engage them in VV during COVID-19 and beyond.

Beyond these aforementioned aspects, LP could also take the opportunity presented by COVID-19 to provide an accessible leisure activity and engage with three groups of individuals: individuals with disabilities, youth, and older adults. First, VV does not ignore a neglected, yet valuable group of individuals within the volunteer population in an effort to offer leisure opportunities. As the majority of volunteer opportunities are specific for individuals without disabilities, VV enables for individuals with disabilities to partake in a leisure activity. Thus, this leisure activity does not discriminate against individuals with disabilities, but instead provides them with an accessible opportunity for leisure.

Second, youth represent the largest portion of VV. While this may come as no surprise given their technological upbringings and surroundings, this pandemic can also provide an accessible leisure activity to youth. As students are unable to seek employment due to COVID-19, VV can allow them to be involved, gain work experience, and develop skills and knowledge for future endeavors. For instance, the Canadian government has advocated for youth to get involved in volunteering during COVID-19 as the "need is there [among practitioners], but it will also reduce the number of young people who are sitting around" (Aiello, 2020). This group's involvement in VV could easily be completed through virtual spaces given their interest and comfort with technology in an effort to provide assistance to leisure practitioners.

Finally, and despite being motivated to partake in VV (Mukherjee, 2011), older adults are not a prominent group in this type of volunteering. Beyond issues, such as surfing browsers, login onto platforms, communicating via email and video software, and small font text, older adults can be considered as very experienced and knowledgeable individuals in their respective fields (Liu et al., 2016; Mukherjee, 2011). Such experience and knowledge is valuable for LP as certain voids could be filled by engaging older adults in VV opportunities. However, there are also benefits for older adults to partake in VV during COVID-19. For instance, as older adults seek leisure opportunities, VV could lead to outcomes such as involvement, meaningfully engagement, and enhanced life satisfaction (Nimrod, 2007). Thus, LP should market VV opportunities to older adults as an accessible opportunity to apply relevant skills and past experiences and/or search for new experiences and development of skills.

Challenges

Despite opportunities, VV challenges LP in their management process. More precisely, the management process is challenged in terms of recruitment, engagement, and retention of VV. Each of these challenges will be discussed below.

Recruitment

For recruitment, LP have yet to take advantage of VV as few have created roles specific for this volunteer type (Liu et al., 2016). Further, LP have reported using other strategies (e.g., in-person interviews) as opposed to technology to recruit volunteers. The lack of willingness of LP to use technology (Murray & Harrison, 2005) for recruitment is ironic given the fundamental nature of VV and an abundance of websites that promote positions for this volunteer type (e.g., Volunteer Canada's Pan Canadian Matching

Platform). This can also be explained by the limited use of technology by LP in comparison to other industries where technology is more prevalent (e.g., education, software design, engineering).

During COVID-19, LP should (a) conduct an internal analysis of their organization or event, and (b) partner with volunteer-related agencies to assist with the recruitment of VV. The internal analysis (e.g., strengths, weaknesses) would enable LP to determine potential needs (e.g., social media, strategic planning, governance) based on their current available resources. For instance, and as strategic planning is often lacking in community sport organizations (e.g., Misener & Doherty, 2009), LP could create VV positions to fill such voids (e.g., Board committee member, business development advisor/consultant). For social media, a relevant group to pursue would be youth given their interests and knowledge of various platforms (e.g., Twitter). LP could provide information about positions or advertise on social media platforms to recruit youth for VV. These recruitment strategies would enable LP to maintain operations virtually, and continue to work toward the achievement of goals and objectives despite COVID-19.

However, determining needs to create VV positions is not enough for LP. To enhance the recruitment of individuals during COVID-19, LP should communicate and partner with volunteer-related agencies at the national- (e.g., Volunteer Canada), provincial- (e.g., Volunteer Alberta), and local-levels (e.g., Volunteer Ottawa). These agencies, which are often overlooked and underutilized, could assist LP with advertising their available positions, and provide additional knowledge and resources to promote best practices. These agencies can also assist LP with the search for specific groups of individuals to be involved in VV (e.g., individuals with disabilities, youth, older adults), and offer strategies to engage undervalued individuals in the volunteer population.

Engagement

For engagement, LP have also had challenges communicating with VV, such as individuals taking prolonged periods of time to provide responses on task progress or follow-up emails, while others even leave their role without notice (Liu et al., 2016). While this can also be possible in traditional volunteering, VV adds an additional barrier (i.e., technological medium) for LP to communicate with its volunteers on a regular basis and to properly engage with them through virtual spaces as opposed to in-person. However, and despite these communication issues, VV have also discussed the need for increased communication and task-load than currently provided by LP (Liu et al., 2016). This juxtaposition creates a challenge for LP to effectively engage their VV.

To combat engagement challenges among VV during the pandemic, LP should be more involved and communicative with its volunteers. First, LP should incorporate weekly meetings with its VV where updates could be given regarding current and ongoing tasks. Such updates could be completed through video platforms (e.g., Zoom), and would enable for communication issues to be less prevalent than before.

Second, communication is important to determine the level of engagement and experience of VV. For instance, if individuals feel as though their tasks are not appropriate or not meaningful, LP should make modifications (e.g., change of position, additional tasks) to promote greater engagement. The assigned role is critical in maintaining a positive volunteer experience as improper role-fit and performance can have negative outcomes (Lachance & Parent, 2020). Providing meaningful engagement and opportunities for VV begins with properly assessing the individual's needs, motives, skills, and past experiences to determine an appropriate role. Thus, LP are encouraged to discover individuals' characteristics through virtual interviews during the recruitment process for VV.

Retention

Finally, VV retention is problematic for leisure practitioners (Murray & Harrison, 2005). In comparison to traditional volunteers, VV are believed to be more difficult to retain as their tasks are primarily project-based and short-term in nature (Murray & Harrison, 2005). As such, LP are challenged to create meaningful opportunities for VV to be involved in more long-term roles and tasks in an effort to encourage retention (Liu et al., 2016). However, volunteer retention is problematic and not a simple undertaking (Hoye et al., 2020).

The circumstances of COVID-19's unpredictability enables LP to combat a major challenge in VV; establishing long-term roles. As current VV opportunities are short-term, leisure practitioners have the unique opportunity to engage individuals for longer periods of time. For instance, a previous volunteer involved in communications could be tasked with a VV opportunity related to the development of policies or operations for social media platforms, a social media strategy, and/or marketing. Additional examples of long-term roles could include policy development (e.g., recruitment and orientation of VV, by-laws, codes of conduct), project management (e.g., financial analyses, marketing and communications), or assisting with editing, proofreading, and translation of operational documents and policies (Volunteer Canada, 2019).

Given the unpredictability of COVID-19, retention of VV is critical for LP to sustain organizational and event operations. If VV are able to be retained, LP will reap the benefits of having knowledgeable and experienced individuals, and spend less time searching for new individuals to fill vacant positions. The operations of organizations and events will look drastically different than before COVID-19, and LP may be forced to continue some additional operations off-site due to safety measures. This highlights the need for VV to be retained and engaged in long-term roles to continually assist with operations and transitions due to COVID-19, and its eventual aftermath.

Conclusion

The relevancy of VV for LP during the COVID-19 pandemic is at the forefront and arguably more relevant than ever. LP must transition some operations virtually, while individuals are forced to be away from one another. Yet these individuals still strive for leisure activities. This essay discussed the major opportunities and challenges for LP to implement VV during the COVID-19 pandemic, and how these opportunities and challenges might be navigated beyond this pandemic. VV offers individuals the opportunity to pursue their desired leisure activity (i.e., volunteering), and enables LP to navigate transitions and maintain operations, all while respecting imposed social distancing measures.

Given the current digital age, technology is not something we can escape, but instead, a tool LP should seek to leverage through its most indispensable resource; volunteers.

VV represents the future of volunteering as a leisure activity, which is ripe for both inquiry and implementation during COVID-19 and beyond. Currently, research on VV in organizations and events is limited. It is thus imperative for us as leisure scholars to advance our understanding of VV in these contexts, aid LP to effectively implement VV, and investigate its relationship with broader topics such as the volunteer experience. This would advance knowledge of the volunteer experience in virtually spaces as current research and understanding of this phenomenon is limited to traditional in-person volunteering experiences (e.g., Lachance & Parent, 2020).

ORCID

Erik L. Lachance 🆔 http://orcid.org/0000-0003-4935-5833

References

Aiello, R. (2020, April 22). PM Trudeau announces $9B in new COVID-19 funding for students. *CTV News*. https://www.ctvnews.ca/canada/pm-trudeau-announces-9b-in-new-covid-19-funding-for-students-1.4906564

Callos, N. (2020, January 25). Volunteer at the Olympics: 2020 Tokyo Summer Olympic Games, 2022 Beijing Winter Olympic Games and beyond. *Volunteer Forever*. https://www.volunteerforever.com/article_post/volunteer-at-the-olympics-2020-tokyo-summer-olympic-games-2022-beijing-winter-olympic-games-and-beyond/

Government of Ontario. (n.d.). *Stopping the spread of COVID-19*. https://www.ontario.ca/page/stopping-spread-covid-19

Hoye, R., Cuskelly, G., Auld, C., Kappelides, P., & Misener, K. (2020). *Sport volunteering*. Routledge.

Lachance, E. L., & Parent, M. M. (2020). The volunteer experience in a para-sport event: An autoethnography. *Journal of Sport Management*, 34(2), 93–102. https://doi.org/10.1123/jsm.2019-0132

Liu, H. K., Harrison, Y. D., Lai, J. J. K., Chikoto, G. L., & Jones-Lungo, K. (2016). Online and virtual volunteering. In D. H. Horton, R. A. Stebbins, & J. Grotz (Eds.), *Palgrave handbook of volunteering, civic participation, and nonprofit associations* (pp. 290–310). New York, NY: Palgrave Macmillan.

McGregor-Lowndes, M., Crittall, M., Conroy, D., & Keast, R. (2017). *Individual giving and volunteering: Giving Australia 2016*. Brisbane, Australia: Australian Government Department of Social Services.

Misener, K., & Doherty, A. (2009). A case study of organizational capacity in nonprofit community sport. *Journal of Sport Management*, 23(4), 457–482. https://doi.org/10.1123/jsm.23.4.457

Mukherjee, D. (2011). Participation of older adults in virtual volunteering: A qualitative analysis. *Ageing International*, 36(2), 253–266. https://doi.org/10.1007/s12126-010-9088-6

Murray, V., & Harrison, Y. (2005). Virtual volunteering. In J. L. Brudney (Ed.), *Emerging areas of volunteering* (pp. 33–50). Indianapolis, IN: Association for Research on Nonprofit Organizations and Voluntary Action.

Nimrod, G. (2007). Retirees' leisure: Activities, benefits, and their contribution to life satisfaction. *Leisure Studies*, 26(1), 65–80. https://doi.org/10.1080/02614360500333937

Volunteer Canada. (2019). *Virtual volunteering*. https://volunteer.ca/index.php?MenuItemID=419

Volunteer Canada. (2020). *Virtual volunteering*. https://volunteer.ca/vdemo/ResearchAndResources_DOCS/Virtual%20Volunteering%20Mar2020.pdf

"Washing Hands, Reaching Out" – Popular Music, Digital Leisure and Touch during the COVID-19 Pandemic

Eric T. Lehman

ABSTRACT

Through the lens of contagion theory, this paper examines the act of sanitizing tactile references in popular music at a time of legislated and extreme isolation. "Sweet Caroline" is an infectious tune that embraces togetherness and intimacy both lyrically and through its live performance. However, on March 22, 2020, Neil Diamond posted on Twitter a clip of himself, alone in front of a fireplace, singing a modified version of his hit song which reworked the lyrics of "touching hands" to "washing hands" and "touching me, touching you" to "don't touch me, I won't touch you." More viral than COVID-19 itself, the revised "Sweet Caroline" has spread to over five million viewers in a couple of short weeks. Touch, during the COVID-19 pandemic, has become devalued at a time when it should be celebrated as a point of comfort in the present and as hope for the future.

Using "Sweet Caroline" as its soundtrack, an advertisement for the 2018 Hyundai Sonata promotes closeness and comradery as two drivers in neighboring cars, caught in a traffic jam, sing along to Neil Diamond's famous song. Noting that "happy drivers make better drivers" and by asking the viewer to "make [their] commute a little sweeter" (Trayvids, 2017), the ad proposes that when you are stuck and have nowhere to go, you can always depend on music (or your Sonata which is branded after a classical music composition form) to find freedom and human connection.

Fast-forward two years to March 2020 and the idea of being "stuck and having nowhere to go" has been taken to unprecedented levels. With the streets empty and everything eerily still, there is little need for music or other happy neighboring drivers to accompany us on our morning commute. During the COVID-19 pandemic, individuals are encouraged to stay home and, when they can't, they are expected to practice safe distancing as a means of combating the virus.

Even singing along to "Sweet Caroline" is not as "sweet." On March 22, 2020, Neil Diamond tweeted a video of himself sitting by a fireplace with guitar in hand and singing an adaptation of his hit song for a shut-in online audience with the lyrics "touching hands" altered to "washing hands" and "touching me, touching you" to "don't touch me, I won't touch you." Diamond introduces the song stating, "I know we're going through a rough time right now, but I love ya, and I think maybe if we sing together, we'll feel just a little bit better" (Diamond, 2020). While *Rolling Stone* likened this action to "a public service announcement" (Kreps, 2020), there is something else at play here. Diamond is not only participating in civic duty, but as a subject to COVID-19 lockdown legislation, he is also participating in a form of digital and musical leisure to pass the time. Engaging in music and social media as digital leisure is not strictly a private activity and Diamond's new rendition of "Sweet Caroline" has contagious possibilities. Unfortunately, by denouncing "touch," an essentially human means of communication and affect, this adaptation of "Sweet Caroline" further isolates those who need connection and contact most.

Theories surrounding the importance of music, community, and leisure are well documented and date back to the philosophy of Aristotle who noted that music was not merely a point of pleasure but was useful in the education of youth as a leisurely and relaxing activity and as a counterbalance to business. Just as it is important to take care of the body through exercise, Aristotle argues, the soul also seeks strengthening through musical leisure (Aristole et al., 1998; Destrée, 2018). Moving beyond restorative qualities, Bennett (2005) notes that popular music, although it may be ubiquitous and fade into the urban soundscape, is far from a passive endeavor. Popular music acts as a powerful agent in spreading alternative ideologies, bringing forth memory and creating affect. Henderson and Spracklen's (2018) study of music promotion and digital spaces demonstrate that music-making and music listening are important for building communities in physical and online spaces. Music is not simply made for personal enjoyment, as Aristotle's contemporaries had believed, but is embedded into our social being and is a crucial part of connecting with others.

Under the global pandemic, where connections are less likely made though physical proximity in public spaces than through touchscreens, musical leisure is still crucial to communities and personal growth. Spotify (2020) published an article highlighting changes to listening habits during the COVID-19 pandemic. People were listening more at home and choosing playlists that complimented other domestic activities such as cooking or cleaning and there was even a boost in certain listening selections. Songs that were chanted from balconies in support of front-line workers in Spain and Italy saw an increase of 820% and the Police's "Don't Stand So Close to Me" saw 135% more plays. Furthermore, while musical leisure may be confined to the private home, the development of musical communities within these private spaces is ongoing. This is evident through the success of virtual concerts. While major summer music festivals like Coachella, Glastonbury and the Montreaux Jazz Festival have been canceled (Billboard Staff, 2020), the "One World: Together at Home" online concert featuring Lady Gaga (who performed Charlie Chaplin's "Smile"), Lizzo (Sam Cooke's "A Change is Gonna Come") Taylor Swift ("You'll Get Better Soon"), and the Rolling Stones ("You Can't Always Get What You Want") was filmed and transmitted from the artists' homes and raised $127 million for COVID-19 research (Peters, 2020).

Like the artists of "One World: Together at Home," Diamond could have chosen other, perhaps better suited, selections from his vast songwriting catalog to campaign for social distancing without modifying "Sweet Caroline." His first hit single, "Solitary

Man" ("I'll be what I am/A solitary man"), or his Golden Globe-nominated number "Lonely Looking Sky" ("Lonely night, lonely looking night/And being lonely/Never made it right") from the soundtrack to *Jonathan Livingstone Seagull* would have been suitable for this purpose without adaptation. So why target "Sweet Caroline" to send a message of social distancing?

One possibility is that "Sweet Caroline" has accumulated a significant amount of "contagious magic." "Contagious magic," as Roberts (2014) suggests, is the "rubbing off" (p. 17) of symbolic capital to maximize consumption across cultural industries and activities (Roberts, 2014). Much like its effective use in the Hyundai ad, "Sweet Caroline" has become part of leisurely and everyday life. It has become a fan favorite at baseball games and has been claimed as an anthem for the Boston Red Sox (Millard, 2007; Willman, 2018). Campfire Collective (2018) rated it as their number one campfire song stating, "good times really never seemed so good when you're belting this song out with friends and family beside the warmth of a bonfire." It remains a staple in Karaoke bars as a sing-along. In direct reference to "Sweet Caroline," Brown (2015) notes that "[t]he sing-along is the ultimate karaoke high … It guarantees an amazing adrenaline rush, because it is the embodiment of the metaphorical merging of the self with the community" (p.114). "Sweet Caroline" finds its way into parties, into dances at wedding receptions, and even into our bedrooms as expressed through the love poetry of Ron S. King (2010): "This night, as the flames of love grew higher/We heated our bodies in passions, more strong/Than the flames of that amorous log-burning fire/While Neil Diamond softly sang his sweet song" (p. 37). Remarkably, "Sweet Caroline" embraces togetherness and intimacy like few other songs have making it the ideal candidate for reaching out as a public service message.

However, changing the lyrics of "Sweet Caroline" alters the ingredients to the "contagious magic" of the song. By replacing "touching hands" to "washing hands" and inserting "don't touch me" and "I won't touch you," the new lyrics negate physical and emotional intimacy in favor of emphasizing the importance of personal hygiene and distancing in the time of the COVID-19 pandemic. Much like the Storybots do in their children's song "Wash Your Hands" ("Because itty bitty germs can get you sick/They're sneakier than you think/So step right up to that marvelous marvel of science/Simply known as a sink") (Netflix Jr., 2020), "Sweet Caroline" becomes an instructional tune to teach citizens to stay healthy in uncertain times. Touch, seemingly, is to be feared and avoided as a reality of COVID-19.

Historically, touch was already conflated with disease and contagion. While the term "contagion" is now associated with the concept of "spreading," it was derived from the Latin *continguous* meaning "touching" and, with a growing understanding of epidemiology, some medical books have discontinued using "contagious" to describe disease transmission adopting instead the terminology of "communicable diseases" (Pernick, 2002). Medical historian Margaret Pelling (2001) expands beyond the medical definition of contagion stating that, "[i]deas of contagion are inseparable from notions of individual morality, social responsibility, and collective action" (p. 17). Like Richard Dawkins (2006) concept of the "meme" or cultural gene which replicates the morals of a society, Wald (2008) notes that contagion is "a foundational concept in the study of religion and of society, with a long history of explaining how beliefs circulate in social interactions" (p. 2). Finally, my own research on the potential spread of computer viruses through digital rights management software shows that the threat of digital contagions is not isolated, but highly connected to concerns regarding public health and national security. Computer viruses not only infect digital bodies, but can jump to biological, political and social bodies as well (Lehman, 2018). Similarly, COVID-19 and touching are not merely matters for public health. They have a myriad of overlapping and interrelated meanings and functions beyond biological contagion which spread though our social, emotional, political and digital networks.

Like contagions, touch has the power to communicate more than just physical illness. Moder (2019) proposes three ontological understandings of touch: the sensual, the geometrical, and the conceptual. The sensual encompasses both physical and tactile touch, but also embodies the emotional understanding of this word – to feel touched. The second category, geometrical, is an understanding of touch in relation to proximity. For example, Modor explains how a "mountain touches the sky" or how we "keep in touch." Finally, conceptual touch is an abstraction and purely metaphorical understanding of the word; "touching on" something equates the concepts of talking with touching. The consideration of a fourth category of touch related to contagion is omitted. Nixon and Servitje (2016) propose the useful concept of "contagious contact" to understand this type of touch and define it as "the material realities of a physically connected world transcribed in their most extreme form" (p. 9). Contagious touch, like conceptual touch, is an abstraction but it is also sensual in that it is embodied and felt. Neil Diamond seems to have leaned on this fourth understanding of "touch" as "contagious contact" in his reworking of "Sweet Caroline". While during the COVID-19 pandemic people wear gloves and sanitize their hands as a matter of personal protection and good citizenship, it is perhaps important to be reminded that not all touch is contagious, and not all touch leads to sickness. Touch is emotive, sensual, metaphorical and connecting. Even Diamond's biographer understands this, and writes, "Diamond took a mere hour to write 'Sweet Caroline,' and today there are few countries in the world where this song is not instantly recognized. He is *touched* by that fact" (Jackson, 2005, p. 61).

Another possibility is that Neil Diamond is not only doing his civic duty in offering up "Sweet Caroline" as a public service announcement but instead is himself participating in a form of digital music leisure through digital contagion (i.e. going viral) to keep occupied during the COVID-19 lockdown. Kreps (2020) connects the COVID-19 "Sweet Caroline" reboot with @actioncookbook's popular tweet posted on February 27, 2020:

NEIL DIAMOND: touching hands

CDC: no don't touch hands

NEIL DIAMOND: reaching out

CDC: please avoid that

NEIL DIAMOND: TOUCHING YOU-

CDC: everyone is Boston is doomed

This tweet, which was circulating in the early stages of social distancing, has received many replies mimicking similar imagined conversations between the Centers for Disease Control and Prevention (CDC) and artist song lyrics including MC Hammer's

"U Can't Touch This," The Beatles "I Want to Hold Your Hand," and Robert Palmer's "Bad Case of Loving You (Doctor, Doctor)." If Diamond had seen this meme, which was retweeted 22,000 times and liked 105,000 times as of April 20, 2020, he could be sanitizing his lyrics for the benefit of @actioncookbook in a digital game of call and response. Brown (2015) notes that anthropologically speaking, in prehistoric times, call and response was functional "to mark in-group/out-group distinctions among other groups of humans" (p.109). In music, it is a gesture and a means of musical communication between two performers or the performer and the audience where one musical phrase is stated and then responded to by a complimentary musical phrase. When Neil Diamond performs live and sings "Sweet Caroline," the audience responds with "bom bom bom." Likewise, when @actioncookbook tweets "touching you – everyone is doomed," Diamond responds with "washing hands."

The message of "washing hands" did not go unnoticed. At the time of writing (April 20, 2020), Neil Diamond's "Sweet Caroline" tweet was watched 5.1 million times, making it more than twice as contagious as COVID-19 itself. On the same day, Worldometer.info reported 2.4 million confirmed cases of COVID-19 ("Coronavirus Cases," 2020). On March 30, 2020, Britney Spears gave a "response" of her own by revising the lyrics for "Hit Me Baby (One More Time)" on Instagram. The post shows a caricature of Spears holding a bottle of hand-sanitizer and posing next to the lyric "This loneliness is *saving me*" with the original "killing me" lyric crossed out (Aniftos, 2020).

While COVID-19 related loneliness and Neil Diamond's latest rendition of "Sweet Caroline" are unlikely to be with us forever, it is important to consider what is being spread presently. On the transmission of social media, Jenkins et al. (2013) stated: "As material spreads, it gets remade: either literally, through various forms of sampling and remixing, or figuratively, via its insertion into ongoing conversations and across various platforms" (p. 27). Similarly, while Neil Diamond's plea came in the early stages of the pandemic and may have been initially interpreted as an act of public service, as we enter deeper into COVID-19 self-isolation, the "remaking" of Diamond and Spears' adaptations which transform "touch" into pestilence and embrace "loneliness" seem misguided. Being told to wash your hands and not to touch others, as the adaptation of "Sweet Caroline" conveys, reinforces state-sanctioned isolation when touch, community and human connection are needed more than ever. Studies have begun to research the social and psychological effects of self-isolation during the COVID-19 pandemic and there is speculation that physical isolation, while it may be useful in combatting the spread of COVID-19, has created an echoing "epidemic of loneliness" (Altschul, 2020). Therefore, touch through safe physical contact in our homes, feeling touched by listening to music or experiencing art and literature, or keeping in touch though social media and telecommunications should be celebrated and encouraged to prevent loneliness in the time of COVID-19.

Personally, "Sweet Caroline" exemplifies family and togetherness as it stands amongst "Cracklin' Rosie," "Cherry Cherry," that girl who would soon be a woman, and Neil Diamond's other muses who would visit my childhood home through my father's turntable. While others may be following and retweeting Neil Diamond's COVID-19 reboot, I will be experiencing "Sweet Caroline" in the pandemic by dusting off an old copy of Diamond's best-selling live album *Hot August Nights* that I picked up for a dollar at the local thrift shop. As the needle glides along the vinyl record, I will close my eyes and listen to the audience celebrating proximity, unity and togetherness. I will imagine myself there, and dream of future hot, August nights when social distancing vanishes and connecting returns around the cottage campfire.

References

actioncookbook [@actioncookbook]. (2000, February 27). NEIL DIAMOND: touching hand CDC: no don't touch hands NEIL DIAMOND: reaching out CDC: please avoid that NEIL DIAMOND: TOUCHING YOU- CDC: everyone is Boston is doomed. Twitter. https://twitter.com/actioncookbook/status/1233220136431124482

Altschul, B. (2020, April 22). What Puts People at Higher Risk for Loneliness [blog]. *Psychology Today*. Retrieved April 24, 2020. https://www.psychologytoday.com/ca/blog/reverse-causation/202004/what-puts-people-higher-risk-loneliness

Aniftos, R. (2020, April 8). Britney Spears Declares 'My Loneliness Is Saving Me,' Urges Fans to Stay Home. *Billboard*. Retrieved April 20, 2020, from https://www.billboard.com/articles/columns/pop/9353501/britney-spears-loneliness-is-saving-me

Aristotle, Barker, E., & Stalley, R. F. (1998). *The politics*. Oxford University Press.

Bennett, A. (2005). Editorial: Popular music and leisure. *Leisure Studies*, 24(4), 333–342. https://doi.org/10.1080/02614360500200656

Billboard Staff. (2020, April 22). Here are all the major music events canceled due to coronavirus (updating). *Billboard*. Retrieved April 23, 2020. https://www.billboard.com/articles/business/touring/9323647/concerts-canceled-coronavirus-list

Brown, K. (2015). *Karaoke idols: popular music and the performance of identity*. Intellect.

Campfire Collective. (2018, October 2). Top 10 Cottage Campfire Songs [Blog post]. Retrieved April 17, 2020. https://www.thecampfirecollective.com/blog/top-10-cottage-campfire-songs/

Coronavirus Cases. (2020, April 20). *Worldometer*. Retrieved April 20, 2020, from https://www.worldometers.info/coronavirus/

Dawkins, R. (2006). *The selfish gene*. Oxford University Press.

Destrée, P. (2018). Aristotle on music for leisure. In T. Philips & A. D'Angour (Eds.), *Music, text, and culture in Ancient Greece* (pp. 183–202).Oxford University Press.

Diamond, N. [@NeilDiamond] (2020, March 22). *Stay safe out there! "Hands… washing hands."* Twitter. https://twitter.com/NeilDiamond/status/1241584423927074818

Henderson, S., & Spracklen, K. (2018). Plus ça Change, Plus C'est la Même Chose': Music promoting, digital leisure, social media and community. *Leisure Sciences*, 40(4), 239–250. https://doi.org/10.1080/01490400.2017.1378139

Jackson, L. (2005). *Neil Diamond: his life, his music, his passion*. ECW Press.

Jenkins, H., Ford, S., & Green, J. (2013). *Spreadable media: Creating value and meaning in a networked culture*. New York University Press.

King, R. S. (2010). A Neil Diamond love-song. In M. Cox (Ed.), *A compilation of poems by Ron S. King* (p. 370). Lulu Press.

Kreps, D. (2020, March 22). Watch Neil Diamond Transform 'Sweet Caroline' into coronavirus PSA. *Rolling Stone*. Retrieved April 17, 2020. https://www.rollingstone.com/music/music-news/neil-diamond-sweet-caroline-coronavirus-psa-971013/

Lehman, E. (2018). From contagion and revealing to recovery and healing: Examining the lifecycle of ubiquitous control through the Sony/BMG Rootkit. In M. S. Daubs & V. R. Manerolle (Eds.), *Mobile and Ubiquitous media: Critical and international perspectives* (pp. 59–73). Peter Lang.

Millard, P. (2007, December 13). PAULINE'S PICKS: Exploring the inspiration of "sweet caroline" and other songs. *Editor & Publisher*.

Moder, G. (2019). Ontology of touch: From Aristotle to Brentano. In M. Komel (Ed.), *The language of touch: Philosophical examinations in linguistics and haptic studies* (pp. 55–72). Bloomsbury Academic.

Netflix Jr. (2020). 'Wash Your Hands' Song for Kids □ StoryBots | Netflix Jr. [video]. YouTube. https://www.youtube.com/watch?v=MyE_xjcTSkg

Nixon, K., & Servitje, L. (2016). *Endemic: Essays on contagion theory.* Palgrave Macmillan.

Pelling, M. (2001). The meaning of contagion: Reproduction, medicine and metaphor. In A. Bashford & C Hooker (Eds), *Contagion: Historical and cultural studies* (pp. 15–38). Routledge.

Pernick, M. (2002). Contagion and culture. *American Literary History, 14*(4), 858–865. https://doi.org/10.1093/alh/14.4.858

Peters, M. (2020, April 19). 'One World: Together at Home' Concert Helps Raise $127.9M for COVID-19 relief, global citizen announces. *Billboard.* Retrieved April 23, 2020. https://www.billboard.com/articles/news/9361485/one-world-together-at-home-concert-raises-127-9m-for-covid-19-relief-coronavirus

Roberts, L. (2014). Marketing musicscapes, or the political economy of contagious magic. *Tourist Studies, 14*(1), 10–29. https://doi.org/10.1177/1468797613511683

Spotify. (2020, March 30). How social distancing has shifted spotify streaming. Retrieved April 17, 2020. https://newsroom.spotify.com/2020-03-30/how-social-distancing-has-shifted-spotify-streaming/

Trayvids. (2017, September 5). *Hyundai Sonata TV Commercial, Duet Song by Neil Diamond iSpottv* [video]. Youtube. https://www.youtube.com/watch?v=jENwDuoRAi0

Wald, P. (2008). *Contagious: Cultures, carriers, and the outbreak narrative.* Duke University Press.

Willman, C. (2018). Mining for Gold with Neil Diamond: As the storied songwriter is honored, a look back at five of his greatest hits. *Variety, 340*(11), 122.

What Do You (Really) Meme? Pandemic Memes as Social Political Repositories

Shana MacDonald (iD)

ABSTRACT
The commentary examines coronavirus memes circulating around forms of generational conflict that have risen from experiences of self-isolation. Employing participant-observation methods within online spaces of meme circulation, the commentary analyzes the political, social, and affective aspects of the memes considered. The commentary offers insight into how we operationalize our social media spaces in times of deep uncertainty in order collectively bring differing experiences and perspectives into a contingent, shifting, and affectively constituted public sphere.

Introduction: This is fine ...

You've seen it. The drawing of a large-eyed dog sitting at a table in a burning room drinking a cup of coffee with a speech bubble that reads "this is fine." The image has been circulated countless times to comment on a variety of anxiety producing global and local events. This includes one recently where the coffee mug is replaced by a pyramid of toilet paper rolls; referencing how public panic around the coronavirus resulted in a toilet paper shortage across parts of North America (Know Your Meme). The meme, created in 2013 by KC Green, has become internet speak for when "a situation becomes so terrible our brains refuse to grapple with its severity" (Plante, 2016). The image reflects our shared existential dread while infusing unbearable situations with dark humour; as such it a great image for the present moment (Figure 1).

Internet memes encapsulate "some of the most fundamental aspects of contemporary digital culture" (Shifman, 2014, p. 4). By being readily shared, parodied, and remixed, memes encourage forms of intertextuality; mixing together "popular culture, politics" to "underscore the social dynamics" of our online and offline worlds (Shifman, 2014, p. 4). Taking this seriously, I examine a series of internet memes that respond to the coronavirus pandemic, considering how they mix popular culture and politics in order to reflect some of the new lived realities and underlying tensions the pandemic has produced. In particular I examine memes commenting on the generational tensions arising

Figure 1. This is fine.

from differing reactions to self-isolation. I suggest memes are used in times of uncertainty to produce a shared perspective on our contingent, shifting, and affectively constituted public sphere (Warner, 2002).

Theoretical review

As An Xiao Mina argues, "[i]t's difficult to overstate the spread of memes in all corners of life." (2019, p. 6). If memes play an increasingly influential role in our social world (Chen, 2012), then we need to treat them as a significant site of scholarly research within this unprecedented moment of human experience. This certainly is the perspective of the US Library of Congress whose digital archivist team is extensively documenting media ephemera produced in response to the coronavirus, including memes (Kurutz, 2020). Key here is how memes "spread across borders and territories to involve much larger groups of people acting in solidarity than might previously have been possible" (Mina, 2019, p. 7). Their virality allows for "new perspectives and narratives" to be shared amongst large groups of disparate but digitally connected populations (Mina, 2019, p. 12). As examples of ordinary or everyday technologies, what memes offer then is a snapshot of "broader social values and systems that shape the human condition" (Humphries, 2018, p. 6).

Drawing on Aimee Morrison's (2019a) discussion of hashtags, I similarly single out memes out for their ability to "assemble publics" which "are marked not just by their humour but by their bent towards the colloquial, the vernacular, and the anecdotal" (pp. 24–25). As such they fit into the focus of Lee Humphrey's (2018) germinal work on the everyday life of social media. Humphrey's work frames my reading of memes as forms of digital communication that are both connective and contextual (2018). We use memes in our leisure time to connect on affective levels with others. What makes memes viral is their relatability; they often focus on the everyday, the absurd, or sometimes, as in pandemic memes, the everyday absurd. In this way they are also contextual. Our social media experiences are differently curated by algorithms that are individually specific, as such we get very different sets of memes circulating on our feeds. One consequence is that memes produce ingroups and outgroups; you are either in on the joke or you are not. This is useful for those situated within an ingroup as their experiences are recognized and validated by a larger collective. However, it can highlight the normative positions of such ingroups. With this framing of connectivity and context , my exploration of one set of memes that emerged during the COVID-19 pandemic reveals how Generation X employed intertextual popular culture references to express their frustrations against the neoliberal norms now being thrown into question by the halt of the global economy.

Methods

As a research "netographer" (Kozinets et al., 2014), I analyze the socio-political and affective aspects mems offer. Netnography, is the "cultural analysis of social media" that collects data via "the researcher's observation of and participation with people as they socialize online in regular environments and activities" (Kozinets et al., 2014, pp. 262–263). My research on pandemic memes uses a mixed-media, qualitative, small data approach (Morrison, 2019b) centered on a "reading practice [that] is embedded, context-driven, and interpretive" in order to move extensively "across webs of connection, in order discern emergent patterns from a diffuse set of instances" (2019b, p. 44).

Many prominent scholars advocate the need for small data approaches to digital media and yet there is still a need to further develop analytic frames that do not rely on randomization, scaling, and coding of big algorithmic data which largely overlook everyday digital communicative acts (boyd and Crawford 2012). As a response, I attend here to the everyday emotions (e.g., humour, irony, and anger) that memes capture and how these articulate political positions through their circulation. I use observational data that I have collected as participant of social media platforms where the analyzed memes circulate. I collected screenshots between March 13 and April 15 2020 and organized them into different groupings. I also tracked news stories related to pandemic memes by typing "COVID-19 memes" into a search engine during the same period and noted the meme-based themes emerging across a variety of news sites. While data scrapping may be a common approach to collecting internet data, I agree with Kozinets, Dolbec, and Early that "the temptation to "mine" large amounts of data can overshadow real-time engagement with the cultural context" (2014, p. 267) In what follows I explore memes tied to generational conflicts arising from the pandemic. These memes offer insight into the cultural context of those identifying as Generation X (born between 1965 and 1980). This is also known as the "sandwich generation," a cohort running most industries at present, many of whom also actively care for either school-aged children or aging parents, or sometimes both. This brief commentary is not an exhaustive study of generations or their potentially competing positions; instead, it reads how the figure of Gen X is being used rhetorically to voice larger socio-political concerns.

Memes of GenX asserting their pandemic politics

Between mid-March and early April 2020, a variety of news outlets (including NBC News, Newsweek, Upworthy, and Distractify) posted stories about how it was

Figure 2. Andi Ziesler tweet.

Generation X's moment to shine. This was prompted by a series of tweets trending on March 15th outlining how GenX was uniquely qualified to weather out the pandemic as it was the generation of latchkey kids growing up in the Reagan Era; a generation that faced the terror of AIDS, the threat of nuclear war, and the War on Drugs. These tweets reflected middle-aged children bemoaning their very different responses to the pandemic of both their boomer parents, and Millennials and Generation Z (who were problematically collapsed together). Gen Xers felt other generations did not seem to be taking the self-isolation recommendations as seriously as they should (Figure 2).

These tensions were further expressed through a popular meme that places together three separate images, each of which defines a different generation in relationship to each other. In one, there is a picture of Xena warrior princess, with the word "Boomer" in big white letters at the top. Next to it is a picture of the blonde woman from the "woman yelling at cat" meme (a picture of Taylor Armstrong, from *Real Housewives of Beverly Hills* season two, during a heated argument), with the word "Millennials" in big white letters. Beneath is an image of either Karen from *Will & Grace* smugly holding a martini or the Dude from *The Big Lebowski* smoking a joint in a bath, with the word "Gen X" in even bigger white letters. There are variations on this that include Darth Vader or Darth Maul as the boomers, Kylo Ren or Luke Skywalker as the millennials, and Han Solo as Gen Xers; and yet another with Donald Trump as boomers, Mark Zuckerberg for Millennials, and Wayne from *Wayne's World* as Gen Xers. In each variation of this meme, intergenerational tensions are filtered through the lens of popular culture. Clearly, these memes are made by people from Generation X as they use the pop culture icons of their youth as the "heroes" in each grouping. It is Karen, the

Figure 3. (a, b, c) Boomer, Millenial, Gen X.

Dude, Han Solo, and Wayne who are successfully addressing and negotiating the stresses of the pandemic in "preferable" ways, while the images of the other generations are portrayed in various states of rage, terror, and confrontation. All of these emotions are reasonable reactions to the current moment, however the memes suggest that Gen X is managing things the "right way." I would argue there are rhetorical reasons for this that have to do with broader political critiques often levelled at the other two generations (Figure 3a,b,c).

A second set of memes that express similar sentiments around the pandemic rely on music and other movie references central to Gen Xers lived experience. This set of memes is both accusatory of other generations and self-congratulating; employing images from *The Breakfast Club*, *Ferris Bueller's Day Off*, *Twin Peaks*, *Reality Bites* as well as references to musical groups including The Cure, Devo, REM, and Nirvana among others. These memes assert the cynical, defiant, anti-social, self-sufficient, and insouciant nature of Gen Xers. Taken together these memes suggest that these traits make Generation X better equipped to survive the current moment, and thus better than boomers and Millennials and GenZ combined. Take for instance this image of Sherilynn Fenn as Audrey Horne answering a telephone in a still from the original *Twin Peaks* series. It is turned into a meme through the adding of the following words: "It's Kurt Cobain from 1991; he says we're stupid and contagious" (Figure 4).

Figure 4. Stupid and contagious.

As one Tweet circulating this meme notes: "Kurt warned us and we took heed. #GenX" (@upcuntrydegen, March 15, 2020). As a quick snapshot into pandemic memes these offer clues into the affective and cultural sentiments of this particular generational cohort. These memes reflect disdain as well as satisfaction that Gen Xers are finally being recognized for their well-honed skills of self-reliance in the face of daunting circumstances. Of course, a similar argument can be made of Boomers earlier experiences of social political unrest in the 1960s and 1970s, but memes may not be as central a method of communication for them. Thus, Gen Xers are writing this particular script. In the image above, it is the use of grunge-rock icon Kurt Cobain, and counter-cultural text *Twin Peaks* that assert Gen X's cultural superiority and call out other generation's actions as both "stupid and contagious." This is a redirection of the original lyrics in the anthem *Smells Like Teen Spirit* where Cobain actually describes himself.

Beyond name calling and posturing, what do these memes offer? Reviewing the tweets, comments, and think pieces arising over this particular meme event, there is more to it than an ironic in joke amongst a certain ingroup. The conversations surrounding these memes continually reference sites of trauma from this group's childhood including for instance the AIDS crisis mentioned above. For many who lived through the early days of the AIDS crisis, it is distressingly under-historicized in the present moment. While the AIDS crisis certainly impacted queer communities to a greater degree than the broader public, it was also a deeply troubling and politicizing turning point for many youth, including those who did not identify as LGBTQ + at the time. As such, conversations prompted by these present-day memes push those sharing them to collectively recognize the points of history they are drawing on when approaching the present. The fight against the AIDS epidemic was woefully underfunded by governments around the world and the cost was millions of lives that were already marginalized by conservative and homophobic agendas. Part of the signal towards these institutional failures now asserts perhaps more loudly than ever how much distrust Gen Xers have toward democratic processes and seeks parallels with the deprioritizing of lives over economies. Throughout their youth such processes failed and left us with diminished social support systems that encourage even greater forms of inequity worldwide. Alongside their early resistance to self-isolation measures both Boomers and late Millenial/GenZ are depicted as supportive of neoliberalism and excessive work

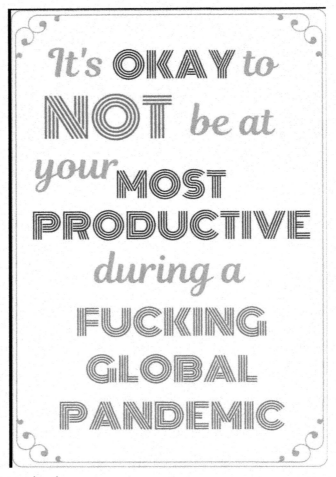

Figure 5. It's ok to not be ok.

productivity. The bravado and glib frustrations of these memes reveal a critique of the generations surrounding them.

Like the figures of the Dude, Han Solo, Karen and Wayne, Gen X considers themselves, whether accurate or not, as rebels who do not uphold the status quo. They cling to an outlier status that largely rejects the self-branding and self-optimization required by our present culture. This is of course not fully accurate; these memes only offer a white, heteronormative vision of rebelliousness that themselves uphold an inequitable dominant cultural position. Further, many within this generational cohort are as tied to neoliberalism as other generations. Why then, would such memes go viral, prompting think pieces and news stories? Memes are everyday acts of communication that articulate identities and political positions. As they circulate, garnering more and more likes and re-shares, they set the tone for conversations and bring into words people's affective sentiments ; these in turn garner greater exposure and engagement. Memes allow for the building of community discourse, which if it circulates enough across our daily social media feeds, becomes a part of our reality. Perhaps this set of slyly critical memes at their core critique outmoded ideological values held fast by other generations. Hopefully through their virality the can, over time, shift into a more productive political discourse. At the very least they have started some important conversations.

Coda: memes as the anti-dote to pre-COVID neoliberal society

On March 16th I took a screen shot of the below image and made it my computer home screen (Figure 5). As an academic mom I am keenly aware of how even in the most equitable of households, women's domestic and emotional labour greatly impacts one's work-life balance on a regular day (Rao, 2019; Slaughter, 2012), let alone during a pandemic. Many people are now both home school support and IT support for our children to the detriment of our research output (Flaherty, 2020). These imbalances reflect how unreasonable the productivity expectations of neoliberal society and the academy are for all involved (and not just parents). As someone sympathetic with (and hailed by) the GenX position outlined above, I was highly critical of the social and work expectations leading up to the pandemic. These expectations thrived on excess; excess competitiveness, excess workhours, excess information to process and wade through; excess burnout and mental health issues. The memes outlined above, as well as those surrounding mental health support and parenting that were circulating at the beginning of the pandemic all seem to call this excess out for what it is – the untenable seeping of neoliberalism into all facets of daily life. Taken together, this collective articulation of how broken our social and institutional systems are is heartening, a small solace in a difficult time. When we name systematic failing, we open up the discursive possibility to imagine life otherwise (hooks, 2012). This includes memes that assert it is okay to not "make the most" of the pandemic and eschew the impulse to be like Einstein and Isaac Newton, who purportedly developed many great theories in quarantine. Perhaps we should instead discuss all the unnamed labour(ers) that supported their efforts? As this pandemic radically shifts our world, we need to resist a return to these excesses and instead re-evaluate what matters to us as scholars and citizens. We need to return to a vigorous and capacious public discourse that speaks to a more equitable world based on collectivity and collaboration (Walcott, 2020). This may remind us our value is more than productivity and individual genius. Memes, like op-eds, public dialogues, and special issues such as this, will keep prodding us in the right direction, my hope is that we listen.

ORCID

Shana MacDonald http://orcid.org/0000-0001-5828-6345

References

boyd, d., & Crawford, K. (2012). Critical Questions in Big Data: Provocations for a Cultural, Technological, and Scholarly Phenomenon. *Information, Communication, & Society, 15*(5): 662–679.

Chen, C. (2012). The creation and meaning of internet memes in 4chan: Popular internet culture in the age of online digital reproduction. *Habitus*, *3*, 6–19.

Flaherty, C. (2020, April 21). No room of one's own: Early journal submission data suggest COVID-19 is tanking women's research productivity. *Inside Higher Ed*. https://www.inside-highered.com/news/2020/04/21/early-journal-submission-data-suggest-covid-19-tanking-womens-research-productivity?fbclid=IwAR0aYDWCH6bD0QJnvwJAxxvmHIhy6HyU5TxXX_7-lDgYOQqwqpmlS5qxEcU

Hooks, B. (2012). *Writing beyond race: Living theory and practice*. New York: Routledge.

Humphries, L. (2018). *The qualified self: Social media and the accounting of everyday life*. Cambridge, MA: MIT Press.

Know Your Meme. *This is fine – coronavirus toilet paper*. Retrieved April 16, 2020, from https://knowyourmeme.com/photos/1781371-this-is-fine

Kozinets, R. V., Dolbec, P.-Y., & Earley, A. (2014). Netnographic analysis: Understanding culture through social media data. In U. Flick (Ed.), *Sage handbook of qualitative data analysis* (pp. 262–275). London: Sage.

Kurutz, S. (2020, April 7). Meet your meme lords. *The New York Times*.

Mina, A. X. (2019). *Memes to movements: How the world's most viral media is changing social protest and power*. Boston: Beacon Press.

Morrison, A. (2019a). Laughing at injustice: #DistractinglySexy and #StayMadAbby as counter-narratives. In D. C. Parry, C. W. Johnson, & S. Fullagar (Eds.), *Digital dilemmas: Transforming gender identities and power relations in everyday life* (pp. 23–52). London: Palgrave Macmillan.

Morrison, A. (2019b). Social, media, life writing: Online lives at scale, up close, and in context. In K. Douglas & A. Barnwell (Eds.), *Research methodologies for auto/biography studies* (pp. 41–48). New York: Routledge.

Plante, C. (2016, May 5). This is fine creator explains the timeliness of his meme. *The Verge*. https://www.theverge.com/2016/5/5/11592622/this-is-fine-meme-comic

Rao, A. H. (2019, May 12) Even breadwinning wives don't get equality at home. *The Atlantic*. https://www.theatlantic.com/family/archive/2019/05/breadwinning-wives-gender-inequality/589237/

Shifman, L. (2014). *Memes in digital culture*. Cambridge, MA: MIT Press.

Slaughter, A. M. (2012, July/August). Why women still can't have it all. *The Atlantic*. https://www.theatlantic.com/magazine/archive/2012/07/why-women-still-cant-have-it-all/309020/

Walcott, R. (2020, April 15). During the coronavirus, academics have found themselves in a crisis of their work. *Maclean's*. https://www.macleans.ca/opinion/during-the-coronavirus-academics-have-found-themselves-in-a-crisis-of-their-work/

Warner, M. (2002). *Publics and counterpublics*. Cambridge, MA: MIT Press.

Self-Isolated but Not Alone: Community Management Work in the Time of a Pandemic

Matthew E. Perks (iD)

ABSTRACT

As the COVID-19 crisis forces individuals to self-isolate, work from home, and find new leisure activities, an increasing number are turning to online gaming. These online communities are often developed by community managers who work to engage communities and establish norms. Community management work, broadly, is considered the "soft-skilled" labor of communication, diplomacy, and empathy within an online community. Despite an obvious need for this work in mediating the myriad of personalities and sheer number of users, community management is often underpaid and precarious. Using early interviews with community managers, conducted during the COVID-19 crisis, I aim to highlight those who work promoting pro-social behavior in leisure spaces online. This work plays a vital role in community well-being, particularly for those who have not previously interacted extensively online. Community management is arguably an essential service during times of self-isolation, as they corral toxicity and shepherd users into positive online communities.

Introduction

The COVID-19 pandemic has led to global mandates for people to self-isolate, leaving many without work, routine socialization, and group leisure activities. Subsequently, many have had to seek out new leisure activities and an increasing number are turning to online gaming (Mostov and Adam 2020; Taylor, 2020). Live streaming platforms, such as Twitch and YouTube, have observed significant global increases in viewership as individuals from around the world tune in to watch others play games, cook meals, and practice drag makeup (Jackson, 2016; Rosenblatt, 2019; Taylor, 2020). For many, this move to online for social connection and leisure is a new experience. Helping to shepherd these newcomers are community managers, those that greet individuals into their communities and establish norms for these spaces. These workers encourage pro-social behavior, and as Kerr (2017) states, they "directly engage with players, they drive engagement through various campaigns, and they respond to problems" (p. 119) to drive commercial sales for game studios. However, the emotional demand of managing pro-social behavior online is draining for community managers, especially when many are socializing online for potentially the first time.

In addition, these communities may not be the best place for people to flock to. Online gaming communities are often hostile to women and people of color, while the games themselves are often full of stereotyped and harmful representations of marginalized people (Gray, 2014). For Gray (2012), games that are initially "fun and enjoyable, frequently become a place full of hatred and intolerance" (p. 412). Sarah T. Roberts (2019) and Tarleton Gillespie (2018) have both offered contemporary looks at content moderation, or the work of removing unwanted, hostile, and toxic content from online platforms. While community management can involve tasks of content moderation, their work is much more than simply removing content that is deemed unacceptable, but also about encouraging pro-social behavior to make these communities less hostile.

Despite this, online gaming allows people to keep up connections while maintaining social distancing. This commentary highlights the work (and workers) behind these communities whose labor promotes pro-social behavior in leisure spaces. While they do not share the same health risks, community management work is arguably necessary during times of self-isolation, similar to the nurses, store clerks, and janitorial staff that continue to work during this pandemic. As Roberts (2019) notes, without the work of moderation and mediation, these platforms would be deserted wastelands, ceasing to function, and be unwelcoming to those seeking leisure and connection during a time of pandemic.

Leisure and sociality in games

Online games have become a site of extensive research into sociality and leisure in virtual spaces (see: Malaby, 2009; Ridings & Gefen, 2004; Taylor, 2006; Simon 2006). As communities begin to form, grow, and experience conflict, there is a need to manage them and establish norms. This has become more prevalent with widespread shifts from public commons to digital ones; much of our media, social-interaction, and sharing has moved into online spaces (Williams, 2006). However, as Ducheneaut et al. (2006) argue, these communities face challenges in creating sustained engagement and social cohesion online. Online interactions have previously been argued to be "empty" as they lacked communal negotiation (see: Putnam, 2000). Later work took this notion further, arguing that the anonymity offered online encourages anti-social behaviors (Cheng et al., 2015; Chesney et al., 2009).

However, as Whitson (2013) argues, games impose social order, even when digital. Games act as a leisurely social experience that becomes homogenized, accessible, and transferable to a wider number of participants, generating meaning and sociality (Whitson, 2013). This is still predicated on the existence of these online spaces, and thus their management and moderation, to bring in users but also maintain social order. Just as Whitson (2013) argues that the coded rules of online games are obscured from those who play them, community management work that occurs behind the scenes, but ultimately structures and makes online community accessible and safe to many, is often rendered invisible and undervalued. Creating and maintaining these spaces requires countless hours of labor and social work, lest they be overrun by toxicity and subsequently deserted.

Building and managing community online

Online leisure spaces have a long history of community building, moderation and management (Dibbell, 1994; Malaby, 2009; Ridings & Gefen, 2004). Often, this work is done by a community manager. Community management work, broadly, is considered the "soft-skilled" labor of communication, diplomacy, and empathy within an online community (Kerr, 2017; Kerr & Kelleher, 2015). While the core of their work is to drive sales across many industries, daily tasks for community management might involve checking social media accounts and responding to inquiries, interfacing with development teams to communicate information to the community, networking and communicating with content creators, scheduling and writing copy for newsletters, social media, or other content, and a myriad of other tasks that can all depend on the stage of development a studio is at.

Community managers often work to combat toxicity and harassment online to maintain safe and open communities. Despite an obvious need for this work in mediating the myriad of personalities and sheer number of users, community management is often underpaid and precarious work (Kerr & Kelleher, 2015; Roberts, 2019). In addition, the games industry is one that is commonly critiqued for the amount of "crunch" forced upon its workers, with upwards of 70 hour work weeks and upper management that seems unconcerned with the physical and mental effects of this trend of working (Campbell, 2019; Consalvo, 2011; Gilbert, 2019).

This work of mediation and empathy is underlined with the need for community managers to be patient with their communities. As part of my larger dissertation research on community management, I had intended to conduct interviews with community managers at the Game Developers Conference (GDC), the largest international gathering of game developers annually, in San Diego in March. Due to the COVID-19 pandemic, this field work was subsequently canceled, and I was forced to follow up with my participants for online interviews. These interviews represent the first 5 that I completed with community managers from the United States, Canada, and the United Kingdom and occurred in March and April of 2020 as many grappled with canceled travel plans for business and networking while adapting to working from home.

In describing their work, Marilyn[1], a communications director for a small independent studio in the United Kingdom, noted that community managers needed "a level head, an ability to not take things personally, a strong moral compass, and a willingness to not be too worried about being unpopular." Asked what frustrates her most as a community manager, Marilyn continued that "no matter how much information or how much content or how many games we give them, it's just never enough. It is a great problem to have […] but there is no end to their hunger. There is no pleasing them." This workload intensifies for community managers during self-isolation due to

---

[1]Pseudonyms are used for all interviewees to maintain confidentiality.

heavy influxes of new players. Many are unfamiliar with the norms and expectations of these communities as they seek outlets for emotional and mental health support.

As the conduit between the community and the developers, community managers are often relaying information that their communities may find unsatisfactory, irrelevant, or just not to their taste. This puts community managers on the frontlines of hostility and toxicity in the communities they are meant to foster and build. These environments are common for community managers online, and is exemplified in the "GamerGate" (2014) controversy which saw individuals (mostly women, queer people, and people of color) and studios receiving what seemed like an endless wave of death threats, women being fired due to outside pressures from "fans," and widespread stalking (Chess & Shaw, 2015; Massanari, 2017; Mortensen, 2018). However, many of the community managers I spoke with noted that they enjoy their work of connecting people and creating community. As Rowan, a community manager for a third-party communications company, says "at its core it's about connecting people [...] we all like to champion things and be passionate about things [...] it's an opportunity to share what you love with people even if it causes you stress."

Community management as essential work

Support during COVID-19 and other pandemic situations are predicated upon gendered, precarious, and underappreciated work (such as store clerks, nurses, and janitors) (Enarson, 2001; Enarson & Pease, 2016; Fothergill, 2003). Online leisure spaces that have uplifted and provided solace during this time, and those that manage them, are arguably no different. Community management has been shifting in its conceptualization for some time, and this pandemic not only highlights the importance of this role but how it has transformed in recent years from simple moderator and censor to caretaker and leader of online communities.

The necessity of this role should not be understated, even under normal circumstances. Many of the community managers I spoke with noted how they were brought on early in the development process to build up communities well before the commercial release of the game. As Marilyn notes "if you launch a game now that doesn't already have an interested community, you can't sell anymore." Under extraordinary circumstances, such as during extended self-isolation, the moderation, mediation, and care work of community management becomes a central facet of everyday life.

While the dangers faced are unequivocally different, there is arguable similarity to workers in grocery stores who struggle to survive on minimum wages while working on the frontlines of a pandemic. Estimates put the average salary of community managers at $49,978 USD, comparable to the median income of $49,348 USD (Indeed.com, 2020; U.S. Bureau of Labor Statistics, 2020). While a modest income, Amelie, a community manager at a mid-sized Canadian games company, reflects that "there is no senior position for community managers. If you want to advance in your workplace you have to change branches" indicating that prospects for community managers looking for more financial security are limited. Despite this, community managers are the enthusiastic workers attempting to bring people together, keep everyone occupied, and keep these online spaces safe during the coronavirus pandemic.

During my interviews with community managers, I end on a question asking them about the future of community management. Amelie notes, "there's not a single industry right now that does not have a community manager. […] It's starting to become more recognized as one of the pillars of a company." It should be no surprise then, conducting these interviews online while they work from home self-isolating, that they think about how their role will look like in the coming weeks, let alone in coming years. As Rowan notes, "I think it is interesting how community managers [during the pandemic] have stepped forward to be the shepherds for online life. […] Adapting and shepherding people into new forms of communication." Amelie notes that through backchannels with other community managers, they are seeing surges in users online during the day, playing their games, and eager to chat and connect with people since widespread self-distancing began. It is these workers who combat toxicity online and help guide users into safe communities online.

Across social media people are being reminded to "be kind" to one another, especially those who are working on the front lines of this pandemic. It is important for us to remember not only to be kind to our delivery drivers, nurses, grocery clerks, janitors, and other essential workers, but also those we interact with online. Questions remain however if everyone is maintaining this same mantra. Ultimately, it is the role of community managers to enact this kindness in their day-to-day work, but also to help others understand how to communicate effectively online as they enter these spaces for the first time. Looking forward to an inevitable return to normalcy, questions remain if they will be recognized for the work they have done to help connect, engage, and provide comfort to those seeking it during this time of self-isolation.

Funding

The author acknowledges that this work was supported by Canada's Social Sciences and Humanities Research Council (grant number 895-2015-1005).

ORCID

Matthew E. Perks ⓘ http://orcid.org/0000-0002-5483-1403

References

Campbell, C. (2019, April 23). How Fortnite's success led to months of intense crunch at Epic Games. *Polygon*. https://www.polygon.com/2019/4/23/18507750/fortnite-work-crunch-epic-games

Cheng, J., Danescu-Niculescu-Mizil, C., Leskovec, J. (2015, April 21). Antisocial behavior in online discussion communities. Ninth International AAAI Conference on Web and Social Media. Ninth International AAAI Conference on Web and Social Media. https://www.aaai.org/ocs/index.php/ICWSM/ICWSM15/paper/view/10469

Chesney, T., Coyne, I., Logan, B., & Madden, N. (2009). Griefing in virtual worlds: Causes, casualties and coping strategies. *Information Systems Journal*, 19(6), 525–548. doi:10.1111/j.1365-2575.2009.00330.x

Chess, S., & Shaw, A. (2015). A Conspiracy of Fishes, or, How We Learned to Stop Worrying About #GamerGate and Embrace Hegemonic Masculinity. *Journal of Broadcasting & Electronic Media*, 59(1), 208–220. doi:10.1080/08838151.2014.999917

Consalvo, M. (2011). Crunched by Passion: Women Game Developers and Workplace Challenges. In Y. Kafai, C. Heeter, J. Denner, & J. Sun (Eds.), *Beyond barbie and mortal kombat. New perspectives on gender and gaming* (pp. 177–191). MIT.

Dibbell, J. (1994). A rape in cyberspace or how an evil clown, a haitian trickster spirit, two wizards, and a cast of dozens turned a database into a society. *Annual Survey of American Law, 1994*, 471.

Ducheneaut, N., Yee, N., Nickell, E., & Moore, R. (2006). Alone together? Exploring the social dynamics of massively multiplayer online games. *Proceedings of the SIGCHI conference on Human Factors in computing systems. 1*, 407–416.

Enarson, E. (2001). What women do: Gendered labor in the Red River Valley flood. *Environmental Hazards, 3*(1), 1–18.

Enarson, E., & Pease, B. (2016). The gendered terrain of disaster. In E. Enarson & B. Pease (Eds.), *Men, masculinities and disaster*. Routledge.

Fothergill, A. (2003). The stigma of charity: Gender, class, and disaster assistance. *The Sociological Quarterly, 44*(4), 659–680. doi:10.1111/j.1533-8525.2003.tb00530.x

Gilbert, B. (2019, May 9). Grueling, 100-hour work weeks and "crunch culture" are pushing the video game industry to a breaking point. Here's what's going on. *Business Insider*. https://www.businessinsider.com/video-game-development-problems-crunch-culture-ea-rockstar-epic-explained-2019-5

Gillespie, T. (2018). *Custodians of the internet: Platforms, content moderation, and the hidden decisions that shape social media*. Yale University Press.

Gray, K. L. (2012). Intersecting oppressions and online communities. *Information, Communication & Society, 15*(3), 411–428. doi:10.1080/1369118X.2011.642401

Gray, K. L. (2014). *Race, gender, and deviance in Xbox Live: Theoretical perspectives from the virtual margins*. Routledge.

Indeed.com. (2020, April 7). Community manager salaries in the United States. *Indeed.Com*. https://www.indeed.com/salaries/community-manager-Salaries

Jackson, G. (2016, December 9). A career waiter's journey to twitch cooking star. *Kotaku*. https://kotaku.com/a-career-waiters-journey-to-becoming-a-twitch-cooking-s-1789931103

Kerr, A. (2017). *Global games: Production, circulation and policy in the networked era*. Routledge.

Kerr, A., & Kelleher, J. D. (2015). The recruitment of passion and community in the service of capital: community managers in the digital games industry. *Critical Studies in Media Communication, 32*(3), 177–192. doi:10.1080/15295036.2015.1045005

Malaby, T. M. (2009). *Making virtual worlds: Linden lab and second life*. Cornell University Press.

Massanari, A. (2017). #Gamergate and The Fappening: How Reddit's algorithm, governance, and culture support toxic technocultures. *New Media & Society, 19*(3), 329–346. doi:10.1177/1461444815608807

Mortensen, T. E. (2018). Anger, fear, and games: The long event of #GamerGate. *Games and Culture, 13*(8), 787–806. doi:10.1177/1555412016640408

Mostov, A., & Adam, M. (2020, March 15). *Could video games and other entertainment help slow the spread of COVID-19?* Scientific American Blog Network. https://blogs.scientificamerican.com/observations/could-video-games-and-other-entertainment-help-slow-the-spread-of-covid-19/

Putnam, R. D. (2000). *Bowling alone: The collapse and revival of american community*. Simon and Schuster.

Ridings, C. M., & Gefen, D. (2004). Virtual community attraction: Why people hang out online. *Journal of Computer-Mediated Communication, 10*(1). https://doi.org/10.1111/j.1083-6101.2004.tb00229.x

Roberts, S. T. (2019). *Behind the screen: Content moderation in the shadows of social media*. Yale University Press.

Rosenblatt, K. (2019, September 29). Meet the drag queen revolutionizing the streaming world on Twitch. *NBC News*. https://www.nbcnews.com/feature/nbc-out/meet-drag-queen-revolutionizing-streaming-world-twitch-n1060021

Simon, B. (2006). Never playing alone: The social contextures of digital gaming. *Proceedings of the CGSA 2006 Symposium*, 13.

Taylor, H. (2020, March 18). Gaming and live streaming rise globally amid COVID-19 crisis. *GamesIndustry.Biz*. https://www.gamesindustry.biz/articles/2020-03-18-gaming-and-live-streaming-rise-globally-amid-covid-19-crisis

Taylor, T. L. (2006). *Play between worlds: Exploring online game culture*. The MIT Press.

U.S. Bureau of Labor Statistics. (2020, April 15). *Usual Weekly Earnings Summary*. U.S. Bureau of Labor Statistics. https://www.bls.gov/news.release/wkyeng.nr0.htm

Whitson, J. R. (2013). Gaming the Quantified Self. *Surveillance & Society*, *11*(1/2), 163–176. doi:10.24908/ss.v11i1/2.4454

Williams, D. (2006). Why game studies now? Gamers don't bowl alone. *Games and Culture - Game Cult*, *1*(1), 13–16. doi:10.1177/1555412005281774

Masturbating to Remain (Close to) the Same: Sexually Explicit Media as Habitual Media

Jonathan Petrychyn (iD)

ABSTRACT

This short commentary surveys the state of sex and leisure during the COVID-19 pandemic. Specifically, it focuses on sexually explicit media and other forms of digitally mediated sex that have received increasing media attention during the pandemic. Though much of this media appears to be new or novel, drawing on the work by Wendy Chun (Updating to remain the same: Habitual new media, MIT Press; 2016), I argue that this sexually explicit media has become habitual media during the COVID-19 pandemic, and helps produce feelings of closeness and sameness during isolation.

"We are forever trying to catch up, updating to remain (close to) the same; bored, overwhelmed, and anxious all at once." (Chun, 2016, p. 1)

On April 18, 2020, social media influencer Rattanak Um (Um, 2020) shared a TikTok video on his social media channels. Captioned "My daily quarantine life," the 18-second video reduces a single day while quarantined during the COVID-19 pandemic into a series of habits. Um wakes up, he jerks off while watching porn on his phone. He plays video games. He scrolls social media. He jerks off again. He plays video games again. He jerks off. He goes to sleep. Each shot is framed the same: the camera is placed at the foot of his bed and moves in arching motion. When the camera moves below the surface of the bed and the image is obscured, the video cuts to the next habit, giving the effect of a never-ending video loop. In each shot, Um either has his phone or his Nintendo Switch in his hand. On the soundtrack the opening lines to the song "Myself" by Bazzi play: "I think I'm losing my mind/Trying to stay inside the lines/It's like I'm running in place/How you keep staying the same?" The video captures three key features of leisure during the COVID-19 pandemic: (1) it is highly routinized and habitual; (2) the internet and our personal devices play central roles in these habits and routines and (3) sex is a recurring habit throughout the day.

This routine is likely familiar to others, with its own variations. Statistics Canada recently found that that 67% of Canadians were spending more time on the internet due to the current COVID-19 pandemic (Statistics Canada, 2020). Given the ways in which digital technologies and the internet have provided us with the ability to be connected not only during this pandemic, but in our everyday lives, this finding is not altogether surprising. As the shot of Um scrolling social media on his phone suggests, many people are using the internet to stay connected with people they cannot be with physically.

These connections are, of course, not always friendly or familial: many of these connections are overtly sexual. PornHub, for example, has reported significant increase in user traffic not only in Canada, but around the world (PornHub Insights, 2020). Dating apps like Grindr, Tinder and Bumble are reporting increased use, and are implementing communications strategies that encourage users to stay home and sext potential matches as opposed to meeting in person (Dockterman, 2020). Circuit party and sex party organizers are hosting digital sex parties using video conferencing software like Zoom (Harris, 2020; Kahn, 2020). Online orders of sex toys are up (Wakefield, 2020) and premium porn subscription services are being offered free or at a discount. On social media sites like Instagram and Tumblr, users are sharing more sexually explicit photos, spawning the genre of the "quarantine nude" (Abad-Santos, 2020). Even friends are sharing nude photos with each other (Jedeikin, 2020). On the darker side of things, UNICEF is warning that the combination of having kids out of school and on the Internet more frequently could open the door for an increase in child sex trafficking online (Blanchfield, 2020), and MPs in the UK are concerned that the increase in porn traffic could lead to an increase in revenge porn and other forms of non-consensual and criminal porn uploaded to the site (Grant, 2020).

These examples suggest that sexually explicit media has become habitual media during the COVID-19 pandemic. Within leisure studies, there is a growing body of scholarship on sex as leisure (Berdychevsky & Carr, 2020; Caudwell & Browne, 2011; Parry & Johnson, 2020). While there has been increasingly more attention paid to such digitally mediated sex within leisure studies (Spracklen, 2015), particularly regarding pornography (McKeown et al., 2018; Valtchanov & Parry, 2020) and dating apps (Cousineau et al., 2018), there is a larger field of digitally mediated sexual practices that this pandemic is bringing to the fore. I want to suggest that what we are seeing now are not necessarily *new* sexual leisure practices, but a *heightened awareness* of already common digitally mediated sexual leisure practices that have become habituated through the current pandemic.

By "habitual media" I am drawing primarily here on the work by Wendy Chun. Chun (2016) argues that "our media matter most when they seem not to matter at all, that is, when they have moved from the new to the habitual" (p. 1). Habitual media is media that has become repetitive, mundane, boring and embedded within the rhythms of everyday life. "Through habits users become their machines: they stream, update, capture, upload, share, grind, link, verify, map, save, trash, and troll. Repetition breeds expertise, even as it breeds boredom" (p. 1). As the pandemic and the social and physical isolation measures remain in place, sex and sexual media, perhaps once situated within the realm of the sometimes, the every now and again, the new and exciting in the ways in which it could intervene in the monotony of our day to day lives, has too become increasing rote and routine. To paraphrase a recent self-help column: sex used to be a fancy meal at an expensive restaurant, but now it has become fast food ("Dear Dad," 2020).

The popularity of Um's video (it has over 250,000 views on Twitter as of this writing) speaks to particular common experience of leisure during the pandemic in which sexual media becomes habitual media akin to video games and social media. Indeed, video game scholars have noted that gaming has played a central role in the pandemic, offering both escapism (Parker, 2020) and task-oriented habituation (Brey et al., 2020). These habituated uses of social media and video games are given a further layer of habituation when they are shared online as part of our routines. Um's video, as a video *about* leisure routines, is part of a broader field of user-generated media content during the pandemic about the new habits and routines of our daily lives. For Waugh and Arroyo (Waugh & Arroyo, 2019), this sort of sharing of our daily routines is key to our experience of the internet: "Confession is the primary modality of the internet. [...] Comment boards, amateur pornography, Snaps, YouTube videos, and all social media – not to mention the gamut of the digital arts – are all fueled by confession" (p. 6). Confession, they note drawing on Deleuze, does not reveal some interiority about the subject, but rather "confessions merely work to swallow one's subjectivity" into the wider field of sociality (Waugh & Arroyo, 2019, p. 11). This echoes Chun's (2016) argument about how habits operate: "Habits are things we learn from others, and they make us 'like' others" (p. xi). These types of social media posts, where users reveal the habits and routines of their lives during the pandemic are less about sharing their unique individual experience, but of reaching out and attempting to find a common connection through isolation. By sharing bits of their own lives online, they are, however ironically, trying to decenter their own experience and have it swallowed into the morass of other leisure experiences during this pandemic.

Within Um's video, masturbation recurs the most of any of the habits he illustrates. We would thus be remiss, as leisure scholars, to ignore the centrality of sex and sexually explicit media in our pandemic leisure lives. The use of sexually explicit media has become habitual and habituated during the pandemic. Serendipitously, Chun (2016) uses metaphors of virality and viral spread to think through the role of habit within the spread of information:

> A focus on habit moves us away from dramatic chartings and maps of "viral spread" toward questions of infrastructure and justice. To take the example of the 2014-2015 Ebola outbreak, a discussion of habit would move us away from what Priscilla Wald has called an "outbreak narrative"—a narrative that manages and diagnoses communicable disease by concentrating on identifying an emerging infection and the global networks through which it travels and is contained—toward understanding the conditions that made this spread possible: from crumbling medical infrastructures to new patterns of mobility brought about by globalization to the lingering impacts of colonialism and civil wars. (p. 15)

An analysis that centers habit is an analysis that orients us toward the conditions that made the spread of information possible, toward the conditions that make us the same: "Habit moves us from the rapid time scale of viral infections and disruptions toward the slower and more stable time frame of homophily" (Chun, 2016, p. 15). Centering habit looks at how things have remained the same through disruption and crisis. By positioning sex as habit, and sexually explicit media as habitual media, we can work to destigmatize sex by underscoring the ways in which we are all routinely doing it during this pandemic. The circulation of sexually explicit media and news articles about sex during the pandemic produces feelings of closeness and sameness within isolation. The habituation of sex and of sexuality explicit media has made it so that masturbating is a way for us to remain close to others, and close to the same.

ORCID

Jonathan Petrychyn ⓘ http://orcid.org/0000-0003-3058-9226

References

Abad-Santos, A. (2020, April 8). Quarantine horniness, explained by a sex researcher. *Vox.* https://www.vox.com/2020/4/8/21210131/coronavirus-nudes-quarantine-sex-instagram.

Berdychevsky, L., & Carr, N. (2020). Innovation and impact of sex as leisure in research and practice: Introduction to the special issue. *Leisure Sciences, 42*(3–4), 255–220.

Blanchfield, M. (2020, April 8). UNICEF warns coronavirus has sparked a rise in online child sexual predators. *The Globe and Mail.* https://www.theglobeandmail.com/canada/article-unicef-warns-coronavirus-has-sparked-a-rise-in-online-child-sexual/

Brey, B., Dolan, P., Lawrence, C., & Stang, S. (2020). Play during quarantine. *First Person Scholar.* https://www.firstpersonscholar.com/play-during-quarantine/

Caudwell, J., & Browne, K. (2011). Sexy spaces: Geography and leisure intersectionalities. *Leisure Studies, 30*(2), 117–122.

Chun, W. H. K. (2016). *Updating to remain the same: Habitual new media.* MIT Press.

Cousineau, L., Oakes, H., & Johnson, C. W. (2018). Appnography: Digital ethnography for app-based culture. In D. C. Parry, C. W. Johnson, & S. Fullagar (Eds.), *Digital dilemmas: Transforming gender identities and power relations in everyday life.* (pp. 95–117). Palgrave Press.

Dear Dad: Quarantine queeries. (2020). *BLOOP.* https://www.grindrbloop.com/zine/2019/7/2/dear-dad-quarantine-queeries

Dockterman, E. (2020, April 11). The coronavirus is changing how we date, perhaps permanently. *Time.* https://time.com/5819187/dating-coronavirus/

Grant, H. (2020, March 25). Urgent action needed as rise in porn site traffic raises abuse fears, say MPs. *The Guardian.* https://www.theguardian.com/global-development/2020/mar/25/urgent-action-needed-as-spike-in-porn-site-traffic-raises-abuse-fears-say-mps

Harris, M. (2020, April 16). Zoom says it uses machine-learning to detect nudity as virtual sex parties spread. *Insider.* https://www.insider.com/zoom-sex-party-machine-learning-to-crackdown-on-nudity-2020-4

Jedeikin, D. (2020, April 4). Trapped in quarantine, friends can't stop sharing their nudes. *MEL Magazine.* https://melmagazine.com/en-us/story/quarantine-friends-sharing-nudes

Kahn, A. (2020, March 24). Coronavirus diaries: I went to a sex party on zoom. *Slate Magazine.* https://slate.com/human-interest/2020/03/sex-party-zoom-coronavirus-quarantine.html

McKeown, J. K. L., Parry, D. C., & Penny Light, T. (2018). My iPhone changed my life: How digital technologies can enable women's consumption of online sexually explicit materials. *Sexuality & Culture, 22*(2), 340–354.

Parker, F. (2020, April 13). *InsightOut: Comfort games.* University of St. Michael's College. https://stmikes.utoronto.ca/news/insightout-comfort-games/

Parry, D. C., & Johnson, C. W. (Eds.). (2020). *Promiscuous perspectives: Explorations of sex and leisure.* Routledge. Manuscript submitted for publication.

PornHub Insights. (2020, April 2). *Coronavirus update.* https://www.pornhub.com/insights/coronavirus-update-april-2

Spracklen, K. (2015). *Digital leisure, the internet and popular culture: Communities and identities in a digital age.* Springer.

Statistics Canada. (2020). *Canadian perspectives survey series 1: Impacts of COVID-19.* https://www150.statcan.gc.ca/n1/daily-quotidien/200408/dq200408c-eng.htm

Um, R. [zaddynak]. (2020, April 18). *My daily quarantine life* [Tweet]. https://twitter.com/zaddynak/status/1251597701248139265

Valtchanov, B. L., & Parry, D. C. (2020). A porn of one's own: feminist complexities with women's consumption of online sexually explicit materials. In Parry, Diana C. & C. W. Johnson (Eds.), *Promiscuous perspectives: Explorations of sex and leisure.* Routledge. Manuscript submitted for publication.

Wakefield, L. (2020, March 18). Sex toy sales surge during coronavirus pandemic as people learn to appreciate their alone time. *PinkNews.* https://www.pinknews.co.uk/2020/03/18/sex-toy-sales-surge-coronavirus-covid19-pandemic-self-isolation-quarantine-womanizer-masturbation/

Waugh, T., & Arroyo, B. (2019). Introduction. In T. Waugh & B. Arroyo (Eds.), *I confess!: Constructing the sexual self in the internet age* (pp. 3–25). McGill-Queen's Press.

#QuarantineChallenge2k20: Leisure in the Time of the Pandemic

Monika Stodolska

ABSTRACT

The purpose of this essay is two-fold. First, it examines constraints on leisure imposed by the global pandemic, how people responded to them, and the lessons it taught us about the place of leisure in contemporary society. Second, it explores the roles of leisure in coping with stress and isolation brought by the COVID-19 outbreak. The essay reveals constraints on travel, social contacts, use of public recreation resources, and access to natural environments imposed by countries, states, and municipalities across the world to control the outbreak of the disease. It then discusses interpersonal and work-leisure relations in the context of leisure in the time of the crisis, and lastly, it examines problem-focused and emotion-focused coping strategies employed by people to deal with the effects of the pandemic.

What began for most people in the West with the images of the train station in Wuhan, China being cordoned off with a metal fence and news of the Spring Festival travel being suspended throughout the country (Linder, 2020a) would soon transform into a worldwide pandemic that would upend lives and bring renewed interest into the roles of leisure in contemporary society. In the weeks and months that followed the outbreak of COVID-19 that began at the end of 2019, hundreds of thousands of people have perished (Worldometer, 2020), the stock markets crashed sparking fears of global recession (Merrill & Day, 2020), millions have lost their jobs (Tappe, 2020), and the social life has undergone a profound transformation. What we have witnessed, however, were also acts of bravery and heroism, communities coming together, and leisure, while severely constrained, gaining a new value for those for whom it brought respite and a renewed sense of hope at the time of the crisis. In this essay, I will 1) examine constraints on leisure imposed by global pandemic, how people responded to them, and the lessons it taught us about the place of leisure in contemporary society, and 2) explore the roles of leisure in coping with stress and isolation brought by the COVID-19 outbreak.

Since early reports have attributed the outbreak to the "wet market" in Wuhan and its spread throughout the world to human travel and mass gatherings (e.g., Champions League soccer game in Milan, Italy) (Associated Press, 2020), leisure-related travel and public assemblies were among the first activities to be curtailed. Spring Festival events in China have been canceled (Salo, 2020), the City of Wuhan, and later the entire Hubei province quarantined (Bloomberg News, 2020), and people were confined to their home sometimes involuntarily and by drastic means (McShane, 2020). Restrictions on travel to the U.S. and mass cancelations or postponements of sporting and cultural events (e.g., the 2020 Tokyo Olympic Games, Cannes Film Festival, MLS, NHL, and NCAA tournaments) soon followed (Cho, 2020). Movie premieres have been canceled, major theme parks such as Disneyland closed (Chubb, 2020a; Duffy, 2020), and many mass entertainment venues, convention centers, hotels, and even parks were converted to field hospitals and testing centers (Palmer, 2020; Rosner & Musumeci, 2020). Within weeks, countries began imposing sweeping travel bans, some U.S. states installed road-blocks to keep out-of-state residents away, and vacation travel across much of the world has come to a complete halt (Aitken, 2020; Tate et al., 2020).

And yet, the hallmark of leisure constraints imposed on the world's population has been dubbed "social distancing" (although the phrase has been criticized for its impre-cise wording) (Menjívar et al., 2020). In order to increase physical distance or to com-pletely eliminate contact between people and thus prevent the spread of the disease, different countries, states, and municipalities have adopted a slew of measures to dis-courage the populace from visiting bars, restaurants, beaches, parks, playgrounds, trails, national parks, golf courses, malls, and shopping centers. From mahjong tables being smashed in China, to cordoning off city parks in the U.S. and forests in Europe, closing off beaches along the U.S. seaboard, removing basketball hoops in New York parks, pouring sand into skate parks in Los Angeles, dying blue lakes with black paint in the UK, and banning public gatherings and family visits, different restrictions have been imposed (Aitken, 2020; Boyle, 2020; Cauguiran & Horng, 2020; Dupree, 2020; Linder, 2020b; Sharp, 2020). While most North Americans and Europeans approached these measures with understanding in the beginning days and weeks of the pandemic, as time went by, concerns began to mount about the arbitrary nature of some of these restric-tions, many of which seemed illogical, contradictory, poorly communicated, and enforced with repressive means (DeMarche, 2020; Duell, 2020). By mid-April, 2020, some people across the U.S. began demanding easing social distancing restrictions, right to return to work and access public spaces, and accused governments of violating con-stitutional rights to public association and assembly, religious freedom, and expression (Warren et al., 2020). While some of the restrictions are beginning to be eased at the time of this essay's writing (Chubb, 2020b) and states begin to "reopen," it remains to be seen how long the pandemic-induced constraints on leisure will last. What the last several months have taught us, however, is that a) what we have taken for granted in the past (e.g., access to public lands, freedom of assembly) can be curtailed or revoked on a moment's notice, b) green spaces such as parks, trails, and beaches have become recognized by much of the public as essential to mental health and quality of life, and that c) societal divisions among those who are willing to endure decreased quality of life and leisure for the benefit of public good and those who put their own hedonistic needs over the welfare of others run deep (Reuters, March 18, 2020). What has also become quickly apparent is that, as George Bernard Shaw said, "a perpetual holiday is a good working definition of hell" (Brightbill, 1960, p. 5) and that crisis situations evoke both the best and the worst in people.

It is to those last two points that I would like to turn to in the second part of this essay. In contemporary societies pressured with the time crunch and ever-increasing demands for productivity, few people have not been dreaming of longer vacations, home relaxation, and more time to spend with their spouses and children. Few of us would expect that this dream may suddenly come true and that the society of leisure we have been yearning for will turn into a burden that will take a long time to recover from and even longer to forget. With their work, home, and childcare routines upended, people found themselves having to restructure their lives, homeschool their children, renegotiate household and work-leisure boundaries, and spend days on end locked in confined spaces with their significant others. And what seemed like a dream in February 2020, by March was met with shock, dismay, and resistance. The lesson that our society was soon to learn was that, as Brightbill (1960) poignantly argued six decades ago, leisure is valuable and necessary to maintain our quality of life, but there needs to be a balance and a boundary between leisure and work. Moreover, most people are ill-equipped to organize their lives around productive leisure pursuits, we all need to have private spaces to enjoy solitude and maintain sanity, work has value beyond providing structure and fulfilling pecuniary needs, and childcare workers, teachers, and recreation providers are more than "essential employees."

The time of the pandemic has also brought to the fore the ugly part of the human psyche that often raises its head at the time of crisis and existential threat. As it happened in the days and years following the attacks of 9/11 (Livengood & Stodolska, 2004), the outsiders were soon blamed for the misfortunes people had to endure. Attacks on Chinese (and any Asian) nationals have been reported across Europe, the U.S., and Australia. Chinese Americans and British have been beaten on the streets, assaulted in subways, and on college campuses (Linder, 2020c, 2020d). Many have feared leaving their homes to attend recreation centers, jog on streets, shop in stores, or even attend college classes in the early days of the pandemic. Racism knows no national boundaries and stereotyping and displacement-induced discrimination (LeVine & Campbell, 1972) have been rampant across the world, including in some areas of China where immigrants from Africa have been forcibly quarantined, denied access to restaurants and even removed from their homes (Tan, 2020; Valinsky, 2020). People also found more subtle ways of displacing their frustration and anger on others. "Coronavirus shamers" have reported women for taking their underage children to stores, families visiting each other, people leaving food on the doorsteps of their elderly relatives, public health workers moving around the city, or residents "illegally" spending time in their backyards (Basner, 2020; Vine, 2020).

The pandemic, however, has also brought the best in people and communities, and has revealed to the public the critical role leisure plays in human life and in helping us cope with traumatic events (Kleiber et al., 2002). Both problem-focused and emotion-focused coping strategies (Iwasaki & Schneider, 2003) have been noted. On the *problem-focused* front, people forced to cancel their leisure travels turned to backyard staycations and invented new ways of playing sports and spending time together (Reuters, April 20,

2020). Zoom, Facetime, and Facebook messenger began to be increasingly used as a communication tool, birthdays were celebrated with families connected via smartphones placed around dinner tables, parties were staged outside of the windows of elderly relatives, weddings were held without guests, and some sports games began to be played without spectators (Linder, 2020e). Despite restrictions on social contact, faced with the fear of the pandemic, people began to flock together and seek solace in the comfort of fellow human beings. While social distancing kept us apart, social media became the medium of choice for reuniting with family and long-lost friends for those seeking the semblance of human touch. People also began to supplement their pantries with home-made goods, learned to bake, make preserves, sew home-made face masks, and grow "Victory Gardens" (Kaur & Luhby, 2020; Morris, 2020).

The *emotion-focused* coping strategies meant to regulate people's emotions and distance from the source of stress were also prevalent. Leisure offered an escape from the stress of the disease, unemployment, and boredom of home confinement. As the pandemic spread through China, Europe, and North America, healthcare workers and first responders would lift their spirits by playing songs and dancing, while community members would donate food, supplies and spread messages of support and encouragement to hospital workers treating COVID patients (Coronavirus Dancing, February 14, 2020; Goldberg, 2020; Reyes, 2020). Quarantined Chinese, Italians, and North Americans played music from their homes and danced on streets, balconies, and rooftops (Alessandro, 2020). Artists began sharing their music for free, orchestras played concerts over Zoom, and museums started organizing "challenges" for people to recreate famous paintings with the items they could find at home (CPR Classical Staff, March 23, 2020; Grinevičius & Keturka, 2020). People all over the world tried to lift their spirits and found creative ways to cope with stress and isolation by putting up Christmas lights, using humor, adopting or fostering shelter animals, and sharing information on available community resources (Caspani et al., 2020). Few things, however, have been quite as iconic as the #QuarantineChallenge2k20 that swept social media in March 2020, where families would gather in their kitchens and living rooms to dance and sing together (Hoffman, 2020). The "challenge" brought quarantining families of all ages to recreate famous songs and routines, lip-synching and dancing to the tunes of Kenny Loggins, Justin Timberlake, B-52's, or Jess Glynne. People learned how to fill the long vacant hours and discover meaning in things they used to take for granted – themselves, their families, and the natural world (Glock, 2020). Fear, stress and uncertainty forced some to reevaluate what really matters in life and realize that freedom and happiness can be found in little things like heartfelt laughter, greening trees in the backyard, and a loaf of bread that came out "just right." Our routines have been broken, jobs lost or suspended, and the leisure revolution that no one thought was possible has quietly taken place in the spring of 2020.

Somehow in the midst of the pandemic and despite the unspeakable hardships and suffering, the world has become a somewhat better and kinder place with pollution receding (Regan, 2020), wild animals roaming city streets, happy birthday messages scribbled in chalk on driveways of our neighbors, and families going together for a walk. Will this pandemic be a watershed moment in our society that will mark a return to the community of the past when, instead of being focused on the consumption of leisure-related goods, people found joy and contentment in the simple pleasures of life such as playing cards, sitting on porches with their families, and dancing together in the house (Glock, 2020)? Or will the lifting of restrictions make people flock to malls, restaurants, and beaches in an attempt to forget the dreadful time of the disease and the warnings of the ensuing Orwellian society of unfreedom (Marcuse, 1964) where the invasion of privacy is condoned, surveillance is the norm, and our civil liberties are curtailed in the name of saving lives materialize (Giglio, 2020)? Only time will tell.

References

Aitken, P. (2020). *Most extreme measures during coronavirus lockdown, state by state.* https://www.foxnews.com/us/coronavirus-most-extreme-lockdown-measures

Alessandro, P. (2020). *Che Meraviglia.* https://www.facebook.com/pianca.alessandro/videos/3192711920748584/UzpfSTY1NjIwMzk0MDoxMDE1Nzc0NTc2NDE4ODk0MQ/

Associated Press. (2020). *Champions League match linked to spread of coronavirus in Italy.* https://chicago.suntimes.com/soccer/2020/3/25/21194015/coronavirus-covid-19-champions-league-italy-atalanta-valencia

Basner, D. (2020). *Moms shuts down coronavirus shamers by putting note on daughter's back.* https://1013thebrew.iheart.com/content/2020-04-16-mom-shuts-down-coronavirus-shamers-by-putting-note-on-daughters-back/?pname=local_social&keyid=WBFX&sc=editorial&fbclid=IwAR02McN37CvswfAOpVXuzmmoc2Z4CaDF9a4BAwl6Fi5iL8KqnLxUV2ITcxY

Bloomberg News. (2020). *China sacrifices a province to save the world from coronavirus.* https://www.bloomberg.com/news/articles/2020-02-05/china-sacrifices-a-province-to-save-the-world-from-coronavirus

Boyle, D. (2020). *La-GOONS! Now the coronavirus cops who stalked walkers with drones ruin picturesque 'blue lagoon' by filling it with BLACK DYE to stop Instagrammers posing for snaps.* https://www.dailymail.co.uk/news/article-8163209/Police-dump-black-dye-blue-lagoon-discourage-Instagram-selfies.html

Brightbill, C. (1960). *The challenge of leisure.* Prentice-Hall.

Caspani, M., Rafferty, A., & Psaledakis, D. (2020). *With songs, screams and recipes, Americans find emotional balm six feet apart.* https://www.reuters.com/article/us-health-coronavirus-usa-communities-idUSKBN21738P?utm_campaign=trueAnthem%3A+Trending+Content&utm_medium=trueAnthem&utm_source=facebook&fbclid=IwAR0z17NIsJcknZIh_oKn0OEYkOpCyfvKCFZ4jE32o0Gbv1GkSFNhubgZTpw

Cauguiran, C., & Horng, E. (2020). *Coronavirus Chicago: Mayor closes lakefront, 606 Trail, Riverwalk to stop spread of COVID-19.* https://abc7chicago.com/health/lakefront-trail-closed-to-public-amid-stay-at-home-order-due-to-covid-19/6051898/?fbclid=IwAR2CjHpeJLHoo6RiPsDsbDyNSWmDpKctK6utNBXPPdInOFN9tJn5HdJwNlE

Cho, D. F. (2020). *A running list of every festival, sporting event and show cancelled or postponed in the wake of the Coronovirus.* https://people.com/health/coronavirus-list-of-every-festival-sporting-event-and-show-canceled-or-postponed/

Chubb, H. (2020a). *Disneyland and Walt Disney World are now closed indefinitely due to coronavirus.* https://people.com/travel/disneyland-to-close-through-the-end-of-the-month-amid-coronavirus-pandemic/

Chubb, H. (2020b). *Florida beaches begin to reopen Friday following coronavirus shutdown.* https://people.com/travel/florida-beaches-begin-to-reopen-friday-following-coronavirus-shutdown/

Coronavirus Dancing. (2020, February 14). https://www.facebook.com/watch/?v=1022536351473288

CPR Classical Staff. (2020, March 23). *WATCH: In isolation, but in unison, The Colorado Symphony performs 'Ode To Joy'.* https://www.cpr.org/2020/03/23/watch-in-isolation-but-in-unison-colorado-symphony-musicians-perform-ode-to-joy/?fbclid=IwAR1SdYFa0826lHQrxKLi8l_axA9w9zqAnwiN_0pF5Xtgo_lvod8UZcBw_O4

DeMarche, E. (2020). *Police in Brazil use helicopter at the beach to disperse crowd amid lockdown: report.* https://www.foxnews.com/world/police-in-brazil-use-helicopter-at-the-beach-to-chase-crowd-amid-lockdown-report

Duell, M. (2020). *The lockdown checklist: From buying alcohol to sitting on a bench ... police detail the things you CAN and CAN'T do as quarantine will continue for at least three more weeks.* https://www.dailymail.co.uk/news/article-8226325/Police-list-things-coronavirus-lockdown-cant.html

Duffy, C. (2020). *Disneyland and Walt Disney World to remain closed because of coronavirus.* https://edition.cnn.com/2020/03/29/business/disney-closures-continue-coronavirus/index.html

Dupree, W. (2020). *WATCH: City of Los Angeles fills Skate Park with sand so nobody can use it.* https://www.lifezette.com/2020/04/watch-city-of-los-angeles-fills-skate-park-with-sand-so-nobody-can-use-it/?fbclid=IwAR2ELetzEt5c67CDUOHvyRGNWR4ybCrX7Fy_La8nC95GPjv-yiWS-P17fQ0

Giglio, M. (2020). *Would you sacrifice your privacy to get out of quarantine?* https://www.theatlantic.com/politics/archive/2020/04/coronavirus-pandemic-privacy-civil-liberties-911/609172/?fbclid=IwAR0IhbAcsR9HfGYx3xIJR59gNgASDEMhIVQ5GfaoDZagzKXZwoTWRd-lS_U

Glock, A. (2020). *Now I finally understand what my grandparents knew.* https://www.cnn.com/2020/03/28/opinions/coronavirus-grandparents-glock/index.html?fbclid=IwAR0cs7-feQnSZh5cfVfFu2Ai_g8WYOyINqcNQwCVgMvsOuPnfVNsXwHJ8uI

Goldberg, B. (2020). *'Here comes the sun' gets U.S. hospitals through dark days of pandemic.* https://www.reuters.com/article/us-health-coronavirus-usa-songs-idUSKCN21U0S0?utm_campaign=trueAnthem%3A+Trending+Content&utm_medium=trueAnthem&utm_source=facebook&fbclid=IwAR1SK5T3NLtQM9bT5-7NVl_8VSFavXYASJ0-ncvPNWxOIc9f7ztXE67IgfE

Grinevičius, J., & Keturka, J. (2020). *Museums ask people to recreate famous paintings at home.* https://www.boredpanda.com/art-recreation-at-home-getty-museum-challenge/?utm_source=facebook&utm_medium=social&utm_campaign=BPFacebook&fbclid=IwAR2aVlAYkE4WX_gMZvLezoy2BJDbnzn9mgqu5hosNbmyD85jnG_peTws2q0

Hoffman, A. (2020). *Day 5 quarantine.* https://www.facebook.com/ali.hoffman3/videos/10157804219590731/

Iwasaki, Y., & Schneider, I. E. (2003). Leisure, stress, and coping: An evolving area of inquiry. *Leisure Sciences, 25*(2–3), 107–113. https://doi.org/10.1080/01490400306567

Kaur, H., & Luhby, T. (2020). *People around the country are sewing masks. And some hospitals, facing dire shortage, welcome them.* https://www.cnn.com/2020/03/24/us/sewing-groups-masks-coronavirus-wellness-trnd/index.html

Kleiber, D. A., Hutchinson, S. L., & Williams, R. (2002). Leisure as a resource in transcending negative life events: Self-protection, self-restoration, and personal transformation. *Leisure Sciences, 24*(2), 219–235. https://doi.org/10.1080/01490400252900167

LeVine, R. A., & Campbell, D. T. (1972). *Ethnocentrism: Theories of conflict, ethnic attitudes, and groups behavior.* John Wiley & Sons, Inc.

Linder, A. (2020a). *China quarantines Wuhan, suspends travel out of city where virus outbreak began.* http://shanghaiist.com/2020/01/23/china-quarantines-wuhan-suspends-travel-out-of-city-where-virus-outbreak-began/?fbclid=IwAR0JtW8swd5YgVHs2NR8vAONyssX-95EipqLjICPzGcwITQyJE9RPx5xZ2U

Linder, A. (2020b). *Police launch crackdown on mahjong, smash tables with hammers amid virus outbreak.* https://shanghai.ist/2020/02/01/police-launch-crackdown-on-mahjong-smash-tables-with-hammers-amid-virus-outbreak/?fbclid=IwAR3TA9LF6fh1Gx3935uUyZlbvy4yUHGaI3FHpDub6NLYRTz77e5eqG8bg7Q

Linder, A. (2020c). *British teens attach Chinese students wearing masks at Southampton University.* http://shanghaiist.com/2020/03/25/british-teens-attack-chinese-students-wearing-masks-at-southampton-university/?fbclid=IwAR2pr0Zce95NL9E5ecSQVPWh3SZY-38cEZJi3R3eazfHjGQGfuOJqliyHSs

Linder, A. (2020d). *"Fucking Chinese!" New Yorker writer tweets about scary encounter with racist on NYC street.* https://shanghai.ist/2020/03/18/fucking-chinese-new-yorker-writer-tweets-about-scary-encounter-with-racist-on-nyc-street/?fbclid=IwAR2ikSAqQBiJaeS2JKcra_8yP_fulBorY3KZjTgaROLFdFKY2m_fkwu5iOc

Linder, A. (2020e). *Shandong couple hold wedding with no guests amid coronavirus outbreak.* https://shanghai.ist/2020/02/10/coronavirus-wedding/?fbclid=IwAR2h5Qn0vGnzUlYMl3cWC 15g6C9RdvhNs0lEe6lN1Z6wJDDbq3ad9OMjHZc

Livengood, J., & Stodolska, M. (2004). The effects of discrimination and constraints negotiation on leisure behavior of American Muslims in the post-September 11 America. *Journal of Leisure Research, 36*(2), 183–208. https://doi.org/10.1080/00222216.2004.11950019

Marcuse, H. (1964). *One-dimensional man.* Abacus Books.

McShane, A. (2020). *Coronavirus: Residents 'welded' inside their own homes in China.* https://www.lbcnews.co.uk/world-news/coronavirus-residents-welded-inside-their-own-home/

Menjívar, C., Foster, J., G., & Brand, J. E. (2020). *Don't call it 'social distancing'.* https://edition.cnn.com/2020/03/21/opinions/physical-distancing-menjivar-foster-brand/index.html?fbclid=IwA R2fiwRtQYVy2TMnLfMKzlxxsXs0r7m-ocS4-XhynoFDpi_XyoWl-snF5Ls

Merrill, D., & Day, E. (2020). *What the Dow's 28% crash tells us about the economy.* https://www.bloomberg.com/graphics/2020-stock-market-recover-dow-industrial-decline/

Morris, J. (2020). *Plant a Victory Garden to combat coronavirus fears and isolation.* https://www.mercurynews.com/2020/03/20/plant-a-victory-garden-to-combat-coronavirus-fears-and-isolation/

Palmer, A. (2020). *Meeting venues to the rescue: Convention centers and hotels become coronavirus emergency care facilities.* https://www.northstarmeetingsgroup.com/News/Industry/Convention-Centers-Hotels-Coronavirus-Emergency-Facilities

Regan, H. (2020). *Air pollution falls by unprecedented levels in major global cities during coronavirus lockdowns.* https://www.cnn.com/2020/04/22/world/air-pollution-reduction-cities-coronavirus-intl-hnk/index.html

Reuters. (2020, April 20). *Italian girls take to rooftop tennis amid coronavirus lockdown.* https://reut.rs/2xRiRs3?fbclid=IwAR0SZc-0MwQ3W6pL3qVg95b3b06zeEKKNA7eNE2W74ouKhw7psbyDwoY7RI

Reuters. (2020, March 18). *Miami spring breakers party on.* https://www.facebook.com/Reuters/videos/2550086665205506/UzpfSTY1NjIwMzk0MDoxMDE1Nzc2MDkxNDEyODk0MQ/

Reyes, A. (2020). *Messages of support for healthcare workers outside of local hospital.* https://www.wkbw.com/news/coronavirus/messages-of-support-for-healthcare-workers-outside-of-local-hospital

Rosner, E., & Musumeci, N. (2020). *An inside look at Central Park's makeshift coronavirus hospital.* https://nypost.com/2020/04/09/central-park-coronavirus-field-hospital-near-capacity/

Salo, J. (2020). *China cancels plans for New Year celebrations as coronavirus spreads.* https://nypost.com/2020/01/23/china-cancels-plans-for-new-year-celebrations-as-coronavirus-spreads/

Sharp, R. (2020). *New York officials take down basketball hoops in courts across the city as Mayor Bill de Blasio warns he might close parks and playgrounds if people don't start following social distancing rules.* https://www.dailymail.co.uk/news/article-8157213/New-York-officials-basketball-hoops-courts-people-ignore-social-distancing-rules.html?fbclid=IwAR2ouNvXv2MG-R4bIX X730YEKwT_HFfAESwIk6zi3j13KkIAOWFy3rFgy60

Tan, K. (2020). *Africans say they're getting evicted from their homes and hotels in Guangzhou.* http://shanghaiist.com/2020/04/10/africans-say-theyre-getting-evicted-from-their-homes-and-hotels-in-guangzhou/?fbclid=IwAR2GS-XkY-rPFyJVlsFUBhtxoVjP6dYkZFXSQHiDcMmACXtX6ATLsgev1Gk

Tappe, A. (2020). *Jobs after coronavirus. The US labor market won't bounce right back.* https://www.cnn.com/2020/04/15/economy/job-market-rebound-coronavirus/index.html

Tate, C., Gilbertson, D., & Hines, M. (2020). *'They're getting pummeled': Travel industry reeling from coronavirus concerns, anxiety.* https://www.usatoday.com/story/travel/2020/03/10/travel-industry-reeling-coronavirus-concerns-anxiety/5000655002/

Valinsky, J. (2020). *McDonald's China apologizes for banning black people from a store.* https://edition.cnn.com/2020/04/14/business/mcdonalds-china-coronavirus-sign-trnd/index.html

Vine, S. (2020). *We might be handling this situation just fine but the lockdown Stasi are coming for YOU.* https://www.dailymail.co.uk/debate/article-8219385/SARAH-VINE-handling-situation-just-fine-lockdown-stasi-coming-YOU.html

Warren, M., Marquez, M., Scannell, K., & Perez, E. (2020). *Conservative groups boost anti-stay-at-home protests*. https://edition.cnn.com/2020/04/20/politics/stay-at-home-protests-conservative-groups-support/index.html

Worldometer. (2020). *COVID-19 Coronavirus pandemic.* https://www.worldometers.info/coronavirus/

Why Don't We Play *Pandemic?* Analog Gaming Communities in Lockdown

Matt Coward-Gibbs (iD)

ABSTRACT
This short response demonstrates the way in which COVID-19 has impacted analog gamers and their leisure practices. Analog gameplay, often referred to by its moniker – tabletop gaming – is jokingly referred to by many of its players as the perfect activity for self-isolation. As such, throughout this response, I consider the resilience of analog play in the wake of a global crisis, considering the way in which digital technologies, gaming lifestyles and humour provide comfort, social interaction and a level of normalcy to their players in the wake of global uncertainty.

Introduction

Just over a week prior to the UK entering a period of lockdown in the wake of COVID-19 I attended and gave a seminar at AireCon, an annual analog gaming festival held in North Yorkshire, England.[1] The paper I gave focused on the way in which analog gamers – otherwise known as tabletop gamers – engaged with and considered the value of their artifacts of play, concentrating on the value and pleasure of tactility within collective leisure experiences. That weekend felt markedly similar to AireCon's previous incarnations albeit for the increased presence of hand sanitizer and the analog gamification of disease prevention and control (in the form of a tongue-in-cheek live-action roll and write game). Analog gaming is a hobby that is primarily concerned with face to face social interaction which is focused around the engagement in ruled play (Bowman, 2010; Woods, 2012). As such, a lockdown brings with it questions around the way in which analog gaming can be performed and a level of normality for its players can be maintained; albeit that with the rise of media coverage around COVID-19 comments within online analog gaming forums suggested that analog play was, in essence, a perfect hobby for lockdown. Following the circulation of a short open-question survey to an online community of analog gamers concerning how their experiences within the hobby have changed since 16 March 2020; forty-eight responses were received which were subsequently thematically analyzed.

---

[1]https://www.airecon.co.uk/

The following discussion centers around three themes. The first – same people, different places – considers the way in which digital technologies and literacies are being used in order to consider the way in which players are, to all extents, attempting to carry on as normal. The second theme – changing player experiences – focuses primarily on the way in which experiences for players have changed and the effect that this is having on their experiences of the hobby. The final theme – a return to the physical – considers the material objects of the analog and the broader economic impacts that COVID-19 may have on the hobby.

Same people, different places

Analog gaming, like many leisure communities, already has a presence on social media platforms, suggesting that hobbyists, at least in principle, act across both physical and digital third places (Yuen & Johnson, 2017). Further, with the rise of the digitization of many contemporary board games (Rogerson et al., 2015; Rogerson, 2018), analog gamers are afforded the opportunity to engage in analog play online. Although these digital tools are available to players, their continued engagement with local gaming stores, conventions and crowdfunding of cultural resources and artifacts of play (usually via Kickstarter) leads to a conclusion that physical play is still favored by the aforementioned *analog* hobbyists. Respondents, unsurprisingly, noted the change in their social engagements in the wake of lockdown, remarking that they are no longer able to attend regular scheduled meetups with public gaming groups, thereby having to change their patterns and practices of social engagement to, where possible, online based mechanisms.

One respondent, who lives alone, explained that it had "been quite a shock to the system" noting that their "friends have all stepped in with regular online interactions" thereby underlying the importance of both regularity and routine in relation to leisure based third spaces (Oldenburg, 1999). In essence, the rise of the use of online platforms such as web conferencing facilities and more gaming-based specific applications including *Discord* (discordapp.com/), *Roll20* (roll20.net/), *Tabletopia* (tabletopia.com/) and *Tabletop Simulator* (tabletopsimulator.com/) demonstrate the ongoing diversification and digitalization of analog play.

Turning to online formats to engage in analog gaming is not always a straightforward translation. Respondents noted that not all games, due to their mechanics (such as hidden information), are suitable for online play. Moreover, even when communicating with other players via a microphone gaming was viewed as "lack[ing] some of the social joy" associated with being in the physical presence of others. As Woods contends, "approaches to space and spatiality in digital games reveal our engagements as multifaceted and multi-layered … [gamers] are active, participating in creating that experience through a combination of engagements … " (Woods, 2012, p. 102).

Comments from several participants also suggested that the sharing of knowledge to aid the formation and continuation of play was critical. In constructing these informal communities of practice (Lave, 1991; Wenger & Snyder, 2000) the learning process which a hobbyist goes through is "configured through the process of becoming a full participant in a socio-cultural practice" (Lave & Wenger, 1991, p. 29). A participant, for example, responded that one of the most difficult aspects of being in lockdown was being unable to "pass on knowledge" about the use of various online services to aid play and social connectivity. This itself, leads to questions concerning individual participants access to digital technologies, emphasizing the persistence of the digital divide (Brabazon, 2013; Warschauer, 2003).

Changing play experiences

As the previous section documented, analog gamers have engaged with several practices in order to retain a sense of normalcy amid ongoing events. However, what also must be recognized is both the effect which lockdown has had and continues to have on the community writ large. Many who contributed their experiences to this survey picked up on the way in which their experiences of play had changed. For some, this was deemed as a positive experience such as increasing the amount of rich social interaction that has taken place with their family through games than before lockdown or, in other cases, where previously uninterested family members and housemates have become more interested in playing analog games, drawing on ideas presented around the levels of relationship closeness between partners of leisure activities (Frye, 2018).

However, for a portion of those consulted, additional pressures in the home environment led to less time, space or energies to engage in play, a factor which was also picked up by Rogerson's work concerning parents who play analog games (Rogerson & Gibbs, 2018). This factor was particularly prominent in cases wherein play primarily takes place outside of the home environment. Issues associated with anxiety and mental health were another factor brought up by individual contributors, leading to diminishing interest in play. In some cases, it was deemed that certain thematic games were now not suitable for play (examples including *Pandemic* as well as *Plague, Inc.*).[2] In other cases players noted that their mental capacity was more limited which meant that they were relying on "tried and tested classics" or titles which were simpler than their usual preferences. The practicalities of lockdown could also lead to a sense of dissatisfaction with a hobbyist's leisure pursuit. As one participant responded, "I can play family games at home but haven't been able to play the new games that I want to play." According to the funological framework of Blythe and Hassenzahl (2003, p. 95), when the hobbyist is playing family games, they are having *fun* which is framed by triviality, rather experiencing the *pleasurable* engrossing and transformative experience of playing what it is that they want to play. In this instance, the usually rewarding pastime of play is replaced with play being enacted as a "distraction factory" (Rojek, 1995, p. 11), performed primarily to fill time.

Writing in the early 1980s regarding fantasy roleplaying games, Fine (1983, p. 1) contended that the interactions that took place within analog play may be conceived as "rather small, perhaps trivial, social world[s]." However, given times of both global and societal uncertainty, engaging with interaction around an unchanging ruleset appears to be beneficial, at least in principle, for many members. Pleasurable (Blythe & Hassenzahl, 2003) or flow-based (Csikszentmihalyi, 2002) experiences, such as game

---

[2]Leacock, Matt. 2008. *Pandemic*. Z-Man Games, Inc (board game): https://bit.ly/3ceWawy; Vaughn, James. 2017. *Plague Inc.: The Board Game*. Ndemic Creations (board game): https://bit.ly/2RZMYV3.

play, exist in such a way that they are transformative and contribute, in one way or another, to an individual's perceived self-worth and value. One respondent reflected this in their note that they were engaging with "longer games … that didn't cause too much anxiety" as they did not really "want to think about what's going on in the real world" while they were engaged in play. Conceptions of flow become paramount here, with the space of play allowing for "deep but effortless involvement" in which the "concern for the self disappears" (Csikszentmihalyi, 2002, p. 49).

A return to the physical

In the wake of lockdown, especially in the UK, it has meant that fervent hobbyists have been afforded the opportunity to work through the backlog of unplayed games in their possession; what several contributors lovingly referred to as either their "pile of potential" (that is, potential pleasurable experiences to be had) or "shelf of shame" ("shame that we've not played that"). Lockdown, in some circumstances, has afforded individuals the opportunity to more deeply engage with their hobby for more extensive periods of time than regular commitments would have allowed for. This is exemplified by one participant who noted that they are making a conscious effort to play though all titles in their collection in order to consider what should be removed from it. Albeit, they continue to reflect, they are unsure what it is they will do with the games that are being removed. Although relatively small in terms of print run size, approximately 3,500 new analog gaming lines are being released annually,[3] leading to a wealth and variety of possible play opportunities. Further, due to the relatively small print-runs, a thriving secondhand gaming market has developed either through public events, social media, or online secondhand retailers. A secondhand market which itself is relied upon by many players in order to bring games, of limited quantities and availability, into their collections.

Of note, however, is the number of individuals who expressed that they purposely bought longer campaign style games (that is, games which continue the same story arc over multiple sessions of play) or purchased games which can be played solo, specifically to play during the lockdown with one participant noting that these titles "probably won't [be] play[ed] again after lockdown ends". In essence, this hints at the levels of transfer and change which takes place within games collections which are augmented and supplemented to fit changing needs as necessary. As such the popularity of games including the extended campaign-based titles such as *Gloomhaven* or even *Pandemic Legacy: Season 1*, align with the current *zeitgeist*.[4] Although the social is vital, gamers still gain pleasure from physical interfacing with games in their possession. At least in principle, this aligns with Woods' (2012, p. 90) sentiment that "A gamer actively participates in producing an experience through a combination of engagements with culturally embedded sound and imagery, a physical relation with a game interface." The importance of these physical engagements and multi-sensory applications cannot be

---

[3]Details taken from an interview with an individual who works for a leading tabletop gaming distributor for my ongoing PhD project *Analog UK: Tabletop Gaming in the 21st Century.*
[4]Childres, Issac. 2017. *Gloomhaven*. Cephalofair Games (board game): http://bit.ly/39m5QUS; Daviau, Rob and Matt Leacock. 2015. *Pandemic Legacy: Season 1*. Z-Man Games, Inc (board game): https://bit.ly/34QI162.

underplayed and figure deeply with Csikszentmihalyi's (2002) work when considering the nature of tactile feeling being both immediate and engaging.

Unsurprisingly, given the lockdown faced by many countries across the globe major events in analog gaming calendars have been either canceled or rearranged. In some cases, this has led to considerable financial uncertainty for their organizers who, at least in the UK, are primarily led by a team of volunteers. Coupled with this are a host of small independent businesses collectively known within the hobby as friendly local game stores who,[5] faced with closure, rely primarily on the goodwill of their patrons and online trade (if possible). As one trader noted, "we're making sales in a week which we would make on a slow day over winter," another responding that "my business has been hit hard" from the closure of a physical store as well as planned event attendance. Hobbyists, however, appear to be aware of the issues that small businesses are facing with participants noting their support along the same lines as a respondent who explained that they would be making a concerted effort to "redirect their saved funds", from non-completed travel and other game expenditure in order to support their local game store. However, there is only an understanding of these issues due to the well-managed social media groups which service the community, and aid interfacing between game publishers, designers, business owners and players.

Playing *Pandemic* in a global pandemic

Across the globe copies of Matt Leacock's *Pandemic* have sold out (Kurzius, 2020; Schelle, 2020; Stewart, 2020). As lockdowns began to be implemented across nations, the forums for *Pandemic's* entry on *Board Game Geek* buzzed with a series of changes, augmentations and fan made errata that can be made to the game in order to simulate COVID-19. Further to this there have also been several games recently crowdfunded which look to document and explore the effects of COVID-19.[6] These two factors taken together suggest that analog gaming offers a space for exploration of social and societal issues. These liminal encounters in relative spaces of safety and exploration may be viewed, in essence, as a "magic circle" (Huizinga, 1949; Salen & Zimmerman, 2003).

Players, as this response has demonstrated, continue to play; albeit in ways that may be both new or innovative to them. However, in some cases technological learning curves and the digital divide, have hindered some individuals ability to engage with analog play. Connections have been made during this time and this is something which will continue, further relegating issues associated with loneliness and social isolation outside of the current lockdown.

Social connectivity is paramount and I, for one, am looking forward to the day that I can once again convene around a physical board with friends (though, maybe I'll leave *Pandemic* away from the table for the time being). However, just prior to writing, I

---

[5]The friendly local game store or FLGS is more commonly associated with being more than just a retailer and usually offers an open play space in which individuals can convene, akin to a third space (Oldenburg, 1999).
[6]*COVID Survival* (https://bit.ly/34NuzQE), *Corona Battle Against Covid-19* (https://bit.ly/2yoYour) and *Infected! – The Covid-19 Board Game* (https://bit.ly/3a7rzj2).

joined a new roleplay group online, working with the very services listed by my participants. My own social circles have extended, with my play group now comprising of individuals from across the globe. Analog play, as it seems, goes on, albeit in newfound ways and can offer an element of normalcy for its players who look forward to once again convening around physical boards and playing tables.

Acknowledgements

I would like to thank the forty-eight participants who contributed their opinions to the short survey which aided the formation of this paper. I would also like to thank my wife, Emma, who commented on a draft of this paper and has proved to be a practically perfect lockdown partner.

ORCID

Matt Coward-Gibbs ⓘ http://orcid.org/0000-0002-5982-7630

References

Blythe, M. A., & Hassenzahl, M. (2003). The semantics of fun: Differentiating enjoyable experiences. In M. A. Blythe, A. F. Monk, K. Overbeeke, & P. C. Wright (Eds.), *Funology: From usability to enjoyment* (pp. 91–100). Kluwer Academic Publishers and Springer.

Bowman, S. L. (2010). *The function of role-playing games: How participants create community, solve problems and explore identity.* McFarland & Company, Inc.

Brabazon, T. (2013). *Digital dieting: From information obesity to intellectual fitness.* Routledge.

Csikszentmihalyi, M. (2002). *Flow: The classic work on how to achieve happiness* (Revised ed.). Rider.

Fine, G. A. (1983). *Shared fantasy: Role-playing games as social worlds.* University of Chicago Press.

Frye, N. E. (2018). Let's do *what* together?!" Shared activity perceptions and relationship closeness. *Leisure Sciences,* 40(5), 374–386. doi:10.1080/01490400.2016.1240052

Huizinga, J. (1949). *Homo ludens: A study of the play-element in culture.* Routledge & Keegan Paul.

Kurzius, R. (2020, March 13). Local board game store labyrinth has seen sales of pandemic quadruple. *Dcist.* https://bit.ly/2VwMdnx

Lave, J. (1991). Situating learning in communities of practice. In L. B. Resnick, J. M. Levine, & S. D. Teasley (Eds.), *Perspectives on socially shared cognition,* (pp. 63–82). American Psychological Association.

Lave, J., & Wenger, E. (1991). *Situated learning: Legitimate peripheral participation.* Cambridge University Press.

Oldenburg, R. (1999). *Great good place: Cafes, coffee shops, bookstores, bars, hair salons and other hang- outs at the heart of community.* Marlow & Company.

Rogerson, M. J., & Gibbs, M. (2018). Finding time for tabletop: board game play and parenting. *Games and Culture,* 13(3), 280–300. doi:10.1177/1555412016656324

Rogerson, M. J. (2018). *Between cardboard and computer: The hobbyist experience of modern boardgames* [PhD thesis]. The University of Melbourne.

Rogerson, M. J., Gibbs, M., & Smith, W. (2015). Digitising boardgames: issues and tensions. In Diversity of Play: Games-Cultures-Identities. DiGRA 2015.

Rojek, C. (1995). *Decentring leisure: Rethinking leisure theory.* Sage Publications.

Salen, K., & Zimmerman, E. (2003). *Rules of play: Game design fundamentals.* MIT Press.

Schelle, C. (2020, March 31). Pandemic board game sells out as coronavirus sweeps across Australia. *7NEWS.* https://bit.ly/3cnK846

Stewart, A. (2020, March 22). Pandemic and Virus board games sell out across the UAE. *The National*. https://bit.ly/34QC5KF

Warschauer, M. (2003). *Technology and social inclusion: Rethinking the digital divide*. MIT Press.

Wenger, E., & Snyder, W. M. (2000, January–February). Communities of practice: The organizational frontier. Harvard Business Reivew.

Woods, S. (2012). *Eurogames: The design, culture and play of modern European Board Games*. McFarland & Company, Inc.

Yuen, F., & Johnson, A. J. (2017). Leisure spaces, community, and third places. *Leisure Sciences*, *39*(3), 295–303. doi:10.1080/01490400.2016.1165638

By Bread Alone: Baking as Leisure, Performance, Sustenance, During the COVID-19 Crisis

Gwyn Easterbrook-Smith (iD)

ABSTRACT

As the coronavirus crisis worsened, a series of news stories documented "panic buying" on grocery staples, including bread, yeast, and flour. News outlets began reporting what I had already concluded based on my own social media: in response, many people had started baking bread. Baking specialty bread, like sourdough, is a time-consuming process, which pre-COVID-19 was a leisure activity for some. Baking bread during isolation is an activity whose purposes are threefold: providing sustenance; filling newly available leisure time; and offering a way to demonstrate one's skill and activities on social media. I consider the sudden attention given to this niche area of cooking, and the ways that bread-making-as-identity is already being disputed online, with attempts to frame an increased interest in what is, ultimately, successful completion of domestic labor, as a threat to 'authentic' interest in specialty bread as culinary capital.

Panic buying and the swift rise of breadmaking

One of the first indications that western countries were taking the coronavirus seriously was a rush to stockpile various consumer goods: hand sanitizer, facemasks, and antibacterial wipes went first. In Australia, current affairs website *Junkee* reported on the frenzied buying, often embedding social media posts recording bare supermarket shelves (Rennex, 2020). *The Guardian* documented the sudden change in shopping behavior, with social media posts again featuring heavily in their reporting (Izzard, 2020). As the crisis worsened, stockpiling of nonperishable and staple foods increased, with pasta, rice, potatoes and bread suddenly hot commodities (Shaw, 2020). I encountered this myself, finding my bread options non-existent during a supermarket trip, deciding instead to try my hand at baking a loaf for the first time in years and discovering to my consternation that yeast and flour had also been entirely cleaned out, a problem also facing shoppers in the USA (Heil, 2020).

An article published on March 20 suggested a shopping list for people preparing "in a low-key manner that does not even slightly resemble panic buying" for the possibility of being isolated for some time (Neville, 2020). It continued:

> "[n]ot much of a baker? If you're stuck in isolation for a couple of weeks, you might become one, so you best get some flour … If you've always wanted to get into sourdough, this could be your chance—making your own starter from scratch takes time, but you'll have plenty of that."

It was around this time that my own social media feeds began to indicate that many people had the same idea simultaneously: an awful lot of people were suddenly having a go at baking bread.

This sudden interest in baking bread was not limited to my own social sphere of Australia and New Zealand however: the *New York Times* and *Reuters* similarly reported a sudden uptick in interest in breadmaking (Howcroft, 2020; Marvar, 2020). *The Huffington Post* suggested that while many people would usually be too busy to devote the time to nurturing a sourdough starter, learning to bake was the "perfect use of ample time" producing "a delicious result to feast on" (Severson, 2020). Other outlets reported bakers found that making bread was both a therapeutic outlet for stress (sometimes mentioning the #stressbaking hashtag some users had adopted), and a way to connect with others through social media, specifically Instagram and Twitter (Clifford, 2020; Rogers, 2020). With many people under varying degrees of state- or self-imposed isolation or lockdown, and restaurants and takeaway outlets temporarily closed in some areas, posts about what social media users were eating or cooking proliferated. Current affairs and news websites capitalized on this to provide content, frequently drawing on social media postings to document how people were adapting to the varying constraints of different lockdown arrangements.

As indicated by this small sample of the many similar articles posted in recent weeks, baking bread while under lockdown/isolation conditions was an activity whose purposes are threefold: providing sustenance, on a practical level; filling newly available leisure time and providing distraction and comfort; and offering a way to demonstrate one's skill and activities on social media, allowing connection to wider social groups in the absence of face-to-face contact. These purposes were not always distinct but often overlapped, with breadmaking fulfilling two or even all three simultaneously.

The uses of bread

Bobrow-Strain, discussing the history of bread in the USA, notes that a substantial shift in how and where it was baked occurred between 1890 and 1930—moving from being made in the home, mostly by women, to being baked outside the home, largely by men (2008, p. 20). Burnett places the shift to the commercial manufacture of white wheat bread occurring in the early 1800s in England, writing that by that point "household bread had all but disappeared" (1989, p. 4). Breadmaking has not been part of the standard repertoire of domestic duties in most households for some time, clearly, but during the coronavirus crisis a resurgent interest in it produced friction between the different social meanings given to bread.

Although drawn from a very different context, research into baking as occupational therapy for inpatient mental health programs found it was an activity which was enjoyable and useful for participants (Haley & McKay, 2004). Baking was experienced as beneficial for its ability to fill time, give structure to a day, with the useful end product providing a sense of accomplishment. In a less formal sense, many domestic cooks explain they experience cooking as "therapeutic" or "relaxing" even when it is a necessity—to provide daily meals for their family—rather than exclusively leisure (Szabo, 2013, pp. 631–632). Many news articles referred to baking's resurgence in popularity being due at least partially because of the comfort and stress relief which participants experienced—not only, or even largely, because of the necessity of feeding themselves, their family, or housemates without the options of delivery or takeout food. In these instances, the practical sustenance provided by bread was secondary to its place as an accessible and proximate leisure activity.

Holland, discussing changing attitudes and preferences for different leisure activities, found that the younger women in an analyzed cohort were more likely to consider baking a leisure activity, while their mothers or grandmothers (her research involved interviewing three generations from four families) considered it a "faff" and a chore which easily available ready-made goods had freed them from (2013, p. 313). The ability *not* to partake in food preparation then is one of the mechanisms by which engaging in it is constructed as leisure—and the class position of the sources interviewed is implied in some of the texts about the baking boom. One text reported on the "one-dollar sandwich bread" which was all that remained in-store, according to a source: "[i]t was a sad, pale loaf… not the heartier, artisanal kind she and her family prefer" (Heil, 2020). The newly risen bakers, it is suggested, chose to bake bread partly as leisurely activity but also in rejection of the limited selection of foodstuffs which they viewed as lacking, uninspiring or insufficiently artisanal and authentic.

The way that "upscale" bread is indexed as a marker of social positioning is seen in the colloquial use of 'white bread' as a descriptor to denote bland homogeneity, but also belonging to working class or lower socioeconomic groups (Bobrow-Strain, 2012). The ability to consider and reject white bread as a foodstuff in the coronavirus context specifically encompasses other indicators of economic privilege: indicating the bakers could afford to buy the ingredients to bake for themselves, and had a kitchen which was at minimum equipped with an oven. As the coronavirus crisis has progressed, it has become apparent that many essential workers are low paid service and retail staff, who have continued to work and therefore are not among those with a new-found bounty of leisure time in which to cook.

Hollows argues that the ability to treat baking or cooking as leisure and 'self care' is:

"…based on a classed and gendered distance from the demands of the everyday… for domestic cooking to be experienced as an indulgent leisure activity rests on the ability to experience the home as a site of leisure rather than labour and this, in turn, rests on a relatively clear demarcation of the temporal relations between public and private spheres." (Hollows, 2003, p. 240).

Szabo similarly discusses the importance of a temporal distinction between spaces of leisure and spaces of work in establishing a leisurely state of mind, although her participants often experienced cooking as a blending of the two (2013). The increase in people working from home, or socializing over video chats, means the temporal distinctions between leisure spaces and workplaces, the public and private, have been significantly eroded or removed. Although certainly not uniform in its distribution across class and gendered divides, with the home already being a site of labor for many, the degree to which the home became a blended space of leisure and labor increased during lockdowns.

The news reports about baking bread profiled more women than men, but it was not produced as an *exclusively* feminized activity, although of course this is not based on an exhaustive analysis. I would speculate that this is perhaps related to the blended nature of it: the production of food was incidental rather than central to the activity. This would be different, I suspect, if the discourses about domestic cooking more generally during coronavirus were to be examined. Baking's contingent meaning as predominantly leisurely in the quarantine context may have served to distinguish it from other food preparation.

The meaning of bread

Pre-coronavirus the rejection of the "sad, pale loaf" in favor of labor-intensive and time-consuming sourdough bread (whether bought at a premium price, or home made) served as a class signifier. In the midst of reduced consumer choice across different socioeconomic brackets however new mechanisms of performing class and status arose. Articles about how to make sourdough would sometimes emphasize the author's history with the bread: having made sourdough in the 70s and again in the 90s, or mentioning that they had faithfully kept the same starter alive since 2014 (Barrow, 2020; Chiles, 2020). Amid the blisteringly quick pace of news which characterized the coronavirus pandemic, was a less impactful but similarly swift shift in news about bread making: everyone was buying flour, everyone was making bread, and not long afterwards, the chiding suggestion that most people were not doing the dignified name of sourdough justice. In early April, the *Wall Street Journal* perhaps encapsulated this turn by running an article titled "We're All Baking Bread Now (And Many of Us Are Failing at It)" (Gasparro & Hagerty, 2020).

Competence at baking bread moved into the realm of a skill which could be documented via social media posting, and furthermore a performance which it was possible to fail at. What meaning is being given to proficiency at this kind of cooking? Are postings which documented the successful completion of domestic labor a rarefaction and commodification of skillsets which have not historically been recognized as 'real' work, unless completed 'professionally', outside the home, by men (Bobrow-Strain, 2008)? Or are they instead demonstrating a culinary capital through familiarity with what sourdough should look and feel like? Embedded in some of the texts were apparent attempts to establish the correct affective engagement with "artisanal" bread as a signifier of belonging in a specific social group or class; a kind of gatekeeping of the legitimacy of bread preferences as "an act of social positioning" (Bobrow-Strain, 2012).

The appeal of sourdough in the midst of panic-buying, rather than other kinds of bread, seemed to be that it can be made without yeast: a starter can be grown by anyone with a jar, a kitchen bench, some flour, and a couple of days to spare. Wincott, discussing how heritage or heirloom fruit and vegetables are deployed as a marker of social class and distinction, comments that discourses place them in contrast to "tasteless" supermarket produce—an analogue to the "sad, pale" bread (2018). She adds that "the middle classes use alternative food discourses for the purposes of social differentiation," which is one possible interpretation of authors prefacing their comments about bread with the provenance of their own starter (p. 56). A preference for artisanal bread in this context is not just a question of dietary tastes, but a way of indicating discernment and signaling particular values and privileges: concerns about industrialized food production, for example, and having the consistent leisure time to nurture a starter for years on end. An increased interest in the topic was responded to as though it diluted these meanings.

However, many of the social media posts reproduced in articles about the resurgence of interest in baking did not appear to be made with the class or social implications of a springy loaf in mind. Instead they often treated successful (or partially successful) kitchen experiments as a display of the fruits of newly created leisure time, or a way to connect with other #stressbakers. Some articles included sources mentioning their engagement in group chats to compare notes about their baking successes and failures, or finding a kind of community from relative strangers on social media (Gasparro & Hagerty, 2020; Rogers, 2020).

There is, then, an emergence of competing discourses about a collective interest in what one article called "carb therapy": one discourse which considered it a practical and diverting leisure activity, a way to connect about a seemingly neutral topic in the midst of a disaster, but another displaying anxiety that an increased interest in the topic of specialty bread threatened its status as a marker of the middle classes. "Foodie" culture is social, although participants are often selective about who they discuss their interests with, judging that their opinions and preferences may not be appreciated by their friends and family, instead seeking out others who relate to food in the same way they do (Vásquez & Chik, 2015, p. 233). Johnston and Baumann, discussing the "omnivourousness" of gourmet food writing, note that "high-status culinary consumption emphasizes authenticity and exoticism" which works "to validate a relatively narrow range of foods that require considerable cultural and/or economic capital on the part of individuals" (2007, p. 169). A sudden influx of interest in a formerly reasonably niche area of food culture might be seen to threaten its exclusivity, with the unusual hobby of feeding a yeast culture twice a week no longer in any way exotic. In response, some articles sought to question the authenticity and dedication of newcomers to baking—dismissing them as "trendy" or succumbing to "hype" (Krystal, 2020).

The tension seems to emerge from different meanings being made of the activity of baking bread. As I argue, baking bread during the coronavirus crisis is a leisure activity with multiple purposes. However, for many participants who are new to baking (or newly returned to it) establishing an identity as a 'foodie' or establishing culinary cultural capital does not seem to be among them, or at least is not the predominant motivator. In response, their doing food 'wrong' is perceived and responded to as a threat to the carefully cultivated expertise of people who invested time in a sourdough starter before the supermarkets ran out of yeast.

As I draft this commentary, there is still no yeast to be had at my local supermarket, and the arguments about baking bread have continued to rage across various social media timelines. One of the latest is the suggestion that it is irresponsible to attempt to make sourdough because of the need to feed and discard the starter, using up valuable flour (Krystal, 2020). The reactions often seem curiously disconnected from the actual qualities of the food being produced: its ability to offer literal nourishment, as well as a temporary reprieve from the onslaught of news about the pandemic, the ability to exert a little control over one's surroundings. Instead, they sometimes suggested a horizontal surveillance and attempts at disciplining aspirational baking. Happily, this seems not to have deterred many people from attempting a batch. As I write, one of the top posts under the #sourdough tag on Instagram (2.8 million posts and counting) reads "I made a ton of mistakes… but it tastes great and I'm sure next week's bread will be even better."

ORCID

Gwyn Easterbrook-Smith (iD) http://orcid.org/0000-0001-8621-3733

References

Barrow, C. (2020, March 16). How to make your own sourdough starter for bread, pancakes, waffles and more. *Washington Post.* https://www.washingtonpost.com/news/voraciously/wp/2020/03/16/how-to-make-your-own-sourdough-starter-for-bread-pancakes-waffles-and-more/

Bobrow-Strain, A. (2008). White bread bio-politics: Purity, health, and the triumph of industrial baking. *Cultural Geographies, 15*(1), 19–40. https://doi.org/10.1177/1474474007085783

Bobrow-Strain, A. (2012). *White bread: A social history of the store-bought loaf.* Beacon Press.

Burnett, J. (1989). *Plenty and want: A social history of food in England from 1815 to the present day* (3rd ed.). Routledge.

Chiles, A. (2020, April 8). I have finally mastered the dark art of sourdough baking. Here's how to do it | Adrian Chiles. *The Guardian.* https://www.theguardian.com/commentisfree/2020/apr/08/coronavirus-crisis-loaf-bread-sourdough-bake-off-flour-yeast-lockdown

Clifford, C. (2020, March 28). Why everyone is #quarantine baking their way through the coronavirus pandemic. *CNBC Make It.* Retrieved April 10, 2020, from https://www.cnbc.com/2020/03/27/coronavirus-why-everyone-is-baking-their-way-through-the-pandemic.html

Gasparro, A., & Hagerty, J. R. (2020, April 2). We're all baking bread now (and many of us are failing at it). *Wall Street Journal.* https://www.wsj.com/articles/were-all-baking-bread-now-and-many-of-us-are-failing-at-it-11585837309

Haley, L., & McKay, E. A. (2004). 'Baking gives you confidence': Users' views of engaging in the occupation of baking. *British Journal of Occupational Therapy, 67*(3), 125–128. https://doi.org/10.1177/030802260406700305

Heil, E. (2020, March 24). People are baking bread like crazy, and now we're running out of flour and yeast. *Washington Post.* https://www.washingtonpost.com/news/voraciously/wp/2020/03/24/people-are-baking-bread-like-crazy-and-now-were-running-out-of-flour-and-yeast/

Hollows, J. (2003). Oliver's twist. Leisure, labour and domestic masculinity in The Naked Chef. *International Journal of Cultural Studies, 6*(2), 229–248. https://doi.org/10.1177/13678779030062005

Holland, S. (2013). Three generations of women's leisure: Changes, challenges and continuities. *Journal of Gender Studies, 22*(3), 309–319. https://doi.org/10.1080/09589236.2012.681185

Howcroft. (2020, April 3). Great British lockdown: Bread-making frenzy sweeps the UK. *Reuters.* https://www.reuters.com/article/us-health-coronavirus-britain-baking-idUSKBN21L1XW

Izzard, H. (2020, March 9). Rolling in the aisles: Australians turn to TikTok to mock toilet paper panic-buying. *The Guardian.* https://www.theguardian.com/world/2020/mar/09/rolling-in-the-aisles-australians-turn-to-tiktok-to-mock-toilet-paper-panic-buying

Johnston, J., & Baumann, S. (2007). Democracy versus distinction: A study of omnivorousness in gourmet food writing 1. *American Journal of Sociology*, *113*(1), 165–204. https://doi.org/10. 1086/518923

Krystal, B. (2020, April 9). Why sourdough baking is a non-starter for me right now. *The Washington Post*. Retrieved April 12, 2020, from https://www.washingtonpost.com/news/voraciously/wp/2020/04/09/why-sourdough-baking-is-a-non-starter-for-me-right-now/

Marvar, A. (2020, March 30). Stress baking more than usual? *The New York Times*. https://www. nytimes.com/2020/03/30/style/bread-baking-coronavirus.html

Neville, A. (2020, March 20). So you've forgotten how to cook. *The Spinoff*. Retrieved April 10, 2020, from https://thespinoff.co.nz/food/20-03-2020/so-youve-forgotten-how-to-cook/

Rennex, M. (2020, March 2). Aussies are clearing out grocery store supplies over coronavirus fears. *Junkee*. Retrieved April 10, 2020, from https://junkee.com/coronavirus-australia-stockpiling/244664

Rogers, K. (2020, April 9). Baking during a pandemic can reduce stress and provide comfort. *CNN*. Retrieved April 10, 2020, from https://www.cnn.com/2020/04/09/health/bread-baking-health-benefits-coronavirus-wellness/index.html

Severson, K. (2020, April 7). How to make sourdough bread and starter from scratch. *The Huffington Post*. Retrieved April 10, 2020, from https://www.huffpost.com/entry/how-to-make-sourdough-bread-starter_l_5e878754c5b6332cecbae318

Shaw, A. (2020, March 25). Covid 19 coronavirus: By the numbers—What Kiwis have been panic buying. *NZ Herald*. https://www.nzherald.co.nz/business/news/article.cfm?c_id=3&objectid=12319948

Szabo, M. (2013). Foodwork or foodplay? Men's domestic cooking. *Sociology*, *47*(4), 623–638. https://doi.org/10.1177/0038038512448562

Vásquez, C., & Chik, A. (2015). "I am not a foodie…": Culinary capital in online reviews of Michelin restaurants. *Food and Foodways*, *23*(4), 231–250. https://doi.org/10.1080/07409710. 2015.1102483

Wincott, A. (2018). When carrots become posh: Untangling the relationship between 'heritage' foods and social distinction. In M. Phillipov & K. Kirkwood (Eds.), *Alternative food politics: From the margins to the mainstream*. (pp. 55–72). Routledge. https://doi.org/10.4324/9780203733080-4

Distancing from the Present: Nostalgia and Leisure in Lockdown

Sean Gammon (iD) and Gregory Ramshaw (iD)

ABSTRACT
This paper considers the role of nostalgia-based leisure in the present COVID-19 pandemic. Enforced lockdowns and social distancing initiatives have been met with various media channels replaying famous sport matches, classic films and memorable concerts from the past. Furthermore, social media is full of families interacting more; playing traditional board games and numerous other leisure-related activities such as baking bread and making fresh pasta. Nostalgia may well end up being one of the primary coping mechanisms (for all generations) of enduring isolation, fear - and a general loss of freedom. It is also worth considering whether we are now creating our own future nostalgia where, when the crisis is through, we will long for the social bonds and sense of community the pandemic created.

At this time, millions across the globe continue to endure the many restrictions of movement imposed by their governments, resulting in a renegotiation of how, where, and when leisure takes place. Similarly, the freedom to look back and find comfort in pre-pandemic times has become a welcomed distraction across the generational spectrum. It may appear flippant in times of great crises to explore the behaviors and experiences of people at leisure. Yet, the leisure choices made in times of stress, anxiety, and threat reveals much about the human condition, especially concerning life affirmation and coping strategies. While the therapeutic features of leisure are reasonably well documented (Kleiber et al., 2011), discussions relating to the psycho-social benefits of leisure nostalgia has had little coverage. This commentary observes how nostalgia is influencing leisure choice(s), particularly in the United Kingdom and United States, and how such choices appear to be part of individuals' current coping strategies in the early weeks of the lockdown. It will also examine how the leisure choices made during the crisis may inform the collective nostalgic reflections in the future. It is, of course, difficult to be definitive about leisure choices, behavior, and consumption during this pandemic;

leisure – like much of our daily lives during the pandemic – has changed daily, and often hourly. However, nostalgia – in its many forms – appears to be the leisure of choice for many in the UK and USA during the lockdown, perhaps precisely because it offers a palliative tonic in times of crisis.

There is little doubt that the global lockdown due to the spread of COVID-19 has profoundly affected our leisure choices and activities. It has also influenced with whom we are able to interact with during leisure and perhaps, more crucially, what is to be made with potentially more free time. Numerous commentators on leisure (Iso-Ahola, 1979; Kleiber et al., 2011; Neulinger, 1981) highlight that two critical components of leisure are freedom of choice and self-determination – each of which influences the quality of the experience. The lockdown coupled with social distancing has created a paradoxical situation that, on the one hand, dictates freedom constraint – while on the other seems to offer more time to engage in activities normally associated with individuals' leisure. Such enforced leisure (a term that may be considered oxymoronic) has led many to reflect on the value of leisure, especially in its ability to act as a buffer for stressful situations (Iso-Ahola & Park, 1996; Kleiber et al., 2011) and its propensity to add meaning and purpose in times of distress, loneliness, and anxiety (Routledge et al., 2013; Watkins, 2000). Freedom of choice has not been extinguished – only the extent of its physical and spatial parameters. These restrictions (both real and imagined) have perhaps led to more creative uses of leisure, which unsurprisingly has by neccessity taken place primarily in the home. As a result, the third place can no longer be reserved for those places that offer meaningful interaction '... outside the home and beyond the "work lots" of modern economic production' (Oldenburg & Brissett, 1982, p. 269) but has become – through strict enforcement and social surveillance – the site of all forms of leisure and non-leisure activities. Unsurprisingly, technology has become the vehicle for many forms of leisure – including gaming, media streaming services (such as Netflix), social media, and virtual conferencing technology (such as Zoom). Perhaps more surprising is the role to which nostalgia may have become one of the primary forms of this type of leisure consumption, including viewing old movies and shows, watching past sporting matches and competitions, and connecting with friends and family to share memories and reminisce. Similarly, other "at home" leisure activities such as cooking, baking, and exercise may also have a nostalgic form to them, whether they reflect a nostalgic view of family bonding or, in the case of fitness, attempting to recapture our former, younger selves.

As the demographic of populations in the most developed countries have notably grown older in the last three decades, so has the interest in nostalgia (Gammon & Ramshaw, 2013; Youn & Jin, 2017). In simple terms, nostalgia refers to a sentimental longing for a past that is forever gone. It is often identified as an emotional response brought on by a dissatisfaction or detachment in the present, and an anxiety for the future (Batcho, 1995; Boym, 2008; Davis, 1979). As a result, a seemingly superior, familiar, and stable past is sought that is comprised of happier times which may generate mixed feelings of both joy and loss. While nostalgia is mostly associated with those from older generations, younger people (those under 40 years) may also harken for simpler, less stressful times. Relentless advances in technology, economic recession, dramatic political change, and climate change (not to mention, of course, the "normalcy" of pre-pandemic society) may all be highlighted as triggers for this cross-generational glance back toward calmer periods. Interpretations of nostalgia have changed over time – from a medical ailment in the seventeenth century to an overly romantic condition that was practiced by older generations – though, in general, in recent times nostalgia has been viewed in pejorative terms; to be nostalgic is to be maudlin and unable to cope with the strange and unfamiliar present. Today, however, nostalgia is viewed in more affirmative terms, as generating numerous positive social and psychological functions for both young and old. For example, Sedikides et al. (2008, p. 304) concluded that, "nostalgia generates positive affect, increases self-esteem, fosters social connectedness, and alleviates existential threat," whilst Moore (2002) suggests that nostalgia can have a practical dimension in that positive reflections about past conditions can provide the framework for constructive future developments. Nostalgia has, in short, become an effective coping strategy to many of life's demands, by not only prompting us to recall more pleasant times – but also enabling individuals to remember how they felt during such times.

At time of writing, the lockdown appears to have spawned a significant interest in the past; where young and old reflect on, and vicariously escape to, more predictable times; when friends could meet up, holidays taken, and events attended. Yet the pervasive manner in which nostalgia has been embraced by individuals, families, media, and politicians all point toward a collective anxiety that is bordering on the original pathological nature of nostalgia in the seventeenth century – in short, a "homesickness" which is less mawkish and more medical. Given that many positive experiences in the past are often leisure-related, it is unsurprising that nostalgia can be both a key trigger for leisure participation and an emotional reaction to it (Cho, 2020). In particular, forms of recent popular culture such as music (see Barrett et al., 2010), film and television (see Holdsworth, 2011), and sport (see Gammon & Ramshaw, 2013) are frequently vehicles for popular nostalgia and, by extension, leisure consumption and participation. For example, studies focusing on the experiences of playing sport, watching sport, and visiting sport attractions (Fairley, 2003; Ramshaw, 2020; Ramshaw & Gammon, 2010) together with many forms of tourism illustrate the significance of past leisure events (Dann, 1998). This has led to a commodification of the past that involves either reintroducing previous brands to a market that remembers them the first-time around – or in the *retrofication* of bygone products aimed at more youthful markets who perceive them as ironic, authentic, or edgy. As such, while nostalgia is a coping mechanism which helps to sooth in challenging times, it is also disseminated by various props and products which help us to long for indeterminate – but "better" – times. This is not to say that commercially tinged nostalgia is necessarily harmful, but rather to note various routes to which individuals may come to – or be influenced by – nostalgia. To explore this further, the following section will discuss the numerous manifestations of nostalgia (specifically relating to family, media, and political rhetoric) which appear to be present in the COVID-19 crisis and reflect on their utility as positive coping mechanisms.

Family-based leisure is often considered in positive terms, as an incubator for future life satisfaction, well-being, and socialization. Yet the proliferation of technology in the home has in many cases helped nurture a more isolationist engagement with leisure, with individuals choosing to virtually socialize and interact with others outside the

family than to spend time with them. At the same time, E-leisure is viewed as an insti-
gator of home leisure, offering more opportunities for shared experiences, socializing,
and intergenerational play. Of course, the extent that families engage in leisure is very
much dependent on the age of the children, employment responsibilities of the parents
or parent, and the nature of the housing and home environment. Nevertheless, there
remains a societal pressure to provide meaningful family leisure experiences.
Undoubtedly, many families have shared images on social media engaging in variety of
traditional board and card games, perhaps in an attempt to reconnect to the way families used to play. A recent article in the *Telegraph* underlines the perceived benefits of
spending quality time with the family, citing: *In the era of self-isolation, many of us are
remembering that the chance to spend time with other people, to sit around the kitchen
table with our households, is a treat* (Rear, 2020). A mixture of leisure and nostalgia
during difficult times, for some, perhaps offers a palliative respite through social interaction, distraction, and escape. At present, individuals in the UK for example have government permission to, once a day, "break free" from the confines of the home. Many
families have likely decided to do this together, which perhaps has helped reduce tension and promote conversation – an event likely considered less exceptional forty
years ago.

The media in all its guises has appeared to both fuel and react to this apparent surge
in nostalgic interest by offering reminders of the way things were before the virus
spread. Some TV and radio channels offer repeats of long since forgotten drama series,
and musical artists provide "couch tours" where they rebroadcast past concerts (or perform their beloved repetoir live, in quarantine, from their homes via social media channels), while other broadcasters replay sports matches from both the recent and distant
past. The BBC recently aired the radio commentary for the final day of the cricket
Ashes series (England v Australia) in 2019. Perhaps many viewers tuned in to not only
relive extraordinary sporting moments and performances, but also to switch off from
the grim realities of the present and to be immersed in a perfect, unchanging past. Such
collective nostalgia (see Gammon, 2002) has proved extremely popular with other
recordings of previous games such as famous matches in soccer, rugby, tennis, and
snooker. Social media platforms have also latched onto the nostalgic zeitgeist by offering
users to discuss and vote for their favorite sporting moments, team jersey, or greatest
athlete. In the USA, sports broadcasters have filled much of their now-empty schedules
with rebroadcasts of past matches – some famous (such as championship games or
record-breaking performances) as well as the more mundane (e.g. pre-pandemic competitions from January and February 2020), interspersed with the occasional current
sports story (such as NFL free agency and the NFL draft) and the near-daily speculation
about when professional and collegiate sport will return. Perhaps most notably, ESPN
rushed to-air the documentary series *The Last Dance* about the championship years of
Michael Jordan and the Chicago Bulls basketball team, which quickly became a ratings
hit (Shaw, 2020). While the use and projection of nostalgic imagery in the media is not
a new phenomenon (Niemeyer, 2014), the apparent current celebration of the past may
be indicative of a media keen in promoting and benefitting from current anxieties.
Airtime and column inches that would usually be devoted to sport appear to have been
replaced with reflective narratives and images that fills not only what would otherwise

be a commercial certainty – but also potentially satisfies a public who are missing their beloved sports.

Alongside the nostalgically positioned articles in the press, politicians across Europe and North America seem to have been citing the past in order to rally their nations' resolve in these times of crisis. "Looking out for each other" and the reification of local and national community appear to be the most common messages; reinforced with explicit reminders that we have endured far worse. Such nostalgic rhetoric sits well with the many current political ideologies around the globe that aim to reestablish glories and achievements of the past (Kenny, 2017). A recent national broadcast by Queen Elizabeth also highlighted the importance of support and resolve while adding that future generations will look back at how the current generation coped during the current economic and social restrictions. This observation relates to an often-neglected facet of nostalgia, coined as *nowstalgia* that involves the planning, production, and distribution of visual documents in the present for the purpose of nostalgic refection in the future (Korin, 2016). The ubiquitous cell phone is increasingly used to capture much of our lives as they happen – but at the expense of experiencing them at the time. A focus on involvement and immersion during leisure episodes is being replaced by considerations of how best to capture and share them on social media. This may act as an additional coping mechanism that helps dilute the seriousness of the present situation while optimistically planning for the future – in essence, potentially be creating a "do you remember when?" moment for our future selves to nostalgize and consume.

It appears that, during this crisis, nostalgia-inspired leisure has been widely used, broadcast, and consumed, perhaps as part of a "cocktail for coping" meant to have a palliative affect during the initial stages of the pandemic. For some, the ability to reflect on the knowable and comforting past is perhaps far more enjoyable – and far less anxiety-inducing – than contemplating a traumatic present and a potentially bleak future. The lockdown may also become a source of nostalgia once the pandemic is over, as we may end up having sentimental attachments to the times we watched old movies together, went for walks, baked bread – and, collectively, defeated the coronavirus. Of course, having leisure – and the space (and, perhaps, boredom) to experience nostalgia – is also a privilege that many essential workers have not experienced during the lockout, while for others "sheltering at home" has created or exacerbated feelings of anxiety, helplessness, depression, and, in some cases, risk from domestic violence. Furthermore, many will have lost a loved one during the pandemic – often, without being able to give their final goodbyes in person – and, as such, this time will hardly be viewed through rose-colored glasses. Our immediate social and economic future also appears bleak, perhaps causing some to permanently retreat into the nostalgic past rather than facing an immensely unknowable future. Moreover, to employ an old axiom, nostalgia is not what it used to be, particularly in terms of future commercial consumption and products. For example, mere weeks after the lockdowns in Western Europe and North America, sports leagues turned to broadcasting e-sports competitions with many (such as NASCAR iRacing competitions in the USA) attracting significant viewership (Gastelu, 2020). Other forms of cultural consumption, such as going to museums and galleries, and attending live performances, may only be able to survive on rebroadcasting and repackaging for so long. As such, while nostalgia may have soothed the jangled nerves for many initially, it may also have a limited shelf-life particularly if the lockdown lingers on.

ORCID

Sean Gammon ⓘ http://orcid.org/0000-0001-5053-8763
Gregory Ramshaw ⓘ http://orcid.org/0000-0001-7238-753X

References

Barrett, F. S., Grimm, K. J., Robins, R. W., Wildschut, T., Sedikides, C., & Janata, P. (2010). Music-evoked nostalgia: Affect, memory, and personality. *Emotion (Washington, D.C.), 10*(3), 390–403. https://doi.org/10.1037/a0019006

Batcho, K. (1995). Nostalgia: A psychological perspective. *Perceptual and Motor Skills, 80*(1), 131–143. https://doi.org/10.2466/pms.1995.80.1.131

Boym, S. (2008). *The future of nostalgia*. Basic Books.

Cho, H. (2020). Importance of leisure nostalgia on life satisfaction and leisure participation. *The Service Industries Journal, 40*(1–2), 90–109. https://doi.org/10.1080/02642069.2019. 1567714

Dann, G. M. S. (1998). There's no business like old business': Tourism, the nostalgia industry of the future. In W. Theobald (Ed.), *Global tourism* (pp. 29–43). Routledge.

Davis, F. (1979). *Yearning for yesterday: A sociology of nostalgia*. Free Press.

Fairley, S. (2003). In search of relived social experience: Group-based nostalgia. *Journal of Sport Management, 17*(3), 284–304. https://doi.org/10.1123/jsm.17.3.284

Gammon, S. (2002). Fantasy, nostalgia and the pursuit of what never was. In S. Gammon & J. Kurtzman (Eds.), *Sport tourism: Principles and practice* (pp. 61–70). LSA Publications.

Gammon, S., & Ramshaw, G. (2013). Nostalgia and sport. In A. Fyall & B. Garrod (Eds.), *Contemporary cases in sport* (pp. 201–219). Goodfellow Publishers.

Gastelu, G. (2020). Fox's virtual NASCAR race sets esports record with 1.3 million viewers. *Fox News*. https://www.foxnews.com/auto/foxs-virtual-texas-nascar-esports-record

Holdsworth, A. (2011). Television, memory and nostalgia, Palgrave Macmillan.

Iso-Ahola, S. (1979). Basic dimensions of definitions of leisure. *Journal of Leisure Research, 11*(1), 28–39. https://doi.org/10.1080/00222216.1979.11969373

Iso-Ahola, S., & Park, C. J. (1996). Leisure-related social support and self-determination as buffers of stress-illness relationship. *Journal of Leisure Research, 28*(3), 169–187. https://doi.org/10. 1080/00222216.1996.11949769

Kenny, M. (2017). Back to the populist future?: Understanding nostalgia in contemporary ideological discourse. *Journal of Political Ideologies, 22*(3), 256–273. https://doi.org/10.1080/ 13569317.2017.1346773

Kleiber, D. A., Walker, G. J., & Mannell, R. C. (2011). *A social psychology of leisure* (2nd ed.). Venture Publishing.

Korin, E. (2016). Nowstagia. Articulating future pasts through selfies and goproing. *Medien and Zeit, 4*, 50–60.

Moore, P. (2002). Practical nostalgia and the critique of commodification: On the 'Death of Hockey'and the National Hockey League. *The Australian Journal of Anthropology, 13*(3), 309–322. https://doi.org/10.1111/j.1835-9310.2002.tb00212.x

Niemeyer, K. (2014). *Media and nostalgia. Yearning for the past, present and future*. Palgrave Macmillan.

Neulinger, J. (1981). *The Psychology of Leisure*. Springfield Illinois.

Oldenburg, R., & Brissett, D. (1982). The third place. *Qualitative Sociology, 5*(4), 265–284. https:// doi.org/10.1007/BF00986754

Ramshaw, G. (2020). *Heritage and sport: An introduction*. Channel View.

Ramshaw, G., & Gammon, S. (2010). On home ground? Twickenham Stadium Tours and the construction of sport. *Journal of Heritage Tourism, 5*(2), 87–102. https://doi.org/10.1080/ 17438730903484184

Rear, J. (2020). The best board game to alleviate boredom during lockdown. *Telegraph online.* www.telegraph.co.uk/family/life/best-board-games-alleviate-boredom-lockdown/

Routledge, C., Wildschut, T., Sedikides, C., & Juhl, J. (2013). Nostalgia as a resource for psychological health and well-being. *Social and Personality Psychology Compass, 7*(11), 808–818. https://doi.org/10.1111/spc3.12070

Sedikides, C., Wildschut, T., Arndt, J., & Routledge, C. (2008). Nostalgia: Past, present, and future. *Current Directions in Psychological Science, 17*(5), 304–307. https://doi.org/10.1111/j. 1467-8721.2008.00595.x

Shaw, L. (2020). 'The Last Dance' overtakes 'Tiger King' as the World's top documentary. *Bloomberg.* https://www.bloomberg.com/news/articles/2020-04-29/-the-last-dance-overtakes-tiger-king-as-world-s-top-documentary

Watkins, M. (2000). Ways of learning about leisure meanings. *Leisure Sciences, 22*(2), 93–101. https://doi.org/10.1080/014904000272876

Youn, S., & Jin, S. V. (2017). Reconnecting with the past in social media: The moderating role of social influence in nostalgia marketing on Pinterest. *Journal of Consumer Behaviour, 16*(6), 565–576. https://doi.org/10.1002/cb.1655

Less Sex, but More Sexual Diversity: Changes in Sexual Behavior during the COVID-19 Coronavirus Pandemic

Justin J. Lehmiller ⓘ, Justin R. Garcia ⓘ, Amanda N. Gesselman, and Kristen P. Mark ⓘ

ABSTRACT
Recreational sex is a popular form of leisure that has been redefined by the COVID-19 (coronavirus) pandemic. "Social distancing" rules have imposed limits on sex for leisure while also creating new opportunities. We discuss results from an online survey of 1,559 adults who were asked about the pandemic's impact on their intimate lives. While nearly half of the sample reported a decline in their sex life, one in five participants reported expanding their sexual repertoire by incorporating new activities. Common additions included sexting, trying new sexual positions, and sharing sexual fantasies. Being younger, living alone, and feeling stressed and lonely were linked to trying new things. Participants making new additions were three times more likely to report improvements in their sex life. Even in the face of drastic changes to daily life, many adults are adapting their sexual lives in creative ways.

In an effort to slow the spread and "flatten the curve" of the COVID-19 pandemic in early 2020, governments around the world began implementing sweeping restrictions on movement and social contact. Lockdown orders and "social distancing" guidelines prompted drastic changes in daily life, with significant implications for leisure activities, including sex. Sex—when freely chosen and pursued for pleasure (the single most common motive across age and gender in Western populations; Wyverkens et al., 2018)—is a popular form of leisure that fulfills multiple needs and is beneficial to physical and psychological well-being (Berdychevsky & Carr, 2020). However, in the wake of COVID-19, stringent contact restrictions have limited opportunities for recreational sex. For example, those living alone under lockdown orders are effectively mandated to a period of celibacy to confine the pandemic.

As coronavirus-related restrictions became more widespread, the popular media began reporting on putative shifts in sexual behavior, pointing to a rise in online

Table 1. Demographic characteristics of participants.

	Percentage (N)
Gender	
Female	71.1% (1109)
Male	23.4% (365)
Nonbinary and other genders	4.5% (70)
Sexual Orientation	
Heterosexual	52.7% (821)
Bisexual	19.5% (304)
Queer	7.8% (122)
Pansexual	7.3% (114)
Gay/Lesbian	7.0% (109)
Other sexual identities	5.7% (81)
Race	
Asian/Asian American	2.8% (44)
Black/African American	3.5% (54)
Hispanic/Latinx	5.6% (87)
White/Caucasian	84.1% (1311)
Multiracial	3.5% (55)
Other races	1.3% (19)
Country of Origin	
United States	73.4% (1144)
Canada	6.0% (95)
United Kingdom	5.7% (89)
Australia	2.4% (37)
Other countries	12.5% (194)
Annual household income (in USD)	
Less than $10,000	3.3% (52)
$10,001–$20,000	6.6% (103)
$20,001–$55,000	24.8% (386)
$55,001–$75,000	14.9% (233)
$75,001–$100,000	13.4% (209)
$100,001–$250,000	24.6% (384)
$250,000+	4.4% (68)
Living arrangement	69% living with a partner, 31% living alone
Age	$M = 34.1$, $SD = 10.3$, Range $= 18–81$

pornography searches (Pornhub Insights, 2020), sex toy sales (Smothers, 2020), dating app downloads (Stunson, 2020), and erotic posts on social media (Zane, 2020). This pattern, consistent with the overall integration of the internet and digital platforms into people's sexual lives (Nixon & Düsterhöft, 2018), suggests that when opportunities for the pursuit of in-person, partnered sex are limited, online and solo activities may be used to fill the void.

To the extent that uptake of sexual technology is occurring at the dramatic pace reported by the media, it would suggest that we are in the midst of a sexual revolution—one that could permanently shift the way we approach sex, currently and long after the pandemic subsides. Although this is a tantalizing thought, selective reporting of corporate sales figures and app downloads offers, at best, a partial picture of what is taking place in people's bedrooms. There may be other, potentially bigger, changes taking place that cannot be detected through these metrics.

How many people have actually experienced changes in their sex life since the pandemic began? To what extent do these changes revolve around using technology versus other leisurely sexual pursuits? What has the ultimate impact been, for better or for worse? These questions have not yet been well addressed, and their answers have a

Table 2. Frequency of new additions to participants' sex lives during the pandemic: in-person, part-nered activities.

Sexual behavior	Number who made this addition	Of those making a new addition, % who engaged in this behavior
Tried a new sexual position	49	15.50%
Shared sexual fantasies with a partner	41	13.00%
Acted on sexual fantasies with a partner	27	8.50%
Played with a vibrator/sex toy with a partner	23	7.30%
Gave a partner a massage/back rub	19	6.00%
Took a shower/bath with a partner	18	5.70%
Watched pornography with a partner	17	5.40%
You or your partner wore sexy underwear/lingerie	17	5.40%
Engaged in BDSM activities (e.g., restraints, spanking)	14	4.40%
You or a partner used marijuana before sex	12	3.80%
Had anal sex	11	3.50%
Hooked up with someone from a sex/dating app	9	2.80%
Role-played during sex	9	2.80%
Engaged in a threesome or group sex act	8	2.50%
You or a partner consumed alcohol before sex	8	2.50%
Had sexual contact in a public place	6	1.90%
Made sexy videos with someone	5	1.60%
Filmed yourself and a partner having sex	5	1.60%
Used food during sex (e.g., whipped cream)	4	1.30%
You or a partner took Viagra or a similar drug	4	1.30%

number of important implications, not only for understanding how our sex lives are likely to change once the pandemic ends but also for learning lessons that could potentially help us better navigate future emergency situations.

In this critical commentary, we sought to document people's sexual lives in the time of COVID-19 by exploring changes in sexual behavior patterns since the pandemic began via an online survey. We investigated changes in the frequency of solo and part-nered sexual activities, the types of new additions (e.g., usage of "SexTech") people have made to their sexual repertoires, changes in the quality of people's sex lives, as well as demographic and psychological factors that predict novel sexual pursuits and differing sexual outcomes.

While media reports suggest that the rise of SexTech is ubiquitous, it is likely that some people's sex lives are changing more than others. For example, people living alone may be more likely to use SexTech due to limited opportunities for in-person contact. In addition, feeling more sexual desire, loneliness, and stress could potentially prompt more sexual adaptations to fulfill psychological needs or relieve negative mood states.

Table 3. Frequency of new additions to participants' sex lives during the pandemic: solo and distance-based activities.

Sexual behavior	Number who made this addition	Of those making a new addition, % who engaged in this behavior
Sexted someone	47	14.90%
Sent nude photos to someone	46	14.60%
Watched pornography by yourself	31	9.80%
Had cybersex with someone	29	9.20%
Searched for sex/sexual health information online	29	9.20%
Filmed yourself masturbating	28	8.90%
Had phone sex with someone	26	8.20%
Made sexy videos for someone	21	6.60%
Tried anal stimulation	21	6.60%
Played with a vibrator/sex toy alone	19	6.00%
Tracked your own or a partner's menstrual cycle in an app	10	3.20%
Tracked sexual behavior in an app	7	2.20%
Uploaded content of any type to a pornographic site	5	1.60%
Role-played online (recipient was aware it was role-play)	5	1.60%
Watched a live camming stream	4	1.30%
Subscribed to a camming stream	4	1.30%
Used a coordinated teledildonic accessory with a partner	4	1.30%
Accessed virtual reality pornography	4	1.30%
Uploaded your own personal content to a pornography site	3	0.90%
Visited a "camming" website	3	0.90%
Tracked sexual satisfaction in an app	3	0.90%
Posted sex questions in an online forum	3	0.90%
Interacted with a cam model via audio	2	0.60%
Performed in a camming stream	2	0.60%
Exchanged sexual messages with a chatbot/AI entity	2	0.60%
Tracked STI symptoms in an app	2	0.60%
Role-played online (recipient was not aware it was role-play)	2	0.60%
Uploaded content of someone you know to a porn site	1	0.30%
Interacted with a cam model via video	1	0.30%

Survey overview

The final sample consisted of 1,559 adults who completed an anonymous online survey on "Sex and Relationships in the Time of COVID-19" between March 21 and April 14, 2020. Only those participants 18 years of age or older who completed enough of the survey to address the research questions of interest were included in analyses. See Table 1 for an overview of participant demographics.

Participants were recruited via internet-based snowball sampling. Standardized messages were posted to public social media platforms, which were widely shared by other social media users. Data collection was conducted in accord with our disciplinary and institutional ethical guidelines. All research procedures were approved by Indiana University's Institutional Review Board.

Table 4. Changes in sexual behavior pre- and post-pandemic.

Sexual behavior	Past year frequency	Frequency since the pandemic began	Statistical comparison
Solo masturbation	4.20	3.86	$t(1542)=10.86, p <.001$
Mutual masturbation	2.27	1.97	$t(1542)=10.92, p <.001$
Giving oral sex	3.00	2.37	$t(1542)=19.16, p <.001$
Receiving oral sex	2.80	2.21	$t(1538)=19.70, p <.001$
Vaginal intercourse	3.44	2.81	$t(1539)=18.79, p <.001$
Anal intercourse	1.53	1.25	$t(1527)=15.88, p <.001$

Note: Behaviors were rated on a 1–7 scale, corresponding to 1 = never, 2 = once per month or less, 3 = a few times per month, 4 = once per week, 5 = 2–3 times per week, 6 = almost every day, and 7 = more than once per day.

Participants indicated whether their sex life had improved, stayed the same, or declined since the pandemic began via a single item. They reported frequencies of solo masturbation, mutual masturbation, giving and receiving oral sex, vaginal intercourse, and anal intercourse during the past 12 months and (separately) since the pandemic began on a 7-point scale, from *never* to *more than once per day*. Participants also completed a 49-item checklist of new sexual behaviors they had engaged in since the pandemic began (see Tables 2 and 3).

We also administered the four-item Perceived Stress Scale (Cohen et al., 1983) and two versions of the Revised UCLA Three-Item Loneliness Scale, one of which assessed general feelings of loneliness and another modified to assess feelings of loneliness since the pandemic began (Hughes et al., 2004). Lastly, a modified version of the sexual desire subscale of the Female Sexual Function Index was administered (Rosen et al., 2000); one question asked about sexual desire for one's partner in the last two weeks, and the other about overall level of sexual desire in the last two weeks.

Survey results

How have people's sex lives changed since the pandemic began? Has sexual quality been impacted and has sexual behavior increased or decreased?

Many participants (43.5%) reported a decline in the quality of their sex life, with the remainder reporting that it either stayed the same (42.8%) or improved (13.6%). Average frequency of solo and partnered sexual behaviors significantly decreased compared to past year frequencies (Table 4). Thus, during this period of widespread restrictions on movement and social contact, frequency of sexual behavior—an activity often pursued for pleasure and leisure purposes—decreased on average.

Changes in the quality of one's sex life were unrelated to age, $r(1532) = .05, p = .067$, socio-economic status, $r(1421) = -.03, p = .259$, and gender, $\chi^2 (4, N = 1531) = 1.54, p = .819$. Regardless of gender identity, more than 40% indicated their sex life declined. Statistically significant drops in solo and partnered sexual behavior were observed across genders; the sole exception was that nonbinary participants were the only group for whom rates of solo masturbation did not decrease, $t(74)=0.28, p =.782$.

A small number of participants reported increases in sexual behavior. For example, whereas 20.8% of participants reported masturbating once per day or more during the past year, 23.2% reported this frequency since the pandemic began. Small single-digit increases in daily engagement were also observed for giving and receiving oral sex and for vaginal intercourse; however, changes at the other end of the spectrum were larger.

Table 5. Bivariate correlates of new additions to one's sex life.

	New additions	Desire for partner	Desire for sex	General loneliness	Loneliness during pandemic	Stress	Quality of sex life during pandemic
New additions	–	.11	.16**	.14**	.04	.07	.11*
Desire for partner	.16**	–	.64**	−.14*	−.17**	−.14*	.22**
Desire for sex	.16**	.76**	–	−.03	−.11*	−.06	.15**
General loneliness	.06	−.02	−.03	–	.56**	.34**	−.15**
Loneliness during pandemic	.14**	−.03	.04	.43**	–	.35**	−.29**
Stress	.08**	−.09**	−.07*	.29**	.40**	–	−.18**
Quality of sex life during pandemic	.11**	.28**	.24**	−.09**	−.28**	−.14**	–

Note:
**designates $p < .01$;
*designates $p < .05$. Correlations above the diagonal are for self-identified men; those below the diagonal are for self-identified women. New additions were coded as 1 for making new additions and 0 for making no new additions.

For instance, just 2.4% of participants reported not having masturbated in the past year, while 20.2% reported not having done so since the pandemic began. Results for partnered behaviors followed a similar pattern: whereas most participants reported having engaged in mutual masturbation, oral sex, and vaginal intercourse in the past year, large numbers (41–61%) reported not having engaged in these behaviors since the pandemic began.

How many people have made a new addition to their sex life since the pandemic began? What new additions were made, and who made them?

Approximately one in five participants (20.3%) reported making a new addition to their sex life since the pandemic began. Most (62.7%) reported making one new addition, with 18.4% making two, 7% making three, and 12% making four or more.

The most common new additions included trying new sexual positions, sexting, sending nude photos, sharing sexual fantasies, watching pornography, searching for sex-related information online, having cybersex, filming oneself masturbating, and acting on sexual fantasies (Table 2). New additions that occurred with lower frequency included visiting "camming" sites (as a customer or performer), using apps to track sexual behavior, and using advanced sexual technologies (e.g., teledildonic accessories, virtual reality porn; Table 3).

Making a new addition to one's sex life was unrelated to gender, χ^2 (2, $N = 1550$) = 0.37, $p = .833$, with 20.6% of self-identified women, 19.4% of self-identified men, and 18.4% of nonbinary participants reporting new additions. However, making a new addition was related to sexual orientation, χ^2 (1, $N = 1551$) = 4.20, $p = .040$; 22.3% of LGBTQ + identified participants reported new additions, compared to 18.1% of heterosexual participants. New additions were also related to racial identity, χ^2 (1, $N = 1559$) = 15.33, $p < .001$; racial minorities were more likely to report new additions than White-identified participants (29.4% vs. 18.5%, respectively). Furthermore, age, $r(1551)$ = −.12, $p < .001$, socio-economic status, $r(1435) = -.07$, $p = .010$, and living with a partner were associated with new additions, $r(1203) = .16$, $p < .001$, with those who were younger, less well-off financially, and/or living alone trying more new things.

The fact that those without a live-in partner tried more new activities is not entirely surprising because these circumstances likely necessitated more creativity with respect to pursuing sex for leisure. This likely partially explains why sexual minorities, racial minorities, and younger adults had increased odds of making new additions: all of these groups had significantly elevated rates of living alone. The fact that those with lower household incomes were more likely to make new additions probably also reflects their higher likelihood of living alone, but it may also indicate that those with more financial means buffered the impact to their intimate lives in other ways.

Living with a partner also predicted the types of new sexual repertoire additions participants made. Those who lived with a partner reported higher rates of partnered behaviors than those living along, such as trying new sexual positions and acting on sexual fantasies; by contrast, living alone was linked to higher rates of virtual and technology-based behaviors compared to those with a live-in partner, such as sexting and sending nude photos.

Several psychological variables were linked to new additions; however, some associations differed across gender. Bivariate correlates of new additions are presented in Table 5. For men and women, reporting more sexual desire in the past two weeks was linked to new additions. For men only, loneliness was associated with new additions; for women only, desire for sex with one's partner in the past two weeks, stress, and loneliness during the pandemic were associated with new additions.

It is noteworthy that stress and loneliness, while associated with negative overall evaluations of one's sex life, were linked to trying new activities. This pandemic and the resulting social isolation likely elevated feelings of stress and loneliness, and both of these factors have well-established links to sexual behavior in general. For example, sex has been shown to relieve stress (e.g., Ein-Dor & Hirschberger, 2012), while loneliness has been linked to sexual risk-taking (e.g., Martin & Knox, 1997). Making new additions may therefore partly reflect a coping mechanism for psychological distress or an intentional strategy for warding off further sexual declines.

Which demographic and psychological factors predict maintaining a better sex life during the pandemic?

Participants who made new additions were significantly more likely than those who did not to report that their sex life had improved since the pandemic began, χ^2 (2, $N = 1539$) $= 81.97$, $p < .001$. Among those making new additions, 28.6% reported that their sex life improved, 29.2% reported no change, and 42.2% reported a decline. For those who did not make new additions, 9.8% indicated their sex life improved, 46.3% reported no change, and 43.9% indicated their sex life declined. While the percentage reporting declines was similar in both groups, those who made new additions were about three times as likely to report improvements as those who did not try anything new. This suggests that many adults are finding creative ways to gratify sexual desires and pursue sex for leisure. For some, this has improved their sex life.

Beyond new additions, changes in one's sex life were linked to several other factors across genders (Table 5). Participants reported more positive changes to the extent that they felt more desire for sex and for their partner during the past two weeks, felt less lonely in general and during the pandemic, and felt less stressed.

Implications

The COVID-19 pandemic is impacting people's sexual lives. This is evidenced in our initial empirical multinational data on the impact of lockdowns and physical distancing restrictions on people's intimate lives. These findings are consistent with a smaller simultaneous study demonstrating a decrease in sexual frequency among a sample of young adults in China (Li et al., 2020), but they differ from a report of married people in Southeast Asia who reported unspecified changes in their sexual life but not decreases in sexual frequency (Arafat et al., 2020). Although our sample is not representative and caution is warranted in generalizing broadly, these findings nonetheless make an important and novel contribution to the literature and to our collective understanding of the influence of the COVID-19 pandemic and physical distancing on sociality, leisure, and sex.

There are several important implications of this work. While a majority of our participants reported no new additions to their sex lives, a substantial minority did. This finding adds much-needed complexity and nuance to the popular media narrative surrounding sex during this unusual time. It is clear that many people's sex lives are undergoing a revolution of sorts, in which they are expanding their sexual repertoires; however, this does not appear to be as widespread and as laser-focused on SexTech as the media suggest. In fact, the single most common new addition did not require any technology at all: trying a new sexual position. This suggests that the changes going on in people's intimate lives are broader in scope than assumed.

We also found that more participants said their sex lives declined rather than improved—and while incorporating new activities into one's sex life was linked to improvements, new additions did not eliminate declines. Generally, only partnered activities were linked to improvements, with few technology-based activities showing any association. The new additions most strongly correlated with sex life improvement were trying new positions, acting on fantasies, engaging in BDSM, and giving massages. By contrast, the most common technology-based additions (sexting, sending nudes) were unrelated to sexual improvements. This suggests that while incorporating more technology into one's sex life was common, it did not appear to have been as gratifying as in-person activities.

Consequently, we caution against premature claims that the COVID-19 pandemic will necessarily usher in widespread SexTech use, recreationally and otherwise. It is possible that recent uptake of SexTech is a temporary coping strategy and that once the pandemic subsides, technology usage may decrease in favor of in-person, partnered interactions.

By understanding factors associated with sexual improvements during this unprecedented time, we are also able to identify factors that might help people better navigate their intimate lives and safely pursue leisure activities during future emergency situations. For example, encouraging more novel sexual pursuits with a partner may be a helpful and therapeutic strategy for persons in relationships, particularly those feeling stressed or lonely. Likewise, the fact that SexTech was largely unrelated to sexual improvements points to important areas for future research and education. Are there ways of making these interactions more satisfying? Can SexTech education make usage more fulfilling?

The widespread social restrictions put in place during the COVID-19 pandemic appear to have significantly disrupted sexual routines and the overall quality of people's sex lives. However, even in the face of these drastic changes, it is apparent that many adults are finding creative ways to adapt their sexual lives, including in the pursuit of sex for leisure.

Disclosure statement

The authors have no conflicts of interest to declare.

Funding

This work was supported by The Kinsey Institute at Indiana University.

ORCID

Justin J. Lehmiller ⓘ http://orcid.org/0000-0003-2198-6588
Justin R. Garcia ⓘ http://orcid.org/0000-0002-5198-4578
Kristen P. Mark ⓘ http://orcid.org/0000-0002-0524-3357

References

Arafat, S. Y., Mohamed, A. A., Kar, S. K., Sharma, P., & Kabir, R. (2020). Does COVID-19 pandemic affect sexual behaviour? A cross-sectional, cross-national online survey. *Psychiatry Research*, 289, 113050. https://doi.org/10.1016/j.psychres.2020.113050

Berdychevsky, L., & Carr, N. (2020). Innovation and impact of sex as leisure in research and practice: Introduction to the special issue. *Leisure Sciences*, 42(3–4), 255–274. https://doi.org/10.1080/01490400.2020.1714519

Cohen, S., Kamarck, T., & Mermelstein, R. (1983). A global measure of perceived stress. *Journal of Health and Social Behavior*, 24(4), 385–396. https://doi.org/10.2307/2136404

Ein-Dor, T., & Hirschberger, G. (2012). Sexual healing: Daily diary evidence that sex relieves stress for men and women in satisfying relationships. *Journal of Social and Personal Relationships*, 29(1), 126–139. https://doi.org/10.1177/0265407511431185

Hughes, M. E., Waite, L. J., Hawkley, L. C., & Cacioppo, J. T. (2004). A short scale for measuring loneliness in large surveys: Results from two population-based studies. *Research on Aging*, 26(6), 655–672. https://doi.org/10.1177/0164027504268574

Li, W., Li, G., Xin, C., Wang, Y., & Yang, S. (2020). Changes in sexual behaviors of young women and men during the coronavirus disease 2019 outbreak: A convenience sample from the epidemic area. *Journal of Sexual Medicine*. https://doi.org/10.1016/j.jsxm.2020.04.380.

Martin, J. I., & Knox, J. (1997). Loneliness and sexual risk behavior in gay men. *Psychological Reports*, 81(3 Pt 1), 815–825. https://doi.org/10.2466/pr0.1997.81.3.815

Nixon, P. G. & Düsterhöft, I. K. (Eds.). (2018). *Sex in the digital age*. Routledge.

Pornhub Insights. (2020). *Coronavirus update – April 2*. https://www.pornhub.com/insights/coronavirus-update-april-2

Rosen, R., Brown, C., Heiman, J., Leiblum, S., Meston, C., Shabsigh, R., … D'Agostino, R. Jr. (2000). The Female Sexual Function Index (FSFI): A multidimensional self-report instrument for the assessment of female sexual function. *Journal of Sex and Marital Therapy, 26,* 191–208.

Smothers, H. (2020). Sex toy sales are skyrocketing during the coronavirus pandemic. *VICE.* https://www.vice.com/en_us/article/y3m9bw/sex-toy-sales-up-during-coronavirus-covid-19-pandemic

Stunson, M. (2020). Should you be hooking up during coronavirus pandemic? Tinder, Bumble downloads surge. *The Kansas City Star.* https://www.kansascity.com/news/coronavirus/article242083236.html

Wyverkens, E., Dewitte, M., Deschepper, E., Corneillie, J., Van der Bracht, L., Van Regenmortel, D., … T'Sjoen, G. (2018). YSEX? A replication study in different age groups. *The Journal of Sexual Medicine, 15*(4), 492–501. https://doi.org/10.1016/j.jsxm.2018.02.012

Zane, Z. (2020). The psychological reasons you're horny as hell during the coronavirus quarantine. *Men's Health.* https://www.menshealth.com/sex-women/a31897503/horny-quarantine-coronavirus-covid-19/

Dogs Unleashed: The Positive Role Dogs Play during COVID-19

Rebecca Mayers (iD)

ABSTRACT

The unprecedented COVID-19 pandemic has forced the global community to cope with widespread fear and isolation. However, there are outpourings of kindness and community despite these challenging times. In some cases, mandatory "social distancing" has even strengthened our relationships. One such relationship is the bond between humans and dogs. In this commentary, I leverage visual autoethnography to detail and understand human-dog relationships in the time of COVID-19, highlighting their importance. I then critique the allocation of space for dogs and the rigid restrictions on dogs in public space. Finally, I use my experience with my dog as a lens to question the heavy policing of public space and reflect on broader issues of this enforcement.

Overview

The COVID-19 global pandemic has left the world in a state of great anxiety and instability. As a precautionary measure to *flatten the curve* and reduce the spread of the virus, governments worldwide have mandated that we leave our homes only for essential trips and exercise. Therefore, individuals now spend the majority of their time indoors, but continue to venture outside for leisure activities at a *social distance*. Dog owners, in particular, must venture outdoors to exercise their pets. Through my experiences bonding with my dog and observing the relationships of others with their pets during this pandemic, I discovered three key lessons: (1) The positive benefits of human-dog relationships are critical during a crisis, (2) spaces for dogs are unreasonably controlled by our community and by-law officers, despite these overwhelmingly positive benefits, and (3) laws intended to increase our 'quality of life' may paradoxically negatively affect our communities.

It is well known that dog ownership is associated with many benefits. These benefits include: (1) health benefits for dog owners, (2) increased social capital amongst dog owners and community, and (3) happiness through play with an off-leash dog. First, dog ownership is correlated with important health benefits such as motivation to be physically active and social support (Cutt et al., 2007). Knight and Edwards (2008) found dog ownership to increase the owners physical, social, and psychological well-being. Dogs are also known to support their owners in times of hardship, and their presence has been linked to the secretion of oxytocin and reducing anxiety (O'Haire et al., 2015). This ability to decrease our anxiety is particularly important during a global pandemic, where stressors and changes to our ways of life are common.

Second, there is strong evidence to suggest pet ownership is significantly associated with higher levels of social capital within the community (Graham & Glover, 2014; Wood et al., 2017). Typically seen as a solution to "managing" contested space within parks, dog parks serve as social hubs for the community, as dogs assist in breaking the ice between people and help to build a sense of community (Booth, 2017; Gómez et al., 2018; Matisoff & Noonan, 2012; McNicholas & Collis, 2000). Despite the benefits of dog-ownership and play, Wood et al. (2017) found pets to be under-recognized as a strong conduit for building social capital and often ignored when it comes to policies and community initiatives. When off-leash spaces for dogs are proposed, there is great opposition to the development, as some community members do not want the potential noise pollution near their residence (Schlereth, 2016).

Third, some see off-leash dog walking is an important activity for recreation, sport, and essential for providing adequate care for their dogs (Walsh, 2011). Westgarth et al. (2017) found dog owners reported positive feelings of happiness from walking their dog, specifically, "Walking, in particular off-leash, was a component of providing the dog with a "good life" (p. 6). Despite the benefits of dog ownership and the meaning derived from walking a dog off-leash, there are laws specific to each community that prohibit this activity.

In the context of this commentary, I live in Waterloo, Ontario, Canada, with a population of 104,986 (Statistics Canada, 2016). There are roughly 21,000 dog licenses sold per year, however, the number of dogs is likely more than the number registered (Outhit, 2011). The closest dog park to my residence is an hour's walk, or a 10-minute drive away. This dog park is the only dog park in the City of Waterloo. According to the City of Waterloo by-laws, a dog is considered to be "running at large" if the dog is off-leash, or if the leash exceeds 2.4 meters (8 feet) (2017, p.27). An owner found violating this by-law may be fined $180 (City of Waterloo, 2017, p. 5). When I bring my dog to the park, I often see dogs off-leash. I sometimes talk with the owners and our dogs play. When I chat with them, they always mention the need for us to have a dog park in the area, and some even mention local petitions to city council for a dog park close by. Therefore, there is clear evidence of demand for people who want to play off-leash with their dogs in the area.

I identified and now present the lessons learned through visual autoethnography, in which I use photographs and narrative to explore a typical day in 'lockdown' with my dog. By doing so, I contextualize my encounters more effectively than using either medium in isolation, and communicate the meaning derived from these lived experiences (Ownby, 2013). I use this narrative as a lens to critique by-laws intended to manage contested space, yet negatively impact the quality of life of the community.

Figure 1. Own Hope: Note received on our apartment door "You are not alone. Be safe, kind, and stay strong #ownhope.

Ruff times: typical day during COVID-19 with my dog

Due to COVID-19, I spend more time with my dog than ever (Figure 1). Previously I had taken his rigid walking schedule and exercise requirements for granted; now, they provide a much-needed sense of structure. Every day, he eagerly wakes me up for his morning walk and breakfast, always cheerful despite the circumstances. We start the day with a cuddle, the daily news, a big cup of coffee, and a quick breakfast for each of us. Next, we ride the elevator in our 22-story apartment building. Occasionally, the elevator stops at other floors to let people board. We smile and wave awkwardly while the doors close, as it is prohibited to ride with others during the coronavirus pandemic. My dog doesn't mind the stops; he patiently waits for the doors to close, despite his obvious desire for others to pet him. Now, we step outside and walk 200 meters to the entrance of the local park trail, where I unleash him and begin to throw a ball back and forth. He jumps for joy, running as the ball bounces and ricochets off the surrounding trees. The trail is empty as far as the eye can see, and it seems as though I am alone with thoughts and my dog (Figure 2). I watch his face beaming as he runs back to me with a smile from ear to ear and his tongue flapping lazily in the wind.

Then, signs of life. A few people bike past us, others running, and I call my dog back before we get close to anyone. I exchange waves and smiles with those passing by, while he waits by my feet. Such positive exchanges would normally happen with only other dog owners, but during the pandemic, our community has become much more neighborly. After an hour, we walk back home, and I begin working from home on my

Figure 2. Where have all the people gone: Waterloo Park, Ontario, Canada.

Figure 3. Puzzling Times: Indoor activities with company.

laptop. In the afternoon, we will venture outside again; Our daily walk schedule is two 30–60-minute walks and a quick walk before bed (Figure 3).

Where to play in a pandemic?

Despite the positive benefits, owning a dog during COVID-19 comes with its own set of challenges. Before the pandemic began, I would bring my dog to the dog park so he

Figure 4. Pre-COVID-19 Bechtel Dog Park: The only dog park in Waterloo.

could socialize with other dogs, run, and play without fear of being ticketed by by-law enforcement officers.

Dog parks are currently closed in Waterloo and the surrounding area, compelling dog owners to go elsewhere to exercise their dogs (Figure 4). Although walking a dog on a leash may provide enough exercise for its owners, some dogs also require time to run. Playing with a dog off-leash is an efficient way to exercise them, especially when you need to work from home with few disturbances from a bored dog. As the saying goes, *a tired dog is a good dog* (Figure 5).

As I live in a small apartment, there is no backyard space to throw a ball or run without disturbing my neighbors. With the dog park closed, I now risk the fine for exercising my dog off-leash. However, these experiences call into question why I should travel to the dog park when a perfectly fine park is located right beside my apartment. Other dog owners feel similarly, given the number of circulated petitions to create an off-leash dog area in the local park and the number of owners flagrantly disobeying the bylaw. Why is it unacceptable for people to do the activity of their choice and co-exist in the park? More broadly, provided their chosen activity does not negatively affect others, why is it not acceptable for people to use the public park space as they see fit?

These questions were brought into sharp relief in the second week of April. As I walked through the local park trail, I noticed a by-law enforcement officer cycling through the park. Despite my clearly off-leash dog, he cycled past without ticketing me, and instead, waved and called out "have a great day!". On the same day, I noticed the local newspaper had an article on the man going through the park, and he was a by-law officer ticketing people for ignoring social distancing orders. Clearly, the by-law officer

Figure 5. My Coworker: Working from home.

Figure 6. Heel position: He heels to my left-hand side and looks up to await instruction.

did not care to enforce the rules regarding my off-leash dog that was not bothering anyone yet was concerned with people ignoring public health messaging about how to keep our community safe and healthy (Figure 6).

Selective enforcement of a law suggests that it should not be a law in the first place. Instead, laws governing the negligence of dog owners in the case that their dogs are a nuisance should be applied. Certainly, untrained and aggressive dogs should not be "running at large" in the park, but any damage they cause can be prosecuted or penalized through other laws rather than prohibiting all dogs via blanket legislation. This experience begs a broader question: What other types of leisure are we "leashing up" through unnecessary policing of space? If we examine the origin of by-laws and the policing of public space, we observe a direct influence of the "quality of life" laws imposed by those in power. "Quality of life" laws typically consist of low-level, nonviolent offenses to "regulate uncivil behaviour" such as drinking in public, sleeping in parks, and having a dog un-leashed (Herring & Yarbrough, 2015, p. 6). These activities are seen as "deviant" and immoral in some areas of the world. However, these activities are not criminalized in other areas, e.g. drinking in public space (Dixon et al., 2016) and marijuana usage (Greer et al., 2019). Furthermore, "quality of life" laws disproportionately affect those who are poor, people of color, and people who are homeless (Herring & Yarbrough, 2015). Moreover, those who do not have a private property to participate in these activities and do so in public parks are disproportionately criminalized. Besides, these "quality of life" laws fail to take into consideration the quality of life for those participating in the activity. In my case, my quality of life is better when I have some off-leash time with my dog—without bothering anyone.

To conclude, we see the strong relationship between myself and my dog through a visual autoethnography, but also how my experience during the pandemic has prompted questions of contested space. In particular, I reflected on how public space is used by humans and their dogs, especially when allocated space is closed. Moreover, this commentary highlights new avenues for research on contested leash laws and how we "leash up" other leisure activities in public space. Finally, this paper continues our discussion on how we negotiate and co-exist with others in our community, just as we are successfully doing during this pandemic.

ORCID

Rebecca Mayers (iD) http://orcid.org/0000-0001-6793-4674

References

Booth, A. L. (2017). Dog eat dog world: public consultation and planning on contested landscapes, a case study of dog parks and municipal government. *Community Development Journal*, *52*(2), 337–353.

Cutt, H., Giles-Corti, B., Knuiman, M., & Burke, V. (2007). Dog ownership, health, and physical activity: a critical review of the literature. *Health & Place*, *13*(1), 261–272.

Dixon, J., Levine, M., & McAuley, R. (2006). Locating impropriety: Street drinking, moral order, and the ideological dilemma of public space. *Political Psychology*, *27*(2), 187–206.

Gómez, E., Baur, J. W., & Malega, R. (2018). Dog park users: An examination of perceived social capital and perceived neighborhood social cohesion. *Journal of Urban Affairs*, *40*(3), 349–369.

Graham, T. M., & Glover, T. D. (2014). On the fence: Dog parks in the (un) leashing of community and social capital. *Leisure Sciences, 36*(3), 217–234.

Greer, A. M., Ritter, A. (2019). It's about bloody time Perceptions of people who use drugs regarding drug law reform. *International Journal of Drug Policy, 64*, 40–46.

Herring, C., & Yarbrough, D. (2015). Punishing the Poorest: How the criminalization of homelessness perpetuates poverty in San Francisco. *Available at SSRN 2620426.*

Knight, S., & Edwards, V. (2008). In the company of wolves: The physical, social, and psychological benefits of dog ownership. *Journal of Aging and Health, 20*(4), 437–455.

Matisoff, D., & Noonan, D. (2012). Managing contested greenspace: Neighborhood commons and the rise of dog parks. *International Journal of the Commons, 6*(1), 28–51.

McNicholas, J., & Collis, G. M. (2000). Dogs as catalysts for social interactions: Robustness of the effect. *British Journal of Psychology, 91*(1), 61–70.

O'Haire, M. E., Guérin, N. A., & Kirkham, A. C. (2015). Animal-assisted intervention for trauma: A systematic literature review. *Frontiers in Psychology, 6*, 1121.

Outhit, J. (2011). Dog licences: fair fee or cash-grab? Waterloo Region Record. https://www.therecord.com/news-story/2585722-dog-licences-fair-fee-or-cash-grab-/

Schlereth, N. (2016). An examination of dog parks and recommendations for development in the community. *Journal of Facility Planning, Design, and Management, 4*(1), 13–24.

Statistics Canada. (2016). Census profile: waterloo city. https://www12.statcan.gc.ca/census-recensement/2016/dp-pd/prof/details/Page.cfm?Lang=E&Geo1=CSD&Code1=3530016&Geo2=PR&Code2=47&Data=Count&SearchText=La&SearchType=Begins&SearchPR=01&B1=All

The City of Waterloo. (2017). By-law no. 09-47: being a by-law to regulate animals. https://www.waterloo.ca/en/government/resources/Documents/By-law/Animal-control-bylaw.pdf

Walsh, J. M. (2011). *Unleashed fury: the political struggle for dog-friendly parks.* Purdue University Press.

Westgarth, C., Christley, R. M., Marvin, G., & Perkins, E. (2017). I walk my dog because it makes me happy: a qualitative study to understand why dogs motivate walking and improved health. *International Journal of Environmental Research and Public Health, 14*(8), 936.

Wood, L., Martin, K., Christian, H., Houghton, S., Kawachi, I., Vallesi, S., & McCune, S. (2017). Social capital and pet ownership–a tale of four cities. *SSM-Population Health, 3*, 442–447.

Queer Isolation or Queering Isolation? Reflecting upon the Ramifications of COVID-19 on the Future of Queer Leisure Spaces

Austin R. Anderson (iD) and Eric Knee (iD)

ABSTRACT

The introduction of "social distancing" and quarantine orders in response to the COVID-19 pandemic have temporarily limited the ability for queer communities to engage in physical forms of social leisure. This pandemic also serves as a reminder of the importance of leisure spaces for queer communities and their unique leisure experiences. Given this opportunity to (re)examine the importance of queer leisure spaces, this paper will take a critical look at the impact this pandemic has had on queer leisure provision and the ramifications for queer leisure and queering leisure in a post-pandemic world. This paper will examine the current absence of queer leisure outlets, portrayal of public queer spaces, how the response to the sudden elimination of queer leisure spaces can inform our current understanding of leisure, and potential lessons about the connection between physical social engagement and queer leisure spaces.

The 2020 global COVID-19 pandemic has brought a sudden halt to numerous aspects of life and has impacted social leisure expressions through the closure of spaces due to government-mandated orders and the introduction of "social distancing." Bars and restaurants have closed to patrons, amateur and professional sport has come to a halt, schools and universities have been dismissed, music festivals have been canceled, and health and economic concerns have, perhaps understandably, taken precedence over community leisure engagement. While this has had tremendous impacts on communities across social and demographic classifications, this paper will examine the impact that the pandemic has had on queer leisure spaces. Additionally, this paper will examine the impact that the pandemic has had on queer communities, (re)examine the importance of physical queer leisure spaces, review media representations of social queer leisure during the pandemic and consider ramifications for the future of queer leisure spaces in a post-pandemic world.

Queer[1] community impact

The COVID-19 pandemic has had a significant impact on queer communities both inside and outside of leisure participation. Often, LGBTQ people experience marginalization in healthcare and in the provision of competent treatment and these issues are likely to be exacerbated during a pandemic. This marginalization takes the form of active discrimination, insensitivity and denial of treatment, fear of sexual stigma, and trans-identified persons can experience particular challenges in accessing adequate medical treatments (Patel et al., 2020). LGBTQ populations also experience microaggressions within healthcare settings through the use of heterosexist terminology, disapproval of LGBTQ experiences, and endorsement of heteronormative culture and behaviors (Dean et al., 2016). The population of homeless persons is also at-risk during the time of a pandemic, and this has significant overlap with LGBTQ populations, particularly in the United States. For instance, 20-45 percent of homeless youth identify as LGBTQ (Romero et al., 2020) and LGBTQ individuals between the ages of 18 and 25 are over two times more likely to be homeless than their non-LGBTQ peers (Morton et al., 2018).

Within leisure engagement, many common and popular forms of queer leisure have a dual reliance on social gathering and physical space. Celebrating at PRIDE events, visiting gay bars, drag shows, participating in LGBTQ sport clubs, LGBTQ community centers, and school-based queer clubs/events are all common queer leisure activities, and all rely on gathering in social settings. In part, this is because leisure spaces have historically been used by queer communities to "provide safe and appropriate contexts for the expression of gay identities" (Markwell, 1998, p. 116). This dependence on physical space for leisure is not unique to queer populations. However, given the (hetero)normative nature of many publicly provided leisure spaces, the queer community often relies on these safe spaces for leisure to negotiate queer identity (Krane et al., 2002).

Shifting queer leisure spaces pre-pandemic

While contemporary queer leisure spaces include a diverse range of offerings, the gay bar has historically represented the central socializing institution for the LGBTQ community (Chauncey, 1995). This was particularly true in urban areas where LGBTQ individuals flocked in large numbers in search of queer community. Indeed, gay bars often represented the only public place where gay men and lesbian women could freely congregate (Faderman, 2016), thus marking them as sites of resistance to heteronormative structures (Cattan & Vanolo, 2014).

Contemporary society promotes a culture of increasing tolerance toward segments of the LGBTQ population (Walters, 2014), yet queer neighborhoods and gay bars remain central to queer communities as sites of alternative discourse (Greene, 2014; Mattson, 2019a). Paradoxically, the number of gay bars in the U.S has declined by approximately 36% in the last decade (Mattson, 2019b). Three intersecting explanations detailing the

---

[1]We use "queer" as an umbrella term inclusive of all minoritized sex, gender, and sexual identities that draws distinction from hegemonic/heteronormative society. The acronym "LGBTQ" (lesbian, gay, bisexual, transgender, queer) is also used as a whole or in part throughout the article to specify segments of the community.

rapid transformation of queer spaces have been offered to explain this decline. The first suggests that as society becomes more accepting of the LGBTQ community, we are entering a "post-gay" era in which finding queer enclaves is no longer necessary (Ghaziani, 2011, 2015). This conceptualization assumes a declining importance of sexual orientation in the lives of the LGB community and a desire to assimilate and participate in mainstream social spaces that were once denied to them.

"Post-gays" also favor using technology to form their community (Collins & Drinkwater, 2017). Indeed, the increased use of technology to form community provides the second explanation behind the decline in queer spaces. Online platforms have been both a replacement for and a complement to physical queer spaces (Zablotska et al., 2012), particularly for younger generations (Collins & Drinkwater, 2017). Although it is largely beyond the scope of this paper's focus on physical leisure spaces, it is worth noting that virtual space created by queer social-based smartphone applications has undoubtedly played an important role in queer leisure during the time of the COVID-19 pandemic. The proliferation of location-based social applications in the last ten years has allowed queer populations to become comfortable creating and maintaining social connection virtually, and this is certainly worthy of further exploration as it relates to queer leisure during the pandemic.

Renninger (2019) argues that these conceptualizations fail to consider the larger politic of urban development. The gentrification of cities has put pressure on queer neighborhoods and establishments making them less friendly to LGBTQ individuals and businesses in favor of attracting a wider audience (Doan & Higgins, 2011). While these spaces were historically in under-developed areas, the growth of LGBTQ acceptance in mainstream society correlates to the commercialization of once queer spaces in an attempt to attract new (heterosexual) residents seeking "hip" physical locations centered in consumptive practices (Kanai, 2014). Such spaces were rebranded to emphasize assimilationist heteronormativity, what Orne (2016) calls the creation of Gay Disneyland. This third explanation therefore is centered in the neoliberal, homonormative shift in the broad LGBTQ community (Duggan, 2002). The consequences of homonormative gentrification include the displacement of queer establishments and persons (Mattson, 2015). This is particularly true for queer individuals who are nonwhite or upper-class (Knee, 2019; Rosenberg, 2017).

The changing nature of queer leisure spaces, and indeed the decline of some, does not diminish the role that such spaces play in the lives of queer persons. Recent leisure scholarship continues to demonstrate the importance of queer spaces in the development of identity and community, even given the above concerns (Fenton, 2018; Lewis & Johnson, 2011; Mock et al., 2019; Vo, 2020). While technological capability has eased some trepidation brought upon by the pandemic, the sudden loss of physical social leisure spaces has likely impacted the ability of queer people to create counter-normative spaces of acceptance within hegemonic communities.

Social identity and queer leisure

The physical social spaces where queer communities come together to experience leisure are important to the creation of community and interpersonal social bonds (group membership). Social identity theory emphasizes the importance of in-group membership (and out-group identity) to an individual's sense of identity and identity formation (Turner & Tajfel, 1986). The theory emphasizes that individuals have multiple layers of identity associated with affiliated social groups and this can have significant impact on behaviors within social environments. This is especially applicable to individuals of non-normative identification, as popular queer leisure spaces are a main way in which group membership and bonds are formed and cultivated (Krane et al., 2002). Individuals with queer identities have experienced a sudden and significant loss of these leisure spaces. This loss of physical social space may have impacts on queer leisure behavior and queer persons' sense of self. It is through this lens of social identity formation that the loss of queer leisure spaces can be explored and lessons about the future importance of these spaces within queer communities can be learned.

Absence of queer leisure outlets - Queering isolation

Media representations of queer leisure during the pandemic have reported virtual variety hours, drag performances, support groups for at-risk LGBTQ populations (Shen-Berro, 2020), and even plans for digital pride celebrations as the summer of 2020 approaches (Haynes, 2020). These have been engaged in to satisfy the need for the community to connect without opportunities for physical congregation. Social media representations of queer leisure modifications during the pandemic and the future of queer leisure spaces after the pandemic have, expectedly, been given from a variety of perspectives. However, there is undoubtedly some apprehension being expressed about the future of these spaces on social media sites. These include advertising/marketing attempts to make LGBTQ nightlife virtually accessible during the pandemic (Hereford, 2020) and the creation of funds to assist those whose livelihoods depend on LGBTQ social spaces (Hammack & Watson, 2020).

In localities with large queer populations, individuals are expressing personal concern about what the future looks like for America's largest gay communities. One local Facebook post in Chicago's Boystown district said, in response to the sudden shuttering of local queer establishments,

> It's pretty sad in Chicago. It's likely that many won't be able to reopen due to financial strain … it's been cool to see the drag community's resilience by moving shows to live digital platforms without skipping a beat. I'd love for things to get back to 'normal', but who knows what that means. If bars do reopen, I'm sure there will be new capacity regulations that will most likely forever change the vibe. (D. Beers, personal communication, April 12, 2020)

While this is simply one expression of opinion among millions on social media, it does underline the importance of these physical spaces, particularly in geographical areas that have become dependent on queer social leisure for their existence. A thorough study of social media expressions related to the loss of queer leisure during the pandemic is outside the scope of this essay, but it is one that should be undertaken to better understand the future impact of the pandemic.

The convergence of modified queer leisure programs in an online format and concerns for the future of physical leisure spaces presents an interesting case in which we simultaneously see the queering of isolation and the continued need for physical social connection. Rapidly providing leisure opportunities and social services via technology harkens to the idealization of queering leisure practices that are based in an ethos of care. Certainly, this is a romantic re-telling of the queer response to isolation – or the queering of isolation – and a cynical, yet valid, argument can be made that these forms of leisure are little more than shallow attempts to raise funds for continued homonormative leisure forms. However, particular examples from the online response by queer leisure providers might more closely represent the potential for radical, post-capitalist, care-based services that Brown (2009) argues remain prevalent within diverse gay economies. Indeed, responses have included online political action campaigns and fund-raising for marginalized communities, specialist sexual and mental health services, youth support groups, and performances by independent artists, including drag performers. Importantly, each of these are hallmarks of services traditionally offered in physical queer leisure spaces; however, they represent only a small portion of what is typically available. This outpouring of support in digital format, when framed from a social identity standpoint, presents a need for community engagement that continues to be well-served in physical queer leisure spaces – even given the pre-pandemic threats from post-gay, assimilationist conceptualizations of community.

Ramifications for post-pandemic queer leisure

COVID-19 has undoubtedly changed the perception of social leisure engagement, particularly for communities that have a history of reliance on this type of engagement. The queer community's increasing reliance on technology for leisure connection over the past decade has, perhaps, never been more important than during this time of social isolation, while simultaneously exposing a premature under-reliance on physical community building. Technology has aided in the creation of community, but it has always worked in *conjunction* with physical gathering space, not in *replacement*. That is, social isolation has emphasized a renewed importance on physical forms of leisure and queer spaces. Technology has made it easier to connect with others, but it is clear that physical spaces are important, perhaps even more so than LGBTQ community members suspected prior to the pandemic. COVID-19 has brought this relationship between technology-based queer social leisure and physical queer leisure spaces into specific relief. The pertinent post-pandemic questions include whether there will be a renaissance in queer leisure spaces when societal operations normalize and what the future of the gay bar, PRIDE festivals, LGBTQ sport clubs, and community centers might look like. Has the pandemic impacted attitudes toward these traditional queer leisure spaces?

While this may be impossible to answer with clarity, there is a real concern that many queer social leisure spaces may be lost due to the pandemic amongst a realization that these spaces are possibly more necessary today than ever before. The hyper-growth of technology during the past decades, in conjunction with liberalizing and "post-gay" attitudes, helped usher in assumptions that the need for queer physical leisure spaces were of a past generational era and that the "death" of the gay bar was a natural byproduct of societal changes. Renewed declarations for the need for physical leisure spaces during the pandemic have underscored their importance in contemporary queer leisure expression. While virtual leisure has queered isolation, the (re)queering of physical leisure spaces will depend on the extent to which the values and attitudes of participants toward such spaces are impacted by their experiences during the pandemic.

ORCID

Austin R. Anderson (iD) http://orcid.org/0000-0003-0890-5341
Eric Knee (iD) http://orcid.org/0000-0003-0681-4817

References

Brown, G. (2009). Thinking beyond homonormativity: Performative explorations of diverse gay economies. *Environment and Planning A: Economy and Space, 41*(6), 1496–1510. https://doi.org/10.1068/a4162

Cattan, N., & Vanolo, A. (2014). Gay and lesbian emotional geographies of clubbing: Reflections from Paris and Turin. *Gender, Place & Culture, 21*(9), 1158–1175. https://doi.org/10.1080/0966369X.2013.810603

Chauncey, G. (1995). *Gay New York: Gender, urban culture, and the making of the gay male world, 1890-1940*. Basic Books. https://doi.org/10.1086/ahr/100.5.1706

Collins, A., & Drinkwater, S. (2017). Fifty shades of gay: Social and technological change, urban deconcentration and niche enterprise. *Urban Studies, 54*(3), 765–785. https://doi.org/10.1177/0042098015623722

Dean, M., Victor, E., & Guidry-Grimes, L. (2016). Inhospitable healthcare spaces: Why diversity training on LGBTQIA issues is not enough. *Journal of Bioethical Inquiry, 13*(4), 557–570. https://doi.org/10.1007/s11673-016-9738-9

Doan, P. L., & Higgins, H. (2011). The demise of queer space? Resurgent gentrification and the assimilation of LGBT neighborhoods. *Journal of Planning Education and Research, 31*(1), 6–25. https://doi.org/10.1177/0739456X10391266

Duggan, L. (2002). The new homonormativity: The sexual politics of neoliberalism. In R. Castronovo & D. D. Nelson (Eds.), *Materializing democracy: Towards a revitalized cultural politics* (pp. 175–194). Duke University Press.

Faderman, L. (2016). *The gay revolution: The story of the struggle*. Simon & Schuster.

Fenton, L. (2018). You can see their minds grow': Identity development of LGBTQ youth at a residential wilderness camp. *Leisure/Loisir, 42*(3), 347–361. https://doi.org/10.1080/14927713.2018.1535276

Ghaziani, A. (2011). Post-gay collective identity construction. *Social Problems, 58*(1), 99–125. https://doi.org/10.1525/sp.2011.58.1.99

Ghaziani, A. (2015). *There goes the gayborhood?* Princeton University Press.

Greene, T. (2014). Gay neighborhoods and the rights of the vicarious citizen. *City & Community, 13*(2), 99–118. https://doi.org/10.1111/cico.12059

Hammack, P., & Watson, S. (2020, March 31). *The show must go on: Nightlife in the age of COVID-19.* https://www.gaycities.com/outthere/50837/the-show-must-go-on-nightlife-in-the-age-of-c

Haynes, S. (2020, April 3). *'There's alwas a rainbow after the rain.' Challenged by coronavirus, LGBTQ communities worldwide plan digital pride celebrations.* https://time.com/5814554/coronavirus-lgbtq-community-pride/

Hereford, A. (2020, April 9). *Gone clubbing: Coronairus is pushing LGBTQ nightlife online and into homes.* https://www.metroweekly.com/2020/04/gone-clubbing-coronavirus-is-pushing-lgbtq-nightlife-online-and-into-homes/

Kanai, J. M. (2014). Whither queer world cities? Homo-entrepreneurialism and beyond. *Geoforum, 56*(1), 1–5. https://doi.org/10.1016/j.geoforum.2014.06.012.

Knee, E. (2019). Gay, but not inclusive: Boundary maintenance in an LGBTQ space. *Leisure Sciences*, *41*(6), 499–515. https://doi.org/10.1080/01490400.2018.1441767

Krane, V., Barber, H., & McClung, L. R. (2002). Social psychological benefits of Gay Games participation: A social identity theory explanation. *Journal of Applied Sport Psychology*, *14*(1), 27–42. https://doi.org/10.1080/10413200209339009

Lewis, S. T., & Johnson, C. W. (2011). But it's not that easy": Negotiating (trans)gender expressions in leisure spaces. *Leisure/Loisir*, *35*(2), 115–132. https://doi.org/10.1080/14927713.2011.567062

Markwell, K. (1998). Playing queer: Leisure in the lives of gay men. In D. Rowe, & G. Lawrence (Eds.), *Tourism, leisure, sport: Critical perspectives* (pp. 112–123). Hodder Education.

Mattson, G. (2015). Style and the value of gay nightlife: Homonormative placemaking in San Francisco. *Urban Studies*, *52*(16), 3144–3159. https://doi.org/10.1177/0042098014555630

Mattson, G. (2019a). Small-city gay bars, big city urbanism. *City & Community*, *19*(1), 76–97. https://doi.org/10.1111/cico.12443

Mattson, G. (2019b). Are gay bars closing? Using business listings to infer rates of gay bar closure in the United States, 1977–2019. *Socius: Sociological Research for a Dynamic World*, 5, 237802311989483–237802311989482. https://doi.org/10.1177/2378023119894832

Mock, S. E., Misener, K., & Havitz, M. E. (2019). A league of their own? A longitudinal study of ego involvement and participation behaviors in LGBT-focused community sport. *Leisure Sciences*, 1–18. https://doi.org/10.1080/01490400.2019.1665599

Morton, M., Samuels, G., Dworsky, A., & Patel, S. (2018). *Missed opportunites: LGBTQ youth homelessness in America*. Chapin Hall at the University of Chicago.

Orne, J. (2016). *Boystown: Sex & community in Chicago*. University of Chicago Press.

Patel, S., Cuneo, C., Power, J., & Beyrer, C. (2020). Topics in global LGBTQ health. In J. Lehman, K. Diaz, H. Ng, E. Petty, M. Thatikunta, & K. Eckstrand (Eds.), *The equal curriculum: The student and educator guide to LGBTQ health* (pp. 261–288). Springer.

Renninger, B. J. (2019). Grindr killed the gay bar, and other attempts to blame social technologies for urban development: A democratic approach to popular technologies and queer sociality. *Journal of Homosexuality*, *66*(12), 1736–1755. https://doi.org/10.1080/00918369.2018.1514205

Romero, A., Goldberg, S., & Vasquez, L. (2020). *LGBT people and housing affordability, discrimination and homelessness*. Williams Institute.

Rosenberg, R. (2017). The whiteness of gay urban belonging: Criminalizing LGBTQ youth of color in queer spaces of care. *Urban Geography*, *38*(1), 137–148. https://doi.org/10.1080/02723638.2016.1239498

Shen-Berro, J. (2020, April 1). *Queer festivals, drag performances and LGBTQ meetups turn digital*. https://www.nbcnews.com/feature/nbc-out/queer-festivals-drag-performances-lgbtq-meetups-turn-digital-n1173281

Theriault, D. (2014). Organized leisure experiences of LBGTQ youth: Resistance and oppression. *Journal of Leisure Research*, *46*(4), 448–461. https://doi.org/10.1080/00222216.2014.11950336

Turner, J., & Tajfel, H. (1986). The social identity theory of intergroup behavior. In S. Worchel & W. Austin (Eds.), *Psychology of intergroup relations* (pp. 7–24). Nelson-Hall.

Vo, T. D. (2020). Rejection and resilience in a "safe space": Exploratory rapid ethnography of Asian-Canadian and Asian-American men's experiences on a gay cruise. *Leisure Sciences*, *42*(3-4), 340–318. https://doi.org/10.1080/01490400.2020.1712278

Walters, S. D. (2014). *The tolerance trap: How God, genes, and good intentions are sabotaging gay equality*. NYU Press.

Zablotska, I. B., Holt, M., & Prestage, G. (2012). Changes in gay men's participation in gay community life: Implications for HIV surveillance and research. *AIDS and Behavior*, *16*(3), 669–675. https://doi.org/10.1007/s10461-011-9919-9

This Must Be the Place: Distraction, Connection, and "Space-Building" in the Time of Quarantine

Marko Djurdjić

ABSTRACT

Philosopher Henri Lefebvre claimed that exultations such as "Change life! Change society!"—or, more appropriately, "Change your habits!"—mean nothing "without the production of an appropriate space" where these changes can occur. Adapting Lefebvre's theories on the production of space to leisure, this paper celebrates how our participation in collectivistic online communities helps reconcile our need for distraction and connection during quarantine, aided by the practice of "space-building." Through this process, leisure develops as both a visual and physical practice, the apathy (and boredom) resulting from inertia circumvented by space-building. By constructing relatable spaces that strive to mimic "real-world" locales, the dissonance created by the dialectical relationship between the objective truth (I'm stuck at home ...) and our subjective projections is temporarily resolved.

I *like* going out.

That may seem redundant, but at least it helps me remember,

این نیز بگذرد

This must be the place ...

Since the onset of COVID-19 and its related quarantine measures, there has been a proliferation of online events and gatherings that serve to replicate the act of "going out." Our participation with our fellow quarantiners in these communal "inside-outings" reveals a fascinating—yet unsurprising—conclusion: people like to do stuff *together*! *I'm* not drinking alone, *WE'RE* drinking alone! And in these times, that's a reassuring dichotomy.

Philosopher Henri Lefebvre (1991) claimed that exultations such as "Change life! Change society!"—or, more appropriately, "Change your habits!"—mean nothing "without the production of an appropriate space" (p. 59) where these changes can occur. Adapting Lefebvre's theories on the production of space to leisure, this paper celebrates how our participation in collectivistic online communities helps reconcile our need for distraction and connection during quarantine, aided by the practice of "space-building." Through this process, leisure develops as both a visual and physical practice, the apathy (and boredom) resulting from inertia circumvented by space-building. By constructing relatable spaces that strive to mimic "real-world" locales, the dissonance created by the dialectical relationship between the objective truth (I'm stuck at home …) and our subjective projections is temporarily resolved.

Employing Erykah Badu's livestreamed "Quarantine Concert Series," and Club Quarantine—"a 🖤 *queer* 🖤 online dance party [taking place] every ◐ day ◐ of ◐ the ◐ quarantine" (Club Quarantine, 2020a)—as my central case studies, this paper will examine how "space-building" utilizes spatial reconfiguration in order to (re)establish place. By repurposing personal spaces to suit the needs of online "outings," our homes become facsimiles of "real-world" locations where these events would normally take place—a process I call "*Spatial Approximation*."

Lefebvre and the paradox of space

In his 1974 opus *The Production of Space*, Henri Lefebvre (1991) established that "(Social) space is a (social) product," possessing a "social character" defined by the "social relations it implies, contains and dissimulates" (pp. 26, 27, 83). Each individual member of a society "relates oneself to space, situates oneself in space, [confronting] both an immediacy and an objectivity of one's own. […] One is, in short, a 'subject'" (Lefebvre, 1991, pp. 182–183). Although spaces personify certain codes which signify their meaning, they are also *signified*, imbued with meaning by every "subject" who enters that particular space. And this is the inherent duality of spaces, producing meaning while simultaneously having meaning placed on them.

Space is therefore *subjectively* determined.

For Lefebvre (1991), social space is neither exclusively mental, abstract space, nor physical, perceptible space. Instead, it is a combination of the two. When we enter, experience, or participate in a space, our mental conception of that space "is 'realized' [through] a chain of 'social' activities" (p. 251), amalgamating the "imaginary" with the "real." The *physical* becomes essential in order to give a space, and its user, "reality": we actualize spaces, and spaces, in turn, actualize us (Lefebvre, 1991). We give each other *meaning*, these spaces becoming part of both our lived experience, *and* our perceived/conceived experience. Thus, the spatial approximation that you "construct" inside your home acts as a tangible representation of *your interpretation* of an "outside" space.

Through spatial approximation, our spaces can take on new meanings and "emerge in a new light" (Lefebvre, 1991, p. 27). Whether historical, social, or political, under quarantine, spaces are not determined by their stereotypical functions; rather, a space's purpose can be redefined to fit the needs of the user. Through space-building, we appropriate and realize "outside" spaces in our homes, thus avoiding the "ideological error [and illusion]" (Lefebvre, 1991, p. 95) that space is fixed, our homes consciously becoming the "*Everyspace*."

Quarantine qoncerts

All spaces hold nostalgic and practical properties which are associated with memories, actions, and/or activities. Whether symbolic or practical, people have always assigned meaning to spaces (Lefebvre, 1991), particularly gathering spaces, imbuing them with a significance exceeding their intended function. While a record store is a place to buy records, it is also a space of congregation where individuals can loiter, debate, or simply flip through records in a tranquil, meditative state. In these gathering spaces, we simultaneously participate and observe. Simply by virtue of being *in* that space, we mimic and interact, either directly or indirectly, with every other person who has ever been, or ever will be, in that space.

Although space is saturated with "signs and meanings" (Lefebvre, 1991, p. 136), these don't necessarily explain the *feeling* of a space, or the feelings one experiences *in* a certain space. Spaces exhibit unexplainable, intangible vibrations and energies that cannot always be put into words, and these become paramount to how we understand a space, and how we define our lived experience within a space (Lefebvre, 1991). Spaces, therefore, represent something *unique* to each and every individual.

This is especially true of concert venues, and live music.

With audiences relegated to their homes, artists ranging from indie-punks (Dogleg, 2020) to The Rolling Stones (Global Citizen, 2020) have begun streaming performances through various platforms in order to imitate the live experience at home, projecting the image of a "concert" from their living rooms, home studios, and basements. Less mosh pits, more couch sits (unfortunately). While these "concerts" lack *corporeal* interaction, they nevertheless present the artist in their own habitat, performing in their version of an "intimate space," a sought-after experience for any concertgoer.

Of all the streamed "home experiences," the most unapologetically ambitious is soul-hip-hop-jazz-gospel-spoken-word-whatever-else-you-can-think-of artist Erykah Badu's *Quarantine Concert Series: Apocalypse, Live from Badubotron.*

During a recent Zoom press conference, Badu (2020) was candid about her inspired approach:

> I'm not just putting an iPhone up on a tripod and streaming on a live free platform. I am creating a world for people that they haven't seen me in. [...] I hope that I am designing a blueprint.

Badu's spatial approximation is therefore deliberate, done in direct response to the multitude of solo living-room shows on YouTube and Instagram. Reimaging her live show as a "scaled-back" bedroom experience, Badu and her five-piece bandana-and-facemask-wearing band performed amidst instruments, equipment, lighting, and the many comforts of home. These pay-per-view concerts (which have ranged from $1 to $3) utilized "majority-rules" audience polls to give fans unprecedented access to her home, where she gave tours, did song-requests, and provided multiple complex (moving!) camera angles of the performance, upscaling the production values in order to fully immerse her audience in the "Badubotron" experience (Badu, 2020). Thanks to Dallas's 20-person group-gathering limit (and some rigorous home sanitation), Badu and her team were able to put this system together in just a few days (Badu, 2020).

By developing her artist-owned livestream site, baduworldmarket.com, Badu has set herself apart by constructing an entirely new space *of her own*, removing the intermediary streamers and connecting the audience directly to the artist. In doing so, she has gained full control of the monetization of her streams, initiating a "trailblazing solution for musicians who are accustomed to making a living off touring" (Sayej, 2020). While Badu's popularity plays a crucial role in her ability to draw a crowd (and their cash), this system can nonetheless act as a buffer between touring and quarantine for artists, including smaller, independent ones hoping to recoup *some* lost revenue from canceled live shows (and all from the comfort of one's bed!). While Badu's approach requires some investment on the part of the performer, so too does touring!

As Lefebvre (1991) states, no space is "'neutral', 'objective', fixed, transparent, innocent or indifferent" (p. 94). There is always purpose behind a space, whether altruistic, capitalistic, political, or otherwise. For Badu (2020), performing live is a way of healing. But concerts are also a *commercial* enterprise, regardless of how one views the "artistry" of live performance. By hybridizing the physical (her bedroom) and the philosophical (the website), Badu has presented us with a tangible approximated space (the concert "venue"), and a transparent purpose behind the space (getting paid!). Badu's World is therefore both symbolic *and* practical. It *denotes* something, while also *accomplishing* something, coupling her art-philosophy with her need to support herself and the "ecosystem" of people in her circle (Badu, 2020). And so far, it's worked: the first three shows drew in over 100,000 *paying* viewers (Aswad, 2020).

Badu (2020) believes this system will be integral to the future of "live" performance, and like any concert experience, she is offering this service for a fee: it is entirely up to the audience whether they want to "enter the space," or not. By investing her own money in order to actualize this experience, Badu is reclaiming the live space while simultaneously making it experientially worthwhile for the audience.

And she wants the audience to do the same: give a dollar, and invest in Badu.

Although these streams can never truly *replace* the feeling of a live concert experience (lest we forget the giant man blocking your view, the shirtless dude slamming into you, or the couple embracing for the ENTIRE concert...), space-building and spatial approximation, as both physical *and* mental processes, can undoubtedly counter isolation by connecting audiences to their favorite forms of distraction, thus positioning these practices as Essential Quarantine Coping Mechanisms[TM]. For Badu (2020), space-building is mutually beneficial, appeasing an audience hungry for performance *and* keeping herself and her dependants paid. Through space-building, Badu has brought people into her home, and offered them creative control, thus celebrating her audience as an integral and irreplaceable part of the "live" experience.

Club Quarantine and the pleasures of spatial approximation

Successful home-based spatial approximations don't just symbolize "outside" spaces, they *become* these spaces. They *are* these spaces. By upholding the material and symbolic value of the "outside" spaces they mimic, spatial approximations simultaneously physicalize and reimagine collectivistic spaces, and in the process, disrupt the alienating effects of quarantining. Thus, the personal needs fulfilled by these "outside" spaces are realized in the home.

In examining the "utopia" of communal living, Lefebvre (1991) conceded that these spaces "dedicated to sensual delight have existed," even if they have been "few and far between" (p. 379). These predominantly literary and/or imaginary spaces fail to invent a "new life" because of "the absence of an appropriated [physical] space" (Lefebvre, 1991, p. 379). And yet, thanks to the internet and space-building, these sensual, delighting, ultimately reaffirming spaces can be both imaginary *and* tangible.

And nowhere is this more apparent than at Club Quarantine.

Founded by four friends and artists from Toronto, Club Q held its inaugural party March 16th, 2020, "the first night Toronto's bars and clubs were told to close," with a promise that the party would keep going "every night until the quarantine was lifted" (Sharp, 2020).

According to cofounder Brad Allen, the impetus for starting Club Q came from the organizers' collective need to "connect with each other" (Xtra Staff, 2020). Streamed through Zoom, users connect to Club Q using a meeting code released every night through the club's Instagram page. The party can hold 1000 attendees, with queues forming to get in (just like a "real" club!). Although free, Club Q incurs $500-to-$3000-a-night expenses for its organizers, which are supplemented through voluntary audience donations—"an approximation of a cover charge" (Kong, 2020)—as well as brand-collaborations and sponsorship deals (Lhooq, 2020), including a weekly "hump day" party-collab with Paper Magazine called "PAPER x Club Quarantine" (Club Quarantine, 2020a). With 66k+ Instagram followers, celebrity performers, and global press coverage, Club Quarantine has established itself as the preeminent online queer dance party for people craving connection (and fun!) during quarantine.

Through this online experiment, Club Q has helped maintain a positive, supportive queer club scene, even in isolation. It is a moderated, accessible, inclusive and interactive space that encourages participation and (respectful) loss of inhibition. Speaking to CBC, cofounder Andrés Sierra explained how Club Q "prioritizes marginalized communities and [that] there is zero tolerance for hate" (Knegt, 2020): if you break the rules, a bouncer will "eject" you, and they've brought on "more moderators to keep the space safe" (Sharp, 2020). Ultimately, "the community joining in nightly really determines what the space can be" (Xtra Staff, 2020). As clubgoer and Toronto event producer Marisa Rosa Grant describes it, "It's just a virtual party, and I think it's the future" (VICE, 2020).

Since its inception, Club Q's attendees have subverted the aforementioned boredom and apathy by employing nostalgia and memory, renegotiating what it means to "go out" and imbuing Club Q with a *practical* impact beyond simply "partying" (Lefebvre, 1991). As cofounder Mingus New succinctly puts it, "Club Q is helping" (VICE, 2020).

This notion of helping, preserving, and distracting is the power—and necessity—of producing "approximate" spaces while people are socially distanced. These virtual concerts, parties and get-togethers are not simply ways to unwind; there is a *need* for these spaces, as well as every activity associated with these spaces (Decorating! Dressing up! Etc!). As one clubgoer gets ready while enacting everyone's favorite prelude to going out (the "pre-drink"), another poses and drinks in a boa-adorned bathtub (VICE, 2020).

Club Q has become a *safe space* for its attendees, and it has been successful precisely because people need this kind of positive distraction. Since we can't physically *go* to a club, spatial approximation allows us to manifest our version of the "The Club Experience" in our homes.

"Utopian" spaces such as Club Q are *representations* of "real" spaces which can be lived, imagined and reinvented (Lefebvre, 1991), offering some reprieve from our current situation, and personifying safe, legal acts of rebellion against quarantine measures; a protest against isolation. These approximations, however, are not meant to be permanent replacements: they are merely a temporary solution for a (hopefully) temporary problem. Although Club Q can remind clubgoers of "real-life" queer parties and events (VICE, 2020), there are nevertheless limitations: "I miss actually partying with my girls," laments one Club Q attendee. "I miss all the dancing and the hugs. But this is as close as we get right now" (VICE, 2020).

Approximated spaces *do not* replace physical contact, "real" spaces, or leaving the home to experience culture. They can't. People still need hugs! Instead, these approximations act as placeholders, where participants can connect with others and share in their need for a given culture, space, or activity. "We have to keep our physical distance from people in this moment," Grant says, "but every night from nine to 12, you feel connected" (Kong, 2020). And *that* is the best we can do *right now*: through spatial approximation, we can get *close* to the spaces and people we miss most. Space-building is an act, a movement. It is something *we must do*.

So, construct a facsimile.

Make-believe.

Pretend you're there.

And *actually* enjoy yourself!

Because this isn't a club: it's Club Quarantine.

Conclusion

Although leisure has always been centered in certain spaces, rarely is it so perpetually (and forcibly) centralized in a *single* space. Yet, by repurposing our homes as "The Concert Venue," "The Club," and other "spaces devoted to encounter and gratification," we embrace and celebrate the collapse of the "partitions between inside and outside" (Lefebvre, 1991, pp. 137, 147). By reproducing these "longed-for" spaces inside the home, we reignite our connection to these spaces through nostalgia, emotions and memories, engaging in what Lefebvre (1991) calls "the freest creative process there is" (p. 137).

Space-building thus acts as a synecdochical approach to, and protection against, the isolating nature of quarantining. Although "going out" has both conceptually *and* physically been taken from us, we still want to *feel* like we are in a space that we are missing, and we want to keep our spaces (and our conceptions of these spaces) "alive" during quarantine.

And *this* is why we must replicate these spaces in our homes. *Of course* we miss the people we are distancing from, but we also, inevitably, miss the spaces where our relationships flourish, places where we gather, commute to, and spend time in. Although we must all practice social distancing, by creating spatial approximations, we are able to "leave" our homes, and party!

Lefebvre (1991) believed that a singular "planet-wide space [could act] as the social foundation of a transformed everyday life open to myriad possibilities" (p. 422). Through the internet and space-building, we are able to reinterpret—and recreate—the spaces we can't live without. You feel most alone when you *think* you're alone, but the internet has helped change that, and the countless viewing, dancing, and participating parties are a testament to the type of community that the internet is supposed to foster.

For although we may be *insulated*, we are never truly isolated.

References

Aswad, J. (2020, April 17). How Erykah Badu created her own livestream company for 'Quarantine Concert Series'. *Variety*. https://variety.com/2020/music/news/erykah-badu-quarantine-concert-livestreams-business-1234582892/

Badu, E. (2020, April 16). *Zoom Press Conference*. https://baduworldmarket.com/pages/stream

Club Quarantine. (2020a). [@clubquarantine]. Instagram. https://www.instagram.com/clubquarantine/

Club Quarantine (2020b, May 3). Club Quarantine zoom stream [Screenshot].

Dogleg. (2020). [@doglegband]. Instagram. https://www.instagram.com/doglegband/

Global Citizen. (2020, April 18). *The rolling stones perform "you can't always get what you want." || One world: Together at home* [Video]. YouTube. https://www.youtube.com/watch?v=N7pZgQepXfA&feature=emb_title

Knegt, P. (2020, March 24). *Four Toronto artists have created social isolation's hottest queer dance party: Club Quarantine*. CBC. https://www.cbc.ca/arts/four-toronto-artists-have-created-social-isolation-s-hottest-queer-dance-party-club-quarantine-1.5507310

Kong, S. L. (2020, April 24). *Online dance parties are curbing loneliness, building community and reviving clubbing*. Globe and Mail. https://www.theglobeandmail.com/life/style/article-online-dance-parties-are-curbing-loneliness-building-community-and/

Lefebvre, H. (1991). *The production of space* (D. Nicholson-Smith, Trans., 1st rev. ed.). Blackwell (Original work published 1974).

Lhooq, M. (2020, April 14). *People are paying real money to get into virtual zoom nightclubs*. Bloomberg. https://www.bloomberg.com/news/articles/2020-04-14/virtual-nightlife-grows-past-dj-livestreams-to-paid-zoom-clubs

Sayej, N. (2020, April 17). *Erykah Badu on the frontier of paid concert streaming: 'It's possible'*. Forbes. https://www.forbes.com/sites/nadjasayej/2020/04/17/erykah-badu-on-the-frontier-of-paid-concert-streaming-its-possible/#3835a3367b95

Sharp, A. (2020, April 17). *Club Quarantine: Queer love from Toronto to the world*. National Observer. https://www.nationalobserver.com/2020/04/17/features/club-quarantine-hits-one-month-nightly-queer-parties

Xtra Staff. (2020, March 19). COVID-19: Your communities in action. *Xtra Magazine*. https://www.dailyxtra.com/covid-19-lgbtq-communities-action-mar-19-168660

VICE. (2020, April 9). *Inside Club Quarantine: The future of nightlife* [Video]. YouTube. https://youtu.be/a-t-McubS0c

Club Quarantine, 9:13pm (Club Quarantine, 2020b).

Club Quarantine, 10:59pm (Club Quarantine, 2020b).

Two screenshots from Club Q's 50th consecutive night, May 3rd, 2020. Participants imbibe, wear costumes, design sets, affix digital backgrounds, and party, all while connecting with like-minded clubgoers.

(Including me! Top row, second from left. I even changed 'locales' halfway through.)

Neighboring in the Time of Coronavirus? Paying Civil Attention While Walking the Neighborhood

Troy D. Glover

ABSTRACT

Whereas physical distancing slows the spread of COVID-19, tactics associated with it have the potential to exacerbate social isolation in our societies. Far from withdrawing from one another during this period, however, engagement in sanctioned localized leisure, particularly neighborhood walking, has facilitated a welcome resurgence in neighboring, an active engagement in authentic social interactions with neighbors, albeit from a safe distance. What existed as a social contract of civil inattention in public space appears to have shifted with the pandemic to greater civil attention. With this in mind, this critical commentary aims to explore how, in this time of crisis, neighborhood walking appears to have facilitated a rediscovery of our social connectedness as neighbors. While there is no guarantee the resurgence of neighboring will survive the pandemic, it warrants recognition that, at least early on in this crisis, leisure affordances play a role in strengthening social connections among familiar strangers.

As much as a global pandemic can devastate communities, it can also bring communities together. What Cooper (2007, p. 217) described more generally as an "unexpected temporal rupture" imposes a sudden shared experience upon people that can affectively inspire them to strengthen their social ties to cope collectively with the crisis they are facing. To be sure, the overwhelming and seemingly sudden emergence of COVID-19 and its accompanying states of emergency have undoubtedly disrupted the lives of individuals and entire communities in negative ways across the globe. Even so, despite physical distancing measures to slow the spread of the virus, including canceling social gatherings and events, closing outdoor recreational amenities, and encouraging people to remain at home, people are finding ways to connect and build solidarity to buffer themselves from the social impacts of the pandemic. In my observation, neighborhood walking, one of the few sanctioned localized leisure activities permitted outside of the home during this crisis, has facilitated a welcome resurgence in neighboring[1], the active

---

[1] This term was first introduced to me by Mervyn Horgan (University of Guelph) who cited it in a newspaper article for which he was interviewed. The citation for the article is: Quan, D. (2020, March 29). 'Tiny acts of solidarity' are

engagement in authentic social interactions with neighbors, albeit from a safe distance. What has long existed as a social contract of civil inattention in public space appears to have shifted slightly to reflect greater civil *attention* with a genuine concern for the well-being of others and a resultant thickening of thin ties among "familiar strangers" within our neighborhoods. With this social phenomenon in mind, this critical commentary aims to explore how, in this time of crisis, neighborhood walking facilitates a rediscovery of our social connectedness as neighbors.

Keeping your distance

Undoubtedly, as a practical matter, anonymity necessarily characterizes the endless number of encounters we experience in modern urban life (Hirschauer, 2005). It is impossible to know everyone, so most social interactions among urban inhabitants in public spaces resemble something Goffman (1963) referred to as *civil inattention*, a normalized display of disinterestedness without contempt. Civil inattention, Goffman (1963, p. 84) explained, gives "to another enough visual notice to demonstrate that one appreciates that the other is present ... while at the next moment withdrawing one's attention." By being inconspicuous, users of public space make their intentions to avoid social interaction clear, thereby transforming public spaces into quasi-private ones (Cooper, 2007). Remaining unknown to others sidesteps any meaningful interaction to deter the possibility of "acquaintanceship" and inhibit any obligation produced by the encounter (Goffman, 1963, p. 112). Not surprisingly, then, treating each other like strangers in public—that is, maintaining social distance—normalizes strangeness among people (Hirschauer, 2005) to ultimately spawn our modern society of strangers.

By now, a widespread recognition pervades that tactics to reduce the spread of COVID-19, though commonly referred to as "social distancing," in actuality aim to minimize the physical distance associated with "copresence," the sociological term used to describe when people are "physically proximate, but socially distant" (Horgan, 2012, p. 608). We are copresent, in other words, when we occupy the same physical space at the same time, but remain aloof or disinterested to stay unknown to each other intentionally. Outward appearances may indicate two people are ignoring one another, but it "implie[s a] mutual understanding of the nature and degree of social distance by which the relationship ought to be characterized" (Horgan, 2012, p. 616). Given this state of interaction, Simmel (1971, p. 146) defined copresence as a synthesis of "nearness and remoteness." Accordingly, the copresence of strangers signifies "a social and spatial relation" (Marotta, 2012, p. 585).

As Klinenberg (1999, p. 242), noted, events such as a pandemic reveal "social conditions that are less visible, but nonetheless present in everyday life." Indeed, the emergence of the coronavirus makes perceptible how inattentive we are from those with whom we are copresent. Individuation and the desire for quasi-anonymity (Florida, 2002) appear to characterize modern communities of propinquity, giving rise to the widespread pervasiveness of relations of "familiar strangers" (Ahmed, 2000). While a

---

bridging our social distance. Can they last? *Toronto Star*. Retrieved from https://www.thestar.com/news/canada/2020/03/29/tiny-acts-of-solidarity-are-bridging-our-social-distance-can-they-last.html

stranger refers to "someone who has not been knowingly encountered before" (Cooper, 2007, p. 205), a *familiar stranger* denotes "an individual who is recognized from regular activities, but with whom one does not interact or communicate" (Jackson et al., 2017, p. 9). Also referred to as "invisible ties" or "nodding relationships," these anonymous, albeit recognizable social connections "become known over time and are no longer interchangeable" (Felder, 2020, pp. 7–8). Such relationships are quite common to our neighborhood experiences.

To be sure, neighborhoods represent familiar environments in which relationships with neighbors can span the spectrum of social ties, from strong to weak to invisible (Felder, 2020) or, put differently, from thick to thin. Neighbors can be close friends, acquaintances, or nominal individuals whom we fail to see at all (Felder, 2020; Rosenblum, 2016). They can also be negative or hostile. Whatever the nature of our ties, our expectations of our neighbors, as Rosenblum (2016, p. 11) suggested, is usually reduced to being nothing more than "decent folks." Decent here describes someone who acts respectful toward others, but remains at a friendly distance. The neighbors we identify in our neighborhoods register with us, not just because of their physical proximity to us, but also because we have *knowledge* of them. Consequently, some fit into the imagined geography of our neighborhood (Rosenblum, 2016), while many others do not. In my observation, the imagined geography of our neighborhoods has expanded with emergence of the global pandemic because of our need to connect socially during this time of crisis.

Bridging the distance

For many people affected by the pandemic, the physical isolation measures adopted to "flatten the curve," while aimed paternalistically at reducing exposure to the virus, threaten to exacerbate the already alarming pervasiveness of social isolation in our societies (Glover, 2018). Limiting mobility, restricting people to isolate at home (sometimes by themselves), and keeping them from seeing their family and friends in person can have damaging health consequences, for meaningful social ties and the support they provide boost our wellbeing in tremendous ways, as increasing evidence demonstrates (Holt-Lunstad et al., 2015). And so, ironically, while encouraged to engage in mislabeled "social distancing," people need more than ever to connect socially with others. And not just online; face-to-face interactions, even if from a safe distance, matter tremendously in terms of our health and wellbeing (Pinker, 2014).

Perhaps not surprisingly, then, the longing for connection, familiarity, and security during an extraordinary generational event like the current global pandemic drives people to interact with familiar strangers in their neighborhoods (Paulos & Goodman, 2004), the people closest and most accessible to them geographically. Far from being trivial, the familiar strangers in our neighborhoods provide a sense of familiarity, establish our geographic surroundings as "comfort zones" (Blokland & Nast, 2014, p. 1147), and contribute to a greater sense of security (Felder, 2020). Thickening thin neighborhood ties—that is, strengthening our weak and invisible neighborhood connections—allows neighbors to build their stockpiles of social capital to facilitate access to economic and informational resources (Gil-Rivas & Kilmer, 2016) as neighbors make themselves available to help if needed. In so doing, neighbors activate the taken-for-granted systems and hidden networks of support that exist within their neighborhoods. Engaging in greater civil attention in the public spaces of our neighborhoods, therefore, increase our capacity for resilience by improving our functioning and adaption during times of adversity (Norris et al., 2008).

Giving greater civil attention reduces social distance, even when socializing takes place six feet apart. When neighbors stop to talk with each other from across the street, they invite meaningful social interaction and create an opening to build a relationship, even if only superficially. They no longer see themselves as familiar strangers participating in random encounters. By noticing, acknowledging, and engaging with neighbors (i.e., neighboring), "feelings of solidarity, increases in emotional energy, creation of symbols, and feelings of morality all stem from [the] interaction" (Campos-Castillo & Hitlin, 2013, p. 170). Welcoming a neighborly interaction, even if only for a brief, but authentic, moment establishes a bond of mutual obligation, which opens the relationship up to future engagement and potential favors (Rosenblum, 2016).

The walking web

So what enables greater civil attention when our mobility is so limited by physical distancing measures? In my view, the sanctioned localized leisure activity of neighborhood walking plays a particularly meaningful role in facilitating neighboring—that is, active engagement in authentic social interactions with our neighbors. Not surprisingly, many people are taking up neighborhood walking during the pandemic to give themselves a change of scenery from their imposed self-isolation at home. Walking a neighborhood route, though perhaps undertaken for physical activity or fresh air, brings about increasing encounters with neighbors, including those who are previously unknown or recognized from regular activities, but with whom one does not typically interact or communicate. As a slow-moving activity that lets walkers "take in" their neighborhood as they walk through it, neighbors attend to what is going on in their neighborhood, thereby creating opportunities for social interaction and the strengthening of neighborhood ties. At worst, when neighbors repeatedly subject themselves to and observe each other while walking the neighborhood, the minimal social contact involved (e.g., nodding or a simple "hello") increases their public familiarity (Rietveld et al., 2019). The shared daily path of a neighborhood walk makes neighbors more recognizable. Moreover, neighbors who see each other routinely become more visible, potentially transforming into familiar strangers or possibly even acquaintances or eventually friends, as time goes by. Connections thicken as interactions become more regular and frequent. Stopping to ask if neighbors are okay and offering them assistance if needed reflects pro-social behavior that often arises in response to collective adversity (Dovidio et al., 2012). What begins as "routinized relations" established during casual walks can turn into something more meaningful. But even if walking only leads to greater familiarity with others, that familiarity forms the core of well-functioning neighborhoods (Rietveld et al., 2019, p. 306). Greater familiarity generates what Horgan (2012, p. 619) referred to as soft solidarity, a form of mutuality recognized and sustained without a requirement for explicit recognition. Ultimately, irrespective of the outcome, neighborhood walking expands our imagined geographies, making our neighborhoods better places to live.

Given the important role walking plays in facilitating interactions among neighbors during the pandemic, we ought to recognize sidewalks and neighborhood streets as important *social infrastructure*, physical places that shape the way neighbors interact. In his description of social infrastructure, Klinenberg (2018, p. 5) wrote:

> When social infrastructure is robust, it fosters contact, mutual support, and collaboration among friends and neighbors; when degraded, it inhibits social activity, leaving families and individuals to fend for themselves … People forge bonds in places that have healthy social infrastructures—not because they set out to build community, but because when people engage in sustained, recurrent interaction, particularly while doing things they enjoy, relationships inevitably grow.

Neighbors come to know each other, in other words, not necessarily because they intended to do so during their neighborhood walk, but because they live in neighborhoods where casual interactions are facilitated by the socio-material environment. Not surprisingly, then, neighborhood and mobility (e.g., walkability) characteristics support the quality of social interactions (van den Berg et al., 2017; for counter evidence see Du Toit et al. (2007), which explains why the observations I report in this commentary do not apply to every neighborhood. Admittedly, the poor physical and social conditions of social infrastructure in many neighborhoods makes neighboring prohibitive.

Interestingly, while leisure scholars may focus on the constraints produced by physical distancing measures, such as park and playground closures, employed during the pandemic, the limited opportunities available to people for public leisure introduce the notion of *affordances* to our field. Affordances recognize that an "environment is characterized by both [its] social and material aspects, and can be best understood as one socio-material environment offering many different possibilities for action, including possibilities for social interaction" (Rietveld et al., 2019, p. 300). Sidewalks, in this case, offer social affordances insofar as they make possible social interaction and cultural exchanges within neighborhoods, or what Jacobs (1961) referred to as "sidewalk ballet." They serve as what Wickes et al. (2019, p. 230) called "local exposure conduits" open to a relatively diverse range of users that support encounters with others and encourage social exchange. The spatial-temporal rhythms of neighborhood social life during the pandemic reflect social interactions that occur and reoccur on our neighborhood sidewalks and streets. As a result of our engagement with our local environment while walking, neighbors emerge from the background of our neighborhoods to affect the quality of our lives (Rosenblum, 2016).

The walk ahead

The pandemic caused by the spread of the coronavirus has the potential to change the character of our communities, including our neighborhoods. So far, the seeming upsurge in neighboring appears to be an encouraging sign. By offering greater civil attention to others in public spaces, neighbors seem to be strengthening their capacity to cope during the pandemic. Neighborhood walking facilitates these connections by bringing neighbors into contact with one another. As one of the few sanctioned localized leisure activities in which people can participate during the crisis, walking, though perhaps not engaged in for any other reason than to get outside and away from home, represents an important activity with tremendous individual and community benefits.

Of course, along with acts of neighborly kindness, I must acknowledge the incidence of more complicated moments of neighboring that have emerged during the pandemic, specifically calling out (i.e., "social distance shaming) and reporting to the authorities neighbors who are violating (or perhaps interpreting differently) physical distancing rules (i.e., virus vigilantes). While neighbors appear to be looking out for one another, they also appear to be engaging in surveillance because they fear their neighbors' actions will potentially expose them and vulnerable others to coronavirus. Sadly, under such circumstances, incivility replaces the civility associated with our civil inattention of the past, therein creating more tensions within a neighborhood.

Ultimately, crises can be turning points for communities. The coronavirus pandemic could well be the moment when neighbors rediscover one another, when cities reinvest in social infrastructure, and city policies enable more affordances to encourage positive social interaction. Alternatively, neighborhoods may revert back to isolation and passivity that characterized our communities prior to the pandemic or transition into landscapes of incivility in response to fear of transmission. With these outcomes in mind, the observations described in this commentary represent "an experiment without guarantees" (Amin, 2013, p. 7), for civilities can be "fragile and contingent" (Amin, 2013, p. 6). Whatever the case, while there is no assurance that the resurgence of neighboring described in this commentary will survive the pandemic, it warrants some recognition that, at least early on during this crisis, leisure affordances played a role in strengthening social connectedness in many neighborhoods.

References

Ahmed, S. (2000). *Strange encounters: Embodied others in post-coloniality*. Routledge.

Amin, A. (2013). Land of strangers. *Identities*, *20*(1), 1–8. https://doi.org/10.1080/1070289X.2012.732544

Blokland, T., & Nast, J. (2014). From public familiarity to comfort zone: The relevance of absent ties for belonging in Berlin's mixed neighbourhoods. *International Journal of Urban and Regional Research*, *38*(4), 1142–1160. https://doi.org/10.1111/1468-2427.12126

Campos-Castillo, C., & Hitlin, S. (2013). Copresence: Revisiting a building block for social interaction theories. *Sociological Theory*, *31*(2), 168–192. https://doi.org/10.1177/0735275113489811

Cooper, D. (2007). Being in public: the threat and promise of stranger contact. *Law & Social Inquiry*, *32*(1), 203–232. https://doi.org/10.1111/j.1747-4469.2007.00056.x

Dovidio, J. F., Piliavin, J. A., Schroeder, D. A., & Penner, L. A. (2012). *The social psychology of prosocial behavior*. Psychology Press.

Du Toit, L., Cerin, E., Leslie, E., & Owen, N. (2007). Does walking in the neighbourhood enhance local sociability? *Urban Studies*, *44*(9), 1677–1695. https://doi.org/10.1080/00420980701426665

Felder, M. (2020). Strong, weak and invisible ties: a relational perspective on urban coexistence. *Sociology*. https://doi.org/10.1111/0038038519895938

Florida, R. (2002). *The rise of the creative class … and how it's transforming work, leisure, community, & everyday life*. Basic Books.

Gil-Rivas, V., & Kilmer, R. P. (2016). Building community capacity and fostering disaster resilience. *Journal of Clinical Psychology*, *72*(12), 1318–1332. https://doi.org/10.1002/jclp.22281

Glover, T. D. (2018). All the lonely people: Social isolation and the promise and pitfalls of leisure. *Leisure Sciences, 40*(1–2), 25–35. https://doi.org/10.1080/01490400.2017.1376017

Goffman, E. (1963). *Behavior in public places: Notes on the social organization of gatherings.* Free Press of Glencoe.

Hirschauer, S. (2005). On doing being a stranger: The practical constitution of civil inattention. *Journal for the Theory of Social Behaviour, 35*(1), 41–67. https://doi.org/10.1111/j.0021-8308.2005.00263.x

Holt-Lunstad, J., Smith, T. B., Baker, M., Harris, T., & Stephenson, D. (2015). Loneliness and social isolation as risk factors for mortality. *Perspectives on Psychological Science : A Journal of the Association for Psychological Science, 10*(2), 227–237. https://doi.org/10.1177/1745691614568352

Horgan, M. (2012). Strangers and strangership. *Journal of Intercultural Studies, 33*(6), 607–622. https://doi.org/10.1080/07256868.2012.735110

Jackson, L., Harris, C., & Valentine, G. (2017). Rethinking concepts of the strange and the stranger. *Social & Cultural Geography, 18*(1), 1–15. https://doi.org/10.1080/14649365.2016.1247192

Klinenberg, E. (1999). Denaturalizing disaster: A social autopsy of the 1995 Chicago heat wave. *Theory and Society, 28*(2), 239–295. https://doi.org/10.1023/A:1006995507723

Klinenberg, E. (2018). *Palaces for the people: How to build a more equal and united society.* Random House.

Marotta, V. (2012a). Theories of strangers: Introduction. *Journal of Intercultural Studies, 33*(6), 585–590. https://doi.org/10.1080/07256868.2012.739133

Marotta, V. (2012b). Georg Simmel, the stranger and the sociology of knowledge. *Journal of Intercultural Studies, 33*(6), 675–689. https://doi.org/10.1080/07256868.2012.739136

Norris, F. H., Stevens, S. P., Pfefferbaum, B., Wyche, K. F., & Pfefferbaum, R. L. (2008). Community resilience as a metaphor, theory, set of capacities and strategy for disaster readiness. *American Journal of Community Psychology, 41*(1–2), 127–150. https://doi.org/10.1007/s10464-007-9156-6

Paulos, E., & Goodman, E. (2004, April). *The familiar stranger: anxiety, comfort, and play in public places* [Paper presentation]. Proceedings of the SIGCHI Conference on Human Factors in Computing Systems (pp. 223–230).

Pinker, S. (2014). *The village effect: How face-to-face contact can make us healthier and happier.* Random House Canada.

Rietveld, E., Rietveld, R., & Martens, J. (2019). Trusted strangers: social affordances for social cohesion. *Phenomenology and the Cognitive Sciences, 18*(1), 299–316. https://doi.org/10.1007/s11097-017-9554-7

Rosenblum, N. L. (2016). *Good neighbors: The democracy of everyday life in America.* Princeton University Press.

Simmel, G. (1971). The stranger. In D. N. Levine (ed.), *Georg Simmel: On individuality and social forms* (pp. 143–150). University of Chicago Press.

van den Berg, P., Sharmeen, F., & Weijs-Perrée, M. (2017). On the subjective quality of social Interactions: Influence of neighborhood walkability, social cohesion and mobility choices. *Transportation Research Part A: policy and Practice, 106*, 309–319. https://doi.org/10.1016/j.tra.2017.09.021

Wickes, R., Zahnow, R., Corcoran, J., & Hipp, J. R. (2019). Neighbourhood social conduits and resident social cohesion. *Urban Studies, 56*(1), 226–248. https://doi.org/10.1177/0042098018780617

Rural-Urban Interdependencies: Thinking through the Implications of Space, Leisure, Politics and Health

Kyle Rich

ABSTRACT
The collective experience of social distancing will undoubtedly have implications for our social, cultural, and political practices. In this critical commentary, I consider the implications of these experiences by focusing on rural-urban relationships in Canada. Drawing from accounts published in online newspapers, I reflect on how social distancing highlights the interdependencies of urban and rural Canada and the role of space and leisure in shaping our broader social and political discourse. Reflecting on issues related to class, space, mobility, and freedom of choice, I suggest that rural-urban interdependencies is a productive framework for considering these relationships and how we might rethink them moving forward. In conclusion, I offer hopeful speculations on how social distancing may indeed bring us closer together.

It also illustrated a social dynamic playing out across Canada, from the Kootenays to the Outaouais, as the affluent take advantage of their private rural isolation opportunities, local snitches call in reports of city folk, mayors try to keep a lid on it all with earnest appeals to social conscience, and provincial governments impose travel bans that fall short of enforceable legal orders (Brean, 2020).

On Friday, March 27th, 2020, Highway 400 north of Toronto, Ontario, was packed. Despite clear directives from the provincial government, many wealthy residents of southern Ontario were headed north, to cottage country, to ride out the period of social distancing at their second homes, cottages, and cabins scattered in the rural parts of central and northern Ontario. Unfortunately, these regions lack both the health infrastructure and supply chain networks to support extra populations outside of typical tourist seasons. This however, did not discourage wealthy residents of southern Ontario from heading north. These unprecedented times provide us with an opportunity to critically reflect on the state of urban-rural[1] relationships in Canada, North America, and indeed across the world. In this critical commentary, I consider the implications of

---

[1]There are many definitions used to define rural across disciplines. It is beyond the scope of this paper to delineate these thoroughly here. I use rural broadly to refer to areas located outside of urban centres. It should also be noted that I do not use rural in reference to Indigenous communities in Canada. The history Indigenous peoples in Canada extends far beyond our contemporary urban and rural definitions, and Indigenous communities have social, cultural, an political issues which are distinct (yet sometimes intertwined) with other parts of what we now call rural Canada.

space and leisure in shaping the relationship between urban and rural communities. I frame the commentary with the idea of rural-urban interdependencies (Caffyn & Dahlström, 2005) and discuss the roles of leisure and tourism in shaping rural communities as spaces which are desired for consumption framed by a poorly developed understanding of the circumstances under which rural citizens live. Drawing from examples published in online newspapers, I discuss the spatial implications of leisure and how leisure practices shape our understanding of rural regions and the implications for broader social and political discourse.

Leisure and Urban-Rural relationships

Tensions surrounding the state of urban-rural relationships have been building for a number of years. In Canada, rural spaces and landscapes were fundamental in settlement and development histories, and these spaces continue to play an important role in Canadian ideas if citizenship, gender, and belonging (see Laurendeau, 2020). However, following processes of urbanization and modernization, rural spaces play an increasingly precarious role. Framed with the rise of neoliberal policy agendas, rural regions have experienced: economic restructuring (Halseth & Ryser, 2006); a loss of resources and social infrastructure (Markey & Heisler, 2011), and; outmigrations of youth (Macdonald, Sinclair, and Walsh, 2012). These changes occurred as the world was becoming increasingly interconnected through globalized economies and widespread access to the internet - which has yet to be realized in much of rural Canada. Subsequently, many rural areas have redefined themselves through economic diversification and innovation, challenging our often idyllic perceptions of rural as quiet, wholesome, hinterlands (Yarwood, 2005).

In many ways, leisure is implicated in these rural transformations. Leisure serves as a context for families to learn about rural heritage, but also to prepare for uncertain futures (Trussell & Shaw, 2009). Sport clubs in rural communities function as important sites of sociability where social infrastructure is otherwise lacking (Mair, 2009). And, sport and leisure practices are implicated in constructing ideas of rurality and community (Rich, Bean, & Apramian, 2014; Rich & Misener, 2021). Important for this commentary, tourism emerged as a way that many rural communities are redefining themselves and re-invigorating their economies in response to regional, national, and global transformations (George et al., 2009). The mobilities or flows of people to and from rural spaces are inextricably bound up with the relationship between urban and rural citizens. Indeed, cottagers, tourists, and weekend warriors (among other monikers) occupy a paradoxical role in regards to their social and environmental impacts in rural areas (Lait, 2018; Michels, 2017). While flows of people bring resources which are important for rural economies, they also impact the social, cultural, and environmental resources in rural communities in complex and sometimes insidious ways.

Divisions to interdependencies

Unpacking the current status of rural-urban relationships in Canada is no simple task given the diversity of both rural and urban areas in Canada. However, similar to other countries around the world, the tensions of these relationships have recently been highlighted in the spatial dimensions of national politics (Speer & Jivani, 2017). This idea is often called the urban-rural divide and it is reflected in the geographical divisions of intra-national culture, politics, and social life - what political commentator Barone (2017) calls the politics of *capital vs. countryside*. Although opinion surveys suggest that differences are more regional than neatly organized along an urban-rural dichotomy (Parkin, 2019), and the narrative presented is certainly not applicable to all regions, decades of uneven development, austerity measures, globalization, and the rise of cosmopolitanism have created very different social and cultural practices in urban and rural parts of Canada.

These problems however, are not new. Rather, they are old issues repackaged in a new temporal and political context. Now often discussed in terms of western (Canada) alienation, these sentiments informed a political movement to separate the northern portion of the province of Ontario in the 1940s - a movement that is still alive today as some feel as though the north is "treated like a colony... as miners to get the ore" (Brean, 2018). The apparent divisions between urban and rural Canada stem from economic and political systems which symbolically situate powerful political decision makers in urban centers which are physically (and socially) far away from rural citizens. It is not surprising that rural ways of life are then positioned as backwards or outdated and conversely, urban people - sometimes referred to as *citiots* (Rosewater, 2017) - are loathed for their inability to adapt their lifestyle to include basic rural skills and social practices. These tensions or divides, some might argue, are prominently reinforced during the great seasonal waves of migration when urban Canadians flock to rural hinterlands for their leisure practices (Michels, 2017).

In this commentary, I challenge the idea of the urban-rural divide and echo calls of planners and regional development scholars to consider these issues as rural-urban interdependencies. Caffyn and Dahlström (2005) suggest that urban-rural relationships are complex and that compartmentalizing urban and rural policy issues does a disservice to understanding these relationships. Rather, we might consider the relationships as complex layers of flows and counter-flows of people, resources, and ideas. I draw from these discussions to examine the events emanating from the social distancing directives imposed in Ontario in the spring of 2020. Drawing from examples published in online newspapers, I provide a commentary on these flows. In considering these interdependencies, I reflect how these events can help us consider the roles of leisure in situating and reinforcing interdependencies in our broader socio-political discourse.

Outcomes of social distancing directives

The directives imposed in early 2020 were unprecedented. The spatial implications however, are particularly interesting. As governments and public health officials released clear messaging to "stay home," many wealthy Canadians clearly perceived their rural cottages, getaways, and summer retreats as second "homes." As a result, rural areas were undeniably perceived as a sanctuary and classist issues surrounding these leisure spaces became evident. While many regions accustomed to seasonal flows of temporary residents appealed to these residents to stay away, it was evident that people were continuing to access these spaces recreationally (Flanagan, 2020; Martin, 2020). Within these broader discussions (e.g., see comments sections), it is clear that, for many urban dwellers, the individual right to property (even a recreational one) trumps a more collective or pluralistic obligation to protect (rural) citizens who are already vulnerable due to insufficient supply chains and meager health care capacity (Society of Rural Physicians, 2020).

Following these initial events, several policy responses were introduced. At the local level, communities enacted creative responses such as municipal orders directing tradespeople to refrain from providing services such as turning on water to seasonal properties (Gowan, 2020). Provincially, Ontario and Québec imposed restrictions on short-term rentals to curb unnecessary flows of people to rural areas (Gray, 2020), and several maritime provinces (with a high proportion of rural municipalities and aging populations) implemented border checkpoints in order to prevent unnecessary or social interprovincial travel (Gollom, 2020). However, as many rural residents learned, at the local level, these directives or regulations fall short of being enforceable (Brean, 2020).

For a (albeit brief) moment, rural regions and their relationship with urban centers appeared to be front and center in provincial politics. The outcomes of which, highlight the ways that urban and rural regions are intertwined or interdependent. Slowed flows of people through rural spaces are impacting economies (MacDonald, 2020), and tourist regions are bracing for what could be a devastating summer season. Small businesses in the agri-food sector (many of which occupy rural spaces) have stepped up production to address deficiencies in our (often globalized) food systems (Duchesne, 2020). In some cases, anonymous urban donors have even made substantial contributions to help address the lack of capacity in health systems in rural areas (National Post, 2020). Collectively, some of the fundamental issues leading to the inequalities experienced by many rural citizens are being given airtime and serious consideration in politics as well as popular media.

Moving forward: reflections on space, leisure, and interdependencies

The collective experience of social distancing will undoubtedly have implications for our social, cultural, and political realities moving forward. In this commentary, I have attempted to highlight some of the spatial aspects of these implications by focusing particularly on rural-urban relationships. In conclusion, I offer a few final reflections on space, leisure, and urban-rural interdependencies.

First and foremost, these events have highlighted spatial issues related to class and leisure. At the crux of these issues is the freedom of choice inherent in leisure pursuits. While cottagers/tourists have the choice of where to distance themselves from others, many rural citizens do not. Without these choices, empty shelves at grocery stores and overtaxed health systems are a much more concerning issue. Conversely, choices not to visit rural areas during expected tourist seasons pose a serious threat to rural economies and ways of life. Therefore, while flows in and out of rural areas are essential for many communities, we must recognize issues related to agency and how we can value diverse contributions that rural areas make to our broader economic and social systems and choose to support these regions in normal times.

Second, it is apparent from much of the discussion surrounding the issues identified above that there is clear lack of understanding and empathy for the implications of rural-urban interdependencies. Urban folks, in search of their weekend getaways, do not appreciate the real impacts of decades of policy which have disproportionately impacted social services in rural regions. Rather, rural landscapes are spaces ripe for consumption and ownership. Rural folks in some cases, have also bought into austerity politics and may espouse an ethos of individualism and even libertarianism that would see a further reduction in social services. They also may view tourists or seasonal residents as commodities which they hope to turn on and off like a supply chain that is no longer wanted when times are tough. Both groups need to recognize the complexity of their relationships and value them accordingly. This may involve a shift to thinking about these relationships as symbiotic rather than exploitative.

Collectively, these issues are reflective of the broader neoliberal context in which they emerged, of which leisure of course, is not immune (Arai & Pedlar, 2003). In this context, flows of people and resources in and out of rural areas are often transactional and viewed solely as an opportunity for individual gain (e.g., a source of income, a space to enjoy, or a new community and sense of belonging). However, these trying times offer an opportunity to re-think the nature of these relationships and the impacts of leisure on our broader social and political discourse. It is my hope that we emerge from this period of social distancing with a new appreciation for the interdependent nature of urban and rural Canada and the impacts that leisure choices have on social and political systems. There are several ways in which this might be achieved. Cottagers/tourists might come to be considered as valuable members of rural communities, whose contributions to community life are measured and valued. We might find ways to provide equitable access to social services in rural areas, even if they cost more and require a disproportionate contribution on behalf of urban citizens. And finally, we might develop platforms of communication where both urban and rural perspectives can be heard in order to develop mutual understandings. Rather than distinct urban and rural classes, it is my hope that these experiences lead to a reinvestment in a common good, a reevaluation of rural spaces, and a recognition that leisure practices associated with rural regions can become a mechanism for establishing common ground and mutual understanding.

Acknowledgement

I would like to thank Dylan Odd for his insightful feedback of an early draft of this commentary as well as the anonymous reviewers for their comments and feedback.

References

Arai, S., & Pedlar, A. (2003). Moving beyond individualism in leisure theory: A critical analysis of concepts of community and social engagement. *Leisure Studies*, *22*(3), 185–202. https://doi. org/10.1080/026143603200075489

Barone, M. (2017). The new/old politics of capital vs. countryside. *National Review*. https://www. nationalreview.com/2017/04/le-pen-brexit-trump-colombia-farc-elections-outsiders-countryside-elites-capital-establishment/

Brean, J. (2018). Northern Ontario's dream to secede, reborn: 'We're treated like a colony.' *National Post*. https://nationalpost.com/feature/northern-ontarios-dream-to-secede-reborn-were-treated-like-a-colony

Brean, J. (2020). 'They are here': Weekend warriors dodge COVID-19 and shaming by hiding out in cottage country. *National Post*. https://nationalpost.com/news/0415-na-cottage

Caffyn, A., & Dahlström, M. (2005). Urban–rural interdependencies: joining up policy in practice. *Regional Studies*, 39(3), 283–296. https://doi.org/10.1080/0034340050086580

Flanagan, R. (2020). Don't head to your cottage to wait out COVID-19 pandemic, Canadians warned. *CTV News*. https://www.ctvnews.ca/health/coronavirus/don-t-head-to-your-cottage-to-wait-out-covid-19-pandemic-canadians-warned-1.4873267

George, E. W., Mair, H., & Reid, D. G. (2009). *Rural tourism development: Localism and cultural change*. Channel View Publications.

Gollom, M. (2020). Many provinces, territories enforcing border checkpoints and travel restrictions. *CBC News*. https://www.cbc.ca/news/canada/coronavirus-checkpoints-travel-restrictions-border-province-1.5522467

Gowan, R. (2020). Huron-Kinloss issues order against turning on water for cottagers. *Owen Sound Sun Times*. https://www.owensoundsuntimes.com/news/local-news/huron-kinloss-issues-order-against-turning-on-water-for-cottagers

Gray, J. (2020). Ontario joins Quebec in restricting short-term rentals during coronavirus pandemic. *The Globe and Mail*. https://www.theglobeandmail.com/canada/toronto/article-ontario-joins-quebec-in-restricting-short-term-rentals-during/

Halseth, G., & Ryser, L. (2006). Trends in service delivery: Examples from rural and small town Canada, 1998–2005. *Journal of Rural and Community Development*, 1(1), 69–90.

Lait, M. (2018). The paradox of nature and elite second homes: Examining the eco-social impacts of Meech Lake cottagers in Gatineau Park, Québec. *Annals of Leisure Research*, 21(3), 302–323. https://doi.org/10.1080/11745398.2018.1426366

Laurendeau, J. (2020). "The stories that will make a difference aren't the easy ones": Outdoor recreation, the wilderness ideal, and complicating settler mobility. *Sociology of Sport Journal*, 37(2), 85–95. [online first]. https://doi.org/10.1123/ssj.2019-0128

MacDonald, R. (2020). Rural Maritime communities hurt by a lack of traffic due to COVID-19. *CTV News*. https://atlantic.ctvnews.ca/rural-maritime-communities-hurt-by-lack-of-traffic-due-to-covid-19-1.4883426

MacDonald, M., Sinclair, P., & Walsh, D. (2012). Labour migration and mobility in Newfoundland: Social transformation and community in three rural areas. In J. R. Parkins & M. G. Reed (Eds), *Social transformation in rural Canada: community, culture and collective action* (pp. 110–130). UBC Press.

Mair, H. (2009). Club life: Third place and shared leisure in rural Canada. *Leisure Sciences*, 31(5), 450–465. https://doi.org/10.1080/01490400903199740

Markey, S., & Heisler, K. (2011). Getting a fair share: Regional development in a rapid boom-bust rural setting. *Canadian Journal of Regional Studies/Revue Canadien Sciences Régionale*, 33(3), 49–62.

Martin, M. (2020). Southwestern Ontario cottage country pleads for outsiders to stay away amid COVID-19. *London Free Press*. https://lfpress.com/news/local-news/southwestern-ontario-cottage-country-pleads-for-outsiders-to-stay-away-amid-covid-19/

Michels, J. (2017). *Permanent weekend: nature, leisure, and rural gentrification*. McGill-Queen's Press.

National Post. (2020). Anonymous Muskoka cottagers donate $135k to local hospital's emergency response fund. *North Bay Nugget*. https://www.nugget.ca/news/anonymous-muskoka-cottagers-donate-135k-to-local-hospitals-covid-19-emergency-response-fund/wcm/34668271-ecdb-4167-8f52-9b0c1e26749e?video_autoplay=true&fbclid=IwAR1dF3oGQNQ4O9lTau_8T6qOeIT6Tt346pswj-rYpeENuXQ5Vi805ptXzQ4

Parkin, A. (2019). Is there an urban-rural divide in Canada? *Policy Options*. https://policyoptions.irpp.org/magazines/october-2019/is-there-an-urban-rural-divide-in-canada/

Rich, K., Bean, C., & Apramian, Z. (2014). Boozing, brawling, and community building: Sport-facilitated community development in a rural Ontario community. *Leisure/Loisir, 38*(1), 73–92. https://doi.org/10.1080/14927713.2014.933511

Rich, K. A., & Misener, L. (2021). Resisting, reproducing, and recreating rurality: Leisure in contemporary rural communities. In T. D. Glover & E. K. Sharpe (Eds.), *Leisure communities: Rethinking mutuality, collective expression, and belonging in the new century.* Routledge.

Rosewater, H. (2017). How to behave now that you are upstate: A guide for citiots. *Hudson Valley One.* https://hudsonvalleyone.com/2017/06/13/how-to-behave-now-that-youre-upstate-a-guide-for-citiots/

Society of Rural Physicians. (2020). *Rural Emergency Departments & COVID-19.* [press release] https://www.srpc.ca/resources/Documents/PDFs/CAEP%20SRPC%20Rural%20ED%20COVID%20statement.pdf

Speer, S., Jivani, J. (2017). The urban/rural divide and a more inclusive Canada. *Policy Opinions.* https://policyoptions.irpp.org/magazines/june-2017/the-urbanrural-divide-and-a-more-inclusive-canada/

Trussell, D. E., & Shaw, S. M. (2009). Changing family life in the rural context: Women's perspectives of family leisure on the farm. *Leisure Sciences, 31*(5), 434–449. https://doi.org/10.1080/01490400903199468

Yarwood, R. (2005). Beyond the rural idyll: images, countryside change and geography. *Geography, 90*(1), 19–31.

From Gym Rat to Rock Star! Negotiating Constraints to Leisure Experience via a Strengths and Substitutability Approach

D J Williams

ABSTRACT

This commentary shares my recent personal experience of having to find a new and realistic way to strength-train, my longstanding serious physically-active leisure preference, during the recent gym closures and widespread social restrictions in place due to the coronavirus (COVID-19) pandemic. While thoroughly considering how to negotiate specific leisure experience constraints, I incorporate familiar concepts and processes from the strengths perspective, identity, and leisure substitutability theories. The result of this process led to a creative solution that retained, or perhaps even amplified, my motivation and ability to continue to progress at my preferred serious leisure activity while also experiencing the activity quite differently.

Background: my strength-training as serious leisure

During the summer of 1984, at the age of 17 years, I began strength-training in order to add some bodyweight to my skinny frame. For the first several weeks, I struggled to lift relatively light weights. However, I quickly came to love this new physically active leisure pursuit. Over the next few months or so, my intention changed from simply adding a bit of bodyweight and then quitting the activity to incorporating strength-training as an enjoyable exercise staple. I discovered that while the physical benefits were apparent, the psychological benefits were probably more salient and personally meaningful. My gym routines seemed to help mitigate occasional bouts of melancholy and depression while regularly adding feelings of confidence and empowerment. There were social benefits, too. I have made dozens of new friends, fellow "gym rats," simply due to sharing the same leisure space and enjoying a similar challenging brand of physical fitness.

For well over 30 years now, strength training at the gym has functioned for me, personally, as a primary serious leisure activity, which according to Stebbins' (2001, 2015) classic attributes, is associated with having particular costs, acquiring specialized knowledge and skill, requiring perseverance, developing in a career-like process, becoming an identity, having a unique ethos, and providing durable benefits and rewards. In August 2010, when I became a grandfather at age 43, I celebrated by doing a particularly strenuous two hour workout, prior to concluding that day with a 15 mile jog. Perhaps somewhat arrogantly, I was hell-bent on staying as fit as I could be, even as a grandpa. However, as I age, I have tried to apply wisdom in modifying my training by resisting urges to lift extremely heavy weight, increasing recovery time, paying closer attention to diet, and changing my training ratio to higher percentages of cross-training and cardio exercises.

Leisure constraints: insights on negotiating desired experience

The rapid spread of COVID-19 has obviously necessitated lifestyle changes to people worldwide. Tragically, many people are struggling simply to survive. Probably like most of us, I did not anticipate a time in my life when businesses, schools, churches, and various economic and social entities across the globe would shut down and the economy would abruptly halt. In considering my typical daily routine and acknowledging my particular position of privilege, I am reminded that I am extremely fortunate compared to hundreds of millions of other people. Besides privilege associated with social positioning (White, middle-class, male, professor, etc.), my physical health is excellent. I am relatively financially secure, and unlike millions, my employment continues. There would, of course, be some minor personal inconveniences—regular travel to cities would be postponed, my daily visit to the coffee shop would end, and more work would need to be done at home instead of campus and community spaces.

It was when my gym closed that I felt a more significant sense of uneasiness to my lifestyle. Of course, I realize that I can survive without any gym, yet that particular space is my leisure staple and has been a huge part of who I am for most of my life. It is a significant part of my lifestyle and an inseparable part of my personal identity, and the gym has helped me cope with the difficult stretches that inevitably occur from time to time in life. Would my mental health now suddenly diminish? What about my social network? Perhaps I can become more active on social media, but for me, personally, it's not the same as being together in person, engaged in the same meaningful activity, with those also who share this salient leisure identity. Of course, I realized that purchasing weights and/or doing pushups and various basic body exercises at home was an option to negotiate the structural constraint of strength-training as a simple *activity,* yet such possibilities were associated with additional problems. Barbells, dumbbells, and basic equipment cost money, and more importantly, require space to use and store, which I don't really have. Much more importantly, I am not motivated to exercise at home, perhaps because I spend so much time engaged in other aspects of my life there, including intentional relaxation and rest. For whatever reason, I have never enjoyed exercising at home and just can't get myself to do it.

In thinking about various constraint negotiation strategies, I gained new appreciation for considering the differences in serious leisure, in this case my own strength-training, as a basic *activity* versus serious leisure as a complex *experience* (Gallant et al., 2013).

Perhaps common social meanings have emphasized fundamental kinesiology of strength-training, while perhaps neglecting other, more dynamic and multidimensional, details. At the same time, I am aware that classic leisure substitutability theory (Iso-Ahola, 1986) also focuses on leisure activity (behavior), rather than experience, and my present situation seemingly required substituting the desired leisure experience of strength-training in a gym environment but not necessarily the raw activity itself. I began to realize that successfully negotiating my current leisure-as-experience constraints would be more challenging than considering strength-training as a fundamental activity. Put simply, leisure meanings and contexts matter, sometimes substantially, and are inextricably connected to personal motivation and leisure costs and benefits.

Considering the strengths perspective in constraints negotiation and substitutability

In trying to brainstorm a solution to negotiating a structural constraint to frequent gym attendance, thus preventing my strength-training as typical leisure experience, I first focused on retaining engagement as a simple activity. I did not have to stop strength-training altogether, but find a very different, yet enjoyable, way to do it. The far edge of my back lawn has a partial boundary made of rocks, which I considered lifting for resistance to keep by back muscles strong. I could also do pull-ups on the post of an old clothesline, and pushups for chest muscles, though I preferred much more resistance. However, working out at home doing exercises without sufficient resistance was not at all appealing. I needed to think more creatively to try to find an appealing experience. I decided to apply a familiar strengths perspective (Saleebey, 2013) to the negotiation process, which is consistent with both positive psychology and leisure science (see Williams et al., 2020). The core premise of the strengths perspective is that individuals, families, and communities all have existing strengths, assets, and resources that can be identified and utilized (at those specific levels) to solve problems that may arise at any of those levels, which is in contrast to focusing directly on problems and deficits (Saleebey, 2013). In my case, the primary question became: What assets and positive attributes do I have personally, in my family and circle of friends, and in my community that can be identified and harnessed to create a new, appealing, version of strength-training experience?

Applying the strengths perspective is routine for me. In fact, I guide my students through this process every semester as part of their required coursework. I am well-aware of several of my own key personal strengths, including self-motivation, personal awareness, self-management, creativity, and being comfortable in social situations or alone. I realize that my other leisure interests, such as hiking and reading, can also be useful strengths. Obvious strengths in my community include living in a geographic region with abundant natural resources, terrific outdoor leisure opportunities, friendly community residents, and a low cost of living. These community strengths are why I continue to live and work in this small city with its clean air and beautiful mountain landscapes. Much of my personal leisure is tightly connected to these place-specific benefits.

In theoretically exploring leisure substitutability, Harmon and Woosnam (2018) recently emphasized the importance of thoroughly considering past experience in future leisure choices, while showing how different leisure activities may be connected. After evaluating my numerous available strengths at multiple levels, along with my past and present leisure repertoire, I arrived at an exciting solution: I would become a rock star! Although the thought of lifting small rocks in my backyard was not appealing, that initial thought did spark some creative possibilities. In the vast nearby foothills, where I have often hiked, is a long mesa containing concentrations of innumerable igneous rocks and boulders of every shape, size, and mass. That natural environment is familiar, rugged, and unique, and I can enjoy the challenge of finding and selecting the perfect sized rocks to move in various ways to bring physical and psychological satisfaction. That remote area, only ten minutes from my house, is my new "gym."

By combining my love of outdoor leisure interests, including frequent hiking, with the creative challenge of finding the perfect rocks to lift in various ways, I could really enjoy the experience of strength-training in a whole new way. With rocks, I can carefully execute modified squats, deadlifts, rows, bicep curls, tricep extensions, and various presses. Additionally, I have long enjoyed listening to hard rock music, as a casual leisure preference. I grew up learning to play drums, so connecting different meanings of the same word (rock) across different leisure activities and contexts served to connect multiple leisure identities, which then added fun and novelty to the new strength-training experience. It's now been a month since my transition from my familiar indoor gym to my new outdoor workout space, which I dubbed "Rocky's." While considerable care is, of course, required to move heavy rocks while avoiding injury, I am very much enjoying this new version of my physically active leisure staple. So far, I have incurred only one minor injury in my quest to become a rock star—accidentally smashing the tip of my ring finger while slightly miscalculating the position of a rock when setting it down on the hard ground. A rare smashed fingertip seems to be one of the few noteworthy costs of my trying to become a rock star!

Conclusion

Widespread protective measures necessitated to prevent the spread of COVID-19 have, of course, introduced substantial constraints to numerous leisure opportunities. Like millions of people worldwide, these barriers have impacted my leisure repertoire significantly. I realized that although I could find a way to continue engaging in a preferred serious leisure activity, specifically strength-training; current structural constraints necessitated trying to find a way to negotiate leisure constraints attached to preferred experience. Similarly, although substituting an entirely new leisure activity was not necessary, what became necessary was to substitute numerous, detailed, qualitative features of the same basic activity. A familiarity with constraints and negotiation (see Schneider, 2016) and classic substitutability (Iso-Ahola, 1986) theories was valuable in implementing a creative process to explore potential solutions.

In considering the complexity of serious leisure experience relative to activity (behavior), Gallant et al. (2013) insightfully point out the need for awareness regarding the impact of sociopolitical context of leisure experience. They note that leisure experience, as a concept, is socially constructed within discourses of gender, sexuality, race, class that operate normatively within societal institutions and structures (Gallant et al., 2013). In addition to political and discursive approaches, scholars have also approached conceptualizing leisure experience via phenomenological and social psychological approaches (see Kivel et al., 2009). Thus, Kivel et al. (2009) suggest that diverse theories and methodologies are needed to address the complexity of leisure experience.

Because of the current need to explore the complexity of leisure experience via diverse methodologies and theoretical approaches, it seems to me that the strengths perspective would be particularly valuable in helping individuals negotiate a variety of potential constraints to leisure as experience. Put more directly, the strengths perspective can be applied across diverse theories and methodologies that inform an understanding of experience. Indeed, potential strengths can seem endless. For example, there are strengths pertaining to individuals, their biology, personalities and identities; there are strengths related to interpersonal relationships, families, and social systems. Communities, organizations, physical and geographic environments also can be assessed for strengths that can be harnessed to help negotiate constraints to desired leisure experience. Various narratives and discourses have limitations, but also potential strengths and value that can be positively recognized and utilized. Of course, the major strength of the strengths perspective is its breadth, yet this breadth may simultaneously function as its primary limitation. Nevertheless, the strengths perspective can be valuable in helping people begin to creatively re-think and re-assess situations when constraints to desired leisure experience subjectively warrant negotiation. Perhaps I am a slow learner, but regardless, my multidisciplinary expertise occasionally produces new insights to ponder.

References

Gallant, K., Arai, S., & Smale, B. (2013). Celebrating, challenging, and re-envisioning serious leisure. *Leisure/Loisir*, *37*(2), 91–109.

Harmon, J., & Woosnam, K. (2018). Extending the leisure substitutability concept. *Annals of Leisure Research*, *21*(4), 424–439.

Iso-Ahola, S. E. (1986). A theory of substitutability of leisure behavior. *Leisure Sciences*, *8*(4), 367–389.

Kivel, B. D., Johnson, C. W., & Scraton, S. (2009). (Re)Theorizing leisure, experience, and race. *Journal of Leisure Research* , *41*(4), 473–493.

Saleebey, D. (2013). *The strengths perspective in social work practice* (5th ed.). Allyn & Bacon.

Schneider, I. E. (2016). Leisure constraints and negotiation: Highlights from the journey past, present, and future. In G. J. Walker, D. Scott, & M. Stodolska (Eds.), *Leisure matters: The state and future of leisure studies* (pp. 151–161). Venture.

Stebbins, R. A. (2001). *New directions in the theory and research of serious leisure*. Edwin Mellen Press.

Stebbins, R. A. (2015). *Serious leisure: A perspective for our time*. Transaction.

Williams, D J, Prior, E. E., & Vincent, J.(2020). Positive sexuality as a guide for leisure research and practice addressing sexual interests and behaviors. *Leisure Sciences*, *42*(3–4), 275–288.

Leisure Matters: Cross Continent Conversations in a Time of Crisis

Mark Havitz, Mark P. Pritchard, and Frédéric Dimanche

ABSTRACT

Months after COVID-19 emerged as a newsmaker in Asia, a new strain of March Madness emerged in North America. Incredulity followed as leisure activities, hallowed as venues and expressions of individual and collective identity were closed. Freedoms, real and perceived, were curtailed. Like others, we sought to maintain social connections. For the first time in decades, our weekly on-line conversations became normative. Two authors remain working to sustain the academy's work during this crisis and the other is retired. Spatially we reside in a major metropolitan area of 6 million, a small west coast college town, and a Great Lakes region vacation community. Our discussion connects leisure research and the context of basic rights that North Americans have long taken for granted. This commentary emerged from integrated discussion regarding how the crisis affects and may change leisure behavior from multiple perspectives.

A world-wide pandemic was declared on March 11, 2020 by the World Health Organization. Governments worldwide imposed regulations and recommendations restricting people's movements and ability to gather. Some countries enforced strict national confinement orders (e.g., Italy, France) while others had a looser approach (e.g., Canada, USA). Within days, people's lives changed dramatically: Teleworking and *"telesocializing"* became, for an unknown period of time, the norm. Impacts are expected to be momentary, but if we cannot control the virus, changes to our work, social, and leisure activities may last. Leisure scholars need to rethink existing theories, precepts, and assumptions. Our discussion took place over weekly Sunday evening Zoom conferences, and wine.

FSD's March 22 e-mail: I'd like to convene an apéritif get-together via Zoom at 8:00 (5:00 west coast). We can have a drink and a video-chat! I hope you're available. Considering our current social options, we all should have time!

MEH: Last month I received a return-envelope from a survey my research team mailed 2009 for our "lifelong longitudinal running study." Chuck was a state high-school champion in the 1960s and an accomplished intercollegiate athlete. Now 70-something, he's battling Parkinson's and a serious heart condition. Former teammates pray as he fights for his life. Something compelled him to retrieve and complete the survey while in hospital. His wife wrote, "Since Chuck has been hospitalized all he talks about is his experiences running, college teammates, and post-collegiate races. He loves it all!" His action and her comments drew me back to when we lived in Eugene, and our work related to involvement and commitment. Chuck exemplifies individuals who remain highly involved and committed from adolescence into older adulthood, with identity, position involvement and social bonding intact (Wilson et al., 2019). His story is a reminder that leisure matters. Deeply.

MPP: With mountains to the north and Mount Rainier to the west, getting out for a breath of fresh air in our county's open space had never been a problem. However, laws constrain freedom and safety at any price takes a toll. While some states sought moderation, others used sweeping restrictions. Town mayors closed beaches, imposed curfews, evicted tourists, and warned beach house owners to stay away or be pulled aside and fined (KOIN 6 News, 2020). Local landowners chased hikers and bikers off unclosed irrigation trails, in many cases ignoring civil liberties.

Perceived freedom, long taken as a defining characteristic in leisure (Ellis & Witt, 1984), plays a much grander role across U.S. history. Nevertheless, reflecting on limits to personal leisure travel and free-time activity ties back to how these alter wider civic life. Perceptions of freedom draw from a wider sense of volition. In work or leisure, this entails a "freedom from" constraints and a "freedom to" act that allow personal meaning and self-responsibility to develop (Steiner, 1970; Pritchard et al., 1999, p. 336). Handling tensions between "freedom to" and "from" in our society is a significant issue. Much like managing perceived and actual risk/competence (McIntyre & Roggenbuck, 1998), the right balance of perceived and actual freedom is vital for human flourishing.

FSD: Doubtless, freedom is currently lacking. Holiday travel, among the world's favored leisure activities, is suddenly out of the question for people across the world. In fact, since mass international travel grew starting in the 1950s, the travel and tourism sector has come to an unprecedented halt. The sector is not dead, but it only survives because of economic support strategies that governments are putting in place to help large companies such as airlines and hotels groups, and small entrepreneurs who are at its heart. The industry is on life support. Many private stakeholders are sick and some will die of COVID-19. But just opening things up is overly simplistic. Uncertainty, health risk, and government-imposed restrictions don't engender consumer confidence needed for people to book leisure trips.

MPP: I believe not opening the economy carries another cost. It is not just simply a tradeoff between economics and lives saved. If we take Case and Deaton (2020) work seriously, there are costs either way. Lives lost to addiction, suicide, and deaths of despair will hit working class Americans hard. In Washington, we entered lockdown almost two months ago under the Governor's "Stay Home Stay Healthy" proclamation. Significant warnings of loss emphasized an "abundance of caution" that resonated with many citizens. Personal adjustments meant moving exams and classes online and canceling speaking engagements abroad. Our university's board of trustees quickly declared financial exigency, cutting salaries for senior administrators and laying off staff.

Despite such changes, reality of the shutdown for our small town of 21,000 took time to sink in. A triage tent went up in our hospital's parking lot, yet despite tragic loss of life in many cities, most rural counties and states saw little effect. Over the next month, the state's website confirmed 14 recoveries and no fatalities for our town. One study argued mass transit and population density play a heavy role in escalating impact. Despite distinct regional differences, shelter in place orders universally closed all public space, state and city parks. Authoritative sources ruled entire states as unable to open. Counties and regions with vastly different population densities were treated as one-and-the-same.

MEH: But does urban escalation mean that rural areas need not worry or does it just mean that the curve will be flatter, that the overall infection rates will eventually even out?

MPP: Curves are flatter and, in many cases, receding. Isn't the *land of the free and the home of the brave* more than just sentiment? Shouldn't we bravely take precautions so that we can be free? Large rural states abroad, like Western Australia, are opening back up, yet the same is not true in Washington. Separated by 100 miles, Kittitas and Seattle's King counties have similar footprints (2297 and 2115 sq. miles) yet vastly different populations (47,935 and 2,252,782, respectively). There is a 50-fold difference in density. Achieving physical distancing not an issue in one but challenging in the other. These differences explain why people in rural counties are protesting the state's closure of fishing on lakes and the Columbia River (Dunne, 2020). Like Sweden, with few deaths and the lowest case/mortality ratio in the country, South Dakota imposed no stay home order. The governor there argued that individuals, not government, should decide whether "to exercise their right to work, to worship and to play. Or to even stay at home" (Freeman, 2020).

FSD: As of April 20, South Dakota had the 12th-highest COVID-19 case rate per million people in the nation trailing only 11 urbanized states, and Sweden also has a higher infection rate than its neighbors. It also seems that with this virus, freedom for some will mean loss of life for others.

MEH: We know about relationships between volition and other aspects of commitment. But other than some early work by Unger and Kernan (1983), few appear to have explicitly studied connections between ego involvement and perceived freedom. Anecdotally, given current circumstances, I suspect highly involved people are more likely to be frustrated by constrained freedom. Last year I joined Sue in retirement. We moved full-time to our "cottage" in a vacation town of 13,700 permanent residents. Population doubles in summer and triples on holiday weekends. Currently, travel to cottages as escapes from cities where physical distancing challenges facilitate rapid spread of the virus, positions cottages as attractive nuisances from the perspective of small resource-strapped host communities. Parallels between this phenomenon and playgrounds, pools, sport events and concerts suggest that leisure events and amenities as attractive nuisances warrant future research. Restrictions are more difficult to impose and enforce in Western democracies than in autocratic countries. The United States' Declaration of Independence and Canada's Charter of Rights and Freedoms speak broadly and explicitly to freedom of movement and choice as basic human rights (Valiante, 2020).

MPP: The Declaration along with amendments explicitly speaks to liberties like the "right to travel." Although ratified after the Civil War, the 14th Amendment also extended economic protections in the early 1900s with the "liberty-of-contracts" doctrine that prevented states from interfering with labor contracts in the name of protecting the health of workers (Legal Information Institute).

MEH: It's worth remembering that life expectancy for white Americans at birth in 1900 was about 50 years and for visible minorities about 35. Our discussion boils down to balancing "living" versus "life." I admit that, following WHO's pandemic declaration, my personal responses lagged several days behind recommendations of lead physicians and health experts. This despite my acceptance that the pandemic is real and my demographic placement as vulnerable based on age and preexisting (heart) conditions. Recalling 15 years of commuting between our city home and our cottage, I was skeptical of our mayor's request and premier's directive that people physically distance at home rather than here, thus burdening our small hospital with seasonal residents (Charbonneau, 2020). Questions abounded. Don't cottagers pay property taxes? Doesn't it make sense for people to relocate to places where it's easier to maintain physical distance? Is it morally ethical that overwhelmed urban hospitals bear the brunt of COVID-19 cases while rural hospitals sit relatively empty? After sleeping on it, I fell in line.

Nevertheless, our town swelled during "spring break" week. Our block illustrates: Cottagers at seven of nine seasonal residences joined those of us occupying nine full-time residences. Despite daily suggestions from government officials and health experts discouraging such movement, most cottagers remain. And many full-timers and cottagers welcomed overnight guests, usually adult children and grandchildren, who don't live under the same roof. In the absence of an official stay-in-place policy, enforcement of those directives has been non-existent. It's different a block away where seasonal trailer park residents are officially barred: Physical barriers and signage block entrance to the park. So, restrictions have been unevenly implemented and applied, tending to favor wealthier people like us over people of more modest means.

FSD: Some Canadian First Nations reserves, by banning visitors outright, have thrown that last observation on its ear by asserting a degree of sovereignty more powerful than that of local governments. Good for them!

But many people who experience confinement find themselves bored and without the things that kept them busy: work and entertainment. Our society is based on relationships with work and leisure, structured by activities that are not possible anymore: outdoor recreation with family and friends, going out to bars and restaurants, watching sports or attending concerts. We are now at home, without our usual distractions, possessions, and excuses.

MPP: As this first wave subsides, additional waves are predicted. Financial anxiety among those prohibited from working is understandable and balancing this is probably top-of-mind for many Governors staggering the reopening of their state economies (Miller, 2020).

MEH: Growing protests at various state and provincial capitols suggest many citizens resent constraints on both leisure and work-related activity, despite overwhelming epidemiological evidence that distancing remains necessary. I've been thinking about MPP's reference to the land of the free and home of the brave. In this pandemic, those clamoring loudest for freedom predominate from low-risk demographic groups fixated on personal lifestyle and economic interests; the brave are front-line workers, caregivers and most medically vulnerable.

FSD: Now more than ever in our lifetimes, we are constrained. Should we ask again with Jackson (2005) how leisure constraints research contributes to our understanding of leisure and travel behavior? People find themselves confined and restricted in their freedom to move because of risks of going outside and traveling, because of public policy that imposes immobility, and because of financial reasons as a result of the devastated economy.

Of course, we'll eventually travel again, but it will be different. Risk perceptions for leisure activities (Cheron & Ritchie, 1982) and travel (Roehl & Fesenmaier, 1992) must be reassessed. Tourists may favor regional destinations to avoid risks inherent in crowded airports and beach destinations, flying, or being packed into cruise ships, not having access to adequate medical facilities abroad, or having to quarantine when back. But even regionally, urban dwellers may find themselves in undesirable crowds as they commute to second homes or shared countryside accommodation … where everyone else wants to escape, and where they will encounter irate locals (Onishi & Méheut, 2020). Travel and hospitality operators work hard to reassure travelers, but doubt and suspicion remain.

MEH: It'd be ironic if the present pandemic spurs another wave of research into relationships between involvement and risk. Perhaps someone will tackle reliability problems, validity questions and resulting frustration that prompted us to abandon study of those connections (Kyle et al., 2007).

FSD: Yes, the old Dimanche et al. (1991) paper may find new life! Leisure travel may become less frequent and more expensive, and therefore more appreciated and valued. Although motivations for pleasure vacations (Crompton, 1979) may remain, priorities will change. After weeks or months of immobility, many will favor visits to friends and family as opposed to going to busy beach resorts.

MEH: I doubt that pandemic impacts will be equally felt in various leisure realms.

FSD: Impact will clearly differ across sectors and activities. The cruise industry experienced significant growth in the past 20 years, but must reinvent itself because cruises are currently considered risky and unhealthy. Cruises are, by definition, non-essential and their well-documented environmental and social problems, in addition to the current health-related trouble, could lead them to sink.

MPP: Safety is extremely important, but we know more about the pandemic now. A case for balancing risks that allow people to choose is there. Policies could adjust to the terrain rather than use blunt proclamations that undermine the confidence of the governed. For many people of faith, complying with stay home orders meant not attending synagogue or church for Passover or Easter celebrations. With alternate "conditions of belief" (Taylor, 2007, p.3) in place, many state lockdowns took a distinctly "secular" (Fish, 2010) view, classifying events as non-essential. Ironically, these same shelter-in-place proclamations stopped millions from celebrating the "release of the captives" with Moses' charge to Pharaoh, to "*Let my people go …*" (The English Standard Version

Bible, 2009, Exodus 9:1), and Jesus' finished mission *"to proclaim liberty to the captives..."* (The English Standard Version Bible, 2009, Luke 4:18).

MEH: I see the irony, although my church and many others celebrated Easter with on-line services, and Christ's apostles socially isolated after the Resurrection up until Pentecost!

FSD: You mention religion, but we have to face ourselves without other pillars that shape social identity: work and leisure activities. Current escapes include shouting across the street with neighbors, Zoom or Skype with friends and families and virtual meetings and apéritifs. Of course, we can still play and read, watch movies and the evening news. It isn't easy to look inward when our main activities have disappeared and need to be substituted. The crisis is making us face ourselves. We may not like what we see because many of us have been shaped by a work life and leisure activities that we don't have access to anymore.

MEH: So, research into perceived freedom and its impact on individuals and society is warranted. Likewise, a re-birth of focus on constraint, with specific focus on volition (or lack thereof), and physical, social and psychological risk; all of which apply to the present situation. Ego involvement may be a mediating variable because so much of what we currently miss most is tied to our identity and the centrality of those activities to our lives. This brings us full-circle to my opening premise. In early April, another of my 2009 survey respondents passed unexpectedly from COVID-19. The day after, his wife wrote this humbling note: "Jerry received your wonderfully crafted book last month (Havitz, 2020). He sat in his recliner and poured over volume two, recalling historical events, friendships and passion these friends shared during those wonderful years; friendships continued to this day. We've been sustained by prayers and kindnesses of many who remember Jerry and his career coaching young men and women. We'll truly miss him, but your book will bring many together in thoughtful remembering. Jerry is resting in peace." So, I return to my original statement. Leisure matters. It's ironically frustrating that society's intense longing for leisure in all its manifestations becomes problematic in these difficult times. We dedicate our commentary to the memory of Sue's mother, Anne Shantz, who passed in Kitchener, Ontario on April 18, 2020 from Covid-19.

References

Case, A., & Deaton, A. (2020). *Deaths of despair and the future of capitalism.* Princeton University.

Charbonneau, L. (2020, March 24). COVID-19 update: Saugeen shores declares state of emergency. https://www.saugeenshores.ca/Modules/News/index.aspx?newsId=890b4222-52a4-4985-8692-8a9e51090e28

Cheron, E., & Ritchie, J. (1982). Leisure activities and perceived risk. *Journal of Leisure Research,* 14(2), 139–154. https://doi.org/10.1080/00222216.1982.11969511

Crompton, J. (1979). Motivations for pleasure vacation. *Annals of Tourism Research,* 6(4), 408–424. https://doi.org/10.1016/0160-7383(79)90004-5

Dimanche, F., Havitz, M., & Howard, D. (1991). Testing the Involvement Profile (IP) scale in the context of selected recreational and touristic activities. *Journal of Leisure Research,* 23(1), 51–66. https://doi.org/10.1016/0160-7383(79)90004-5

Dunne, I. (2020, April 22). Fishing protest planned for Saturday in Wenatchee. *Wenatchee World*. https://www.wenatcheeworld.com/news/coronavirus/fishing-protest-planned-for-satur-day-in-wenatchee/article_9c3e75e4-84c3-11ea-a08c-3f756d06fed3.html

Ellis, G., & Witt, P. (1984). The measurement of perceived freedom in leisure. *Journal of Leisure Research, 16*(2), 110–123. doi: 10.1080/00222216.1984.11969579

Fish, S. (2010, February 22). Are there secular reasons? *The New York Times*. https://opinionator.blogs.nytimes.com/2010/02/22/are-there-secular-reasons/?hp

Freeman, J. (2020, April 15). South Dakota vs. Coronavirus: Statewide shutdown is not the only way to protect public health. Wall Street Journal. https://www.wsj.com/articles/south-dakota-vs-coronavirus-11586967498

Havitz, M. (2020). *One hundred ten years running on the banks of the Red Cedar: A social history of Michigan State University cross country*. Self-published.

Jackson, E. (Ed.). (2005). *Constraints on leisure*. Venture.

KOIN 6 News Staff. (2020, March 21). 'Don't come here': Warrenton mayor evicts tourists. *KOIN 6 News*. https://www.koin.com/news/health/coronavirus/dont-come-here-warrenton-mayor-tells-tourists-to-vacate/

Kyle, G., Absher, J., Norman, W., Hammitt, W., & Jodice, L. (2007). A modified involvement scale. *Leisure Studies, 26*(4), 399–427. https://doi.org/10.1080/02614360600896668

McIntyre, N., & Roggenbuck, J. (1998). Nature/Person transactions during an outdoor adventure experience: A multi-phasic analysis. *Journal of Leisure Research, 30*(4), 401–422. doi: 10.1080/00222216.1998.11949841

Miller, H. (2020, April 30). Reopening America: A state-by-state breakdown of the status of coronavirus restrictions. *CNBC*. https://www.cnbc.com/2020/04/30/coronavirus-states-lifting-stay-at-home-orders-reopening-businesses.html

Onishi, N., Méheut, C. (2020, March 29). Rich Europeans flee virus for 2nd homes, spreading fear and fury. *New York Times*. https://www.nytimes.com/2020/03/29/world/europe/rich-coronavirus-second-homes.html

Pritchard, M., Havitz, M., & Howard, D. (1999). Analyzing the commitment-loyalty link in service contexts. *Journal of the Academy of Marketing Science, 27*(3), 333–348. https://doi.org/10.1177/0092070399273004

Roehl, W., & Fesenmaier, D. (1992). Risk perceptions and pleasure travel: An exploratory analysis. *Journal of Travel Research, 30*(4), 17–26. https://doi.org/10.1177/004728759203000403

Steiner, I. (1970). Perceived freedom. *Advances in Experimental Social Psychology, 5*, 187–248.

Taylor, C. (2007). *A secular age*. Belknap.

The English Standard Version Bible. (2009). Oxford University Press.

Unger, L., & Kernan, J. (1983). On the meaning of leisure: An investigation of some determinants of the subjective experience. *Journal of Consumer Research, 9*(4), 381–392. doi: 10.1086/208932

Valiante, G. (2020, April 4). 'The Charter still applies': Canadians urged to monitor civil liberties during pandemic. https://www.ctvnews.ca/canada/the-charter-still-applies-canadians-urged-to-monitor-civil-liberties-during-pandemic-1.4882742

Wilson, A., Havitz, M., Mock, S., & Potwarka, L. (2019). A retrospective analysis of the influence of ego involvement on adult running participation(s) and preference(s) among post-collegiate varsity athletes. *Leisure/loisir, 43*(4), 523–541. https://doi.org/10.1080/14927713.2019.1699439

Where Is Leisure When Death Is Present?

Karen M. Fox and Lisa McDermott

ABSTRACT

For many, the COVID-19 pandemic is the overwhelming, ever-present reality of dying—of loved ones, close family members, dear friends, colleagues, or patients. Fear, avoidance of or lack of time for essential conversations, physical separation during final moments, and lack of rituals for these contingencies leave individuals alone with loss, mourning, and grieving. How is leisure relevant during such realities? Historically, leisure has been present across diverse cultural dying and death practices: art, music, dance, theater, play, contemplation, rituals, and somatic practices. These connect individuals with life forces even as some are absent in the flesh. In truth, we are all experiencing dying-death-mourning-beginning again during the COVID-19 pandemic. Josef Pieper's (2017, 2016, 2011, 1999, 1988) philosophy hints of leisure as context for the meaning, purpose, and comfort in such trying times: contemplating one's place in a changing world/universe and celebrating or affirming that relationship in community.

For many, the COVID-19 pandemic foregrounds leisure pursuits (e.g., virtually mediated physical activity, creative game interactions, baking, home crafts) as mainstays of everyday life. They divert, satisfy, or fulfill an individual and create forms of happiness and self-empowerment. For other individuals, the pandemic brings hardship and existential fear. These states of being are further compounded by occurrences of death, where normative rituals for dying have been undermined leaving people both with and without COVID-19 alone and desperately searching for an anchor. Such realities require something different from leisure than happiness or self-empowerment. How is leisure relevant during these times?

As the pandemic evolves, how does leisure address the uncertainties and changes wrought by COVID-19? Devastating mini-death-like transitions that engender processes of mourning and grieving: loss of a job and identity, security, human contact, or sense of control, reminding us of life's ephemeral nature. Escapist coping practices such as hours of computer surfing, movie streaming, drinking, or endless sleeping do not support facing death and working through these transitions. Too often, seeking happy, optimistic experiences obscures insights and resilience gained from engaging difficult emotions and setbacks. Death, as part of life's cycle, ultimately undermines our discourse of self-determined control. And while some leisure practices help weather these times, they may not directly address the issues related to being *present* for dying and the accompanying mourning and grieving.

While the leisure literature highlights physical activity's contribution to healthy *living*, little space is devoted to considering how vital leisure is and experiencing *all* that life brings, including dying. Josef Pieper's (2009) theologically entwined philosophy of leisure and writings on death provide a structure to understanding how leisure is critical during times of great change and loss (Holba, 2017).

Pieper (1904–1997) posited that leisure was an end in itself and the necessary corollary of the deliberate pursuit of useful work. Grounding his leisure discussion in Plato and Thomas Aquinas, Pieper (2007, 1999) focused on ultimate questions (e.g., what is the meaning of life and death?) requiring continual rethinking and serendipitous inspiration. We suggest his concepts of leisure, conceived as a *philosophical act* of the "philosophizing person" receptive to contemplation and celebration, and "assenting to the world as is" speak directly to leisure's potential role and significance in the midst of the pandemic.

Guilbeau (2018) suggests Pieper understood leisure "not according to its external appearance, but according to its interior reality" (p. 42), as a "resting" to take contemplative delight in *being*. It is an affirmation of existence and a contemplative union with the whole of being. Happiness thus arises from the *experiencing* of reality instead of *using* reality as resources for human interest, whether that be work- or leisure-related. The resting sustains a "self-opening encounter with reality, often in the form of amazement, a neglected essential of human existence" (Hoye, 2004, p. 18). *Contemplation* exceeds ordinary perspective, leading to unequivocal signs that the universe "is more profound, more commodious, more mysterious than it appears to our everyday understanding" (O'Higgins, 2014, p. 149–50). *Celebration,* or affirmation of being, is contemplation's twin that occasions a community's avowal of the individual's place within the universe. The arts, of which all cultures have variations, gesture to the more-to-be-pondered because they are "so close to the fundamentals of human existence" (Pieper, 1990, p. 39).

At the core of contemplation and celebration is the philosophical act, a receptive capacity that entails simply seeing (*simplex intuitus)* and an openness to the experience of reality and its unexpected outcomes. Significantly, Pieper (2007) does not privilege the cognitive aspects of contemplation; rather he says contemplation involves the entirety of one's being—cognitive, physical, sensoria, and spiritual. Consider how, for example, cross-stitching, music, physical movement, or being with plants and animals can lead to wonder and inspiration.

Pieper focused on the "philosophizing person" whose engagement in a philosophical act, in all its diverse manifestations, seeks to unite and "hold in unity different elements of experience" (O' Higgins, 2014, p. 148). For Pieper, the goal of unifying different experience modalities is always an unfinished, reiterative process.

Pieper believed people reach full potential through awareness of the totality of human experience and a willingness to "assent to the world as is," to *being* with the "whole of reality" rather than insisting it conform to our desires. Assenting to the world as is accepts that the universe was created by forces outside humans' control. Yet this does not remove their obligation to act ethically within it. The assent moves humans to see that reality encompasses *both* good and bad, life and death, and the lessons they contain. This willingness to assent arouses a disposition "to break through the world of the ordinary (i.e., work and human-made cultures/objects) to the satisfying world of the extraordinary (i.e., all things created and beyond human beings' creation)" (Austenfeld, 2000, Sec II). While Pieper argues factual knowledge offers evidence of how things work, it does not answer "why." To assent to the whole of reality is, therefore, "to understand that the world and Being itself are a mystery, and for that reason inexhaustible" (Pieper, 2007, LOC 5165).

The "whole of reality," in all its plenitude, involves difficult and often uncomfortable circumstances including pain, suffering, and dying that typically move humans to raise with particular urgency questions of "why." Pieper's experience of losing his son to a cerebral hemorrhage after a day spent hiking at Mount Rainier reinforced his understanding of suffering as an integral part of humans' inability and struggle to know the truth of things, and his theologically informed interpretation of hope as a "not-yet" that propels seeking deeper insight. His "assenting to the world as is" thus acknowledges the reality of considerable personal duress (cited in Austenfeld, 2000, Sec V).

Pieper (1999) postulated underneath every celebration is an affirmation extending to the whole of existence—both its joy *and* sorrow. Affirming sorrow as worth celebrating comes from engaging and/or being present to the horrors in this world. Honoring, accepting, and moving through grief requires piercing the heart by sorrow—not avoiding or shutting it out—thereby transfiguring it into something beautiful and sustaining if we flow through its painful currents (Anderson, 2014) to consolation.

Leisure's role during dying, death, mourning, and grieving

In the leisure literature, death implicitly appears through poor health habits—the absence of exercise and good eating, the use of harmful substances, the lack of family and community support, and so on. The one explicit engagement with it is an article focused on a recreation professional who was dying yet spoke little to this process; her conclusion: leisure was not relevant toward the end of life (Carpenter, 2002).

While various professionals administer specific skills during dying, family, friends, and community have an equally essential role. Historically, attending the dying person and preparing the body for burial remained within the family or community context; it culminated in public celebration and mourning (i.e., funerals, wakes, etc.) that served as venues for expressing and moving through grief. In recent times, communal practices are less evident, although changing with the emergence of Death Doulas (who assist with the dying process especially at home), community deathcare (volunteer organizations who support re-engagement with meaningful, holistic, dying and death care in environmentally sustainable ways), and death cafés (nonprofit organizations that host discussions over food and drink about death, helping others become familiar with life's end).

To varying degrees, all humans are affected by the pervasiveness of dying and the specter of death brought about by the COVID-19 pandemic, triggering a sense of vulnerability and susceptibility to the porous nature of life and death. While assenting to dying and philosophizing neither hold definitive nor unchanging universal answers, death highlights life's value and joy. COVID-19 survivors, for example, speak of wanting "to help people more than I ever have before" (Chavez, 2020), a sentiment connecting them to the web of life with a purpose beyond utilitarian actions. Pieper's (2009) concept of leisure as contemplation, philosophizing, and celebration stretches across spiritual and secular positions, contributing to both individual and community resilience, renewing who they are becoming (Holba, 2017). However, his conceptualization entails reenvisioning who leisure professionals and scholars are and how they engage leisure.

First, the relationship between leisure and dying requires academic explication. Death is a natural process all animate beings experience; therefore, it is something to which leisure is present. Within Westernized nations, the medical and funeral industry's colonization of the care and burial of the deceased has limited frank public discussions about dying and surviving loss. The emergence of alternative approaches to dying and death are renewing and creating traditions and practices allowing people to celebrate a life and grieve its loss. As this cultural shroud around death lifts, Pieper's leisure becomes especially relevant.

Second is the need for leisure scholarship and practice to shift, enabling the philosophizing individual to seek meaning and capacity to engage the whole of reality through leisure. Frank Ostaseski (2019), the Zen Hospice Project founder, demonstrates the relevance to holding space for professionals, including leisure. He begins with an attentive *presence* to the existing moment, where curiosity, love, and *akroatic listening* (i.e., embodied hearing, harmonic and rhythmic responsiveness) link being to one's attunement with the context of people dying or grieving: a family called Ostaseski to assist with their child's home death. Ostaseski entered the child's room, kissed his forehead, and said "hello." The parents dissolved into tears; neither had touched him after he died. Ostaseski suggested they bathe their son, normally a pleasurable and playful activity. Ostaseski held space for the parents to know both sorrow and joy, nodding encouragement to continue despite deep grief. He enabled them to be present and care for their child while Pieper's leisure surrounded them.

Presence and *akroatic* listening focus on observing and comprehending from a state of awareness, a place "from which human beings can both *be* and *become*" (Lipari, 2014, p. 348). We offer two non-COVID-19 examples illustrating leisure's potential to be present to dying. Newspaper accounts of the pandemic give cursory examples of leisure (e.g., describing flowers blooming, reading stories, reminiscing) without details of its significance to dying for leisure professionals. We therefore selected examples directly relevant to leisure.

Keening, a form of singing and wailing during Irish wakes, reveals a way of holding space. In a room where the body is displayed, the keeners modulate the mourners' grief through intensifying songs and wailing to tap into, express, and navigate waves of intense grief; soft, rhythmic sections engender a solace engaged in remembrances pulling them forward, and reconnecting with life. When the keening is over, mourners move to a room that has food, music, and dancing. (Toolis, 2018). Notice the leisure contexts holding space for grieving and returning to the pulse of life; a space allowing survivors' presence to death and life, and reenvisioning their relationship with the deceased.

Differing funeral practices around the world replicate this pattern interweaving death with life (e.g., fantasy coffins of planes for pilots) and serious ritual with leisure activities (e.g., jazz burials in New Orleans), sustaining contemplation and celebration. Music, dance, storytelling, and art engage and communicate beyond the literal performance of these activities through letting go and accepting inspiration. Pieper's philosophizing individual is one who moves between these visible and invisible aspects of life.

Jayson Greene's (2019) progression through grieving the death of his 2-year-old daughter, Greta, exemplifies the mystery of these processes that come when we are at leisure (Pieper, 2007). Greene avoided his regular practice of running for months after her death. Finally, the old desire returned. Steeling himself for the route through Greta's favorite park, he found himself in a different state of being:

> There at the park's mouth, my heart stirs, and I feel a peculiar elation. *I recognize her.* Greta is somewhere nearby. I feel her energy, playfully expectant. *Come find me, Daddy,* she says. Tears spring and run freely down my face. *I hear you, baby girl,* I whisper. *Daddy's coming to get you ....* Elated, I enter the park and immediately spot her; she is waiting for me hiding behind the big tree in the clearing … giggling, just like in our old game…. Standing in the park, staring at her, I make a strange and primal sound, deep and rich like a belly laugh, hard and sharp like a sob. *You are here. You picked the park. Good choice, baby girl.* Oblivious to the people around me, I run to her…. Stooping down, I scoop her up … into the sky. She is invisible to passerby…. But she is not here for them; she is here for me…. I feel her presence filling up my heart, and with it comes a strange exhilaration that I have felt often in the weeks after her death. Grief at its peak has a terrible beauty to it, a blinding fission of every emotion. The world is charged with significance, with meaning, and the world around you, normally so solid and implacable, suddenly looks thin, translucent. I feel like I've discovered an opening. I don't know quite what's behind it yet. But it is there. (Greene, 2019)

Greene's poetic, insightful, and emotionally charged piece resonates with Pieper's sense of leisure. The morning run loosens the body, places it moving through life, encountering it beyond human existence, and seeing the "terrible beauty" of grief. This was not a run just for the sake of exercise, but movement toward assenting to the whole of life death. The movement, the change in awareness, was a gift, "not without our own efforts but nevertheless not through those efforts. Rather, we will obtain them only if we can accept them as free gifts" (Pieper, 1990).

Celebrations are essential in times of dying because they remind us how our lives are enriched by another's life and move us to honor those within our lives. Pieper (1999) posits a celebration worthy of leisure affirms a person's relationship and role to the universe. Furthermore, it reinforces humans' interconnection within the mysterious web of life. What gives meaning and love are interconnections with others and being present to life.

The COVID-19 pandemic has produced major changes in how people both die and struggle to celebrate and mourn those deaths at a distance. While the current focus is on technological adaptations for delivering modern funeral practices, communal relationships and actions supporting end-of-life decisions, mourning, and grieving are critical. As Pieper et al. (2009) describes, contemplation and affirmation are sustained by community. The more we imagine a connection between community, embodiment, and technological practices, the more we bring the power of leisure to sustain people during the pandemic. For example, mobile phones and tablets are enabling people to communicate and be "present" for last moments with family and friends: as a 74-year-old great grandmother lay ventilated in a New York hospital, a healthcare worker readied a tablet with Spanish praise music chosen by the dying woman's loved ones; a social worker made a Zoom call to family across the United States and in Colombia: "Ms. Toro was breathing but unconscious…. A chorus of voices range from the tablet greeting her, telling her how beautiful she was, thanking her, expressing love…. 'You were the soldier, strong for all of us'" (Fink, 2020, p. 13). Maintaining "contact," even if it is only to hear their beloved breathing (Waldrop, 2020), is vital as a person slips further away from life since hearing is the last sense to go; opportunities for a final connection through voice or music can be quite powerful. Equally important such 'contact' allow survivors to move together through processes of grieving facilitating their movement into the realm of living once more.

Final thoughts

Leisure, as Pieper et al. (2009) imagined it, is essential during the COVID-19 pandemic, as it sustains people, provides a visceral connection to life, and opens space for them to contemplate and celebrate life while facing the reality of death. Pieper's leisure calls leisure scholars and professionals to reimagine another path relevant to sorrows and horrors of life. This leisure accepts people as they are, walks alongside them, provides comfort and support in challenging times, and points toward both life *and death*.

References

Anderson, E. M. (2014). The celebration of sorrow in the roman rite. *Sacred Music, 141*(3), 27–34.
Austenfeld, T. (2000). Josef Pieper's contemplative assent to the world. *Modern Age, 42*(4), 372–382.
Carpenter, G. (2002). Leisure behaviors and perceptions when mid-life death is imminent: A case report. *Journal of Park and Recreation Administration, 20*(4), 12–36.
Chavez, N. (2020). *They won the fight against coronavirus. Here's what life looks like on the other side.* www.cnn.com/2020/04/23/us/coronavirus-survivors-recovery/index.html
Fink, S. (2020, May 3). With matriarch ill, a family prepares for the end. *The New York Times*, pp. 1, 12–13.
Greene, J. (2019, April 10). *Once more we saw stars.* www.vulture.com/2019/04/jayson-greene-memoir-once-more-we-saw-stars-book-excerpt.html#comments
Guilbeau, A. (2018). The courage to rest: Thomas Aquinas on the soul of leisure. *Nova et vetera, 16*(1), 39–46.
Holba, A. M. (2017). Groundwork for an ethics of death: Leisure, faith, resilience. *Journal of Communication and Religion, 39*(3), 1–17.
Hoye, W. J. (2004). Josef Pieper: The four cardinal virtues. *America, 8*, 16–22.
Lipari, L. (2014). *Listening, thinking, being: Toward an ethics of attunement.* University Park, PA: Penn State University Press.
O'Higgins, E. O. (2014). Josef Pieper, a philosophical style. *Alpha Omega, XVII*(1), 147–156.
Ostaseski, F. (2019). *The five invitations: Discovering what death can teach us about living fully.* New York, NY: Flatiron Books.
Pieper, J. (1990). *Only the lover sings. Art and contemplation.* San Francisco, CA: Ignatius Press.
Pieper, J. (1999). *In tune with the world: A theory of festivity.* South Bend, IN: Saint Augustine's Press.
Pieper, J. (2007). *For love of wisdom: Essays on the nature of philosophy.* San Francisco, CA: Ignatius Press.
Pieper, J. (2009). *Leisure: The basis of culture* (A. Dru & G. Malsbary, Trans.). San Francisco, CA: Ignatius Press. (Original work published 1952)
Toolis, K. (2018). *My father's wake: How the Irish teach us to live, love and die.* Cambridge, MA: Da Capo Press.
Waldrop, T. (2020). *His family stayed on the phone for 30 hours—Until he died.* www.cnn.com/2020/04/21/us/30-hours-phone-call-father-family-coronavirus/index.html

On Not Knowing: COVID-19 and Decolonizing Leisure Research

Bryan S. R. Grimwood (iD)

ABSTRACT

The COVID-19 pandemic has enfolded waves of uncertainty—intense doses of not knowing—into our daily experience. In this commentary, I stutter into the discomfort of not knowing as a mode of relation. Recognizing that the collective uncertainty surrounding the pandemic has marshaled vital desires to know how to respond, to cope, and even to survive, I think and write toward productive possibilities that arise when we tune attention away from knowing more and knowing better. The journey I take hitches to conceptual anchor points from settler colonial studies, and to moments of personal upheaval associated with both the current pandemic and learning to take responsibility for settler colonization. As I navigate this route of not knowing, I churn up potential decolonizing pathways for leisure researchers to debate, discard, pick up, or move through.

I don't know what the COVID-19 pandemic will bring, what it has brought. I don't know the extent of suffering that individuals and families are experiencing. I don't know the burden health care workers are carrying, or the intense threat being felt by communities who are most vulnerable. I don't know how economies will recover, if societies or ecologies will be restored, what power relations will become entrenched or undone. I don't know what or who to believe when I consume media. I don't know when schools and daycares in my community will re-open, or when athletes will next take the field. I don't know what recreation or tourism or sport will become. I sense these domains of our leisure lives, these companion fields of study, are changing, but I don't know how or where, or whom will benefit and lose out.

And I really don't know what to do about all this. I don't know how to be a father, spouse, professor, or friend when physical distancing has warped the spatial and temporal folds of my world. I don't know what it means to be a responsible scholar in this moment. I don't know if the surge of special issues on COVID-19 in social science journals is driven by insatiable desires to raise impact factors. I don't know if these special issues will generate insights or capacities that will do communities much good. For those of us who aren't on the frontlines of health care or essential service provision, I don't know if our best response is to simply slow down: to pause, rest, read, play, play music.

"Not knowing" is the permeating theme of this commentary and something I've been trying to embrace. I understand it as a mode of relating to the world, one that COVID-19 has forced upon us but also one that represents a productive positionality for leisure researchers to adopt and deliberate. My aim in this commentary is to recontextualize the collective experience of not knowing brought on by the pandemic within scholarly movements designed to support decolonization. More specifically, by weaving academic anchor points with personal reflections, I attempt to show and inhabit not knowing as a situated stance for Settler leisure scholars like myself learning to take responsibility for settler colonialism[1]. I do this by tracing some instructive conceptual and political footing for readers, and forging linkages between not knowing during the event of COVID-19 and the larger, longer project of decolonization[2].

Not knowing and decolonial futures

Much of my recent research and writing has concentrated on decolonizing Indigenous-Settler relations in tourism landscapes and encounters (Grimwood, Muldoon, et al., 2019; Grimwood, Stinson, et al., 2019; Grimwood & Johnson, 2019; Stinson et al., 2020). The consistent task haunting this work, haunting my theorypractices (Berbary, 2020), is to take responsibility for unsettling the storm that is settler colonization: a storm that we don't pass through but which passes through us[3]. And that storm is an ongoing twister of forces designed to eliminate Indigenous[4] societies from their ancestral lands so that settler societies are made to feel entirely justified in occupying it and making it their permanent, undisputed home (Coulthard, 2014). The particular violences of settler colonization – something we've hardly named or deliberated in leisure studies – amount to cultural genocide (Truth and Reconciliation Commission of Canada (TRC), 2015). Here, on the land now often called Canada, these violences include exposing Indigenous communities to disease and environmental change, forcibly removing Indigenous children from families, policing Indigenous bodies and language and cultural practices, and establishing and enforcing policies that essentialize identity, infringe on rights, and restrict political and economic opportunities. And these traumas bleed into the present through settler colonial structures (e.g., nation states, advanced capitalism), systems (e.g., Eurocentric regimes of knowledge, law, and truth), and stories (e.g., terra nullius, good intentions) (Lowman & Barker, 2015). The power relations at play operate to erase diverse Indigenous ways of knowing and being from landscapes, and in turn normalize settler identities and states so completely that they seem self-evident, their historical and contemporary complicity in colonial domination and oppression disavowed (Regan, 2010). As a Settler, my entanglement in these politics is so intricate that I don't always know how settler colonialization is performed through me, or how it generates and recasts the relational worlds within which I live.

Decolonization is, similarly, murky terrain that I don't know how to entirely chart or rest comfortably upon. When I do land somewhere, it's only for a moment –

epistemological security wiped away with a disinfectant wipe. Like Cameron (2015), I find decolonization requires an awkward "turn both toward and away from colonial relations" (p. 19). It necessitates emancipatory critiques of colonial conditions, but also the fostering of cultural practices and self-determined lifeways situated beyond colonial command and imaginaries (Mackey, 2015). It also demands the repatriation of Indigenous lands to Indigenous peoples (Tuck & Yang, 2012). I don't know what this might look like, what it might entail, how to get there. And that uncertainty is uncomfortable. More often than I'd like, as I think through or attempt to practice decolonization, I feel like I'm fumbling along with many other non-Indigenous persons making suspect moves to alleviate the atrocities of colonization and interfering with more meaningful alliances, restorations, and transformations (Tuck & Yang, 2012). It's not unlike the fumbling I feel trying to respond amid our current pandemic circumstances.

What I'm learning in relation to decolonization, however, is to situate my efforts and actions in critical proximity to settler colonizing structures, systems, and stories, and peripheral to Indigenous resurgence and revitalization. Borrowing from Carlson's (2017) framework, I'm learning to leverage my skills, relative privilege, and access to resources to help perforate settler colonialism, which in turn might make safer spaces for Indigenous peoples to enact their self-determined worlds. One example from my research is a collective memory work study with non-Indigenous university students designed to critique personal stories of travel, particularly those associated with meanings of "Canadian" and "Indigeneity" (Grimwood & Johnson, 2019). Through the process of recalling, writing, sharing, and restorying these memories, we are locating and troubling harmful narratives like *terra nullius* that condition our identities. The point of this project is not to understand or represent Indigenous ways of knowing and being (Indigenous peoples control these efforts), but rather to "undo" ourselves as Settlers so that we might shoulder greater responsibility for resisting settler colonial relations as a practice of allyship, solidarity, and accountability. My colleague, Trevor Holmes (personal communication, 11/13/2019), aptly described this as doing "unburdening work": that is, relieving some of the weight Indigenous peoples carry as the ones most affected by settler colonial violence and the ones doing most of the work to stop it, all the while struggling also to maintain and revitalize cultures. Others have described this as focusing on the "Settler problem" (Lowman & Barker, 2015; Regan, 2010).

One of most unsettling aspects of this work, particularly for those of us in academia, is that it demands a radical reworking of knowledge. Non-Indigenous scholars—including several in our field—increasingly accept that knowledge and its production is tethered to colonization, yet we tend not to question our epistemological framings that conceive knowledge as information and presuppose our entitlement to know (Cameron, 2015; Jones & Jenkins, 2008). Indeed, while we may have sharpened our collective critical reflexivity skills and commitments to social justice inquiry (Johnson & Parry, 2016), we have remained fixated on accumulating accurate information, framing what is not-known as potentially-knowable, and asserting or interpreting new truths. These pursuits, these assumptions about what knowledge *is* and what knowledge *does*, rest on the belief that everything is in principle knowable, and that our knowing more, or knowing better, will lead to a more progressive and less fragmented world (Cameron, 2015). Knowledge in this hue pivots on the desires for coherence, certainty, order, mastery, authorization, and control that characterize colonial logics and practices (Akomolafe, 2017; Mackey, 2015).

Looking around at the scene of responses to COVID-19, it is clear that our global village values knowledge as the accumulation of more and more accurate information. This is rational of course. Peoples' survival, our herd's health in both the short and long term, are contingent on rendering this novel coronavirus visible, mapping and managing its spread, and discerning and adapting best practices in health care and public health. And then there's the economic and social suffering: individuals, families, and businesses want to know when the financial bleeding will stop; kids want to know if their summer camp or football season will open; universities want to know how admissions will be affected; people want to know that they'll be food secure tomorrow, next month. For these and many other uncertainties, we see public health officials, economists, government leaders, even leisure and tourism researchers, generating and compiling knowledge as information to help settle our anxieties, to determine strategies for restoring or resetting systems.

This pandemic is revealing, however, that even with all the concerted efforts to accumulate knowledge, much remains uncertain. We don't know when the pandemic will end, or what will come after. We don't know if our responses will be helpful or how they'll echo in subsequent pandemics or crises (e.g., mental health, xenophobia). COVID-19, its spread, its impacts, and our responses to it, have marshaled uncertainty into our daily experiences, into our everyday worlds. This is difficult to sit with and, as any cursory read of the news reveals, is grafted in with the layers of impacts and adaptations we're grappling with.

Yet, I wonder if there are potential capacities emerging from this collective uncertainty that might usefully migrate over to imagining and enacting decolonial futures. Specifically, might our present discomfort of not knowing in this pandemic provide us with an experiential basis for embracing and learning from disruptive, decolonizing perspectives? For settler colonial scholars, not knowing has been adopted as a critical positionality to jar colonizing structures, systems, and stories. Mackey (2015) describes it as "a principled, historically aware stance of self-conscious refusal to mobilize the axiomatic knowledge and action that have emerged from settler entitlement and certainty" (p. 38). In the practice of leisure research, this could mean choosing to deny dogmatic methodological procedures, shed allegiances to particular paradigms or theoretical regimes, or avoid representations that imply certainty of truth. Cast in this way, not knowing is a dissenting stance to the "doctrine of discovery" where knowledge, essentialized as information, can be accessed, accumulated, and conveyed outside its relational context (Cameron, 2015; Lee, 2017). It represents not a failure to know, but a way of relating to knowledge as a dynamic, networked process of generating, validating, synthesizing, and critiquing information (Cameron, 2015). Not knowing thus retools us away from mastery, away from any quest "to meet the world by conquering it" (Akomolafe, 2017, p. 2), and toward a practice of refusal that "may open a space for genuine attention to alternative frameworks, and seed possibilities for creative and engaged relationships and collective projects" (Mackey, 2015, p. 38).

There is of course a crucial difference between the not knowing settler colonial scholars advocate and the not knowing associated with COVID-19. The former is a deliberate, situated positionality that welcomes discomfort as a companion, while the latter is a distressing condition imposed upon our experience by the pandemic and those enduring colonial epistemological framings mentioned earlier. I suspect there is a real risk that societies in the post-COVID-19 world will look to double-down on certainty, to fortify knowledge as accumulation and entitlements to know, all the under the guise of marshaling comfort and security. If, however, leisure researchers want to help manifest other futures—futures characterized, for instance, by the creativity, humility, generosity, and solidarity required in the collective struggle to end colonialism and live something other than colonial (Lowman & Barker, 2015)—perhaps we can channel the uncertainty experienced during this pandemic and relate to knowing differently.

Weaving toward some closure here, I'd like story toward some interrelated pathways that not knowing opens up. First, by embracing not knowing as a mode of relation, Settler scholars recast themselves as learners. And if we are serious about decolonization, if we are serious about surviving the multiple ripples of this pandemic or the ones to come, perhaps now is the moment to become better at learning *from* Indigenous peoples (Jones & Jenkins, 2008). The life experiences and cultural knowledges and intergenerational memories of Indigenous peoples include stories of living through and restoring self-determined lifeways in the face of colonialism, and all that has come with it, including pandemics with far more severe consequences than COVID-19. Learning from Indigenous peoples—as opposed to learning about them—reflects an "openness to difference that can provoke meanings beyond our own [Settler] culture's prescriptions—and lead us to new thought" (Jones & Jenkins, 2008, p. 480). This must certainly be a relational engagement, embedded in reciprocity and respectful dialogue with Indigenous colleagues, collaborators, and communities. Learning from is not about Settlers representing or mimicking Indigenous cosmologies, knowledges, or systems. It is instead about listening for stories (Cruikshank, 2005), for ways of being and relating, that differ from dominant colonial ones, and figuring out how these might help us further unsettle what we know.

Relatedly, not knowing may teach us to become humble listeners to the world around us. If there is one thing that the pandemic has burned into my memory, it's that non-humans have agency (Latour, 1993). Indeed, COVID-19 reminds us that other living and non-living things participate in the ongoing emergence of the world – stirring affect, revealing generative capacities, restorying relations, causing trouble. We are presently living witness to the rough reality that we are not always in control: that even with all the information we've accumulated, things happen beyond our awareness, beyond the limits of our perceptions and frameworks. Perhaps the best response is not to shore up on concrete information, but to practice the art of witnessing, feeling, and listening to the influences of nonhumans. In our quest for certainty, we often forget that nonhumans are excellent teachers and guides for learning how to behave and live well[5]. As one illustration, some colleagues and I have been drawing insight from a resident plant teacher to support and enact decolonial justice in tourism (Stinson et al., 2020). Specifically, we've been learning from common plantain (*Plantago major*)—an invasive species to North America that has become "naturalized" to place (Kimmerer, 2013)—about the value of discretion, gentle coexistence, and sharing our gifts when learning to heal wounds.

And so, perhaps at the end of this pandemic, we'll not be so quick to let go of the uncertainty we're experiencing. Indeed, I'm curious if we can channel this collective not knowing into a more engaged practice of leisure research for decolonization. The particularities that I offer herein for moving forward with such a project are intentionally hesitant, vague, and suggestive. I've opted instead to represent in this commentary the tensions of not knowing, how this might serve Settler scholars as a situated stance, and how COVID-19 might open us to this epistemological mode of relation. As I wrestle through this pandemic, I often feel the vulnerability, anxiety, sense of loss. But I'm also often awash with gratitude: for the new stories of care, friendship, ingenuity, and resiliency that are awakening; and for learning from the intensity of this experience in not knowing.

Notes

[1]"Settler colonialism" is a particular form of colonial invasion characterized by the ongoing occupation Indigenous lands exerted through social, political, and economic structures built by settler society. "Settler" refers to a situated, place-based, and process-based identity that connects a common group of people to settler colonization.
[2]Thanks to MK Stinson for helping to clarify my thinking here, and troubling it elsewhere!
[3]Sticky lyrics from *Prairie Lullaby* by JT & the Clouds come to mind here. They sing: "You get who you is from who you was. And we don't pass through storms, they pass through us."
[4]Indigenous peoples in Canada include diverse First Nations, Inuit, and Métis peoples. While I recognize identities as fluid and hybrid, my aim is to respect individuals and communities that self-identify as "Indigenous", especially in and where Indigenous identities mean "being oppositional to colonization" (Lowman & Barker, 2015, p. 14).
[5]I am grateful to Emma Lee of tebrakunna country for providing constructive feedback on an earlier draft of this commentary and for keeping me alert to the teachings of our more-than-human kin. Thanks also to the anonymous reviewer and special issue editors for their thoughtful feedback.

ORCID

Bryan S. R. Grimwood http://orcid.org/0000-0003-1555-7541

References

Akomolafe, B. (2017). *These wilds beyond our fences: Letters to my daughter on humanity's search for home*. North Atlantic Books.
Berbary, L. A. (2020). Theorypracticing differently: Re-imagining the public, health, and social research. *Leisure Sciences*, 1–10. https://doi.org/10.1080/01490400.2020.1720872
Cameron, E. (2015). *Far off metal river: Inuit lands, settler stories, and the making of the contemporary Arctic*. UBC Press.
Carlson, E. (2017). Anti-colonial methodologies and practices for settler colonial studies. *Settler Colonial Studies*, 7(4), 496–517. https://doi.org/10.1080/2201473X.2016.1241213

Coulthard, G. S. (2014). *Red skin, white masks: Rejecting the colonial politics of recognition.* University of Minnesota Press.

Cruikshank, J. (2005). *Do glaciers listen? Local knowledge, colonial encounters, and social imagination.* UBC Press.

Grimwood, B. S. R., & Johnson, C. W. (2019). Collective memory work as an unsettling methodology in tourism. *Tourism Geographies*, 1–22. https://doi.org/10.1080/14616688.2019.1619823

Grimwood, B. S. R., Muldoon, M., & Stevens, Z. M. (2019). Settler colonialism, Indigenous cultures, and promotional landscape of tourism in Ontario, Canada's "near north. *Journal of Heritage Tourism*, 14(3), 233–248. https://doi.org/10.1080/1743873X.2018.1527845

Grimwood, B. S. R., Stinson, M. J., & King, L. (2019). A decolonizing settler story. *Annals of Tourism Research*, 79, 102763–102711. https://doi.org/10.1016/j.annals.2019.102763

Johnson, C. W., & Parry, D. C. (2016). *Fostering social justice through qualitative inquiry.* Left Coast Press.

Jones, A., & Jenkins, K. (2008). Rethinking collaboration: Working the Indigene-Colonizer hyphen. In N. K. Denzin, Y. S. Lincoln, & L. T. Smith (Eds.), *Handbook of critical indigenous methodologies* (pp. 471–486). SAGE.

Kimmerer, R. W. (2013). *Braiding sweetgrass: Indigenous wisdom, scientific knowledge, and the teachings of plants.* Milkweed Editions.

Latour, B. (1993). *We have never been modern.* Harvard University Press.

Lee, E. (2017). Performing colonisation: The manufacture of Black female bodies in tourism research. *Annals of Tourism Research*, 66, 95–104. https://doi.org/10.1016/j.annals.2017.06.001

Lowman, E. B., & Barker, A. J. (2015). *Settler: Identity and colonialism in 21st century Canada.* Fernwood Publishing.

Mackey, E. (2015). *Unsettled expectations: Uncertainty, land and settler decolonization.* Fernwood Publishing.

Regan, P. (2010). *Unsettling the settler within: Indian residential schools, truth telling, and reconciliation in Canada.* UBC Press.

Stinson, M. J., Grimwood, B. S. R., & Caton, K. (2020). Becoming common plantain: Metaphor, settler responsibility, and decolonizing tourism. *Journal of Sustainable Tourism*, 1–20. https://doi.org/10.1080/09669582.2020.1734605

Truth and Reconciliation Commission of Canada (TRC). (2015). *Honouring the truth, reconciling for the future: Summary of the final report of the Truth and Reconciliation Commission of Canada.* Library and Archives Canada.

Tuck, E., & Yang, W. K. (2012). Decolonization is not a metaphor. *Decolonization: Indigeneity, Education & Society*, 1(1), 1–40.

Pandemic Precarity: Aging and Social Engagement

Shannon Hebblethwaite, Laurel Young, and Tristana Martin Rubio

ABSTRACT
Social isolation of older adults was identified as a key public health issue prior to the onset of COVID-19. The current crisis raises serious questions about how societies are organized and function in relation to aging populations. Drawing on resources in critical gerontology on "precarious aging" (Butler, 2009; Grenier & Phillipson, 2018) and an intersectional approach (Crenshaw, University of Chicago Legal Forum, 1(8), 139–167, 1989) that recognizes aging as an axis of oppression, we will (1) outline how this pandemic provides opportunities for candid dialogue about systemic institutional failures within leisure and social services sectors as they relate to older adults, taking important intersections of race, class, gender and ability into account; (2) examine how leisure and the arts have been positioned in response to social isolation of older people during a pandemic and (3) explore the risks of further marginalization inherent in these activities even as they are potentially crucial and transformative social lifelines for older adults. We call the further marginalization of older adults already precariously positioned "pandemic precarity."

Introduction

Discourses surrounding aging often portray social isolation and loneliness as significant challenges, impacting not only social and emotional wellbeing, but also physical health (Brooke & Jackson, 2020). Contrary to this discourse, however, loneliness and isolation affect people of all ages.[1] The COVID-19 pandemic and associated physical distancing practices have brought into relief the experiences of people who are regularly subjected to marginalization and isolation.[2] Tommy Dunne, dementia advocate and person living with dementia said, "This coronavirus will have given many people their first taste of social isolation, being told when you can go out, who and how many you can meet. Having dementia is like this all of the time" (Dunne 2020, April 16).

---

[1] In fact, recent research suggests that 10% of young people aged 16–24 years report often being lonely, compared to 3% of older people (Office for National Statistics, 2018).

[2] Important distinctions exist between isolation and loneliness that are beyond the scope of this paper. We highlight the two terms here because they are often linked and used interchangeably in media discourse related to aging.

This unparalleled crisis, in tandem with restrictions on leisure activities, has exposed, made compelling and aggravated the underlying social pathologies in Canada that contribute to the precarity of older people, including financial instability, precarious housing, lack of social inclusion and health inequalities. In our specific context in Montreal, Canada, older adults are in a position of acute precarity (Grenier & Phillipson, 2018). Thirty-five percent of adults over the age of 65 live alone and 28% report difficulty buying goods and accessing services (Markon et al., 2017). Only 50% of those over the age of 75 access the Internet regularly, pointing to an intergenerational and intragenerational digital divide (CEFRIO, 2018).

Aging, intersectionality and precarity

Once the COVID-19 pandemic was declared, older people, arbitrarily defined as age 70 and over, were the first to have their activities restricted. Although it is true that older adults face relatively higher risks for medical complications due to COVID-19, their risks cannot be reduced to chronological age. Butler's (2009) work provides resources for thinking through the heightened risk older adults disproportionately face in this pandemic as a result of inadequately organized and maintained conditions thereby subjecting them to unjustifiable suffering. As Tremain (2020) argues, *vulnerability* to COVID-19 is not an inherent property of the older body so much *as* a body "rendered vulnerable"—or "vulnerableized"—by systemic attitudinal, institutional and cultural circumstances (e.g., ageism, financial instability, precarious housing, social exclusion and health inequalities). Older lives have been enabled and disabled by politically induced *precarious* conditions that disproportionately expose some populations to different degrees of moral injury and violence (Butler, 2009). Indeed, the COVID-19 pandemic has not created extreme social isolation among older adults or the precarious conditions in long-term care homes as the case may be, so much as forcefully exposed them to the light of day.

Similarly, care providers are made vulnerable by the nature of their working conditions. Indeed, when the majority of carers are themselves "vulnerableized" by the nature of their precarious working conditions, the lives of older adults are devalued. Over the past two decades, austerity measures implemented by governments of all political stripes have decimated the workforce in homecare, hospitals and long-term care thus lowering an already questionable standard of care in many facilities. Provincial governments have established only minimum standards for the provision of leisure services, often only requiring one individual with "related" training to assume a designated lead role, left to depend on volunteers for help. Due to large resident to staff ratios,[3] facilities have resorted to large group leisure programing, which is not suitable for all individuals and unsustainable when physical distancing measures must be implemented. Of course, well organized volunteer programs are important but "care work is skilled work" (Armstrong et al., 2020, p. 5) and a comprehensive and humane realization of care must include a range of professional leisure and arts services that provide meaningful

---

[3]In long-term care facilities in Quebec, each resident is entitled to only 26 minutes of leisure programming per week. Typically, residences employ one full-time employee plus 1 day/week part-time employee in a residence of 100 people.

opportunities for all older adults to fulfill their unique potentials in context, going well beyond meeting their basic physiological needs. Indeed, by treating older people this way, we are effectively saying that older lives matter to different degrees.

Currently, many leisure and arts professionals working with older adults find themselves in a position of precarity,[4] working at several facilities, making low hourly wages (in some cases as low as $15–18 per hour) with no job protection or benefits. This devaluation of care for older adults has resulted in unacceptable tragedy. Better quality leisure and arts services must be enabled to foster the provision of care in a safe way, with job security and appropriate compensation for this work to prevent similar future tragedies.

Policy decisions made during the COVID-19 crisis (e.g., the distribution of ventilators, discharging older adults from hospitals back to long-term care facilities with active COVID-19 outbreaks) have further devalued the lives of older people. Despite the health risks that this posed to older adults, the hospital system was prioritized from the start and little attention paid to the implications of disease spread in long-term care settings until it was too late (Montpetit, 2020, April 15).

This pandemic, therefore, has dramatically brought to light the intertwining of aging and ability as an axis of oppression. Traditionally, intersectionality has the goal of bringing to light the intimate relationship among identities—such as race, gender and class—with the oppressive influence of systems of power that structure them (Crenshaw, 1989) but age (Calasanti & Giles, 2018) and (dis)ability (Tremain, 2020) are often overlooked. However, there can be no understanding of race, gender, ability or class without aging as the harms of racism, sexism, ableism and classism are borne out through time. Aging is not merely the accidental feature of a social identity but rather a structure of being, capable of "othering" of us all.

Gerontological scholars have responded to ageism inherent in the implementation of policy, cautioning that using age alone as a criterion for decision making is fundamentally wrong, stating:

> As a population group, it is wrong and overly simplistic to regard people who are aged 70 and above as being vulnerable, a burden, or presenting risks to other people. Many people in this age group are fit, well, and playing an active role in society. Older people participate in paid work, run businesses, volunteer, are active in civil society and the cultural life of communities, and take care of family members including parents, spouses/partners, adult children (especially those living with disabilities), and grandchildren. (Scharf et al., 2020, March 20)

This calls into question the homogenization of older adults, encouraging us to account for characteristics such as age, gender, ethnicity, race, sexual orientation, disability, socioeconomic status, marital status, place of residence, care roles and associated inequalities (e.g., people who are imprisoned or experiencing homelessness). We caution against policy measures that reinforce ageist discourse that devalues older lives and views all people over a certain age as sharing a particular set of characteristics. Cruikshank (2000, p. 160, 159) instead calls for the practice of "conscious aging," which

---

[4]Like the circumstances of personal support workers, largely racialized women, who because of precarious employment and the need to work in multiple facilities, along with a lack of personal protective equipment for staff in CHSLDs and the structure of the environment (shared living quarters, communal dining, etc.).

involves a "mindful resistance" to age stereotypes. This does not mean setting aside an awareness that with age comes limitations. Rather, it encourages us to stay attuned to changes in capacities and different material conditions of existence that put some older people at more risk than others.

Leisure, arts and aging in a digital age

During this unprecedented time of imposed physical distancing, a wide range of leisure and creative endeavors have been deployed—some in-person but most online—to facilitate coping and maintain some sense of "normalcy" in our daily lives. This involves consuming a continuously expanding range of cultural and entertainment offerings (e.g., virtual art gallery tours, streamed live music performances) and participation in leisure and creative activities, such as singing in virtual choirs, executing cooperative apartment balcony performances and artistic renderings of hopeful messages displayed in windows, to name but a few. It is hard to imagine what our lives would be like during this pandemic if these opportunities for meaningful engagement were inaccessible or unavailable. However, prior to COVID-19, this exclusion was and continues to be the case for many older adults.

Unfortunately, it has taken a pandemic and tragic loss of life to bring more widespread awareness to dire living situations of many older adults. With ongoing reports that basic care needs of older adults are not being met, it may seem trivial to be advocating for better access to high quality leisure and arts programs. However, if we are to move forward with a comprehensive plan that genuinely seeks to address the diverse needs of older adults, leisure and arts initiatives that enable them to flourish in context (Armstrong et al., 2020) are a critical component of this plan.

Like many human beings, older adults can benefit from participating in activities that bring meaning to their lives, going beyond pursuits related solely to basic survival needs (Fortune & McKeown, 2016). Although leisure is not necessarily a universal good, research has shown that meaning in life is associated with higher levels of resilience, which helps older adults to maintain better physical, mental, social and spiritual health (Mohseni et al., 2019). A sense of meaningfulness has been associated with being creative, feeling connected to self and others, having opportunities for choice and self-determination, and engaging in endeavors that reflect and express one's cultural identity (Baumeister et al., 2013; Dattilo et al., 2017).

Admittedly, there have been some recent attempts to address this challenge through the establishment of "cost effective" programs such as Music and Memory[TM] iPod music listening programs for persons living with dementia ("Music & memory," 2020) and social prescribing initiatives where health professionals refer patients to social activities as complementary to more "conventional" medicine ("Social prescribing: Facts and links," 2020). Although these initiatives are well intentioned and can result in some benefits, they are an oversimplification of the myriad ways in which leisure and arts programs can actually support a diverse population of older persons and thus should not be regarded as a "one size fits all" solution. Furthermore, these initiatives risk further marginalizing some older people and do not address crucial issues of accessibility, personalization, contextualization, quality control and safety (Young, 2017). Considering the heterogeneity of older people through an intersectional lens helps to elucidate the precarity that has been heightened for older adults during the COVID-19 crisis, particularly related to technology and online engagement.

Since the onset of public health directives to self-isolate, there have been high hopes for technological progress to address myriad challenges elucidated by the pandemic. There are innumerable heartwarming (or heart wrenching) stories of tablets and smartphones being deployed to connect isolated older adults with their families. To be sure, when used with skill and purpose, digital leisure can facilitate social connections for older adults (Genoe et al., 2018). Online discussion groups have contributed to the cohesion and persistence of community (Leonard & Hebblethwaite, 2017) and a sense of empowerment for older adults (Nimrod, 2009). Older activists have harnessed the power of digital media to facilitate activism and raise awareness of issues such as food insecurity, elder abuse and accessibility (RECAA, 2018).

Often ignored in a time of techno-futurist confidence are the digital inequalities (e.g., internet access and ownership of digital devices) and varied digital literacy among older people that result in increased alienation and social exclusion (Hebblethwaite, 2017). People's desire to maintain social connectedness is adjusted when infrastructure is poor or if they had unpleasant experiences with digital technologies. Furthermore, negative impressions of digital technologies are difficult to change once the infrastructure improves (Melvin et al., 2015).

The "process of digital inclusion should aim to promote the 'good use' (conscious, careful, thoughtful, moderate, unperturbing, relational contexts) of digital technology and not simply the diffusion of computers, tablets, and smartphones" (Colombo et al., 2015, p. 54). We cannot ignore the human and social systems that must also be in place for technology to make a difference, including: physical, digital and social resources and relationships; content and language; literacy and education; community and institutional structures. As Young (2017) argues, the use of personal music listening devices to "treat" the behavioral and psychological symptoms of dementia is an oversimplified "magic pill solution" that in fact can isolate or agitate some individuals and does not fully account for the creative and relational fulfillment that more interactive contextualized music experiences can afford.

Engagement with digital technology, like any leisure or arts practice, should be a collaborative decision that allows individuals to make informed choices about their involvement. Adopting digital media without careful consideration of its implications can not only lead to ineffective practices but may also result in direct harm to participants if issues of privacy and management of personal data are not considered.

Conclusion

The COVID-19 crisis has illuminated the precarity that older people experience in relation to the pandemic. Drawing on theoretical frames of precarity and incorporating an intersectional lens, we call into question the homogenization of older people. We offer this reflection as an opportunity to unsettle ageist discourses, policies and practices that differently value the lives of older adults. By questioning how we foster engagement with leisure and the arts in a digital age, we hope to shed light on the precarity and vulnerabilization of older people and their carers resulting from the ways in which aging is constituted through Canadian health and social service systems. Engaging with the intersecting vectors of age and ability with race, class and gender, we draw attention to ongoing ways that societies are underpaying, undervaluing and exploiting the physical and emotional labor that largely goes unrecognized. Additionally, when planning leisure and arts-based experiences, we need to better account for these intersecting vectors in order to avoid further marginalizing the diverse population of older adults. We encourage the practice of conscious aging (Cruikshank, 2000) to reflect upon the complex ways in which age acts as an axis of oppression both during and beyond the pandemic.

References

Armstrong, P., Armstrong, H., Choiniere, J., Lowndes, R., Struthers, J. (2020). Re-imagining long -term residential care in the Covid-19 crisis. https://www.trentu.ca/aging/sites/trentu.ca.aging/files/documents/2020%20mcri%20covid19%20final.pdf

Baumeister, R. F., Vohs, K. D., Aaker, J. L., & Garbinsky, E. N. (2013). Some key differences between a happy life and a meaningful life. *The Journal of Positive Psychology, 8*(6), 505–516. https://doi.org/10.1080/17439760.2013.830764

Brooke, J., & Jackson, D. (2020). Older people and COVID-19: Isolation, risk and ageism. *Journal of Clinical Nursing,* 1–3.

Butler, J. (2009). *Frames of war: When is life grievable?* Verso.

Calasanti, T., & Giles, S. (2018). The challenge of intersectionality. *Generations, 41*(4), 69–74.

CEFRIO. (2018). *Vieillir à l'ère numérique.* https://cefrio.qc.ca/media/1898/netendances-2018_veillir_avec_le_numerique.pdf

Colombo, F., Aroldi, P., & Carlo, S. (2015). New elders, old divides: ICTs, inequalities and well-being amongst young elderly Italians. *Communicar, 45*(23), 47–55.

Crenshaw, K. (1989). Demarginalizing the intersection of race and sex: A black feminist critique of antidiscrimination doctrine, feminist theory and antiracist politics. *University of Chicago Legal Forum, 1*(8), 139–167.

Cruikshank, M. (2000). *Learning to be old: Gender, culture, and aging.* Rowman & Littlefield.

Dattilo, J., Mogle, J., Lorek, A. E., Freed, S., & Frysinger, M. (2017). Using self-determination theory to understand challenges to aging, adaptation, and leisure among community-dwelling older adults. *Activities, Adaptation & Aging, 42*(2), 85–103. https://doi.org/10.1080/01924788.2017.1388689

Dunne, T. (2020, April 16). *BEM isolation.* https://twitter.com/search?q=tommy%20dunne%20BEM%20isolation&src=typed_query

Fortune, D., & McKeown, J. (2016). Sharing the journey: Exploring a social leisure program for persons with dementia and their spouses. *Leisure Sciences, 38*(4), 373–387. https://doi.org/10.1080/01490400.2016.1157776

Genoe, R., Kulczycki, C., Marston, H., Freeman, S., Musselwhite, C., & Rutherford, H. (2018). E-leisure and older adults: Findings from an exploratory study. *Therapeutic Recreation Journal, 52*(1), 1–18. https://doi.org/10.18666/TRJ-2018-V52-I1-8417

Grenier, A., & Phillipson, C. (2018). Precarious aging: Insecurity and risk in late life. What makes a good life in late life? citizenship and justice in aging societies, special report. *Hastings Center Report, 48*(5), S15–S18.

Hebblethwaite, S. (2017). The (in)visibility of older adults in digital leisure cultures. In S. Carnicelli, D. MacGillivray & G. McPherson (Eds.), *Digital leisure cultures: Critical perspectives.* (pp. 94–106). Routledge.

Leonard, K. C., & Hebblethwaite, S. (2017). Exploring community inclusion in older adulthood through the use of computers and tablets. *Therapeutic Recreation Journal, 51*(4), 274–290. https://doi.org/10.18666/TRJ-2017-V51-I4-8526

Markon, M.-P., Lemieux, V., Lebel, P., Dupont, M. (2017). *Portrait des aînés de l'Île de Montréal. Centre intégré universitaire de santé et de Services sociaux du Centre-Sud-de-l'Île-de-Montréal & Direction régionale de santé publique.* http://collections.banq.qc.ca/ark:/52327/2976961

Melvin, R. M., Bunt, A., Oduor, E., Neustaedter, C. (2015, April). The effect of signal expense and dependability on family communication in rural and northern Canada [Paper presentation]. In *Proceedings of the 33rd Annual ACM Conference on Human Factors in Computing Systems* (pp. 717–726). ACM. https://doi.org/10.1145/2702123.2702301

Mohseni, M., Iranpour, A., Naghibzadeh-Tahami, A., Kazazi, L., & Borhaninejad, V. (2019). The relationship between meaning in life and resilience in older adults: A cross-sectional study. In J Boy, F Detienne, & J. D. Fekete, (eds.), *Health Psychology Report, 7*(2), 133–138. https://doi.org/10.5114/hpr.2019.85659

Montpetit, J. (2020, April 15). Why are Quebec's nursing homes so understaffed, and what's being done about it. *CBC News.* https://www.cbc.ca/news/canada/montreal/quebec-nursing-homes-understaffed-1.5531997

Music & memory. (2020). Music & Memory©. https://musicandmemory.org/

Nimrod, G. (2009). The Internet as a resource in older adults' leisure. *International Journal on Disability and Human Development, 8*(3), 207–214. https://doi.org/10.1515/IJDHD.2009.8.3.207

Office for National Statistics. (2018). *Analysis of characteristics and circumstances associated with loneliness in England using the Community Life Survey, 2016 to 2017.* http://bit.ly/3b8wSzr.

RECAA. (2018). *Ressources ethnoculturelles contre l'abuse envers les aîné(e)s.* http://recaa.ca

Scharf, T., Holland, C., Newman, A., Price, D., Buffel, T., Carney, G., Christopher, G., Devine, P., Hyde, M., Lariviere, M., Marston, H., Martin, W., Musselwhite, C., & Vandravela, T. (2020, April 16). *COVID-19: Statement from the President and Members of the Executive Committee of the British Society of Gerontology.* https://ageingissues.wordpress.com/

Social prescribing: Facts and links. (2020). Culture, Health & Wellbeing Alliance. https://www.culturehealthandwellbeing.org.uk/resources/social-prescribing

Tremain, S. (2020, April 1). *COVID-19 and the naturalization of vulnerability* [Blog post for Biopolitical Philosophy]. https://biopoliticalphilosophy.com/2020/04/01/covid-19-and-the-naturalization-of-vulnerability/

Young, L. (2017, February 11). *Challenging assumptions about how music helps* [Blog post for Oxford University Press]. https://blog.oup.com/2017/02/challenging-assumptions-how-music-helps/

A People's Future of Leisure Studies: Leisure with the Enemy Under COVID-19

Rasul A. Mowatt (iD)

ABSTRACT

To those of us who have been consistently critical of leisure, we have mapped our critique of leisure onto discussions of leisure as a concept, as a tool, or as a social construct in society that has had serious implications on the gendered, the racialized, and the classed as disposable. Leisure is a life-politic that hides: dominant lifestyles, harmful environmental engagement, and political regimes. But in the midst of pandemic, there are two enemies, at the mirco- and macro-level to the life of a person via leisure that are becoming exposed at this time: 1) Person to Person; and, 2) The State to Person. With the coronavirus pandemic, it reveals a need to depart from a happiness and titillation orientation of leisure, and more a collective life-giving requisite in our research, instruction, and advocacy. For with COVID-19, leisure (as it is predominantly conceived) is the enemy.

Whistling past a graveyard, a phrase that connotes the need to be positive in the midst of extremely dire circumstances, and is also not unlike a sentiment to promote the benefits of leisure during a global pandemic with lasting repercussions. Facing this reality is difficult I must admit, but we must set our minds on both the now and the later. Set our minds on what exactly? Well, it is quite easy to think about leisure as an experience that people of varying degrees of complicated privilege engage in. This is a very individualistic perspective, making the affect of leisure never a collective consideration. Leisure, in this conception, begins and ends with the person. By extension, this conception of leisure in society influences researchers to stay proximate to this individualistic perspective of leisure (experiences, choices, and free time). While the individualistic perspective always needed a reckoning, the global pandemic of this coronavirus (SARS2-CoV-2) and its disease (COVID-19) is forcing a philosophical reckoning in startling and immediate ways.

To those of us who have been consistently critical of leisure (in how it is conceived, represented, and discussed), we mapped our critique onto discussions of leisure social construct in society that has had serious implications on the gendered and the racialized disposable class. While the experience of leisure is individualistic, the impact and implications have never been. The focus is not on leisure as what it does for the person, but what it does to society. In no way am I providing a panacean view of leisure as shared. Instead, leisure impacts us as public cultural construct rife with ideals, tastes, and beliefs that we may not share nor want. As a collective reality, I am saying leisure implicates societies as they continuously solidify class divisions in everyday life.

This commentary argues that leisure is more than an experience, it is instead a complicated and problematic reality that is public and collective, and COVID-19 both hides and reveals this toxic reality. Leisure, as your "friend", is challenged in this commentary and is argued as life-threatening and -ending rather than life-giving and -sustaining. What is then highlighted are two (micro- and macro-) enemies to the life of a person via leisure that have been exposed at this time of the coronavirus: 1) *Person to Person*, by way of abuse and violence; and, 2) *The State to Person*, for the explicit purpose of control. With COVID-19, leisure is the enemy.

Person to person

Gaining some attention over the initial weeks of the "shelter-in-place" mandates by public officials has been the concern of violence in the home. Intimate partner violence, child abuse, senior abuse, and even more tragic, domestic abuse killings will have an acute increase if a person must be with one or more abusers for months (and even a projected year). In the United Kingdom, at least 16 incidents (the killing of women by men, including children) occurred just over a three-week period (Grierson, 2020). While in the United States for a portion of March 2020, hotlines like Childhelp National Child Abuse Hotline already saw a "23 percent increase in call and a 263 percent increase in texts compared to March 2019" (Venkatraman, 2020). Long-term sheltering concerns fall in line with research that indicated holidays were accompanied by spikes in domestic violence incidences. In using a broader term, *intimate terrorism,* to include all experiences of violence but also "isolation from friends, family and employment; constant surveillance; strict, detailed rules for behavior; and restrictions on access to such basic necessities as food, clothing and sanitary facilities" (Taub, 2020).

Social distancing at home may keep one safe from the virus, but it only further empowers an abuser. Walker (1979) articulated a battering cycle that included three sequential stages within a repetitive process of violence as long as relational proximity endures: 1) the tension-building phase; 2) the acute battering phase; and, 3) the loving contrition/honeymoon phase. While Williams (2005) noted a four-phased sexual assault cycle: a) build-up phase; b) acting-out phase; c) justification phase; and, d) pretend normal phase (p. 300). Within Williams' (2005) study, recreation was used,

> in the acting-out phase … watching videos, playing pool, and hiking with the victim, and functioned to persuade the victim to participate in planned sexual activities … in the justification phase to provide psychological benefits such as reducing stress, tension and fear associated with the crime … in the pretend normal phase … functioned in various ways to help the offender maintain a normal image to others. (p. 92)

For Walker (2006) warned in situating these actions as deviant, "'healthy' leisure also may play in the larger process of criminogenesis" (p. 92). Even in nonviolent times one is living under the threat of the acute battery stage or the acting out phase. So in fearing threats to one's life: Do you contain your excitement in beating your parent in a video game? Do you stay awake if your partner insists on binge-watching a show on Netflix? Do you workout because your spouse does not like your weight-gain during isolation? As a research aim related to this reality, leisure cannot be the focus because of the potentiality for violence via leisure. Intimate terrorism would need to be the focus of study. Even in the practitioner realm, leisure-based industries could be a viable solution. But this would take quite a different conceptualization and use of leisure spaces similar to how France has converted some hotels specifically for survivors of abuse (Godin et al., 2020). While not all of those facing abuse are gendered as women, women are overrepresented in global cases of intimate terrorism.

If we see women servicing their abusers whims in both leisure and abuse, the undergirding of the lack of legal protections from intimate terrorism is that these incidences are matters of the "home", the private-public space. This idea of the home as the sphere of women only returns us to the 1800s *Cult of Domesticity* virtue of submission to their duty in service to those gendered as men. This especially troubles women in ways that further makes enacting agency now "unvirtuous", if not difficult and impossible. With the additional threat of COVID-19, how does one shelter-in-place without a shelter, especially when it's lost due to abuse? The public health guideline of flattening the curve to protect others unintentionally contributes to the loss of their own protection.

By extension, this undervaluing of women in their homes from intimate terrorism correlates with the abuse of those occupying low wage and gig economy positions. Women, especially women of color, are overly represented in these occupations that are satisfying the shopping needs of the privileged with virtually no financial and health assistance. The relationship to these means of production is also the operating origin for gender and racial discrimination in Western societies. Controlling their labor by situating them in a labor class controls their leisure and wealth, as one must be an owner (member of the Veblen's leisure class) of the means of production to fully enjoy leisure. Women featured as essential workers in TV commercials mask the reality that their essentiality only goes as far as their cost is not a burden to the home and broader society. Capitalism, patriarchy, and conspicuous consumption will only allow this reality to thrive under COVID-19, as gender, Race, and queer identities are only some of the modalities *through which* class is experienced. And, this experience is dangerous in the time of the coronavirus. When the personal (micro-level) becomes deadly, there is a need for the public sector to become the sanctuary.

The state to person

However, the public may be considered equally threatening or deadly depending on one's placement in either a racialized ethnicity or ethnitized racial groups. Revisiting the notion that leisure spaces are effective for the 1) articulation of power; 2) places of demarcation; and, 3) reification of the racial order, the racial geography of COVID-19 can be mapped alongside the ongoing spread of social blame for the virus throughout the world. In a *racecraft* sleight of hand with unsubstantiated claims, the identification of people as vectors for coronavirus leads to retaliatory actions or calls for repressive policies onto those populations. The initial (and still persistent) view that SARS2-CoV-2 was a "Chinese" virus resulted in case-upon-case of hostilities toward Asian-identified tourists on holiday in Canada, France, Italy, and the United Kingdom as early as January 2020 (Giuffrida & Wilsher, 2020). This xenophobic "Kung-Flu" labeling implies a biological and cultural disposition to the coronavirus. But it aids barring "all people coming from China" from entering restaurants and entertainment venues, refusing service from Asian labor in the hospitality industry, and not buying from Asian vendors after such published headlines, as France's "Alert Jaune" (Yellow Alert) became commonplace (Courrier Picard, 2020), much less travel bans to other countries.

The barring of certain people based race in leisure spaces, re-invokes Philipp's (2000) questioning of institutionalized racial discrimination, "how many Whites avoid leisure places and activities because there are too many Blacks present? ... how many Blacks must be present in a leisure space before Whites begin avoiding it?", but specific to this pandemic (p. 122). In Guangzhou, China, African nationals have been ejected from hotels, and other public spaces as they have been blamed for a second wave of COVID-19 (Sun, 2020). While in India, attacks upon Muslim and the Dalit class have only intensified with the spread of the virus. India's health ministry made false claims that the initial ground zero were Muslim tourists at an Islamic Seminary readied as terrorist "corona bombs" for a #CoronaJihad (Frayer, 2020), that recalls anti-Muslim incitement post-September 11th (Livengood & Stodolska). Countries with fraught histories of racial violence could very well see similar actions as the situation worsens.

In March 2020, the United States' Federal Bureau of Investigation ran nearly 3.7 million background checks from gun purchases, and with some states seeing a 1,000% increase in sales (Volpe, 2020). Does COVID-19 present a "trigger" for existing animus toward racialized groups? This is not a far-fetched line of questioning, in post-Hurricane Katrina there were founded allegations of White vigilantes positioned on roof tops shooting African Americans with impunity for "fun" in the name of protecting neighborhoods from "savages" (DOJ, 2019). So, it is concerning to see cases in the United States in which Klan members are grocery shopping with hoods as face coverings (Papenfuss, 2020). Does this return society to a point in which affiliation and affinity to White Nationalist organizations were displayed without restriction in leisure spaces (Mowatt, 2019)? While online activity of anti-government groups indicate preparation for the "Boogaloo" or the inevitable civil war due to the coronavirus and economic collapse (Mathias, 2020), as well as the concerning animation of public space for anti-lockdown protests.

Yet, city officials in Eastern Illinois have asked for residents to "tip your masks" (lowering it slightly) to prevent racial bias because, "if people were to commit a crime, they wouldn't tip ... [and] be caught on camera" (Ricossa, 2020). This is in spite of nation-wide concerns of wearing any facial covering by Black and Brown population. Mayors have sternly condemned social gathering and alluded to the poor health indices of racialized Black and Brown populations as the culprits of the spread, thereby leading to excessive uses of force on "hangouts" and people playing in East Village parks of New York City. But leniency was extended to West Village park attendees despite violations of social distancing; with some cases of police interaction revolving around masks provision to those that were basking in the sun (Noor, 2020), yet 35 of 40 arrests were Black. As society slowly re-opens, so will repressive and life-threatening policing (Maynard & Ritchie, 2020). More troubling are nation-states enacting harsher authoritarian responses for stay-at-home violations because of such things as gathering in parks to exercise and socialize with reports in Brazil, the Philippines, Israel's Gaza Strip, and South Africa of deaths from law enforcement officers acting on orders to shoot violators on sight (Roth, 2020). Racecrafting is the "social alchemy … that transforms racism into race" (Fields & Fields, 2012, p. 262). The will and intent of the State to do and allow harm upon a segment of its populace is skillfully turned into the perception of the attributes of those populations. The articulated rhetoric of State actors that are repeated through news outlets, become the demarcated basis for extra-judicial actions of everyday citizens and for State policy that reifies the racial order. When the State (macro-level) fails at protecting human life, all other nominal recourses become failed endeavors.

A concluding perspective

This perspective of leisure is not about the gleefully free idea of happiness, but more a public assurance on leisure as a life giver. This invokes an idea that leisure is more than a matter of quality of life, but must be the counter to all forms of life-threatening and -ending actions. With the absence of the "bread and circus" in mass spectacle leisure to occupy much of our minds, this pandemic is revealing a reality that wealth and privilege are the vectors most responsible for transmitting the disease, and it will be experienced most through the intimacies of poverty (Taylor, 2020). And it is no surprise that woman, as a gendered whole, and people of color, as a racialized group, are overly represented in lower economic classes. Leisure as a matter of personal growth is a life-politic that hides: dominant notions of lifestyles, harmful environmental engagement, and actions of political regimes. The societies that we have created that bolster the fragile and false lifestyles of leisure are in now in question.

At some point, a vaccine will be produced (that French doctors opined should be tested on Africans). So, will there be a rush back to the old normal that was already untenable for a labor class devoted to all of the provisions of leisure for less than nominal pay with little to no leisure of their own? Will there be a rush to a new normal created by the experiences of the pandemic to create a society more responsible of social inequalities? Or, will there be a quickening to more decay due to environmental non-restrictions that creates exposure to the next pathogen? A since deleted tweet from a New York health official indicated that public parks were being prepped for use as temporary grave sites for the infected dead, however parks have become emergency field-sites for overloaded hospitals (Woodward & Mosher, 2020). Herein lies the irony, *whistling past a park* could very well become the next idiom to convey a critique at not taking things seriously. I hope that you and I are alive.

ORCID

Rasul A. Mowatt (iD) http://orcid.org/0000-0003-4177-0725

References

Courrier Picard. (2020, January 26). À propos de notre une du 26 janvier. https://www.courrier-picard.fr/id64729/article/2020-01-26/propos-de-notre-une-du-26-janvier

Department of Justice. (2019, February 14). New Orleans man sentenced for hate crime in shooting of three African-American men attempting to evacuate after Hurricane Katrina. *The United States Department of Justice, Office of Public Affairs.* https://www.justice.gov/opa/pr/new-orleans-man-sentenced-hate-crime-shooting-three-african-american-men-attempting-evacuate

Fields, K., & Fields, B. J. (2012). *Racecraft: The soul of inequality in American life.* Verso.

Frayer, L. (2020, April 16). Hindu nationalists blame Muslims for India's COVID-19 crisis. *NPR.* https://www.npr.org/2020/04/16/835710029/hindu-nationalists-blame-muslims-for-indias-covid-19-crisis

Giuffrida, A., & Wilsher, K. (2020, January 31). Outbreaks of xenophobia in west as coronavirus spreads. *The Guardian.* https://www.theguardian.com/world/2020/jan/31/spate-of-anti-chinese-incidents-in-italy-amid-coronavirus-panic

Godin, M. (2020, March 31). French government to house domestic abuse victims in hotels as cases rise during coronavirus lockdown. *Time.* https://time.com/5812990/france-domestic-violence-hotel-coronavirus/

Grierson, J. (2020, April 15). Domestic abuse killings 'more than double' amid COVID-19 lockdown. *The Guardian.* https://www.theguardian.com/society/2020/apr/15/domestic-abuse-killings-more-than-double-amid-covid-19-lockdown

Livengood, J. S., & Stodolska, M. (2004). The effects of discrimination and constraints negotiation on leisure behavior of American Muslims in the post-September 11 America. *Journal of Leisure Research, 36*(2), 183–208. https://doi.org/10.1080/00222216.2004.11950019

Mathias, C. (2020, April 24). Amid the pandemic, U.S. militia groups plot "The Boogaloo," aka civil war, in Facebook. *Huffpost.* https://www.huffpost.com/entry/boogaloo-facebook-pages-coronavirus-militia-group-extremists_n_5ea3072bc5b6d376358eba98?guccounter=1

Maynard, R., & Ritchie, A. J. (2020, April 9). Black communities need support, not a coronavirus police state. *Vice News.* https://www.vice.com/en_ca/article/z3bdmx/black-people-coronavirus-police-state

Mowatt, R. A. (2018). A people's history of leisure studies: Leisure, the tool of racecraft. *Leisure Sciences, 40*(7), 663–674. https://doi.org/10.1080/01490400.2018.1534622

Mowatt, R. A. (2019). A people's history of leisure studies: Where the White Nationalists are. *Leisure Studies,* 1–18. https://doi.org/10.1080/02614367.2019.1624809

Noor, P. (2020, May 4). A tale of two cities: How New York police enforce social distancing by the color of your skin. *The Guardian.* https://www.nytimes.com/2020/05/02/nyregion/weather-parks-nyc-nj-coronavirus.html

Papenfuss, M. (2020, May 4). California shopper in Ku Klux Klan hood alarms customers, officials. *Huffpost.* https://www.huffpost.com/entry/santee-san-diego-kkk-grocery-shopper_n_5eaf9fb6c5b639d6e578a543

Philipp, S. (2000). Race and the pursuit of happiness. *Journal of Leisure Research, 32*(1), 121–124. doi: 10.1080/00222216.2000.11949899

Ricossa, M. (2020, April 23). Local group asks you to "tip your mask" to help prevent racial bias. *KWQC.* https://www.kwqc.com/content/news/Why-you-should-Tip-Your-Mask–569907021.html?fbclid=IwAR34VbpH2WnFSq6YQzHuPEDaHgXU4Zz4QL7WIbx7uxdf_0GIo07dsKtXJRo

Roth, K. (2020, April 3). How authoritarians are exploiting the COVID-19 crisis to grab power. *Human Rights Watch.* https://www.hrw.org/news/2020/04/03/how-authoritarians-are-exploiting-covid-19-crisis-grab-power#

Sun, Y. (2020, April 17). COVID-19, Africans' hardships in China, and the future of Africa-China relations. *Brookings Institute.* https://www.brookings.edu/blog/africa-in-focus/2020/04/17/covid-19-africans-hardships-in-china-and-the-future-of-africa-china-relations/

Taub, A. (2020, April 6). A new COVID-19 crisis: Domestic abuse rises worldwide. *The New York Times.* https://www.nytimes.com/2020/04/06/world/coronavirus-domestic-violence.html

Taylor, K. (2020, March 30). Reality has endorsed Bernie Sanders. *The New Yorker.* https://www.newyorker.com/news/our-columnists/reality-has-endorsed-bernie-sanders

Venkatraman, S. (2020, March 27). Experts fear child abuse will increase with coronavirus isolation. *NBC News.* https://www.nbcnews.com/news/us-news/experts-fear-child-abuse-will-increase-coronavirus-isolation-n1170811

Volpe, A. (2020, April 8). A legacy of the COVID-19 pandemic will be that even more Americans own guns. *Rolling Stone.* https://www.rollingstone.com/culture/culture-features/covid-19-coronavirus-pandemic-nra-gun-firearm-ownership-980341/

Walker, L. E. (1979). *The battered woman.* Harper & Row.

Williams, D. (2005). Functions of leisure and recreational activities within a sexual assault cycle: A case study. *Sexual Addiction & Compulsivity, 12*(4), 295–309. https://doi.org/10.1080/10720160500362553

Williams, D. (2006). Forensic leisure science: A new frontier for leisure scholars. *Leisure Sciences, 28*(1), 91–95. https://doi.org/10.1080/0149040050033274

Woodward, A., & Mosher, D. (2020, April 13). Sobering photos reveal how countries are dealing with the dead left by the coronavirus pandemic. *Business Insider.* https://www.businessinsider.com/coronavirus-covid-19-victims-bodies-burials-morgues-cemeteries-photos-2020-4#yet-even-temporary-morgue-facilities-which-expanded-typical-capacity-for-900-bodes-to-more-than-3600-became-so-full-that-officials-began-discussing-alternative-options-including-temporary-interment-in-city-parks-10

Biopolitics, Essential Labor, and the Political-Economic Crises of COVID-19

Jeff Rose (iD)

ABSTRACT
Biopolitics is the power to control life. In the early global reactions to the COVID-19 pandemic, many people's daily labor functions have been placed into stark relief, with a tripartite typology forming between those labor functions that are "essential," those labor roles that have been lost, and those that have transitioned to an online format. For those whose labor has maintained, as well as those who seek to return to pre-COVID-19 labor conditions, a crude biopolitical calculus takes place where the functioning of our capitalist political economy is weighed against the maintenance of life itself. The current pandemic exposes and highlights many of the unsustainable fault lines characteristic of contemporary capitalism, where the uneven exploitation of labor renders lives associated with some labor functions as more expendable than others. This places us in political-economic crisis, where we have choices to enact more just, equitable, and sustainable systems moving forward.

" ... the problem of biopolitics is the problem of life ... ." (Foucault, 2004, p. 78)

British Prime Minister Margaret Thatcher, a key player in the global implementation of neoliberalism, famously quipped, "the trouble with socialism is that eventually you run out of other people's money." In the initial shocks of the COVID-19 pandemic, an increasingly applicable response is that "the trouble with capitalism is that eventually you run out of other people's labor." This oversimplification of the in fact dialectical relationship between capitalism and socialism underlies complex phenomena that are rapidly unfolding in real time in response to this global pandemic. The tension, however, between capital and labor, has been more clearly exposed in the COVID-19 pandemic, and necessitates critical questions about what labor is necessary, what lives are necessary, and how capitalist power relations affect the essence of our lives. Implicit in these questions are reconsiderations of society's labor roles and the ways in which we value labor both during and after this crisis. With a particular focus on the USA, this commentary presents biopolitics as a productive theoretical lens to interrogate labor and life under capitalism, with necessary implications for leisure. Subsequently, labor roles, labor values, and leisure values come into clearer focus through the power dynamics of biopolitics, the power to regulate life itself. The commentary concludes with a discussion of the concept of *crisis* and the opportunities it presents.

Essential labor

Marxist political economy is concerned with the interrelationships between economic, political, and social systems. Capitalism, as Marx emphasized, is not strictly a way of understanding economic exchange; it is also a set of social relations, and a form of social organization, that often mirrors the logics of economic exchange. Surplus value (i.e., profit) is what remains after accounting for labor costs (paying workers) and replenishing both the conditions of production (material and environmental conditions) and the means of production (infrastructure, equipment, machinery). If workers are compensated the full value of their labor, and/or if natural systems are reinvigorated at the same rates at which they are drawn down – in other words, if the social and environmental systems are "sustainable" – then there is little or nothing left for capitalist accumulation. The maintenance of desirable profit rates relies upon the exploitation of labor and/or nature in order to operate, making it economically, socially, and environmentally unsustainable.

What the COVID-19 crisis highlights, then, is the first contradiction of capitalism, which Marx (1990 [1867]) saw as the tendency for capitalism to undermine the very economic conditions required for its existence.[1] The contradiction is that labor must not only produce value but also purchase goods and services. But maintaining safety during the outbreak requires either the absence of labor, or labor to transition to online mechanisms; otherwise, labor reduces their safety margins. Each of these options threaten capital's profit, and further exacerbate it by decreasing workers' purchasing power, another form of alienation characteristic of crises of capitalism (Marx, 1988 [1844]).

The pandemic and our social and political response to it highlights an unjust and inequitable hierarchy of labor in late-stage capitalism. As some aspects of the economy have wound down or even ground to a halt, some types of labor are more indispensable than others. Most obviously, there are the frontline "essential" workers who have not stopped working during the pandemic, and have not lost their jobs or shifted their functions to an online environment. These are workers in warehouses and grocery stores and agricultural fields, in addition to those who serve in the medical, law enforcement, emergency, and other municipal and social services. Other seemingly essential functions are those labor experiences that are noted *in absentia*, the teachers, day-care providers, and service workers who are most appreciated in their now nonappearances in our daily lives. The frontline essential labor and the lost labor are functions that are now highlighted for many of us in our daily existence, where we viscerally feel their immediate contributions to our lived experience. But one would be remiss not to also note those labor functions that are critical to our functioning that we choose not to see, those whose labor is transformed into (lesser) value in locations like homeless shelters, domestic violence transitional housing, and refugee camps, among countless others. In

---

[1]Marx's second contradiction is the tendency for capitalism to undermine its environmental preconditions. This contradiction, too, has come into clearer focus during the times of the pandemic as natural systems respond to rapidly changing rates of extraction, production, consumption, etc.

summary, in the immediate wake of COVID-19, there have emerged three classes of workers: (a) "essential" workers who remain in hazardous, exposed, frontline working conditions, followed by "non-essential" work that is comprised of (b) those that have lost their employment, and (c) a professional class that has transitioned (somewhat) to online environments.[2]

The effects of this new typology are widespread. Many people, in academia, finance, technology, law, and other professional manifestations of labor, have experienced new-found levels of anxiety and dislocation during this pandemic, but are not (immediately) threatened with a loss of a paycheck or, in the USA, loss of access to healthcare (which is often tied to employment). In comparison to the labor that is more clearly and materially expressed as "essential" during the COVID-19 response, the now often-online labor of the professional class is compensated at much higher rates than many of the professions that are desperately needed on a daily basis at this time. Not only are these essential labor functions compensated (on average) much less than those shielded in homes, apartments, and other private spaces, they are also unlikely to receive any kind of increased hazard pay for making themselves physically and materially more vulnerable for an unknown amount of time.[3] While these three categories of employment (essential, lost, and online) do not fit uniformly with rates of remuneration, there seems to be a loosely inverse relationship between wages derived from labor and how essential that labor is to communities' survival. In general, many of the essential laborers are compensated most poorly. During the COVID-19 pandemic, the entirety of the US population is seemingly dependent upon the essential labor provided by the same people we have previously suggested should not be compensated with a living wage. Class inequalities demonstrate that wealthier workers can stay at home, while poorer workers must increase their risk of exposure. We should acknowledge that division of labor results in inequities in who performs what types of labor, requiring interrogation into who performs what, for what reason, and at what costs.

An ironic dissonance expresses itself on a now daily basis for many of us. There is the labor that is essential, that is necessary, that supports life itself during these trying times, but this labor is often valued less than the non-essential labor of financiers, lawyers, tech programmers, bureaucrats, and academics. However, this approximation of who matters and who doesn't, who gets appropriately compensated and who doesn't, is simplistic and unsophisticated. It is imperative (during the pandemic and otherwise) to consider those contributions to society that elude functional and compensatory analyses. For instance, during this highly disruptive time, what is the value of art? Of history? Of communication? Activities that we often position as leisure experiences help us make sense of this strange experience we are living through. Engaging in leisure provides contributions that defy typical (crude) analyses of functionality and remuneration. Essential labor should be considered beyond merely the utilitarian, functional perpetuation of life, but also efforts that contribute to quality of life and a life well lived, traditional interests of leisure philosophers.

---

[2] This typology overlooks those already most economically maligned. Marx and Engels (1970 [1846]) referred to the lumpenproletariat, those who face unemployment, homelessness, vagrancy, and generally lack awareness of their collective oppression. The lumpenproletariat may face high virus exposure, but their labor is difficult to exploit.

[3] Tyner (2019) uses the term "dead labor" to refer to those who die all-too-soon in the making of capitalism, an apt concept for essential employees during the pandemic.

Biopolitics

How do we theoretically situate the supposedly "essential" work that supports life – whether in a utilitarian sense or in a more holistic sense – and the discourses and policies that serve as ideological foundations of the valuation of this labor? In a series of lectures in 1975–1976 titled *Society Must Be Defended*, Foucault (1997) outlined and diagnosed what he considered a new kind of power. Historically, sovereignty had the right "to take life and let live." With the emergence of capitalism in the 1700s, there was the emergence of a "power to make live and let die" (Foucault, 1997, p. 241). At its core, biopolitics is this power *to make live and let die*.

What does the power to make live and let die look like? For Foucault, this was the emergence of a discourse of life as a political problem to be addressed by the sovereign.

> Biopolitics derives its knowledge from, and defines its power's field of interventions in terms of the birth rate, the mortality rate, various biological disabilities, and the effects of the environment… Biopolitics deals with the population, with the population as a political problem, as a problem that is at once scientific and political, as a biological problem and as power's problem. And I think biopolitics emerges at this time. (Foucault, 1997, p. 245)

Foucault would later define biopolitics as "the attempt, starting from the eighteenth century, to rationalize the problems posed to governmental practice by phenomena characteristic of a set of living beings forming a population: health, hygiene, birthrate, life expectancy, race" (Foucault, 2004, p. 317). Biopolitics is a disciplinary intervention designed to modify – at the population level as opposed to the individual level – who lives and who dies. Not solely a technocratic concern, power relations interweave throughout biopolitics, as one mechanism to regulate life is through political-economic considerations, where the power of capitalism and capital-labor relations intervenes to regulate life itself. Biopolitics provides a critical framework to apply during global pandemic.

On March 22, 2020, as the extent of the COVID-19 outbreak began to be digested by the world, as death tolls mounted, businesses and schools closed, economic indicators plummeted, and "social distancing" became practice, the President of the USA proclaimed, via Twitter: WE CANNOT LET THE CURE BE WORSE THAN THE PROBLEM ITSELF. AT THE END OF THE 15 DAY PERIOD, WE WILL MAKE A DECISION AS TO WHICH WAY WE WANT TO GO! Two days later, similarly, Texas's Lieutenant Governor speculated: "Are you willing to take a chance on your survival in exchange for keeping the America that America loves for its children and grandchildren? And if that is the exchange, I'm all in." Australia's Prime Minister voiced similar sentiments, as have a variety of political leaders around the world. Scattered public protests have supported these ideas, and an active debate has ensued, that in a binaried choice between capitalism and life, we should collectively tilt toward maintaining the exploitative unsustainability of capitalism. In these sentiments, capitalism transfers from merely a political-economic system to an unquestionable ideological commitment. Capitalism becomes a religion. Capitalism's labor necessities are prioritized over the recommendations of scientists trying to minimize casualties, and an unknown additional amount of people will die so that capitalism can maintain. A previously unthinkable (or at least unspeakable) strategy becomes an option for governance during COVID-19: the state can "let die"[4] some disadvantaged few so that the fundamental mechanisms and functioning of our capitalist political economy are not further threatened. Foucault (1997) referred to this form of biopolitics as "indirect murder: the fact of exposing someone to death, increasing the risk of death for some people" (p. 256). We are disturbingly close to a sociopolitical situation where our political leaders announce, without nuance or dog whistles or ambiguity, who will be *made live* and who will be *let die*, through a simultaneously technocratic and ideological calculation that prioritizes GDP growth, stock market responsiveness, Puritanical work ethic, and continued capital accumulation and concentration.

It may seem unthinkable, but is it unthinkable? Is it unthinkable that we simultaneously respond to, resist against, and reproduce a political economy – a social system – where some are made live and others are let die?

The question of who will be *made live* and who will be *let die* falls along existing lines of social and political inequality, at multiple geographic scales. For instance, mortality rates are higher in many Global South nations, an increasing concern as the virus spreads. In the USA, the poor are more exposed to COVID-19 due to the material conditions of poverty. People of color, due to racism, are more susceptible to poverty. Susceptibility to poverty is due to capitalism, which maintains racism at structural levels. People of color are overrepresented in minimum wage jobs that kept employees at work after it was safe to do so, and they will return to work too soon. People of color are overrepresented in poverty; they are overrepresented in prisons; they are overrepresented among the uninsured. People of color are more often forced to live in subpar housing, in crowded apartments, in communal living spaces out of necessity. They are more likely to be unable to stockpile necessities. These material conditions disproportionately expose them to harm. It is not new that the labor of people of color is disproportionately exploitative, but the immediacy of the consequences of that exploitation is heightened. Such biopolitical analyses could be applied to many other groups seeking greater equity. Finally, while we should support frontline laborers during this crisis, we should also remember that for the working poor, not working can mean not eating, further underscoring the fundamentally biopolitical nature of labor. The COVID-19 pandemic is a mirror unto ourselves; it has not changed, but only highlighted, trenchant inequities in our society. It both exposes and exacerbates preexisting inequality and marginalization.

As COVID-19 has disrupted so many norms, it has also underscored existing power relations that directly threaten the lives of the exploited. Some labor is essential but hazardous. While non-essential (lost or online) labor transitions to the private sphere, other biopolitical risks increase, like domestic violence, sedentary lifestyles, and mental health effects associated with isolation. In this way, all of us are increasingly exposed during the pandemic, in one way or another, but the likelihood and the ramifications for that exposure is starkly different and at least in part determined by biopolitical considerations.

---

[4]In an exemplary moment, on May 5, 2020, the US President visited a factory where the Guns 'N Roses song, "Live and Let Die" blared over the speakers.

During this surreality, when eschatological anxiety is high, many people look to the future and yearn for when we can "get back to normal." The pre-COVID-19 normal, however, was unjust and exploitative, governed by a political economy with grossly uneven social, health, and environmental outcomes. Back to normal for many of us means returning to the time, space, and materiality of our privileges, perhaps increasing our leisure activities and opportunities, ignoring the exploitation of the lower classes and the labor and environmental mistreatment of the Global South.

Time for crisis

It may be tempting to suggest that during this crisis there is an increased participation and perhaps an increased appreciation for not only leisure, but for some of the supposed simplicities of life: family, close friends, local parks, decreased pace of life, less daily consumption, less pollution, and the like. Without debating the veracity of people's claims or experiences in these matters, we should also acknowledge that such perceived and actual benefits are also biopolitical in nature, built upon those whose (exploited and hazardous) labor continues during the pandemic. Obscene distributions and concentrations of accumulated wealth existed well before COVID-19. Much of that wealth is generated by capitalists' exploitation of social and environmental systems to amass profit, and then limit the sharing of prosperity as much as is politically possible. Such systems are supported by politicians, policy makers, and community members who everyday make biopolitical decisions about their own labor and the labor of others, ultimately determining who is made live and let die.

Perhaps interrogating the idea of *crisis* is helpful here. Typically, crisis connotes a time of intense difficulty or danger. Historically, however, the word, crisis, referred to a time when a particularly important decision needed to be made. A medical patient faced a crisis when doctors had to decide how to proceed. Perhaps the interwoven crises of COVID-19, climate change, and structural inequality present us with a crisis – a time for new decisions on how to proceed. The COVID-19 pandemic is ripe for disaster capitalism (Klein, 2007) to find new opportunities, new markets, new finance mechanisms, and new exploitations, but it is also an opportunity to take stock of the choices we have made, and to then make new and better decisions toward a more just world (Klein, 2020). Crisis is time for choice and opportunity. Leisure is one of a number of domains to support pertinent, critical questions. For instance, how can philosophers critically analyze the work/leisure dichotomy? How can leisure activities support resistance toward productivist labor and neoliberal ideologies? How can leisure be both counter-exploitative and emancipatory for individuals and groups? The COVID-19 crisis is a crisis opportunity to work toward a more sustainable and non-exploitative series of social and environmental relationships.

ORCID

Jeff Rose ⓘ http://orcid.org/0000-0003-3171-7242

References

Foucault, M. (1997). *Society must be defended: Lectures at the College de France, 1975–1976.* Picador.

Foucault, M. (2004). *The birth of biopolitics: Lectures at the College de France, 1978–1979.* Picador.

Klein, N. (2007). *The shock doctrine: The rise of disaster capitalism.* Picador.

Klein, N. (2020, March 16). Coronavirus capitalism – And how to beat it. *The Intercept.* https://theintercept.com/2020/03/16/coronavirus-capitalism/

Marx, K. (1988 [1844]). *Economic and philosophic manuscripts of 1844.* Prometheus.

Marx, K. (1990 [1867]). *Capital: Volume I.* Penguin.

Marx, K., & Engels, F. (1970 [1846]). *The German ideology.* International Publishers.

Tyner, J. (2019). *Dead labor: Toward a political economy of premature death.* University of Minnesota Press.

Mass Hysteria, Manufacturing Crisis and the Legal Reconstruction of Acceptable Exercise during a Pandemic

Brian Simpson (ID)

ABSTRACT

There is a saying in that every crisis is an opportunity. Unfortunately, this seems to be applied more to politicians seeking to extend their powers over citizens, and less to citizens attempting to imagine new forms of accountable government. The Covid-19 pandemic has created an extraordinary shift in people's freedoms in a short space of time, with little interrogation or apparent concern with the legal basis of this shift. Exercise has been one area where citizens otherwise required to stay at home can perform some freedom. Yet many of the directives are confused and contradictory in explaining what exercise is permitted. Australian examples are used to illustrate these points and question whether the law is redefining exercise in ways that are arbitrary and discriminatory for a crisis now that may impact on the future practice of exercise. Is this legal control of exercise the harbinger of new forms of social control?

The Covid-19 pandemic currently affecting the global community has been described by various political leaders as 'unprecedented' (e.g. Guterres, 2020) and a 'war' (e.g. Bishara, 2020). This is often associated with the time being 'above politics'. But politics is always an aspect of infectious diseases (Kapiriri & Ross, 2020) and these narratives serve to both legitimate actions that would not usually be tolerated by citizens while also deflecting attention away from politicians who may have ignored advice to properly prepare for such an event. A public health crisis also becomes a legal problem as laws to control the transmission of the disease are put into place. In many countries these laws have directed people to stay at home and to socially distance from others or face monetary fines or imprisonment. These laws severely curtail people's freedom of movement and association. They also play their own part in adding to the climate of fear and a form of 'mass hysteria' that operates to further justify their need. In the Australian context, even one of the nation's most senior judges has observed that governments often see in 'emergencies', 'crises', 'danger' and 'intense difficulties', such as pandemics, an opportunity to expand their powers that cannot be wasted. (Pape v Commissioner of Taxation, per Heydon, J.: para. 551)

While there may be some justification for creating some level of anxiety to communicate the seriousness of the matter, this climate of fear can also play out in other, often unintended ways. This essay explores some of the consequences that flow from the role and application of law in a public health crisis, in particular by way of the example of 'exercise' as one of the exceptions to the requirement to stay at home. The focus is on Australia but much of the discussion has broader relevance. What is highlighted is the law's ambiguity and the discretion this grants to law enforcement agencies combining with a more general climate of fear that affects how we understand the concept of exercise, and how this benefits some while others suffer discrimination as a result. Beyond this example and the current crisis, it asks the question as to whether these legal narratives of exercise might have a more lasting effect on how we understand both that concept and the role of law.

The legal construction of "exercise" outside the home

In Australia, all States and Territories have issued some form of public health order under relevant legislation requiring citizens to stay at home without a 'reasonable excuse'. In most of those jurisdictions one of the explicit examples of a 'reasonable excuse' for being outside your home is 'exercise' (Boseley & Knaus, 2020). The penalties for breaching these laws include fines of $1334.50 in Queensland, up to $11,000 and 6 months imprisonment in New South Wales, and on the spot fines of $1,652 in Victoria and fines up to $16,800 or 6 months imprisonment in Tasmania (Boseley & Knaus, 2020). The penalties are thus potentially severe.

But what constitutes 'exercise' under these laws? Statutory interpretation always begins with a dictionary definition. In this instance, exercise can be defined as "bodily or mental exertion, especially for the sake of training or improvement." (Macquarie Dictionary) While leisure studies may have its own disciplinary meaning of exercise, in the first instance law translates a term into its world through the medium of a dictionary. The problem is of course that this definition does not readily clarify which forms of activity might come within the term, as many activities require 'bodily or mental exertion' for training or improvement. The vagueness of the law results in claims that 'common sense' and police discretion must be applied (Smith-Lathouris, 2020). Many lawyers would argue that the problem with common sense is that it is neither common, nor always sensible.

Courts can also look to purpose and context when defining words in legislation. The purpose of the public health orders was primarily to contain the spread of the virus while allowing some opportunity for outdoor exercise, provided that social distancing rules were followed. Given this purpose, what constitutes 'exercise' could be interpreted in that light. Exercise undertaken in ways that did not create a risk of transmission could then be regarded as within the exception under this approach. But such recourse to 'purpose' and 'context' does not make this an easy task of legal construction. Purpose can be multi-layered and clearly the idea of staying at home is in tension with leaving home for exercise. Whatever the health purpose of exercise may be, there is also a political compromise at work here that acknowledges the difficulty in retaining legitimacy for laws which lock people up with no exceptions. Retaining some vagueness in the law provides both an appearance of simplicity while also importing some flexibility into it. However, this also allows for many considerations to intrude into how the exception is understood. Thus, the application of discretion - or common sense - can soon evolve into arbitrary and discriminatory judgments about the trustworthiness of certain groups and what constitutes 'proper' exercise in this context.

This can be demonstrated in some of the ways in which the law was subsequently applied across various Australian jurisdictions. In New South Wales, for example, fishing was initially not considered to be a reasonable excuse for leaving home for exercise. The State Police Minister then 'personally intervened' and gained legal advice from the Police General Counsel that fishing was 'passive exercise' (Nguyen, 2020). The NSW Police Commissioner commented on this:

'If you do need a break and if [fishing] is your exercise, then do it sensibly and do it quickly and return home,' he said.

'You can fish but if you end up on a wharf with 50 other people then we get back to safe distancing and getting tickets.' (Nguyen, 2020)

However, this can be contrasted with Queensland where the relevant Minister stated that exercise did not cover "recreational" boating and fishing. He said:

There's no reason for anyone to be taking the boat out — unless it's for essential travel to get to work, to and from your home, to local shops for provisions, or catching fish for your family. (Cassidy, 2020)

In the case of golf, most States allowed it as a form of exercise subject to the following of social distancing requirements (Bamford, 2020). However, in the case of Victoria, golf was not allowed as a form of exercise. The Victorian Premier, was quoted:

'No one likes playing golf more than I do, no one. You don't need to play golf. You might want to play golf, but you don't need to play golf,' he said.

'And no round of golf is worth someone's life. That's the key point here.' (O'Connor, 2020)

This introduces the concept of 'need' into discussions of exercise. Yet this ban had less to do with the public health risk associated with playing golf and more to do with the fear of people clustering and creating a transmission risk. Victoria's Chief Medical Officer, Brett Sutton, 'ruled out not just golf but fishing, boating, hunting, camping and "all recreational activity beyond basic exercise" (Groch et al., 2020). The notion of 'basic' exercise does not appear in the public health order and represents a further reading into the text of words to achieve a particular purpose. The Victorian Chief Medical Officer was later candid that this was more about simplifying the political message to stay home rather than recognizing any inherent risk in the playing of golf.

As for golf - a huge issue in this pandemic – Sutton [the Victorian Chief Medical Officer] doesn't think you'd catch COVID-19 on the eighteenth fairway.

But he knows that it's hard for a suburban dad, or mum, who is allowed to wander around a golf course swinging a stick at a ball, to tell their teenager that they can't go down to the skate park for a grind, or their four-year-old that the swings at the park are off limits (Towell, 2020).

Yet such a judgment about the simplification of the message to stay at home and its acceptance by the population is far from a medical judgment, it is a political judgment for which medical officers can claim no special expertise. What intrudes here into the interpretation of the word 'exercise' is not simply its place in the context of mitigating the risk of infection as a legal question but also political judgments about how people will react to the activity being permitted. This runs the risk of allowing the legal question to dip into a process that creates a climate within which prejudice and even fear of certain groups can take hold.

The concern with how much people can be trusted to observe social distancing also appears in discussions of whether being allowed out of the home to exercise also implies some capacity to travel far for that purpose or to engage in the exercise for an extended period of time. Guidance provided by the Victorian Department of Health stated: 'Yes, you can go to the park to exercise, but visits to the park should be kept short.' (Victorian Health & Human Services, 2020) But is the length of time spent exercising relevant in determining the legality of the reason for being outside your home if the purpose is to reduce the risk of transmission or is it a matter of *how* you exercise? The Victorian advice appears to be confused on this point:

> Yes, you can leave your home to exercise alone, provided it's possible to maintain physical distancing of at least 1.5 metres from others at all times. This includes, walking, running, bike riding or other types of exercise, such as yoga in a park.

> While it may be necessary to leave your immediate neighbourhood to undertake exercise, we're asking Victorians – please use common sense and don't travel any further than you have to. (Victorian Health & Human Services, 2020)

How far you 'have' to travel is arguably a function of the type of exercise a person wishes to engage in, but it seems clear from other statements noted above that the authorities are more concerned with addressing what people may not do when provided with the opportunity to exercise (observe social distancing) than clarifying what is permitted.

There is also in many of the interpretations of exercise a sense that it must be 'active'. Government advice in New South Wales on boating notes that 'a reasonable excuse to use your boat could be to: exercise (for example kayaking, sailing, paddling); go fishing…' (NSW Department of Planning & Industry & Environment, 2020) This guidance groups 'fishing' outside forms of exercise (perhaps as food gathering instead) even though earlier advice categorized it as 'passive' exercise. There are anecdotal examples in Australia of a person being told to return home because they were moving too slowly to be exercising. In another example, a person claimed that he was out for a run and stopped to eat a kebab, and in that moment was fined for being outside home with no reasonable excuse (Offbeat, 2020). In Italy, a person taking their turtle for a walk was not deemed to be justification for being away from home (Squires, 2020).

This latter example appears to be particularly harsh when one considers that 'exercising a dog' seems to have been assumed to be covered by the exercise exemption even though it is not necessarily the case that the human owner is the one exercising. In this way, what is exercise also seems to overlap with what might be termed recreation. For example, New South Wales Department of Planning guidance notes:

Our great parks and parklands are still open so you can enjoy daily exercise, walk animals and spend time among nature, but it's important to follow current health orders and stay close to home when you do go out. (NSW Department of Planning, Industry & Environment, 2020)

Yet the public health order cited only explicitly refers to 'exercise' as a reason for being outside your home, not "walking animals" or "spending time among nature". Indeed, the latter may be a past time that involves some time in a public space and so is at odds with any advice to keep visits to parks brief. Yet, taking dogs for a walk is commonly mentioned in the context of the exercise exemption, both in Australia and overseas, although other animals are not so mentioned. It might be thought that walking a dog implies active exercise on the part of the human companion and so clearly falls within the terms of the health order but could it also be that walking a dog is an activity often undertaken by the middle class and so it is assumed will be done responsibly? Is this an example of a political judgment being made about the persons undertaking this activity being trusted to abide by the social distancing rules and so privileged in how discretion is applied?

Transforming a health crisis into a legal question

The concept of 'exercise' becomes a legal term in the law which enforces public health orders and so must be interpreted. It is a basic proposition in statutory interpretation that words require context to be properly understood and so achieve the purpose of the law. We provide context by in effect adding other words or meaning to single words to clarify meaning. We have thus seen 'exercise' defined, for example, as both 'active' and 'passive', read to embrace walking a dog, to include fishing in some jurisdictions but not others, and to include being in nature - but not for too long a time. We have also observed the political judgments that intrude into the definition that can have the effect of preventing some from their exercise while allowing others to do theirs.

The problem is that in interpreting 'exercise' as a legal term, it is easy to introduce biases, prejudices and preconceived ideas about what exercise is or should be. It becomes enmeshed with other agendas such as whether some groups can be trusted to comply with social distancing requirements when they engage in exercise. Transformed from a public health problem to one of public order, there is a risk that exercise as a reason for being outside your home will be determined by those with power or status in society and will exclude the exercise of those with marginal social status. There is the potential for assumptions based on class, race, age, ethnicity and gender to intrude into such judgments.

Conclusion: reconstructing exercise for the post-pandemic age?

At one level, the law's response to the Covid-19 crisis has led to competing definitions of 'exercise' that can be mocked for the confusion they have caused. But there is a much more subtle and insidious way in which law operates. The concept of 'soft law' (e.g. Sekalala, 2017, p. 50) is relevant here as are other forms of social control (Cohen, 1985) that become embedded in practice. Thus, in recasting what constitutes 'exercise' during a pandemic, hard rules that prohibit certain activity set the tone, but vague words and discretion that appear to offer flexibility enforce certain norms about acting responsibly that discriminate. Without a consensus about the clear purpose and limits of the law in this process, there is a danger that this recasting of the activity has longer term implications for social behavior.

Laws that reconstruct the meaning of exercise may rest on perceptions of who is trustworthy and responsible in their social interactions and so who has their activity granted the badge of acceptable exercise (and with it, free movement). But for those in social groups that are feared or targeted for political purposes, these same laws may have created a model for denying their activities the status of legitimate exercise and their exclusion from the privileges that that status confers.

ORCID

Brian Simpson (iD) http://orcid.org/0000-0002-2986-5601

References

Bamford, M. (2020, April 9). Golf a 'reason to get up in the morning' and keeping Aussies on course amid coronavirus. *ABC Radio Sydney*. https://www.abc.net.au/news/2020-04-09/golf-keeps-aussies-on-course-during-covid19/12119570

Bishara, M. (2020, April 27). The pandemic as a war and Trump, the 'medic-in-chief'. *Aljazeera News*. https://www.aljazeera.com/indepth/opinion/pandemic-war-trump-medic-chief-200427105106026.html

Boseley, M., & Knaus, C. (2020, April 7). Australia's coronavirus social distancing rules explained: State by state guidelines. The Guardian.

Cassidy, T. (2020, April 1). Coronavirus restrictions force recreational boaties and anglers off the water. www.abc.net.au

Cohen, S. (1985). *Visions of social control: Crime, punishment and classification*. Polity Press.

Groch, S., et al. (2020, April 18). 'Stop looking for loopholes': What are the new COVID-19 social rules? *Sydney Morning Herald*. https://www.smh.com.au/national/stop-looking-for-loopholes-what-are-the-new-covid-19-social-rules-20200407-p54hyd.html

Guterres, A. (2020, April 22). COVID-19 pandemic, an 'unprecedented wake-up call' for all inhabitants of Mother Earth. UN News. https://news.un.org/en/story/2020/04/1062322

Kapiriri, L., & Ross, A. (2020). The politics of disease epidemics: A comparative analysis of the SARS, Zika, and Ebola Outbreaks. *Global Social Welfare*, 7(1), 33–45.

Nguyen, K. (2020, April 3). Can I go fishing in NSW? Coronavirus restrictions allow 'passive exercise'. www.abc.net.au

NSW Department of Planning, Industry and Environment. (2020). *A guide to using public spaces during COVID-19*. https://www.planning.nsw.gov.au/Policy-and-Legislation/COVID19-response/A-guide-to-using-public-spaces-during-the-COVID19-pandemic

NSW Government. (2020). *Stay home*. https://www.nsw.gov.au/covid-19/stay-home

O'Connor, T. (2020, April 7). Premier Daniel Andrews: now is not a time for golf. *The Courier*. https://www.thecourier.com.au/story/6715104/andrews-not-a-time-for-golf/

Offbeat. (2020, April 4). Premier loses it over kebab question. *Daily Mercury*. https://www.daily-mercury.com.au/news/premier-loses-it-over-kebab-question/3988941/

Pape v Commissioner of Taxation. (2009). HCA 23.

Sekalala, S. (2017). *Soft law and global health problems: Lessons from responses to HIV/AIDS, malaria and tuberculosis*. Cambridge University Press.

Smith-Lathouris, O. (2020, April 13). Police warned to use "common sense" when enforcing isolation measures. *9News*. https://www.msn.com/en-au/news/coronavirus/police-warned-to-use-common-sense-when-enforcing-isolation-measures/ar-BB12zWHw

Squires, A. (2020, April 16). Italian woman fined for taking her tortoise for a stroll. *The Telegraph*. https://www.telegraph.co.uk/news/2020/04/16/italian-woman-fined-taking-tortoise-stroll/

Towell, N. (2020, May 8). When medicine can't save you, all you have is 'the message'. *The Age.* https://www.theage.com.au/politics/victoria/when-medicine-can-t-save-you-all-you-have-is-the-message-20200508-p54r9h.html

Victorian Health and Human Services. (2020). *Stay at home direction – frequently asked questions.* https://www.dhhs.vic.gov.au/coronavirus-stay-home-directions-frequently-asked-questions#can-i-leave-the-house-to-do-outdoor-exercise-on-my-own

Football is "the most important of the least important things": The Illusion of Sport and COVID-19

Jack Black (iD)

ABSTRACT

In his book, *On the Pleasure Principle in Culture* (2014), Robert Pfaller argued that our relationship to sport is one grounded in "illusion". Simply put, our interest in and enjoyment of sport occurs through a process of "knowing better". Here, one's knowledge of the unimportance of sport is achieved by associating the illusion of sport with a naïve observer – i.e. someone who *does* believe in sport's importance. In the wake of the global pandemic, COVID-19, it would seem that Pfaller's remarks have taken on an added significance. With major sporting events and domestic competitions being indefinitely postponed or canceled, Liverpool manager, Jürgen Klopp, commented that football was "the most important of the least important things". In light of these remarks, this paper will critically locate sport's sudden unimportance in relation to Pfaller's contention that sport reflects an "illusion without owner".

Introduction

It would seem that sport no longer matters. In view of the COVID-19 pandemic, which has resulted in a number of domestic and international sporting competitions being indefinitely postponed or canceled, Liverpool FC manager, Jürgen Klopp, referred to football "as 'the most important of the least important things'" (Wilson, 2020). Notably, Klopp's sentiments have been echoed by other sporting celebrities, such as Tiger Woods, who, in similar fashion, stated that "There are a lot more important things in life than a golf tournament" (Carroll, 2020).[1] But who are these remarks for? Surely, no one would disagree with Klopp or Woods's statements and suggest that sport *is* more important? In fact, amidst an increasing death toll and national "lockdowns" resulting in levels of unemployment unseen since the 2007 financial crash (Strauss, 2020; Tooze, 2020), do Klopp and Woods's remarks even need repeating?

In light of these questions, I wish to expand upon the nature of sport during the COVID-19 pandemic, paying specific attention to the inherent ambivalence that underscores both Klopp and Woods's remarks. This ambivalence will be explored through

---

[1]Woods was referring to the 2020 Masters Tournament.

Robert Pfaller's contention that sport and play provide an "illusion without owner" (Pfaller, 2014). Drawing from Johan Huizinga's "sacred seriousness" (Huizinga, 1955), Pfaller (2014) details how the significance of sport relies upon an inherent illusion, an illusion which presupposes a "naïve observer".

In what follows, it will be argued that the importance of this "naïve observer" proves integral to the above remarks. For example, though no one would openly disagree with either Klopp or Woods's statements, the fact that they are stated, and subsequently reported, relies upon an Other who *does* believe in sport's importance (even in the face of a global pandemic). In the case of sport, leisure and play, the formal significance of this Other will be used to discern what COVID-19 avers: the inherent illusion that underscores our desire for "play"; an illusion that does not belong to any subject – an "illusion without owner".

Enjoy! Your leisure

Certainly, the commodification of leisure and the conflation of work and play is a widely recited theme in academic research (Jameson, 1991), culminating in the "gamification" of working practices (Wark, 2007). This infusion, however, belies a more significant tension. That is, under the neoliberal directive to "Enjoy!", we, paradoxically, have less time for enjoyment (McGowan, 2012; Žižek, 2008). As a result, we become participants in a relentless enjoyment that is never fulfilled, and which inevitably becomes work: an enjoyment that is decidedly unenjoyable. Such demands are evidenced in the extent to which our leisure practices become embroiled in a constant desire for affirmation, as Van Oenen (2018) highlights:

> because … affirmation can no longer be received from traditional sources such as God or nature, or any other self-evident and undisputed source of authority, it can only be procured from man-made social arrangements and be based on assessments by other human beings. It is thus to be expected that individuals will demand such continuous re-affirmation from other individuals, or collectives. (p.114).

For Pfaller (2014), this re-affirmation "holds on to the *illusion* of self-determination", with the subject "pursu[ing] his or her own heteronomy simply for the sake of 'proving' it to be autonomy" (p. 215, italics added).[2]

Unfortunately, what becomes obscured in this desire for self-affirmation through leisure is its attribution to a naïve Other (Boncardo, 2018). Such a naïve Other follows the Lacanian contention (elaborated by Žižek, 2001) that our subjective beliefs are enjoyed through an Other, constituting what Pfaller (2014) refers to as "objective illusions". While objective illusions ground their subscription in a variety of subjects, they are, nonetheless, claimed by no one: They are, in effect, disavowed. Both Pfaller and Žižek relate this unique process to a variety of examples, including when an individual uses their VCR to record films that will never get watched; when an academic photocopies a book, they will never read; or, when the canned laughter on your favorite sitcom laughs for you. In each instance, the subject may never subjectively watch the films, read the

---

[2]According to Pfaller (2017), this process has heralded a decline in "public space".

book or laugh, but instead, they can relax in the objective comfort that the VCR, photo-copier and canned laughter has achieved this for them.

However, what remains unique about this transference is its disavowed status. Notably, in each transference – what Pfaller (2014, 2017) refers to as a form of interpas-sivity – "The illusion is not theirs" (Pfaller, 2014, p. 23); that is, the illusion is *not claimed by the subject*. Consequently, "in full 'knowledge' of the alleged unsuitability of an interpassive process, the actors nonetheless carry it out, and then actually obtain suc-cessful results from it – yet once again conceal these results from themselves" (Pfaller, 2014, p. 23). This is reflected in the case of sport, where the desire to "check the score", and thus stop whatever one may be currently doing, relies upon the subject's open acknowledgement that such "checking" is inherently "silly" ("I know this is silly, but I just have to know the score from yesterday's game").[3] This concealment bears witness to an important ambivalence in cultural practices involving sport, leisure and play. In part, it suggests that the enjoyment we seek through our leisure practices, including watching professional sport, is one in which the interpassive subject deliberately follows a path of self-forgetting.

In order to help explain this act of self-forgetting, we can consider what has been referred to as sport's "mimetic sphere" (Elias & Dunning, 2008; Maguire, 2011). According to Maguire (2011), "'Mimetic' activities … provide a 'make-believe' setting which allows emotions to flow more easily, and which elicits excitement of some kind imitating that produced by 'real-life situations', yet without its dangers or risks" (p. 920). Importantly, "'Mimetic' activities thus allow, within certain limits, for socially permitted self-centredness" (Maguire, 2011, p. 920). In light of the above, we can offer a slight revi-sion to Maguire's (2011) contentions, arguing instead that what these activities collectively provide is a form "self-decentrement", predicated on our own self-forgetfulness.

Sacred seriousness and knowing better

Following Huizinga (1955), Pfaller (2014) outlines how forms of play rely upon a level of secrecy which is shared by those involved in the practice. This is echoed in examples of politeness where, "The fact that niceties are 'not real' is thus a secret that is shared by all participants, and one that is kept secret from others who remain fully unspecified" (Pfaller, 2014, p. 89–90). In these instances, such "secrecy" relies upon an "illusion" that remains "ownerless" (Pfaller, 2014). What is more, it is in upholding this illusion that the enjoyment of play and sport relies upon the knowledge, and subsequent disavowal, that it is merely play. As Pfaller (2014) asserts:

> A player who does not know that the game is play cannot be captured by "sacred seriousness". He or she remains trapped in profane seriousness. This knowledge essential for play consists in "knowing better" about an illusion. Consequently, every game must contain an illusion. (p.91).

Therefore, if we follow Maguire's (2011) contention that the "make-believe" settings of our leisure practices serve as "the 'siblings' of those aroused in 'real-life' situations" (p. 920), then it is clear that such forms of "make-believe" refer explicitly to play's

---

[3]See Pfaller (2014, p. 1).

inherent illusion. Importantly, the fact that such activities are known to be "make-believe" works to accentuate their seriousness. If anything, it underscores play's seriousness in the face of our everyday ("real-life") profanatory (Pfaller, 2014). Furthermore, this is not confusion. One does not simply confuse the "play" as more seriousness than "everyday life"; instead, the sacred seriousness of play occurs when "the players are *not* confused. Only by *knowing* that it is 'just' play is it possible to be more absorbed by it than by other areas of life" (Pfaller, 2014, p. 92, italics added).

As noted, what remains key to such "knowing" is its disavowed status. Play, and its rationalization in a variety of sporting and leisure practices, works off a "suspended illusion"; or, in other words, a suspension of our better knowledge (Pfaller, 2014). For Pfaller (2014):

> Because this knowledge includes the fact that the game is "only a game", the game must contain a counter-illusion, so to speak – namely, that of being "more than just a game". This emerges as an important observation for understanding other, non-representative practices, too (such as abstract, repetitive forms in art, obsessional neurotic acts, and religious rituals that have seemingly lost their meaning): *wherever sacred seriousness reigns, there must be a denied illusion that is kept suspended.* Sacred seriousness is a sign indicating the presence of an illusion of the other. It is its symptom. (pp.99-100).

This affords further clarification on the apparent distinction between sport's inherent tensions and its similarity to other cultural art forms (Elias & Dunning, 2008). According to Maguire (2011), sport's "quest … for battles [is] enacted playfully in a *contrived* context which can produce enjoyable battle excitement with a minimum of injuries to the human participants" (p. 922, italics added). As a result, "Compared with the arts, the scope for the exercise of the imagination involved appears to be of a rather restricted and heavily rule-bound kind" (Maguire, 2011, p. 922). On the contrary, when considered in view of the "illusion without owner", we can begin to see how it is through sport's "contrived context" that our imaginations and our enjoyment in play are interpassively assured. Only a naïve observer would find the restriction of activity, through sport's rule-bound necessity, as in some way inhibiting the opportunity for play. Instead, play's sacred seriousness can occur precisely *because* there are accepted rules that restrict the full opportunity for enjoyment.

Take, for example, a game of football, and ask yourself: Why do we bother restricting the game to the primary use of feet? Why do we add this "rule" which only restricts the opportunity to put the ball in the opposition's net? Certainly, no one who plays football ever questions this rule (in fact, if they did, they may prefer another sport, such as, Rugby Union/League); instead, it is part of the game's "secrecy" – an accepted illusion that allows one to fully participate in the game. Moreover, rather than reflecting an unstable decontrolling of emotional constraint (Elias & Dunning, 2008), this reversal of our knowledge – the knowledge that play is merely play – is what can be identified when certain athletes break "the rules", resulting in suspension or outright castration from sport. Ultimately, such actions only confer play's sacred seriousness (its disavowed illusion): One *must* break the rules to win "the game".

It is in this way that our involvement in sport presents a form of "self-decentrement": indeed, a space *between* sport's objective adherence (i.e. following its rules) and our subjective divestment from the demands of its illusion (an illusion of the Other). In doing so, both sport and leisure can help to confer a form of self-forgetfulness, one that stands apart from the unending and inevitably impossible "self-realization" that the leisure industry so hopefully promotes (Rojek, 1993).

Sport's inherent ambivalence and COVID-19

We can now begin to see the ambivalence which sits at the heart of sport; an ambivalence which is brought to light in the aforementioned comments from Klopp. Indeed, while Klopp's remarks serve as a denouncement of sport in the face of COVID-19, at the same time, he bears witness to the "sacred seriousness" it relies upon (Huizinga, 1955). When Klopp asserts that football remains "the most important of the least important things" (Wilson, 2020), it is clear that football holds *some* importance. Yet, what underscores Klopp's assertions is an inherent ambivalence regarding the "importance" of football; one that remains indebted to a naïve observer who whole-heartedly believes in football's importance. Consequently, such remarks ambivalently herald both positive and negative assumptions: Football *is* the *most* important of the *least* important things. In effect, it is precisely because football is "unimportant" (or the least important) that it remains important. Ultimately, Klopp's remarks help reveal the suspended illusion which underlies football's (un)importance.

Furthermore, it is the contention of this essay that such ambivalence can reveal the significance of play's self-decentrement. Indeed, if we follow Pfaller's (2014) contentions, then it is in the context of play that the illusions we uphold, but disavow, can be deferred to an Other who underpins the illusion's social efficacy. It is in delegating the illusion to a naïve observer that we regain a sense of enjoyment from the process of delegation itself. This is further substantiated by Pfaller (2014) and Žižek's (1998) claims that the delegation of enjoyment can result in a surplus enjoyment.

In the case of sport, such outsourcing of enjoyment functions even when the literal postponement of sport occurs. What the cancelation of sport seems to highlight, therefore, is how "the strongest emotional ties to something can develop precisely when the matter – through real or imagined better knowledge – is declared to be 'foolish' fun or 'mere' play" (Pfaller, 2014, p. 93). Here, the postponement of sport during COVID-19 has resulted in a number of daft examples.

During the first postponement of English Premiership League games, Watford and Leicester City played their fixture via the managerial simulator, *Football Manager* (BBC Sport, 2020). Echoing this, Leyton Orient asked fans to select the team for their game at Bradford City, which included pre-match advice from their manager, Ross Embleton. In addition, Southampton took part in a game of *noughts and crosses* with Manchester City (BBC Sport, 2020). What remains unique to these examples is that they were followed with match reports from the BBC. In fact, despite sport's "official" postponement, Bull (2020) highlighted that "sport [... could] be found in the most unlikely places". He commented upon:

> the viral clips of the two men playing paddle tennis between their neighbouring windows on the fourth floor of their apartment block (their rally lasted 28 shots) and the pair playing ping pong with frying pans and a net made out of pasta boxes. Or Ian Bell lacing a bog roll down the corridor for four ("Don't bowl there, son," he tells his kid) or Lionel Messi doing keepie-uppies with one (which brought to mind Michel Platini's line: "What Zidane does with a ball, Maradona could do with an orange."). (Bull, 2020).

In each example, sport's illusion for the Other proves particularly captivating, resulting in a host of "silly" activities (including the strange proliferation of "online" quiz events),[4] that, in light of play's sacred seriousness, seems only to compel individuals to think up different ways of doing "sport". Accordingly, while governments have undoubtedly struggled with the aim of increasing physical participation among its population, the cancelation of sport, and the subsequent "lockdown", has only resulted in a number of people deliberately taking the opportunity to complete their leisure allocation (Cabinet Office, 2020).

Final comments

To conclude, we can reflect upon the ambivalent satisfaction which these examples seem to infer. As Poulard (2013) asserts, "The displacement of enjoyment can be viewed in two different lights: either as an ineluctable symptom of alienation inherent to mass entertainment or as the opening of a space of relative freedom where (for a change) nothing is expected of me" (p. 306). Set against our pre-COVID-19 reality, where one was expected to join a gym, check the scores and "find time" with the family, it is our present reality – one that goes no further than the basics required for living – which suddenly denotes a "nothing expected" (Poulard, 2013). It is, instead, the unexpectedness of a future that helps to confer a level of self-forgetfulness that is brought to light in our relations with play, leisure and sport. In doing so, play's naïve observer reveals a self-decentrement that remains decidedly collective. Indeed, when sport inevitably returns, when leisure becomes what we do "at the weekend", we can perhaps take greater stock of the interpassivity which underscores our most cherished and self-affirming practices. Practices that are "less encumbered by aggressive demands for recognition and more attuned to truly public questions – questions of distribution, of shared history, and of justice" (Boncardo, 2018, p. 307). It is in this regard that our leisure can offer a more liberating, non-alienated significance.

ORCID

Jack Black http://orcid.org/0000-0002-1595-5083

References

BBC Sport (2020, March 14). *Coronavirus: What happened on a day without Football?* https://www.bbc.co.uk/sport/football/51890573

Boncardo, R. (2018). Interpassivity and the Impossible: From Art to Politics in Pfaller's Interpassivity: The Aesthetics of Delegated Enjoyment. *Continental Thought & Theory, 2*(1), 298–317. http://hdl.handle.net/10092/15482

Brennan, A. (2020, March 30). Virtual pub quiz: The pubs and breweries hosting online quizzes amid coronavirus lockdown. *Standard.* https://www.standard.co.uk/go/london/bars/virtual-pub-quiz-coronavirus-lockdown-a4396276.html

---

[4]See Brennan (2020).

Bull, A. (2020, April 1). From marble racing to balcony marathons: The "sports" filling the void. *The Guardian.* https://www.theguardian.com/sport/blog/2020/apr/01/cabin-fever-agenda-for-housebound-olympics

Cabinet Office. (2020, March 29). *Staying at home and away from others (social distancing).* https://www.gov.uk/government/publications/full-guidance-on-staying-at-home-and-away-from-others/full-guidance-on-staying-at-home-and-away-from-others

Carroll, R. (2020, March 17). Tiger Woods puts coronavirus into perspective by admitting "there are a lot more important things than golf". *The Independent.* https://www.independent.co.uk/sport/golf/coronavirus-tiger-woods-golf-cancellations-the-masters-players-championship-pga-tour-a9405806.html

Elias, N., & Dunning, E. (2008). *Quest for excitement.* University College Dublin Press.

Huizinga, J. (1955). *Homo Ludens: A study of the play-element in culture.* Beacon Press.

Jameson, F. (1991). *Postmodernism, or, the cultural logic of late capitalism.* Duke University Press.

Maguire, J. A. (2011). Welcome to the pleasure dome?: emotions, leisure and society. *Sport in Society, 14*(7–8), 913–926.

McGowan, T. (2012). *The end of dissatisfaction.* SUNY.

Pfaller, R. (2014). *On the pleasure principle in culture.* Verso.

Pfaller, R. (2017). *Interpassivity.* Edinburgh University Press.

Poulard, E. (2013). "After the Takeover": Shakespeare, Lacan, Žižek and the interpassive subject. *English Studies, 94*(3), 291–312.

Rojek, C. (1993). *Ways of escape.* Macmillan.

Strauss, D. (2020, April 2). Years of UK jobs growth wiped out by coronavirus. *Financial Times.* https://www.ft.com/content/9f3661b9-14cb-472a-9246-d784d436ea52

Tooze, A. (2020, March 18) Is the Coronavirus crash worse than the 2008 Financial Crisis? *Foreign Policy.* https://foreignpolicy.com/2020/03/18/coronavirus-economic-crash-2008-financial-crisis-worse/

Van Oenen, G. (2018). Robert Pfaller: Theorist of public grace. *Continental Thought & Theory, 2*(1), 104–131. http://hdl.handle.net/10092/15476

Wark, M. (2007). *Gamer Theory.* Harvard University Press.

Wilson, P. (2020, March 14). Klopp reminds Liverpool fans of what matters most. *The Irish Times.* https://www.irishtimes.com/sport/soccer/klopp-reminds-liverpool-fans-of-what-matters-most-1.4202586

Žižek, S. (1998). Cyberspace, or, how to traverse the fantasy in the age of the retreat of the big other. *Public Culture, 10*(3), 483–513.

Žižek, S. (2001). *On belief.* Routledge.

Žižek, S. (2008). *The sublime object of ideology.* Verso.

Hosting the Olympics in Times of a Pandemic: Historical Insights from Antwerp 1920

Bram Constandt ⓘD and Annick Willem ⓘD

ABSTRACT

Postponing the Tokyo 2020 Olympics due to the global outbreak of COVID-19 marks a unique moment in the history of the Olympic Movement. For the first time since the cancelation of the Olympic Games during both World Wars, the Olympics will not take place as scheduled. This unprecedented postponement strongly impacts the Olympic Movement. Although only the future can tell exactly, the Antwerp 1920 Olympics can offer certain historical insights. Exactly 100 years ago, the Antwerp Olympic Games were the first Olympics organized after World War I and the Spanish flu pandemic. Their value in terms of rising the Olympic Movement from its ashes is vital. Profoundly promoting its identity, newly introduced Olympic symbols then helped avoiding the collapse of the Olympic Movement. Acknowledged as the "Games Reborn", the Antwerp 1920 Olympics were strongly about recovery, helping to heal a wounded society. How could Tokyo 2020 fulfill the same role?

Introduction

On the 24th of March 2020, the IOC and the local organizing committee released a joint statement regarding the postponement of the Tokyo 2020 Olympics because of the global outbreak of COVID-19 (Rich, Futterman, & Panja, 2020). Approximately one week later, the new timing of the Tokyo Olympics was communicated. Tokyo 2020 – which will not be rebranded into Tokyo 2021 to avoid additional costs – will now take place from the 23rd of July until the 8th of August 2021. Although critiques contend that this postponement should have been declared earlier, one can also argue that such unprecedented decision should not be taken lightly and unprepared (Rich et al., 2020). After all, even though the Olympic Movement has been confronted with both internal and external crises on a regular basis (e.g., the hostage taking during Munich 1972 and the Cold War boycotts during the 1980s), no rescheduling of such nature has ever occurred since the start of the modern Olympic Games in 1896.

COVID-19 is however not the first pandemic that impacts the modern Olympics. Hundred years ago, the 1920 Antwerp Olympics were organized shortly after an extremely deathly and interconnected duo of calamities. In parallel with the final stages and the aftermath of World War I, the Spanish flu terminated the lives of tens of million of people all over the world in 1918–19 (Mitschang, 2012). COVID-19, today's society, and the Olympic Movement are significantly distinct compared to the situation of a century ago. However, it can be of great contemporary interest to examine the symbolic role and legacy of the Antwerp Olympics in revitalizing the Olympic Movement as well as helping to heal a wounded global society. Three important Olympic symbols were introduced during the Antwerp Olympics (i.e., the Olympic oath, the Olympic flag, and releasing pigeons). These symbols highlighted the relevance of the Olympic Movement in stimulating international peace and uniting the world. The aim of this commentary is to look back to Antwerp 1920 to consider how Tokyo 2020 can be of similar relevance, as solidarity between nations in reviving the world will be of fundamental importance in the forthcoming years.

Looking backward: Antwerp 1920

The organization of the 1920 Olympic Games was granted to the Belgian city of Antwerp during an IOC session in April 1919. Both before and after this allocation, doubt was raised on behalf of different actors whether Antwerp would be capable of delivering such a complex financial and logistical organization at the start of an early peace (Renson, 1996). World War I had only come to an end with the armistice of the 11th of November 1918. A somehow similar kind of doubt is currently circulating in regards to Tokyo 2020. Today, there is great uncertainty about whether and how the Olympic competitions should and could take place when social (i.e., physical) distancing has become the new global norm. Rather than financial and logistical concerns (as in relation to Antwerp 1920), current critiques strongly relate to safety and public health issues. Yet, the Antwerp Olympics were also confronted with a public health crisis. The planning of the Antwerp Olympics started in a world that experienced the final outbreaks of the horrendous Spanish flu pandemic, which raged over the globe from 1918 until 1919 and resulted in an estimated death toll of 50 million people (Mitschang, 2012). Amplified by malnutrition and a weak health, countless soldiers and civilians died due to the Spanish flu rather than because of direct war violence (De Smet, 2005). Being partly "overshadowed" by the simultaneous First World War and wartime censorship, the Spanish flu can be considered a somehow "forgotten" pandemic (Honigsbaum, 2013). It is therefore no surprise that historical sources refer little to potential or direct consequences of the Spanish flu on the 1920 Olympics.

Nonetheless, the 1920 Olympic Games have clearly operated as a comforting factor for a world that was heavily hurt by the interconnected war and pandemic (Mallon & Bijkerk, 2003). The Antwerp Olympics are symbolized as the rebirth of the Olympic Movement from the ashes of the war (Renson, 1996). At the same time, their value in support of the recovery of the global society (including participating nations and athletes, representing all five continents) should be acknowledged. During the first centuries of the 20th century, the IOC was criticized for being insufficiently inclusive toward women, working class people, and certain ethnic groups (Chatziefstathiou, 2005). With the Antwerp Olympics, the IOC slowly yet meaningfully tried to be more inclusive, while helping the world to find comfort with regards to a recent trauma (Mallon & Bijkerk, 2003; Truyens, 2020). In a similar vein, Tokyo 2020 could unite the world to some extent in dealing with the sorrow caused by COVID-19. As further discussed in this commentary's final section, the Tokyo Olympics can also be used by the IOC to counteract current critique on its operation.

As only a few months had passed since the end of World War I, its impact was seeping into the preparations for the 1920 Olympics (Kluge, 2014). National delegations organizing their departure for Antwerp were continuously confronted with the sore reality of early post war time. The case of the American delegation is telling in this regard. A large part of the American athletes had to travel to Antwerp in a vessel that had shortly before been used to return the bodies of fallen American soldiers back home. Athletes were complaining about the pungent smell of formalin that was still strongly observable (Renson, 1996). Although current obstacles to plan for the Olympics are of course not entirely similar, today's national Olympic Committees (NOC's) have to work in times of uncertainty and difficult preparations. For example, it is unclear whether there will be a vaccine and/or effective medication to fight COVID-19 by July 2021. As such, Tokyo 2020 might get canceled anyways. In addition, a heavy task awaits NOC's in keeping Olympic athletes motivated with their years-long goal being postponed, whilst reassuring them it will be safe to engage in physical contests during the Olympics (bearing the recent cases of COVID-19 infections during Olympic qualifiers in mind, see Panja, 2020).

Little certainties were also present when national delegations arrived in Antwerp in 1920. The impact of the war was still heavily observable when the Antwerp Olympic Games were taking place. Many competing athletes had served their country in the war trenches themselves (Renson, 1996). All official speeches emphasized the peace creating value of the Olympic Movement, in contrast to the horrors of recent war times (Mallon & Bijkerk, 2003; Renson, 1996). During the opening ceremony of Antwerp 1920, athletes carried their national flags "to victory over there on the battle fields of peace, just as they carried our flag to victory on the battlefields of war" (Lucas, 1983, p. 35). One can wonder whether those Olympic athletes wearing their national flag during Tokyo 2020s opening ceremony will be referred to in a similar way. Will these Olympians think about their country's fight against COVID-19 and the human losses caused by this disease? Although it would be naive to merely think of Tokyo 2020 as a celebration of international understanding after having (hopefully) beaten the new coronavirus together, the IOC could use Tokyo 2020 in a strategic manner to promote its underlying values of unity and solidarity.

In summary, the entire 1920 Olympics were symbolized by the societal need to deal with the war and find peace with the horrible things that happened over the past years. Beautifully phrased by Mallon and Bijkerk (2003, p. 12), the Antwerp Olympics "helped the world to recover from the war, and perhaps allowed them to enjoy a sporting spectacle again, instead of having to worry about the future of mankind (sic)". At the same time, the 1920 Olympics helped to restore the Olympic Movement. Eight years had passed since the last Olympic Games of Stockholm 1912, as those of Berlin 1916 had been canceled due to the war. In case the Olympics of 1920 would also not take place, the IOC feared losing the relevance of its movement (Renson, 1996). Nevertheless, the

IOC seized the opportunity and used the 1920 Olympics to strengthen its identity. The peaceful and uniting character of Olympism (i.e., the philosophy guiding the Olympic Movement) was highlighted, whereas new Olympic symbols were introduced. Such are the Olympic flag, the Olympic oath, and releasing pigeons (by soldiers). Although Olympic crises were prevalent during the 1920–30s, these symbols set the stage for a new era of an amplified Olympic Movement (Chatziefstathiou, 2005; Renson, 1996). In the remainder of this commentary, we will analyze more closely how Tokyo 2020 could as well aid to recover a wounded society and strengthen the Olympic Movement.

Looking forward: Tokyo 2020

Although innumerous things have changed when it comes to both the Olympics and society at large, certain aspects of the 1920 Olympics might be interesting to assist our thinking when considering the nature and role of Tokyo 2020. Amply illustrated by the communication of world leaders and by press metaphors, the world is currently "at war" with COVID-19. After considerable external pressures and internal discussions, the IOC and the local organizing committee took the joint decision to postpone the 2020 Olympics (Rich et al., 2020). The Tokyo Olympics will now take place in 2021, which accounts for a rescheduling of exactly one year. Even though its past is laced with crises, a postponement of such size is unseen in the history of the modern Olympic Games. "The Games must go on" as scheduled has long been functioning as one of IOC's leading principles, both before and after its then president Avery Brundage formulated his now infamous words in regards to the Munich 1972 terrorist attack.

This unprecedented decision to postpone the Olympics has been taken in a time in which the Olympic Movement is under heavy fire. Over the past years, the IOC is criticized for its seemingly ever increasing focus on commercialism and gigantism. Canceling instead of postponing the Games appeared impossible because of the associated multibillion interests, while each edition of the Olympics appears to be more profitable for the IOC than its predecessors. Moreover, although more attention has lately been dedicated to sustainability and environmental aspects, and a total new procedure for allocating the Olympics (called "Continuous Dialogue") has been developed, hosting cities and nations are still often facing post-Olympics cost overruns and abandoned infrastructures. Both practitioners and academics also argue in favor of more transparent and democratic decision making processes, illustrated by a plea for strengthening the voice of the athletes (Chappelet, 2020). Some critiques even go as far as claiming that the Olympic Games are "an idea whose time has gone" (Gammelsaeter, 2019). In addition, critiques now also contend that time, energy, and financial resources should be used for societally more important things, instead of planning the Olympics when the new coronavirus is still spreading around the globe. In 1919–20, similar voices were casted in times of worldwide recession and austerity. For example, the British public opinion showed negative feelings toward the allocation of public funds to pay for the participation of a national team in so-called aristocratic and inappropriate Olympic Games (Llewellyn, 2011).

Whilst the entire world is experiencing the harmful consequences of the COVID-19 pandemic, the Olympic Movement is also facing an existential identity crisis. Yet, each crisis offers opportunities. Nonetheless, if the IOC fails to take the opportunity that lies in an adapted, health focused, and downscaled business model, the Olympic Movement might lose its worldwide recognition. Whereas IOC's founding father Pierre de Coubertin insisted that the Antwerp 1920 Olympics would not go down in history as the games of war winners versus losers (although war "losers" such as Germany were not invited, see Kluge, 2014), the current Olympic Movement and society face one clear enemy: the new coronavirus. Today, there is no guarantee at all that the COVID-19 pandemic will be totally under control by the start of the Tokyo Olympics in July 2021. However, an additional year of planning, preparation, and consideration can safeguard the future of the Olympic Movement. Even when no effective COVID-19 vaccine or medication is available by the start of the Tokyo Olympics, the IOC and the local organizing committee can develop a downscaled version of the Olympic Games, yet with a magnified Olympic message to the world. Hence, rather than waiting (in vain?) for the return of old habits that allow a mega sport event, the Olympic Movement can inspire by its strength and resilience with adapted Games (e.g., partly virtual or with spectator limitations). Reinforced by the idea that the ideology of Olympism is in essence about celebrating international understanding, excellence, friendship, and respect, the Tokyo Olympics could play a vital role in uniting the (sporting) world in dealing with a (hopefully then) past trauma (Kidd, 2020). These values were already guiding the Olympic Movement before 1920 (Chatziefstathiou, 2005). However, despite the crisis caused by the First World War, the Antwerp Olympics made some of them more visible (Renson, 1996).

As demonstrated during Antwerp 1920, a revived Olympic Movement needs to be supported by strong symbols. Little brands in the world are as broadly known as IOC's logo with the five rings, which was first shown on the stage of the Olympics during Antwerp 1920 (Ferrand et al., 2012). Symbolizing the colors of all national flags and the five continents, this logo has a strong and global uniting potential that can again be implemented during the Tokyo Olympics. Besides the intrinsic symbolic value of the Olympic logo, developing new Olympic symbols and practices will be required in dealing with recent societal losses and accompanying sorrow. Antwerp 1920 was relatively small in number of spectators but great in symbolism (Renson, 1996). A downsized Tokyo 2020, in which the voice of the athletes and the health of everyone involved is put at the forefront of attention, could give the Olympic Movement a new élan of international meaning and relevance. Looking 100 years back and returning to the early roots of Olympism would certainly contribute to an enhanced understanding of the healing potential of (new) Olympic symbols. By showing massive resilience, the IOC and the local organizing committee of Tokyo 2020 might realize the same legacy as Antwerp 1920 in killing two birds with one stone: offering societal comfort while revitalizing the Olympic Movement.

Acknowledgments

The authors would like to thank Jasper Truyens and Gerben Verbrugghe for sharing their valuable thoughts on a first draft of this paper.

ORCID

Bram Constandt ⓘ http://orcid.org/0000-0002-5630-0745
Annick Willem ⓘ http://orcid.org/0000-0003-3753-2919

References

Chappelet, J.-L. (2020). The unstoppable rise of athlete power in the Olympic system. *Sport in Society, 23*(5), 795–809.

Chatziefstathiou, D. (2005). *The changing nature of the ideology of Olympism in the modern Olympic era* [Unpublished doctoral dissertation]. Loughborough University.

De Smet, S. (2005). *De Spaanse Griep in België* [The Spanish flu in Belgium] [Unpublished master's thesis]. Ghent University.

Ferrand, A., Chappelet, J.-L., & Séguin, B. (2012). *Olympic marketing.* Routledge.

Gammelsaeter, H. (2019, February 6). The Olympic Games: An idea whose time has gone [blog post]. https://panorama.himolde.no/2019/02/06/the-olympic-games-an-idea-whose-time-has-gone/

Honigsbaum, M. (2013). Regulating the 1918-19 pandemic: Flu, stoicism and the Northcliffe press. *Medical History, 57*(2), 165–185.

Kidd, B. (2020, March 26). How the rescheduled Tokyo Olympics could heal a post-Coronavirus world. *The Conversation.* https://theconversation.com/how-the-rescheduled-tokyo-olympics-could-heal-a-post-coronavirus-world-134757

Kluge, V. (2014). Funeral games, heroic groves and an Olympic death knell. *Journal of Olympic History, 3*, 40–48.

Llewellyn, M. P. (2011). Olympic Games are an international farce. *The International Journal of the History of Sport, 28*(5), 751–772.

Lucas, J. (1983). American preparations for the first post World War Olympic Games, 1919-1920. *Journal of Sport History, 10*(2), 30–44.

Mallon, B., & Bijkerk, A. T. (2003). *The 1920 Olympic Games. Results for all competitors in all events, with commentary.* McFarland & Company.

Mitschang, T. (2012). Influenza. Past, present and future. *BioSupply Trends Quarterly, 4*(3), 30–31.

Panja, T. (2020, March 27). The I.O.C. Let an Olympic boxing qualifier happen despite virus warnings. *The New York Times.* https://www.nytimes.com/2020/03/27/sports/olympics/coronavirus-ioc-boxing.html

Renson, R. (1996). *The Games Reborn. The VIIth Olympiad Antwerp 1920.* Pandora.

Rich, M., Futterman, M., & Panja, T. (2020, March 24). I.O.C. and Japan agree to postpone Tokyo Olympics. *The New York Times.* https://www.nytimes.com/2020/03/24/sports/olympics/coronavirus-summer-olympics-postponed.html

Truyens, J. (2020). *Antwerpen 1920. Verhalen van de VIIe Olympiade [Antwerp 1920. Stories of the VIIth Olympiad].* Davidsfonds Uitgeverij.

Festivals Post Covid-19

Karen Davies [ID]

ABSTRACT
Festivals have become a part of the cultural fabric of global society and a tourism and leisure pursuit that is participated in by many. The COVID-19 crisis has meant that many festivals in 2020 have been canceled or postponed. But what are the long term impacts for the future of the industry, and accessibility to these events? Will greater restrictions be placed on licensing, with a maximum number of attendees allowed? Will there be a certification scheme for attendees and participants based on current testing methods for COVID-19? Will festivals become more 'exclusive', or will there be more smaller-scale accessible organizations that work within a new 'sharing economy'? This paper explores some of the issues and possibilities for the future of the festivals industry by using an ecological economist's view of the potential shift in economic paradigms as outcomes of the pandemic.

Introduction

The rapidly developing global COVID-19 pandemic crisis continues to have a severe effect on the ways in which societies operate, both in terms of economic activity and in relation to how people spend their leisure time. Patterns of working life are changing and many businesses are suffering, prompting the biggest global recession since the Great Depression (Rappeport & Smialek, 2020). An insightful piece written by Mair (2020 [online]), an ecological economist, predicted four possible outcomes of the crisis. Put simply, these are "a descent into barbarism, a robust state capitalism, a radical state socialism, and a transformation into a big society built on mutual aid" (Mair, 2020 [online]). These possible outcomes are used in the following commentary to present some potential effects of COVID-19 on the future of the festivals industry.

The state of the festivals industry

Festivals are a social phenomenon that occur in virtually all human cultures and have been defined as "a sacred or profane time of celebration, marked by special observances" (Getz & Page, 2016, p. 67). They are staged in a variety of locations, both indoors and outdoors, as well as in virtual spaces, with a variety of management structures ranging from public sector provision, not-for-profit and privately run organizations. There are a wide range of types from food festivals, to theater, dance, to music or a combination of art forms, ranging from the smallest community festivals to large-scale music festivals with over 100,000 participants. They can be of global reach, diasporic (for example Chinese New Year celebrations), or rooted in local and/or religious traditions (Newbold & Jordan, 2016). Festivals make a huge contribution to the global tourism industry, in a number of ways. In some instances they become the key motivator and driver for tourism (as in the case of the Edinburgh festival series). In other cases, festivals are part of the overall cultural offering of a destination, and in others they are a phenomenon that tourists stumble upon in their travels (Picard & Robinson, 2006). In the UK alone, music events contribute £17.6 billion to the UK economy, and attendance at UK music festivals has increased by some 22% in the last two years with 57% of this number preferring to take part in this tourism activity than to book an annual European holiday (Mintel, 2019).

Studies on what motivates people to attend festivals include escape from everyday life, socialization and family togetherness (Crompton & McKay, 1997; Jepson et al., 2019). In a similar way to Pearce's (1982) 'tourism travel career trajectory' model which considers the holiday choices people make concerning their self-concept, many people aim to attend several different festivals year to year and construct their personal identities via these transformational experiences (Robinson, 2015; Webster & McKay, 2016). These events reinforce social and communal identities or belongingness, where the human need for "frequent, affectively pleasant interactions with others" (Jaeger & Mykletun, 2013, p. 214) can be satiated and where cultural and social capital can be developed (Wilks, 2011; Quinn & Wilks, 2013). Festivals are places where the participants' utopian ideals for society are explored (Small, 1998), but at the same time 'festivity' as a social phenomenon answers the human need for continuity that reaffirms social structure and order (Newbold & Jordan, 2016).

Undoubtedly festivals now play a pivotal role and are part of the fabric of global society. Taking the modern music festival as an example, this is a phenomenon that originated in the 1960s and 70 s as a countercultural movement in the West of Europe and has grown into a global industry (Anderton, 2011; Robinson, 2015) where competition is extremely high. Diversification and market segmentation has naturally occurred and the sector is now engrained into the global economy with fully established supply chains (Ryan & Kelly, 2018). The festivals industry now lies at the sharper capitalist end of the mixed economy of many countries, and its general buoyancy is therefore determined by the market forces of supply and demand, with very limited governmental intervention. The music festival industry in particular has in some ways become the epitome of a capitalist society, with companies such as Live Nation (which controls 25% of UK festivals (Digital, Culture, Media and Sport Committee, 2019)) holding the power to book the bigger name acts, whilst the remainder of the sector often struggles to survive. It has been argued that these more corporate festivals are based on a standardized mode of production (Finkel, 2009) and have moved away from their creative and community-oriented roots, with a focus on profit and economies of scale. Some may argue that this is a natural process of free markets providing more choice for everyone, but the opposing view is based in a concern that as the industry grows, suppliers will increase their prices, inevitably pricing out some of the smaller not-for-profit festivals and creating more exclusivity (Szabo, 2016). This can be seen in the example of headline acts, the cost of which has risen by 50 times in the last 50 years, ten times more than the rate of inflation (The Economist, 2019). Furthermore, in the case of arts festivals that are publicly funded and where a good percentage of the program is available for free (for example Edinburgh Fringe Festival), the rising costs of accommodation makes attendance more difficult for people on lower incomes. These issues have recently led to a more critical approach to research on festivals with the likes of Laing and Mair (2015), Finkel et al. (2019) and Bossey (2020) questioning issues of inclusivity, accessibility and marginalization within the festivals arena.

The potential future(s) for the festivals industry

There is no certainty as to how the future of society as a whole will look, let alone individual sectors. With conflicting news stories concerning an exit strategy from lockdown, some suggest that the pandemic will last way beyond December 2020 and that we will not be 'back to normal' until a vaccine is produced, which realistically could take up to a year to develop (Eyal et al., 2020). Mair (2020), an ecological economist, uses future planning methods to envision some potential futures for society post COVID-19. The basic premise is that response to the crisis will require some form of radical social change, ideally where we produce less (and therefore cause less damage to the environment) and where we understand the economy as being "the way we take our resources and turn them into the things we need to live" (Mair, 2020 [online]), as opposed to using resources to produce unnecessary items. There are four potential outcomes (or any combination or blending of these outcomes); the first is a robust capitalist state where capitalist production continues as it has done in the past, but where the state steps in to support markets in crisis by extending welfare, giving out business loans and providing more credit. In terms of festivals, often their success relies on the exchange-value of the commodity of entertainment, as well as on the use of gig-workers and zero-hour contracted staff who have no job protection. This is an issue which Mair (2020) suggests is a product of the market and exchange-value economies of the UK and the USA in the last 40 years. Festivals, especially the smaller not-for-profit ones, are an extremely high-risk industry in economic terms, at the mercy of market forces more than many others due to the high costs and low profit margins. Festivals are also at a high risk in other ways; due to the sheer number of people that attend, they require a huge focus on health and safety regulations and crisis and risk management (Silvers, 2013; Getz & Page, 2016). Yet, no risk assessment in the world could have prepared the industry for the lock-downs and social distancing measures that we are currently experiencing. Many events companies are not insured against pandemics, many companies in the supply chain are not doing any business and many festivals have been forced to cancel or postpone their 2020 editions (Szatan, 2020). What does this mean for the future of the industry? Unless festival organizations are innovative in developing high-quality online alternatives, have saved for a 'rainy day', or their customers are prepared to roll their ticket purchases over to next year, they are at risk of liquidation without government intervention, as per many of the small-medium enterprises within the tourism and hospitality sectors. In reality, short-term intervention by the government may provide some initial help for the 2020 season, but if the pandemic lasts for any significant length of time, this is not sustainable and a more long-term strategy will be required.

In the second potential scenario – state socialism – the government protects the parts of the economy that are essential to life (for example food, shelter and energy). This idea is far from avant-garde, with ideas of a universal basic income having been mooted as an option to reduce inequalities in society as early as 1516 in Thomas More's book 'Utopia'. The festival environment has often been sociologically analyzed as 'utopic' (Gardiner, 1992) and in that sense it could be argued that these environments should be made more available to everyone in society. As intimated earlier, festivals do play a pivotal role in society in many respects, and are often spaces that are 'ahead of the curve' in terms of highlighting political issues within society, one good example in today's times being our relationship with the planet and the need for a more sustainable way of life (Guttridge-Hewitt, 2020). Whilst festivals will never be considered a 'human need' and therefore will not be fully available for free, if all adults in society were provided an income for securing their basic needs, it is possible that they would have more disposable income to spend on activities such as attendance at festivals. This is turn could reduce the problems relating to accessibility and inclusivity highlighted by the likes of Laing and Mair (2015) and Finkel et al. (2019).

Barbarism, the third potential outcome, is the exact opposite of state socialism, a dystopic world where the economies collapse. This is an unlikely outcome, due to the levels of state intervention currently at play. However, in areas where the disadvantaged in society feel unfairly treated, this may bring out anti-social behaviors amongst certain groups. The festival environment is not excluded from these types of issues, and with a long history of drug and crime-related incidences, it is a possibility that these could be exacerbated. It is likely that some form of evidence of having been tested for COVID-19 as a prerequisite for entry will need to be enforced, which could easily lead to a black market and dangerous levels of fraudulent activity. Although the festival organizations are resilient and well-equipped to deal with such issues, some element of state intervention and legal frameworks would need to be introduced which may deter people from attending larger events.

The last potential outcome for society following COVID-19 is the idea of a society based on mutual aid, where individuals and small groups begin to organize support and care within their communities through building networks that protect the vulnerable (Mair, 2020 [online]). There has certainly been a strong, compassionate and healthy response to the pandemic from communities across the world, where people are offering help and support to each other like never before. With a decrease in air travel, social distancing and more focus on local and virtual communities, there is a potential for a growth in the number and importance of smaller, more affordable community events, as well as virtual or online festivals. These would be based around and run by communities (real or virtual), where 'art for art's sake' are the main motivations to both produce and attend, as opposed to the propping up of celebrities' status and lining the pockets of the intermediaries such as booking agents and ticketing platforms, as is so often the case in the current situation.

Summary

There is some hope for a blend of state socialism and mutual aid where strong, democratic states that mobilize resources to build strong health systems and prioritize the protection of vulnerable people and the environment begin to evolve, and where citizens form mutual aid groups and more equal economies develop. This blend of socialism and mutual aid applied to festivals could be a reality, insofar as smaller community festivals may be a more efficient method of limiting the number of attendees and cutting down costs for the festival hosts and attendees. The fact is, the mixed economies of the world can only be successful in the long term for all members of society with a good blend of 'ethical capitalism' and 'socialist politics', where the state makes good financial decisions on what services to support and where successful companies maintain a sense of responsibility to the wider communities that they serve. The festivals industry could be set to be a leading light in following this path.

ORCID

Karen Davies ⓘ http://orcid.org/0000-0001-5769-7521

References

Anderton, C. (2011). Music festival sponsorship; between commerce and carnival, *Arts Marketing. Arts Marketing: An International Journal, 1*(2), 145–158. https://doi.org/10.1108/20442081111180368

Bossey, A. (2020). Accessibility all areas? UK live music industry perceptions of current practice and Information and Communication Technology improvements to accessibility for music festival attendees who are deaf or disabled. *International Journal of Event and Festival Management, 11*(1), 6–25. https://doi.org/10.1108/IJEFM-03-2019-0022 .

Crompton, J. L., & McKay, S. L. (1997). Motives of visitors attending festival events. *Annals of Tourism Research, 24*(2), 425–439. https://doi.org/10.1016/S0160-7383(97)80010-2

Digital, Culture, Media and Sport Committee. (2019). *Live music, ninth report of session 2017–19.* House of Commons. https://aiforg.com/wp-content/uploads/Digital-Culture-Media-and-Sport-Comittee-Live-Music-Ninth-Report-of-Session-2017-2019.pdf.

Eyal, N., Lipsitch, M., & Smith, P. G. (2020). Human challenge studies to accelerate coronavirus vaccine licensure. *The Journal of Infectious Diseases, 221*(11), 1752–1756. https://doi.org/10.1093/infdis/jiaa152

Finkel, R. (2009). A picture of the contemporary combined arts festival landscape. *Cultural Trends, 18*(1), 3–21. https://doi.org/10.1080/09548960802651195

Finkel, R., Sharp, B., & Sweeney, M. (eds.). (2019). *Accessibility,* diversity and inclusion in critical event studies. Routledge.

Gardiner, M. (1992). Bakhtin's carnival: Utopia as critique. *Utopian Studies, 3*(2), 21–49.

Getz, D., & Page, S. J. (2016). *Event studies; theory, research and policy for planned events* (3rd ed.). Routledge.

Guttridge-Hewitt, M. (2020, February, 25). This is the future of festivals, according to festivals. *DJ Mag.* https://djmag.com/longreads/future-festivals-according-festivals.

Jaeger, K., & Mykletun, R. J. (2013). Festivals, identity and belonging. *Event Management, 17*(3), 213–226. https://doi.org/10.3727/152599513X13708863377791

Jepson, A., Stadler, R., & Spencer, N. (2019). Making positive family memories together and improving quality-of-life through thick sociality and bonding at local community festivals and events. *Tourism Management, 75*, 34–50. https://doi.org/10.1016/j.tourman.2019.05.001

Laing, J., & Mair, J. (2015). Music festivals and social inclusion – the festival organisers' perspective. *Leisure Sciences, 37*(3), 252–217. https://doi.org/10.1080/01490400.2014.991009

Mair, S. (2020, March, 30). What will the world look like after coronavirus? Four possible futures. *The Converstion.* https://theconversation.com/what-will-the-world-be-like-after-coronavirus-four-possible-futures-134085?utm_medium=email&utm_campaign=Latest.

Mintel. (2019). *Raving Mad: UK music festival attendance at highest level of four year.* https://www.mintel.com/press-centre/leisure/raving-mad-uk-music-festival-attendance-at-highest-level-in-four-years.

Newbold, C., & Jordan, J. (2016). Introduction: Focusing on world festivals. In C. Newbold & J. Jordan (Eds.), *Focus on world festivals: Contemporary case studies and perspectives* (pp. xiii–xxi). Goodfellows Publishers.

Pearce, P. L. (1982). *The social psychology of tourist behavior.* Pergamon.

Picard, D., & Robinson, M. (2006). Remaking worlds: Festivals, tourism and change. In D. Picard & M. Robinson (Eds.), *Festivals, tourism and social change* (pp. 1–31). Channel View Publications.

Quinn, B., & Wilks, L. (2013). Festival connections; People, place and social capital. In G. Richards, M. P. de Brito, & L. Wilks (Eds.), *Exploring the social impacts of events* (pp. 15–30). Routledge.

Rappeport, A., & Smialek, J. (2020, April, 14). I.M.F. predicts worst downturn since the great depression. *New York Times.* https://www.nytimes.com/2020/04/14/us/politics/coronavirus-economy-recession-depression.html

Robinson, R. (2015). *Festivals and the politics of participation.* Taylor and Francis.

Ryan, W. G., & Kelly, S. (2018). The effects of supply chain management (SCM) activities and their impact on festival management and the consumer experience. In A. Jepson & A. Clarke (Eds.), *Power, construction and meaning in festivals* (pp. 109–128). Routledge.

Silvers, J. R. (2013). *Risk management for meetings and events* (2nd ed.). Routledge.

Small, C. (1998). *Musicking: The meanings of performing and listening.* Wesleyan University Press.

Szabo, J. Z. (2016). Large festivals – great struggles. In C. Newbold & J. Jordan, (Eds), *Focus on world festivals: Contemporary case studies and perspectives* (pp. 140–151). Goodfellows Publishers.

Szatan, G. (2020, April, 15). Should I stay or should I go: How coronavirus is jeopardising music festivals. *The Guardian.* https://www.theguardian.com/music/2020/apr/15/abort-retry-fail-how-coronavirus-is-jeopardising-music-festivals.

The Economist. (2019, August, 03). Why are music festivals so expensive? [video]. *Youtube.* https://youtu.be/PMfkO3Pv4VQ

Webster, E., McKay, G. (2016). *From glyndebourne to Glastonbury: The Impact of British Music Festivals.* https://ahrc.ukri.org/documents/project-reports-and-reviews/connected-communities/impact-of-music-festivals/.

Wilks, L. (2011). Bridging and bonding: Social capital at music festivals. *Journal of Policy Research in Tourism, Leisure and Events, 3*(3), 281–297. https://doi.org/10.1080/19407963.2011.576870

Purveyors of One Health: The Ecological Imperative Driving the Future of Leisure Services

Daniel Dustin, Gene Lamke, James Murphy, Cary McDonald, Brett Wright, and Jack Harper

ABSTRACT

The coronavirus pandemic, for all of its damage to human health and well-being, has brought to light the wisdom underlying the idea of One Health, whose advocates reason that health is a reciprocal relationship between our species and the environment that sustains us. What is good for people should also be good for the environment, and what is good for the environment should also be good for people. Their preferred future is one in the same. As the recent days, weeks, and months have also shown, leisure is not necessarily a cure for what ails us. Indeed, leisure pursuits may have contributed to the pandemic's spread. What, then, are we to make of leisure in the time of the coronavirus? We believe it is a fundamental lesson in ecology.

The coronavirus pandemic, if nothing else, illustrates the wisdom underlying the idea of human health and the Earth's health as "One Health" (Hendricks et al., 2019). As the Center for Disease Control defines it, One Health is "a collaborative, multi-sectoral, and trans-disciplinary approach—working at the local, regional, national, and global levels—with the goal of achieving optimal health outcomes recognizing the interconnection between people, animals, plants, and their shared environment" (CDC.gov, 2017). It is time to abandon our academic and professional silos to join our colleagues across the allied health professions to promote One Health, and to demonstrate how the field of leisure services contributes to One Health.

Through all of the pain and suffering, the coronavirus pandemic has broadcast one message loud and clear—ecological understanding must provide the future foundation for all planning, management, and evaluation of our social, cultural, economic and political systems, each of which is but a subsystem of the largest system of all—the ecological system. As the pandemic has demonstrated in many devastating ways, healthy people cannot long sustain themselves on an unhealthy planet (*Think of the pandemic's origin.*), and a healthy planet cannot long harbor unhealthy people (*Think of the pandemic's spread.*). Health, at its core, is a symbiotic relationship between people and the larger living world (Dustin et al., 2009; Schwab et al., 2009). Moreover, the pandemic has demonstrated repeatedly that leisure can have both positive and negative effects on this fundamental ecological relationship (*Note that leisure settings have been treated as both a cure for, and contributor to, what ails us.*). The challenge for the leisure services field is to take this lesson to heart and plan for the future accordingly.

> "When we try to pick out anything by itself, we find it hitched to everything else in the universe."
>
> John Muir (1911, p. 110)

What started out as an epidemic in Wuhan, China, has rapidly spread across the globe. The coronavirus has shown no respect for the social, cultural, economic, and political boundaries erected by our species that separate us from one another. On the contrary, the pandemic has brought to light the basic ecological interrelationships and interdependencies that, for better or worse, connect us with one another (Chivian & Bernstein, 2008, 2004). Despite our individual differences, and despite the fact that some among us are more vulnerable to the coronavirus's damaging effects than others, in a larger sense we are all in the same ecological boat, and we are now challenged to put our differences aside in service of a much bigger cause, our collective health and well-being.

Taking this ecological lesson seriously may be the only silver lining in what otherwise will likely be dismissed as merely an unwelcome disruption of business as usual. If we learn nothing else from the coronavirus pandemic, we must understand its ecological implications. Otherwise, we will be ill-prepared to ward off even greater threats to our health and well-being, including the specter of a world reeling from human induced climate change. We need to examine the pandemic's inputs, throughputs, and outputs very carefully, so that we can learn from our mistakes and avoid repeating them. This requires worldwide coordination and cooperation on a scale we have never seen before (*Consider, for example, working with China rather than chastising China for the coronavirus's origin.*). It requires putting aside our individual differences in deference to our ecological inseparability.

The coronavirus's cascading effects have accelerated rapidly. Like a row of dominos falling one after the other, the pandemic's harmful impacts have resounded across our social, cultural, economic and political systems in ways we never could have imagined. Heretofore hidden interconnections and interdependencies reveal themselves on a daily basis, and efforts to prevent or mitigate the coronavirus's spread are confounded by multitudes of interacting factors (*Recall the unintended impacts of transcontinental, national, regional, and local travel on the coronavirus's transmission.*).

For a short while it seemed like leisure pursuits might be immune from the coronavirus's harmful effects. Indeed, it appeared we could take refuge in them. "Go outdoors. Get some fresh air. Take a walk." But the need for physical distancing to prevent the spread of the coronavirus quickly compromised the ability of outdoor pursuits to serve their therapeutic function of restoring our physical and mental health. As people flocked in large numbers to the out-of-doors to benefit from nature's healing powers, those very numbers were feared to fuel the virus's spread, and public officials grudgingly closed many park and recreation areas and facilities (*Remember those images of congested parks, sporting events, and dining establishments.*). The refuges, it seemed, may have been contributing to, rather than thwarting, the pandemic's spread.

Of even greater irony has been the opportunity lost to strengthen family bonds through stay-at-home leisure pursuits. While self-isolating families may not have had to worry about physical distancing, families whose members have continued working outside the home have had to worry about bringing the coronavirus home with them. And while there have been encouraging reports describing many creative ways other families have surmounted the physical distancing barrier, it is disappointing nonetheless to think that the opportunity for families to accept the challenge of entertaining themselves rather than being entertained by others has frequently been inhibited by the need for physical distancing (*Reflect on those images of glass panes separating people from human touch.*). Clearly, leisure as an antidote for what ails us has been constrained by the coronavirus's omnipresence.

> "Recreational development is a job not of building roads into the lovely country, but of building receptivity into the still unlovely human mind."
>
> Aldo Leopold (1949, p. 26)

The overarching lesson for leisure services is self-evident. We must plan for and promote leisure pursuits based on the ecological principle of reciprocity—what is good for people must also be good for the environment, and what is good for the environment must also be good for people (Dustin et al., 1991). We must encourage leisure pursuits that contribute to a healthy environment and discourage leisure pursuits that jeopardize a healthy environment (Zajchowski & Brownlee, 2016). Through leisure education, we must teach the citizenry to recreate in ways that are, above all else, socially and environmentally responsible. Leisure pursuits, at their best, must be manifestations of a healthy symbiotic relationship between our species and the environment that sustains us. That is the goal of One Health.

This orientation to service requires moving away from a highly individualistic view of leisure to a community-centered view of leisure; moving away from seeing people as separate and distinct from one another to seeing people as connected and part of one another. As the coronavirus pandemic has shown, each of us is indeed part of something larger than ourselves, and our individual health depends on our ability to see one another not as separate, autonomous and independent beings, but as connected, communal and interdependent beings. This realization, in turn, points to our growing collective responsibility to look out for one another when engaging in leisure.

This ecological understanding also demands that we step down from our anthropocentric pedestal to adopt a more humble station in life (Leopold, 1949). It demands that we take more responsibility for the consequences of our leisure choices. The coronavirus pandemic has made it clear that our freedom to choose what we find joy in doing can sometimes encroach on the freedom of others to be free of harm from our choices (*Picture crowded beaches right now.*). The freedom central to leisure decision-making carries with it both an opportunity and an obligation. The opportunity rests in our freedom to choose. The obligation rests in answering for our choices. Ecology teaches us that everything is interconnected, our individual actions have far reaching consequences, and we are ethically obliged to conduct ourselves in a manner that respects this interconnectedness.

Furthermore, and perhaps just as importantly, no longer can the leisure services field interpret its mandate as simply serving popular tastes for recreation (Sax, 1980) if those tastes lead to significant harm to others (*Think about those leisure pursuits that are highly consumptive of limited nonrenewable natural resources, severely damage fragile ecosystems, or otherwise harm other species.*) Leisure service professionals are duty bound to employ their expertise to encourage leisure pastimes that are socially and environmentally responsible. The coronavirus pandemic is a wake-up call to take these professional obligations more seriously.

> "*A thing is right when it tends to preserve the integrity, stability and beauty of the biotic community. It is wrong when it tends otherwise.*"
>
> Aldo Leopold (1949, pp. 224–225)

Now is the time for leisure service professionals to promote leisure pursuits that contribute to the health and well-being of everyone, including planet Earth—the ground of our being. Now is the time to recognize leisure's preventative, restorative, and rehabilitative power for health promotion (*Note the emerging Park RX programs springing up across the globe.*). Now is the time to capitalize on our leisure expertise to promote health as a public good. This requires prioritizing the beneficial outcomes of leisure services and promoting leisure pursuits that contribute most to the health and well-being of people and planet considered together. To advocate for one at the expense of the other misses the point. The point is their preferred future is one in the same. We do not mean to suggest that leisure service professionals must dictate what good and bad leisure behavior is; neither are we suggesting we can completely eliminate our footprint on the natural world. But we do mean to suggest that leisure service professionals have an obligation to "nudge" people in the right direction (Thaler & Sunstein, 2009), and to structure leisure opportunities in ways that fully support programs, services, and management that foster One Health (Dustin et al., 2019).

We still have much to learn about what the field of leisure services should do in response to the coronavirus pandemic, as well as how to go about doing it. As a first step, we might listen to the kinds of learning nature has to teach us. Other members of the community of life have existed a lot longer than our species, and have learned how to live in harmony with the larger living world. Indeed, biomimicists have identified a canon of nature's laws, strategies, and principles that characterize the successful working of things, including: "nature runs on sunlight; nature uses only the energy it needs; nature fits form to function; nature recycles everything; nature rewards cooperation; nature banks on diversity; nature demands local expertise; nature curbs excesses from within; and nature taps the power of limits" (Benyus, 1997, p. 7).

The challenge for our field is to mimic nature's lessons in the work we do as well. How, for example, might we run leisure services on sunlight? Use only the energy we need? Fit form to function? Recycle everything? Reward cooperation? Bank on diversity? Demand local expertise? Curb excesses from within? And tap the power of limits? And more broadly, how might the field of leisure services—in the name of One Health—

promote individual, familial, communal, national, and international health, as well as biodiversity conservation, in the design and implementation of our work? Sustainable answers to these questions will provide the foundation for our field's contributions to an Earth-friendly form of health promotion (Dustin et al., 2019).

> *"The greatest achievement of our flight to the moon is the picture of the Earth, a living blue-green planet whirling in the dark, endless void of space, and the realization that this is home."*

Sigurd Olson (1976, p. 59)

The picture Sigurd Olson leaves us with is a stark reminder that from space there are no social, cultural, economic or political boundaries subdividing planet Earth. From space there is only one ecological reality within which we must learn to live our lives (Dustin, 1991). As we move forward into the future together, our mission should be to model ecologically sustainable practices through the design and delivery of leisure services in ways that lead to One Health. The coronavirus pandemic, for all of the harm it has done to our species, is a clarion call for our field to lead by example.

References

Benyus, J. (1997). *Biomimicry: Innovation inspired by nature.* William Morrow and Company, Inc.

CDC.gov. (2017). *One health.* (pp. 25–35). International Institute for Environment and Development. https://www.cdc.gov/onehealth/basics/health

Chivian, E., & Bernstein, A. (2004). Guest editorial: Embedded in nature: Human health and biodiversity. *Environmental Health Perspectives, 112*(1), A12–A13.

Chivian, E., & Bernstein, A. (Eds.). (2008). *Sustaining life: How human health depends on biodiversity.* Oxford University Press.

Dustin, D. (1991). Peace, leisure and recreation. *Parks & Recreation, 26*(9), 102–104.

Dustin, D., Bricker, K., & Schwab, K. (2009). People and nature: Toward an ecological model of health promotion. *Leisure Sciences, 32*(1), 3–14.

Dustin, D., McAvoy, L., & Schultz, J. (1991). Recreation rightly understood. In T. Goodale & P. Witt (Eds.) *Recreation and leisure: Issues in an era of change* (3rd ed., pp. 97–106). Venture Publishing, Inc.

Dustin, D., Zajchowski, C., Gatti, E., Bricker, K., Brownlee, M., & Schwab, K. (2018). Greening health: The role of parks, recreation, and tourism in health promotion. *Journal of Park and Recreation Administration, 36*(1), 113–123.

Dustin, D., Zajchowski, C., Lackey, Q., Tysor, D., Pagano, K., Bennett, T., & Taylor, M. (2019). Libertarian paternalism and the park, recreation, and tourism profession. *Journal of Park and Recreation Administration, 37*(1), 95–104.

Hendricks, W., Schwab, K., Bricker, K., Zajchowski, C., and Dustin, D. (2019). The future of parks and recreation: One health. *Journal of Park and ZRecreation Administration, 37*(1), 141–145.

Leopold, A. (1949). *A sand county almanac.* Oxford University Press.

Muir, J. (1911). *My first summer in the Sierra.* Houghton Mifflin Company.

Olson, S. (1976). *Reflections from the North Country.* Alfred A. Knopf, Inc.

Sax, J. (1980). *Mountains without handrails.* University of Michigan Press.

Schwab, K., Dustin, D., & Bricker, K. (2009). Parks, recreation, and tourism's contributions to Utah's health: An ecologic perspective. *Utah Leisure Insights, 29*(1), 12–14.

Thaler, R., & Sunstein, C. (2009). *Nudge: Improving decisions about health, wealth, and happiness.* Penguin Books.

Zajchowski, C. A. B., & Brownlee, M. T. J. (2016). Decreasing degrees of freedom: Ethical recreation in a changing climate. *River Management Society Journal, 29*(2), 10–11.

Thinking through the Disruptive Effects and Affects of the Coronavirus with Feminist New Materialism

Simone Fullagar and Adele Pavlidis

ABSTRACT

The disruptive biocultural force of the coronavirus highlights the value of more-than-human perspectives for examining the gendered effects and affects on our everyday lives and leisure practices. Pursuing this line of thought our article draws upon the insights of feminist new materialism as intellectual resource for considering what the coronavirus "does" as a gendered phenomenon. We turn to this body of feminist scholarship as it enables us to attune to what is happening, what remains unspoken and to pay attention to "the little things" that may be lost in a big crisis. Writing through the complexity of embodied affects (fear, loss, hope), we focus on the challenge to humanist notions of "agency" posed by these shifting timespace relations of home confinement, restricted movement and altered work-leisure routines. We explore the tensions arising from "home" as an historical site of gendered inequality and a new site of enhanced capacity.

A place of confining freedom

Taking a shower
first cold, then warm, then too damn hot
but I like it that way, just bearable.
Shrinking, making smaller, contained in that hot, wet cubicle
this containment the only moment of freedom in this tough day.

As people die and mothers struggle
people of Asian descent are on the receiving end of hateful, violent attacks.
My own children struggle to fall asleep, his small heart aches
from a panic attack brought on by this wildfire.
Extinguished for a moment by the hot water,
the steaming room and a minute alone.

Time alone, the water washes over me
for a moment there is nothing else but the heat, the wet
my own body being washed clean.
Thoughts intrude; make-shift morgues, children in poverty,
women scared in their own homes
Little pockets and small leisure moments created
so we don't feel 'shut down',
imprisoned
not quite in prison, but confined.
The future murmurs, moving us ever so slightly.
(AP)

COVID-19 presses against our thinking, highlighting the value of leisure practices in supporting survival and flourishing as both individual and collective concerns. Loss, death, and trauma have intensified the affective relations and gendered inequities of "home" as a particular leisure site – a timespace of confinement *and* freedom. Our opening poem offers a creative analytic (Parry & Johnson, 2007) murmuring, inspired by Deleuze and Guattari's "sound of a contagious future, the murmur (*rumeur*) of new assemblages of desire, of machines, and of statements, that insert themselves into the old assemblages and break with them" (1987, p. 83). Leisure worlds have become saturated with the affective intensities of a relentless corona news cycle that permeate and disrupt living rooms and digital devices. Words and images of sickness and graphs of infection rates do not simply "represent" the external world, they are produced through an affective economy (Ahmed, 2004) that circulates fear, anger, loss, and frustration with political (in)action.

These dynamic affects and sleepless nights have moved us to write this commentary to think our way through with the intellectual resources of feminist new materialism (Barad, 2007; Coole & Frost, 2010; Fullagar, 2017; Haraway, 2016; Kumm et al., 2019; Lupton, 2019; Thorpe et al., 2019). It is an analytic approach that orients us toward the "moments of affirmation and moments of dissonance" afforded by changing leisure practices, policies and provision - in the effort to counter sexism, racism, poverty, homophobia, transphobia and environmental degradation (Bargetz, 2019, p. 193). However, these disturbing affects are also countered by connectedness, belonging and hopefulness that emanate from an array of creative social media moments via "home" as a private-public and gendered leisure site; music, dance, yoga, cooking, art, fitness practices and shared humor reassert their embodied value (Fullagar et al., 2018b). Arbitrary divisions between private and public, home and work, digital and physical, human and nonhuman, self and other, are collapsing and reconfiguring leisure in lockdown through a radically different *timespacemattering* (Barad, 2007).

Gendered leisure in materializing worlds

We need different ways of conceptualizing leisure beyond individualized models of "human agency," to enable a deeper grasp of the embodied, *affective* relations that produce leisure phenomena as an assemblage of gendered forces (Braidotti, 2013; Fullagar et al., 2019). Feminist new materialism offers a relational approach to leisure that is attuned to ambivalence and the multiplicity of meaning; the gendered experience of despair and trauma enacted in highly normalized ways, alongside the "performative tactic[s] of counter-feelings ... counter-manifestation" (Bargetz, 2019, p. 193). This is a multiscalar endeavor. It's the little things, and the big things at once. And everything in-between. It is the tiny pleasures of hot showers, hugs from a toddler or dog, your favorite comedy show, growing or making things, a walk in the park, or a good cry with a friend. To borrow from Barad (2007) we suggest that such affective practices are about "making worlds ... materially engaging as part of the world in giving it specific material form" (p. 91). Feminist materialisms have us thinking about disrupting this disruption.

As a disruptive knowledge practice feminist theory seeks multiplicity while undoing the binary thinking that continues to marginalize and "fix in place" material and discursive forces (including policies, practices, ideologies and affects). The pandemic evokes these tensions for us to think with – how does COVID-19 come to matter in gendered ways and for different women (recognizing cis, trans and fluid gender identifications, intersectionality and more-than-human worlds)? How does leisure scholarship grapple with the affects of loss and joy, as well as the limitations of humanist assumptions about agency? Today we face COVID-19, yet the a/effects of global warming and inequality related climate crises loom large in our planetary future.

Gendered risk and entangled agency

Governments have been largely silent about the gendered effects of the virus (Gaweda, 2020), while activists and women's organizations, such as UN Women, have called for feminist perspectives to examine the impacts of the pandemic and governmental responses on gender inequalities (Stephenson & Harris-Rimmer, 2020). A recent survey by the Australian Bureau of Statistics found that women were statistically more likely than men to be experiencing anxiety and/or depression in the mid-March to mid-April time period (Australian Bureau of Statistics, 2020). Statistics from the United States show that younger women (20 to 29) and African Americans are experiencing higher rates of infection (Statista, 2020), potentially due to their role in front line services. The conditions of everyday freedom are not only gendered, they are also shaped by intersectional forces – the entanglements of class, race, sexuality, age, illness/disability (Hinton et al., 2015). Within such entanglements, Barad (2007, p. 32) poses a key feminist question that shifts from what gender differences exist to "how differences get made, what gets excluded and how these exclusions matter" with respect to gender justice.

Across the globe feminized labor holds up the essential work of the health, care, food provision and education sectors. Many women have lost their casualized jobs, feminized poverty increases housing and food pressures. Women of color are subject to racial abuse and structural racism, while an increasing number are experiencing the horror of gender-based violence or "domestic terrorism" in the homes they are confined to (Gearing, 2020). The defensive borders created around the ownership of homes, bodies, nature, countries, territories – have fueled racism, sexism and exploitation for profit and patriarchal pleasure. As (eco)feminist, Indigenous and scholars of color have argued the human experience of vulnerability, uncertainty and precarious living, is profoundly biopolitical. Precarity exacerbated by the crisis is bound up with an ontological politics premised upon the othering of difference (nature-culture, self-other, mind-body, etc.)

(Barad, 2007; Butler, 2004; Gilson, 2014; Haraway, 2016; Nxumalo, 2020). Watene (2020) noted New Zealand's effective response to the crisis (led by Prime Minister Jacinda Ardern as one of several effective women leaders in the crisis) invoked "the well-known Māori phrase He waka eke noa (we are all in this together)" and yet there exist inequities in social life and higher rates of infection for Māori people.

Dominant masculine fantasies of mastery "over" others (nature, the body, death, other bodies …) are embodied by male leaders such as US President Trump and Brazilian President Bolsonaro, who recently responded with "so what?" to questions about Brazil's rising death toll (Phillips, 2020). Yet, humans are nature; living microbiomes that host and transmit a diverse range of helpful and harmful microorganisms and non-living agents, such as viruses. COVID-19 is thought to have emerged from human-animal transmission through the consumption of infected wildlife; animals that are increasingly threatened by profit motives. An invisible non-living agent becomes alive in bodies and halts the flow of capital, people and commodities, causing global supply chains to faulter. The fantasy of masculine privilege has failed, revealing a profound vulnerability with higher death rates for men. This death rate is largely framed through biological theories, suggesting that the lower risk for females is related to "traits that enhance their ability to care for young, hence their stronger immune system" (Graves, 2020). These kinds of explanations ignore the biocultural question of how transmission is mediated through the micro-politics of space. Masculine body comportment has been shown to claim more entitlement to space (Young, 1980). While thousands were dying in Italy and China during March, crowds of mainly men gathered to attend the Melbourne Grand Prix. Even Australia's Prime Minister announced in self-assured fashion that he would be "going to the footy" (Speers, 2020). Public pressure from varying groups shut down the Grand Prix and the football at the 11th hour: with its large crowds men's sport became identified by public health experts a key vector of disease.

Rethinking leisure through relational capacities

Turning to feminist new materialism, the question of change (and leisure choice) is conceived of as complexity and emergence. Attention is focused on multiple affects and (digitally mediated) interrelationships that produce expanded or limited agentic capacities, rather than atomistic agents (Barad, 2007; Fullagar et al., 2018a). Rational choice models (Simpson & Harrell, 2007) have long assumed a static notion of the self and world as separate entities where leisure practices appear to be *chosen* and enacted through sheer will. The ontological assumptions of such theories fail to grasp complexity and in the current context the radical revision of "home" as an intense site of practically everything. Thinking beyond the atomistic individual we argue that it is through the human and nonhuman, global and local relations that leisure practices are assembled, producing particular affects and meanings in historically specific ways (that plug into related formations involving un/paid work, care, community, consumption etc.) (Deleuze, 1986). Leisure is a multi-scalar phenomenon and not simply constituted in terms of the macro or micro. From this perspective relational power is understood to work through different scales connecting global flows with the micropolitics of gendered patterns in everyday life. Importantly, agentic capacities are not conceptualized as residing "within" individual humans but rather are distributed relationally. The generative force of human and nonhuman "matter" is recognized as an emergent and gendered relation instead of an inherent property or source of agency (Coole & Frost, 2010).

Nowhere has this been clearer than in this current pandemic and the distributed agency at play. Governments and leaders around the world have institutionalized responses to the invisible threat of COVID-19, via new policies with lock-downs, emergency powers and criminalizing seemingly innocuous leisure practices (sitting with another on a park bench for example) (see for example, the Queensland Government's Home Confinement, Movement and Gathering Direction from the Chief Health Officer, Queensland Health, 2020). This "state of exception" creates new legal and political parameters of agentic capacity that intersect with the material and affective conditions we find ourselves in at home.

Gendered homes and affective capacities

Home as a safe place to retreat from contagion is an assumed ideal in many government responses, being for some a privileged location and others a reminder of dispossession, nonbelonging and loss. As an historical site of gendered inequality home is being configured as a new site of enhanced capacity where governments and employers assume a "costless," "largely frictionless" space (and time) for work, leisure, sport, sustenance, care (and childcare), and education (Jenkins, 2020). These shifting boundaries of life alter how we experience home through material and discursive forces, condensing memories, sensory moments and future desires into what Barad (2007) calls *timespacemattering*. Physical distancing measures and digital communication are transforming the social relations of leisure via new ways of becoming "together/apart." As familiar leisure routines disappear, the quickening pulse of anxiety and the painful realization of loss generate different ways of affectively re-organizing everyday life. Such disruptions are not simply gender neutral "behavioural" changes, they are profoundly political and visceral, affecting how we feel, relate and respond in the context of *privatepublic* life enacted via digital media. Small homes or apartments impede movement, large homes with the privilege of gardens provide moments of reprieve and time in nature. There are jobs which can be easily done at home, jobs lost or income reduced, high speed internet connection (or not), mental health challenges and more. Home is profoundly entangled with leisure-work-care-assemblages that reconfigure choices and gendered relations that press upon us in ways that intensify or relieve anxieties.

Ahmed's (2004) writing on the affective economy of fear resonates strongly with our current situation in which the personal is political. She argues that, "emotions play a crucial role in the 'surfacing' of individual and collective bodies through the way in which emotions circulate between bodies and signs" (Ahmed, 2004, p. 117). The home-leisure-work-care-assemblage is a complex multiplicity of emotions, constituted through forces that produce movement and tension. Leisure relations with home are gendered configurations of timespacemattering; experienced as safe (from the virus and contagion) *and* dangerous (from domestic violence, coercive control); stressful (juggling care of young children with domestic work, paid work, self-care and more) and comforting (to be close with those you love during this crisis).

These multiple affects shape agentic capacities for different women with respect to their material and discursive conditions. Losing a job, or losing access to work-place routines, community-based leisure relationships or time spent with or without others can be felt and embodied through a particular kind of dislocatedness or grief (Kalaichandran, 2020). Home confinement thus constitutes self-world relationships anew as immobility is felt through reduced capacity to access leisure sites and sensory connection (cafes only offer takeaway, sports clubs are closed, parks and paths enable movement only for "exercise" at a distance etc.). We are yet to understand the differential impact of collective anxiety arising from living with the constant "threat" of COVID-19 and the loss of agentic capacities in the enactment of leisure lives, or how to respond to the potential trauma as home-world relations shift again.

Gendered contours of a post-COVID world

In wealthy settler nations such as Australia, responses to the gendered risks of COVID-19 have played out in both normative and surprising ways. The conservative male dominated government has engaged in an ideological backflip with new funding allocated to provide free childcare, domestic violence prevention, mental health and increased unemployment benefits, as the state is repositioned as an intervening force in a collapsing global market - the effect of an invisible virus that permeates the borders of bodies and nation states. Yet this support and social infrastructure, has been set to "snap back." Australia's current Prime Minister, Scott Morrison has been clear that the $200 billion or more of special funding will be turned off and life returned to "pre-pandemic normality" post-COVID-19 (Farr, 2020). Yet any return to business as usual is an impossible fantasy, as Barad (2014, p. 9) suggests, a feminist return is a process of renewal, "re-turning – not by returning as in reflecting or going back to a past that was, but re-turning as in turning it over and over again." Notions of "snapping back" or a return to "normal" fail to grasp how affective relations are transforming gendered experiences, environments and social institutions in the COVID-19 world (Fullagar, 2020). Revitalizing leisure lives and services will require a deep appreciation of the affective assemblages that will profoundly shape the gendered contours of public spaces and embodied engagement.

References

Ahmed, S. (2004). Affective economies. *Social Text*, *22*(2), 117–139. https://doi.org/10.1215/01642472-22-2_79-117
Australian Bureau of Statistics. (2020, April 14–17). 4940.0 - Household impacts of COVID-19 survey [webpage]. https://www.abs.gov.au/ausstats/abs@.nsf/Latestproducts/4940.0Main%20Features114-17%20Apr%202020?opendocument&tabname=Summary&prodno=4940.0&issue=14-17%20Apr%202020&num=&view=
Barad, K. (2007). *Meeting the universe halfway: Quantum physics and the entanglement of matter and meaning*. Duke University Press.
Barad, K. (2014). Diffracting diffraction: Cutting together-apart. *Parallax*, *20*(3), 168–187. https://doi.org/10.1080/13534645.2014.927623
Bargetz, B. (2019). Longing for agency: New materialisms' wrestling with despair. *European Journal of Women's Studies*, *26*(2), 181–194. https://doi.org/10.1177/1350506818802474
Braidotti, R. (2013). The posthuman. Cambridge: Polity Press.
Butler, J. (2004). *Precarious life: The powers of mourning and violence*. Routledge.

Coole, D., & Frost, S. (Eds.). (2010). *New materialisms*. Duke University Press.

Deleuze, G. (1986). *Kafka: Toward a minor literature* (Vol. 30). University of Minnesota Press.

Deleuze, G., & Guattari, F. (1987). A Thousand Plateaus, Capitalism and schizophrenia. Minneapolis: University of Minnesota Press.

Farr, M. (2020). Morrison reminds us nothing lasts forever – Especially the coronavirus spending spree. *The Guardian Australia* [online article]. Retrieved April 22, 2020, from https://www.the-guardian.com/australia-news/2020/apr/02/morrison-insists-nothing-lasts-forever-especially-the-coronavirus-spending-spree

Fullagar, S. (2017). Post-qualitative inquiry and the new materialist turn: Implications for sport, health and physical culture research. *Qualitative Research in Sport, Exercise and Health, 9*(2), 247–257. https://doi.org/10.1080/2159676X.2016.1273896

Fullagar, S. (2020, May 6). Recovery and regeneration in community sport: What can we learn from pausing play in a pandemic? *The Machinery of Government, Griffith Policy Innovation Hub.* https://medium.com/the-machinery-of-government/recovery-and-regeneration-in-community-sport-9a217bd70aef

Fullagar, S., O'Brien, W., & Pavlidis, A. (2019). *Feminism and a vital politics of depression and recovery.* Springer.

Fullagar, S., Parry, D., & Johnson, C. (2018a). Digital dilemmas through networked assemblages: Reshaping the gendered contours of our future. In D. Parry, C. Johnson, & S. Fullagar (Eds.), *Digital dilemmas: Transforming gender identities and power relations in everyday life* (pp. 225–244). Palgrave Macmillan.

Fullagar, S., Pavlidis, A., & Francombe-Webb, J. (2018b). Feminist theories after the post-structuralist turn. In D. Parry (Ed.), *Feminisms in leisure studies: Advancing a fourth wave* (pp. 34–57). Routledge.

Gaweda. (2020, April 17). The politics of the missing gender perspective: Responding to the Coronavirus pandemic through parliamentary politics. *EUGENDE Gender, party politics and democracy in Europe: A study of European Parliament's party groups.* Tampere University [online article]. Retrieved April 22, 2020, from https://research.uta.fi/eugendem/the-politics-of-the-missing-gender-perspective-responding-to-the-coronavirus-pandemic-through-parliamentary-politics/

Gearing, A. (2020, April 1). Coronavirus and 'domestic terrorism': How to stop family violence under lockdown, *The Conversation.* https://theconversation.com/coronavirus-and-domestic-terrorism-how-to-stop-family-violence-under-lockdown-135056

Gilson, E. (2014). *The ethics of vulnerability: A feminist analysis of social life and practice.* Routledge.

Graves, J. (2020, April 20). Coronavirus kills up to twice as many men as women and the reason is in ourgenes. *The Conversation.* Retrieved April 22, 2020, from https://theconversation.com/why-do-more-men-die-from-coronavirus-than-women-136038

Haraway, D. (2016). *Staying with the trouble: Making kin in the Chthulucene.* Duke University Press.

Hinton, P., Mehrabi, T., & Barla, J. (2015). *New Materialisms_New colonialisms* (New Materialism. Networking European Scholarship on 'How Matter Comes to Matter', New Materialisms on the Crossroads of the Natural and Human Sciences, position paper). https://doi.org/10.1215/9780822392996

Jenkins, F. (2020, April 4). Did our employers just requisition our homes? *The Canberra Times.* https://www.canberratimes.com.au/story/6701054/did-our-employers-just-requisition-our-homes/

Kalaichandran, A. (2020, April 13). We're not ready for this kind of grief: The coronavirus pandemic will leave lasting emotional scars. *The Atlantic.* https://www.theatlantic.com/ideas/archive/2020/04/were-not-ready-for-this-kind-of-grief/609856/

Kumm, B. E., Berbary, L. A., & Grimwood, B. S. (2019). For those to come: An introduction to why posthumanism matters. *Leisure Sciences, 41*(5), 341–347. https://doi.org/10.1080/01490400.2019.1628677

Lupton, D. (2019). Things that matter': Poetic inquiry and more-than-human health literacy. *Qualitative Research in Sport, Exercise and Health*, 1–16. https://doi.org/https://doi.org/10.1080/2159676X.2019.1690564

Nxumalo, F. (2020). Situating indigenous and black childhoods in the anthropocene. In A. Cutter-Mackenzie-Knowles, K. Malone, & E. Barratt Hacking (Eds.), *Research handbook on childhoodnature: Assemblages of childhood and nature research* (pp. 535–556). Springer.

Parry, D. C., & Johnson, C. W. (2007). Contextualizing leisure research to encompass complexity in lived leisure experience: The need for creative analytic practice. *Leisure Sciences*, *29*(2), 119–130. https://doi.org/10.1080/01490400601160721

Phillips, T. (2020). "So what?": Bolosonara shrugs off Brazil's rising coronavirus death toll. The Guardian [online article]. Retrieved April 29, 2020, from https://www.theguardian.com/world/2020/apr/29/so-what-bolsonaro-shrugs-off-brazil-rising-coronavirusdeathtoll?CMP=fb_gu&utm_medium=Social&utm_source=Facebook&fbclid=IwAR07kPkayKS3RSygHov5M_5ZvTnieICKa-Czyi-WvgIght0ybXCxoCzpU_M#Echobox=1588168827

Queensland Health. (2020). Home confinement, movement and gathering direction, [legislation], effective April 2, 2020. Retrieved April 21, 2020, from https://www.health.qld.gov.au/system-governance/legislation/cho-public-health-directions-under-expanded-public-health-act-powers/home-confinement-movement-gathering-direction

Simpson, B., & Harrell, A. (2007). Rational choice theories. *The Blackwell encyclopedia of sociology*. John Wiley & Sons.

Speers, D. (2020, April 6). Scott Morrison's 'f-word' misread the public mood on the coronavirus pandemic. *ABC News* [online article]. Retrieved April 22, 2020, from https://www.abc.net.au/news/2020-03-15/coronavirus-scott-morrison-footy-next-information-campaign/12054174

Statista. (2020). *Number of COVID-19 cases in Australia April 27, 2020, by age and gender* [webpage]. https://www.statista.com/statistics/1104012/australia-number-of-coronavirus-cases-by-age-group/

Stephenson, E., Harris-Rimmer, S. (2020, March 31). Covid-19 responses: Why feminist leadership matters in a crisis. *The Interpreter*. Lowy Institute. https://www.lowyinstitute.org/the-interpreter/covid-19-responses-why-feminist-leadership-matters-crisis

Thorpe, H., Clark, M., & Brice, J. (2019). Sportswomen as 'biocultural creatures': Understanding embodied health experiences across sporting cultures. *BioSocieties*, 1–21. https://doi.org/10.1057/s41292-019-00176-2

Watene, K. (2020, April 24). Caring for community to beat coronavirus echoes Indigenous ideas of a good life. *The Conversation*. https://theconversation.com/caring-for-community-to-beat-coronavirus-echoes-indigenous-ideas-of-a-good-life

Young, I. M. (1980). Throwing like a girl: A phenomenology of feminine body comportment motility and spatiality. *Human Studies*, *3*(1), 137–156. https://doi.org/10.1007/BF02331805

Adventure in the Age of COVID-19: Embracing Microadventures and Locavism in a Post-Pandemic World

Susan Houge Mackenzie and Jasmine Goodnow

ABSTRACT

Unprecedented mobility restrictions due to COVID-19 have frozen the adventure travel and tourism industry. These restrictions have forced many to embrace 'hyperlocal' approaches to adventure and provided an opportunity to reimagine our adventure travel philosophies and practices. Despite claims that traditional adventure travel could address some of the "world's most pressing challenges", it has largely failed to realize its potential to provide a range of social, economic, and environmental benefits. Conversely, microadventure, which espouses adventures in nearby nature that are low-carbon and human-scaled, is an enticing alternative for both current and post-pandemic conditions. This essay first critiques pre-pandemic adventure travel and describes the hazards of this approach in age of COVID-19. It then explores creative 'lockdown' microadventures; envisions what post-pandemic adventure may look like; and explains why we not only *need* to embrace microadventures in a post-pandemic world, but also why we may *prefer* them to traditional adventure travel.

It is time to reimagine adventure. The COVID-19 pandemic fundamentally questions the importance of discretionary travel for leisure and personal well-being. Prior to recent unprecedented mobility restrictions, adventure travel (e.g., travel to undertake novel, physically challenging activities in remote natural environments) experienced significant growth. This growth was fueled not only by demand from individual's seeking adventure benefits (e.g., nature connection, self-development, well-being), but also by proposed supply-side benefits. Adventure travel was touted for its "vast potential … to address some of the world's most pressing challenges, including socioeconomic growth, inclusive development and environmental preservation" (WTO, 2014, p. 10). Nevertheless, the rationale for extended travel requiring significant equipment, finances, and emissions to fragile environments and communities for personal development is questionable across environmental and social justice fronts. The 'microadventure' movement, which has gained traction in Europe and North America since 2016, emerged in response to these dilemmas. It espouses "adventure that is close to home, cheap, simple, short, and … effective. It still captures the essence of big adventures, the challenge, the fun, the escapism, the learning experiences and the excitement" (Humphreys, 2014, p. 14). This movement reconceptualises adventure from being 'out there' (i.e., remote, time and resource intensive) to 'right here' (i.e., local, attainable) and reflects broader calls for *locavism*: short distance, lower-carbon travel that retains financial and social capital locally (Hollenhorst, Houge Mackenzie & Ostergren, 2014).

COVID-19 has forced many to embrace *locavist* approaches to adventure on the most micro level. Some have rediscovered opportunities for nearby nature-based adventures via human-scaled mobility. In contrast, traditional adventure travel practices in the age of COVID-19 have potentially disastrous outcomes for public health systems, particularly in remote communities. These juxtaposed approaches are epitomized by reports of wilderness areas overrun by visitors seeking remote nature-based adventure at any cost during lockdowns. In addition to seeking adventure in remote areas, the increasing numbers of people seeking refuge from COVID-19 in isolated communities has sparked debates regarding the ethics of tourism in these areas. At the crux of these debates are issues of social responsibility in relation community quality-of-life, the livelihoods of people dependent on tourism, and the rights of second home owners in vulnerable areas. This commentary critiques traditional, pre-pandemic adventure travel in the age of COVID-19 and explores the benefits of microadventures for a post-pandemic world.

Past: pre-pandemic adventure

Pre-pandemic, adventure travel was experiencing significant global growth. The adventure travel industry grew by 195% from 2010 to 2014 and was forecast to grow a further 33% by 2023 (Allied Market Research, 2018; WTO, 2014). While 'adventure' has various academic and popular definitions, uncertainty, skill development, novelty, unique physical and mental challenges (often framed as 'risk'), and natural environments are oft cited elements (e.g., Boudreau et al., 2020). Traditionally, it has also involved extended travel to remote environments and communities (e.g., Rantala, Rokenes, & Valkonen, 2018). Increases in adventure travel were largely driven by the individual benefits attributed to these novel experiences, such as personal transformations; enhanced self-esteem, self-confidence, intrinsic motivation, resilience, and well-being; and, more recently, ecocentric perspectives (e.g., Brymer & Schweitzer, 2013; Ewert & Yoshino, 2011; Houge Mackenzie & Brymer, 2020). Adventure travel was also fueled by desires for escape and liminality, a state of transition characterized by the absence of boundaries, social conventions, and daily constraints (Turner, 1966). As liminality is achieved by either physically entering a novel environment and/or cognitively disconnecting from normal environments and thought processes, the natural environments and immersive activities inherent in adventure are highly conducive to liminality (e.g., Bloom & Goodnow, 2013; Goodnow & Bordoloi, 2017; White & White, 2004).

In addition to promising personal growth, adventure travel was portrayed as an archetype of environmentally sustainable, socially responsible travel amidst the antipathy of mass tourism. This idealized form of travel was promoted on the basis of its triple-bottom line benefits by bolstering local economies, preserving pristine environments, and empowering communities (e.g., Dwyer, 2005; Stoddard, Pollard, & Evans, 2012; WTO, 2014). Despite these utopian ideals, adventure travel has been critiqued for contributing to the very environmental, social and economic issues is purports to mitigate. This type of resource-intensive travel, largely undertaken by well-off Western clients, presents a host of environmental and social justice issues, ranging from commodification of cultural artifacts and destruction of fragile ecosystems, to modern day colonialism (e.g., Williams & Soutar, 2005).

The microadventure movement evolved in response to many issues posed by traditional adventure travel. Microadventures are rewarding short-term adventures completed close to home "in normal places for Normal People" (Humphreys, 2014, pp. 16 17). Allister Humphreys coined this term when, after decades of adventure travel, he began a family and replaced extended, remote adventures with shorter, closer family-friendly adventures that retained the spirit of 'grand adventure' and core benefits, such as liminality, novelty, perspective shifting, and escape. Microadventure concepts and practices, ranging from solo to multi-generational adventures, have since been increasingly embraced across all ages, abilities, and family stages, particularly by time-poor Europeans (Euromonitor, 2016). This approach is more inclusive as it addresses three primary hurdles to traditional adventure (mobility/access, time, and money) and avoids common criticisms such as carbon emissions, damage to unique ecosystems, social disruptions, cultural commodification/exploitation, and economic leakage (e.g., Roberts, 2018; Williams & Soutar, 2005). There is also evidence that microadventures facilitate similar psychological benefits to traditional adventure experiences (e.g., Goodnow & Bordoloi, 2017; Roberts, 2018). Rather than relying on extended durations and exotic environments to achieve traditional adventure benefits, microadventures hinge on activity novelty and participant mindset (e.g., degree to which participants' cognitively or emotionally disconnect from everyday life). Microadventures also exemplify Hollenhorst et al.'s (2014) broader calls for *locavism*: bioregional tourism undertaken close to home. Locavism was proposed as a climate-friendly antidote to fast, high-carbon travel predicated on superficial experiences in long-haul destinations. Critically, this slow, terrestrial travel called for attentional shifts "from distant, exotic places to our own backyards" (p. 314).

Present: adventure in the age of COVID-19

The worldwide pandemic lockdowns in January to May 2020 exponentially accelerated these attentional shifts and brought tensions associated with traditional adventure modes into stark relief. Globally, 91% of the population has experienced restricted movement, ranging from strict (e.g., China, Italy, New Zealand) to more fragmented, *laissez-faire* approaches (e.g., Brazil, USA) (Pew Research, 2020). In the age of COVID-19, traditional adventure travel is not only more difficult, but unethical given the imminent threat it poses to humanity. This is not hyperbole considering government admonitions to refrain from activities involving heightened risks or remote environments, such as backcountry hiking, mountain biking, and water-based activities (e.g., surfing, swimming), in order to avoid straining health systems or exposing emergency responders.

Transmission concerns have also manifested in widespread closures of public parks and forest areas where adventure activities often unfold (e.g., NPS, n.d.).

Ironically, these restrictions have engendered a surge in adventure pursuits despite these activities being prohibited. People are taking refuge from the global crisis by seeking nature and adventure benefits. Media worldwide report unprecedented visitation at national parks and wilderness areas. In the UK, for example, grave concerns were raised over people converging on Snowdonia National Park and the potential devastation this could cause for rural health facilities. Park authorities reported their "busiest ever visitor day in living memory" and that "significant crowding on the mountain summits and trails [made] it impossible to maintain effective social distancing" (BBC, 2020). In the USA, most national parks closed following a flood of visitors coinciding with removal of entrance fees to make it "easier for the American public to enjoy the outdoors." This decision prompted outcry from park staff and condemnation by officials, "Encouraging mass park visitation amid a pandemic is irresponsible and endangers visitors and local communities" (Castleman, 2020). Even top government officials have breached adventure travel guidelines, resulting in removal from office or demotion. Possibly the most glaring of these was committed by the New Zealand Minister of Health who, on separate occasions, drove to undertake mountain biking and beach activities after issuing prohibitions on such activities (Otago Daily Times, 2020). These breaches, often at great personal or potential community costs, underscore the value we place on nature contact and adventure for our well-being and the need to identify sustainable ways of engaging in adventure moving forward.

As lockdowns have extended and restrictions on adventure travel have been clarified or tightened, we have seen creative microadventures flourishing in the most unlikely places. Sierra Club encourages people to explore their backyard, not the backcountry. Local councils promote 'isolation adventures' via webpages with adventure opportunities in nearby nature (e.g., DunedinNZ.com) and urban guidebooks revealing secret pathways connecting neighborhoods to green spaces (e.g., Jaramillo, 2012). Neighborhood 'bear hunts' have sprung up internationally; social media overflows with images of backyard camping; and people are encouraged to "skip the climbing crag and rig a … station in [their] backyard" (Castleman, 2020). On a personal level, the first author has discovered trails around the corner and shifted focus to 'pre-schooler paced' adventures exploring the local stream, identifying birdsongs, and practicing outdoor travel skills with her family 'bubble'. However, the pinnacle of microadventure creativity may be epitomized by parents who built a homemade ski slope descending from their backyard treehouse, complete with pulley ski lift to hoist children atop (Gibbons, 2020).

Future: post-pandemic adventure

The pandemic is teaching us it is time to reimagine adventure. As our mobility and access to adventure travel gradually increase, we cannot forget these important lessons. Microadventures are not a stop-gap novelty 'for (global) emergencies only'. Rather, our vision of adventure places the microadventure philosophy and practices at the heart of post-pandemic adventure. Here we optimistically envision what post-pandemic adventure could look like, and why we may not only *need* to embrace microadventures in a post-pandemic world, but also why we may *prefer* them to traditional adventure travel.

What microadventures will look like. Post-pandemic adventure entails a back-to-basics approach focused on the psychological experience of adventure predicated on human-scaled mobility and locavism. An emphasis on simplicity, personal skill development, immersion in nature, curiosity, and personal insight will facilitate a return to the core of what adventure is about, elements increasingly lost in modern day adventure travel. Rather than pursuing 'more, further, faster' with advanced equipment and technology, adventure can be built around the challenges and uncertainty inherent in self-supported human-powered travel (e.g., biking, rowing/paddling, walking). Locavism and microadventures present opportunities for enhanced community connections in local places by going 'deeper' not further. These approaches retain social, psychological and financial capital for local benefit, something that is lost when community members invest psychological and financial resources in disparate, faraway places.

The pandemic will also help us reconsider the true value and ethics of exoticising far-off lands and peoples, as opposed to creating enduring place attachments in our own communities. Globalization has taught us to view our 'ordinary' neighborhoods as far less worthy of our attentional resources than fanciful distant destinations. Our current restricted mobility may unveil the overlooked natural beauty and wonders in our everyday environments. Indeed, this already seems to be unfolding in wonderfully surprising ways during lockdowns, as evidenced by an outpouring of reports highlighting people's renewed appreciation for, and engagement with, nearby nature (e.g., Hauser, 2020). The secret, understated local spots we never had the time or energy to notice are suddenly of immense value. Small trails or green spaces we never made time to explore, because we were imagining or engaging in 'grander' adventures, are now center-stage in our minds. If the pandemic has done nothing else of value, hopefully it has revealed what our own bioregion has to offer and illustrated that fulfilling adventures can be found much closer than we thought.

For historically disadvantaged populations, restricted mobility has underscored inequities in access to natural areas. People experiencing inequity and limited access to safe greenspace have creatively sought adventure in devalued local places by transforming abandoned churches, rooftops, and streets into *wildscapes* (e.g., Mug, 2012). Rather than romanticizing this creativity born of inequity, these endeavors highlight the importance of ensuring equal access to nature via urban planning and conservation in lower-income and highly urbanized areas. The current crisis underlines the need for greater social, psychological and financial investment in local places, particularly for disadvantaged nieghborhoods, in a post-pandemic world.

Why we need microadventures. While this pandemic may be resolved with a vaccine, climate change will not. Even if we eschew the microadventure approach, in order to mitigate climate change and avoid future pandemics, global travel must change. One clear result of the pandemic is the need to embrace domestic/bioregional travel more than its sought-after, more glamorous cousin: international tourism. The momentum of economics has prevented this shift in many popular adventure destinations, such as Queenstown, New Zealand, touted as the global 'adventure capital' (Destination

Queenstown, n.d.). Queenstown experienced double-digit tourism growth prior to the pandemic, resulting a booming economy coupled with community uproar about visitor impacts (e.g., Jamieson, 2018). This tourism-dependent economy has screeched to a halt in a matter of weeks and the industry has called for a "serious rethink" of tourism to benefit communities and environments, with an emphasis on domestic/regional travel (Littlewood, 2020). The pandemic has done what communities the world over could not: stop economic momentum and unlock the time and space to redesign adventure destinations.

In a post-pandemic world, we envision people adventuring closer to home for a number of reasons. On the supply side, many adventure operators are small-to-medium sized businesses that may not survive travel restrictions and associated economic fallout, resulting in decreased supply of adventure travel options. Governments will be more cautious about incentivising and over-investing in tourism. On the demand side, many people will not have pre-pandemic disposable income levels necessary for traditional adventure travel. They may also worry about health risks of long-haul travel for them or their families. Even for those still seeking traditional adventure travel, global restrictions may dictate significant changes to where, how, and if they can adventure. Emirates Airlines, for example, has implemented on-site COVID-19 testing for all passengers and requires facemasks throughout boarding and flight. In addition, airport kiosks monitoring temperature, heartrate, and respiratory rates are being trialed, and it is predicted that some countries will require COVID-19 certificates and/or two-week quarantines upon arrival for all travelers (Wamsley, 2020).

Why we may prefer microadventures. In addition to these external factors that will drive a microadventure approach post-pandemic, a range of internal factors may also fuel this change. In the age of COVID-19, many people will reprioritise how they spend their time, money, psychic energy, and efforts. The (enforced) opportunities for reflection and contemplation afforded by the pandemic, and subsequent changes in economic and life situations, may create greater awareness of the intrinsic value of our immediate surroundings, of slowing down, of traveling at 'human' speeds. It may also provide more frequent adventure opportunities. Experiencing adventure more often (e.g., weekly), rather than via an extended trip every 6–18 months, may result in more consistent and enduring psychological benefits. These shifts in how we approach the world, and the values we prioritize, may mean we are not only forced to adopt microadventures, but that we may actually prefer them to pre-pandemic adventure.

Proust (1913/1982) long ago articulated a core philosophy underpinning microadventures: *the real voyage of discovery consists not in seeking new landscapes but in having new eyes.* If we shift our frame of reference, we can find adventure closer to home than we imagined. We can enhance well-being and reduce environmental impacts by focusing on microadventure experiences that are close by, low carbon, low consumption, and result in deeper connections to local people and places. If we can learn to seek adventure where we are, rather than in distant places, the outlook for post-pandemic adventure is hopeful.

References

Allied Market Research. (2018). Adventure tourism market overview. Retrieved from https://www.alliedmarketresearch.com/adventure-tourism-market on 24 October 2019.

BBC (2020). Coronavirus: 'Unprecedented' crowds in Wales despite warnings. https://www.bbc.com/news/uk-wales-51994504

Bloom, K., & Goodnow, J. (2013). Insight and the travel experience: An exploration into the contributions of liminality. *Journal of Travel and Tourism Research*, 13(1/2), 143–157.

Boudreau, P., Houge Mackenzie, S. & Hodge K. (2020). Flow states in adventure recreation: A systematic review and thematic synthesis. Psychology of Sport and Exercise, 46, 101611.

Brymer, E., & Schweitzer, R. (2013). Extreme sports are good for your health: A phenomenological understanding of fear and anxiety in extreme sport. *Journal of Health Psychology*, 18(4), 477–487. doi: 10.1177/1359105312446770

Castleman, A. (2020, March 26). Ride out the coronavirus in your backyard, not the backcountry. https://www.sierraclub.org/sierra/ride-out-coronavirus-your-backyard-not-backcountry

Destination Queenstown. (n.d.). *How Queenstown became the adventure capital of the world.* https://www.queenstownnz.co.nz/stories/post/how-queenstown-became-the-adventure-capital-of-the-world/

Dwyer, L. (2005). Relevance of triple bottom line reporting to achievement of sustainable tourism. *Tourism Review International*, 9(1), 79–93. doi: 10.3727/154427205774791726

Euromonitor (2016). *World travel market travel trends report.* https://news.wtm.com/wp-content/uploads/2016/11/GTR-FINAL-FINAL-ok.pdf

Ewert, A., & Yoshino, A. (2011). The influence of short-term adventure-based experiences on levels of resilience. *Journal of Adventure Education & Outdoor Learning*, 11(1), 35–50. doi: 10.1080/14729679.2010.532986

Gibbons, T. (2020, April 12). Dad builds backyard skilift after Easter trip cancellation over coronavirus. https://www.radio.com/news/dad-builds-ski-lift-after-cancelled-easter-holiday

Goodnow, J., & Bordoloi, S, (2017). Travel and insight on the limen: A content analysis of adventure travel narratives. *Tourism Review International*, 21(3), 223–239. doi: 10.3727/154427217X15022104437701

Hauser, C. (2020, April 10). *Quarantined runners log miles in backyards.* https://www.nytimes.com.

Hollenhorst, S. J., Houge Mackenzie, S., & Ostergren, D. M. (2014). The trouble with tourism. *Tourism Recreation Research*, 39(3), 305–319. doi: 10.1080/02508281.2014.11087003

Houge Mackenzie, S., & Brymer, E. (2020). Conceptualizing adventurous nature sport: A positive psychology perspective. *Annals of Leisure Research*, 23(1), 79–91. doi: 10.1080/11745398.2018.1483733

Humphreys, A. (2014). *Microadventures: Local discoveries for great escapes.* Williams Collins.

Jamieson, D. (2018, August 5). It's crunch time for Queenstown - let tourist numbers double, or shut the gate? https://www.stuff.co.nz/business/industries/105768339/its-crunch-time-for-queenstown–let-tourist-numbers-double-or-shut-the-gate

Jaramillo, J. (2012). *Secret stairway walks.* Mountaineer Books.

Littlewood, M. (2020, April 19). Call for serious rethink of New Zealand's approach to *tourism.* https://www.stuff.co.nz/timaru-herald/news/121112865/call-for-serious-rethink-of-new-zealands-approach-to-tourism

Mug, K. (2012). Nature, nurture; danger, adventure; junkyard, paradise: The role of wildscapes in children's literature. In R. Keenan & A. Jorgensen (Eds.), *Urban wildscapes* (pp. 80–96). Routledge.

National Park Service (NPS). (n.d.). *NPS public health update.* https://www.nps.gov/aboutus/news/public-health-update.htm

Otago Daily Times (2020, April 7). *PM on Clark: 'I expect better, so does New Zealand.'* https://www.odt.co.nz/news/national/pm-clark-i-expect-better-so-does-new-zealand

Pew Research (2020, April 1). More than nine-in-ten people worldwide live in countrieswith travel restrictions amid COVID-19. www.pewresearch.org

Proust, M., & Chatto, W. (1982). *Remembrance of things past* (C.K.S. Moncrieff, trans.) (Original publication 1913).

Rantala, O., Rokenes, A., & Valkonen, J. (2018). Is adventure tourism a coherent concept? A review of research approaches on adventure tourism. *Annals of Leisure Research, 21*(5), 539–552. doi: 10.1080/11745398.2016.1250647

Roberts, J. W. (2018). Re-placing outdoor education: Diversity, inclusion, and the microadventures of the everyday. *Journal of Outdoor Recreation, Education, and Leadership, 1*(10), 20–32.

Stoddard, J. E., Pollard, C. E., & Evans, M. R. (2012). The triple bottom line: A framework for sustainable tourism development. *International Journal of Hospitality & Tourism Administration, 13*(3), 233–258.

Turner, V. (1966). *The ritual process: Structure and anti-structures.* Cornell.

Wamsley, L. (2020, April 15). Emirates Airline begins conducting rapid COVID-19 tests for boarding passengers. https://www.npr.org.

White, N. R., & White, P. B. (2004). Travel as transition: Identity and place. *Annals of Tourism Research, 31*(1), 200–218. doi: 10.1016/j.annals.2003.10.005

Williams, P., & Soutar, G. (2005). Close to the "edge": Critical issues for adventure tourism operators. *Asia Pacific Journal of Tourism Research, 10*(3), 247–261. doi: 10.1080/10941660500309614

World Tourism Organisation (WTO) (2014). *Global report on adventure tourism.* Retrieved from https://www.unwto.org/archive/middle-east/publication/global-report-adventure-tourism

The Future is Unwritten: Listening to the Rhythms of COVID-19

Brian E. Kumm, Joseph A. Pate, and Callie S. Schultz (iD)

ABSTRACT

This article asks us to listen critically to the rhythms of our time. COVID-19 has altered the pace and tempo of contemporary life; however, rhythm asks that we engage our moment in ways that account for the seismic shifts in how we live, how we teach and how we learn. We call leisure scholars to listen to the rhythms of our current pandemic, to consider how rhythm may suspend pace, tempo and meter to open space for a reparative leisure and critical appreciation of our current moment. Ultimately, we relate a learning activity whereby students reminded us that we are still alive. We present this learning experience, in candid, honest and vulnerably ways, to encourage our field to rhythmically engage our "new reality" within this pandemic.

"I have no other message than don't forget you are alive"—Joe Strummer (n.d.)

Joe Strummer, the rock "n" roll legend who adopted his moniker from the motion of rhythm guitar players, is a reminder of the type of rhythm we hope to inspire within these pages[1]. Rhythm has nothing whatsoever to do with tempo, meter or pace. In music, that which commonly passes as rhythm—the beat—can become as rigid as a military march. Tempo and pace signal a metered dogmatism, a potential fascism inherent to music that can take us lock-step into the abyss and beyond (cf, Bogue, 2003; Deleuze & Guattari, 1980/2011; Kumm & Johnson, 2017). And we would be wise to take a step back and listen to rhythm during this time. Contrary to meter, "rhythm is critical; it ties together critical moments, or ties itself together in passing from one milieu to another" (Deleuze & Guattari, 1980/2011, p. 314).

Certainly, our current pandemic qualifies as a "critical moment." Rhythm occurs within these moments insofar as particular milieus edge toward intersecting with

---

[1]We celebrate Strummer, the front man for the Clash, not because of the beats-per-minute by which his tunes can be measured (i.e., meter), but by the *immeasurable* social commentary that found voice within his tunes (i.e., rhythm). He pressed the edges of a milieu (e.g., rock "n" roll) to intersect with social commentary and sonic expressions of other milieus (e.g., reggae, ska, rockabilly) and/or chaos (e.g., first wave, punk, hardcore), producing a sonic clash of meanings, relevancy, and rhythm.

incommensurable "others," be they different milieus[2] or chaos[3] (Deleuze & Guattari, 1980/2011). Heterogeneous and predicated upon differential, incommensurable relations, rhythm is expressed, for example, where sea meets shore. The intermixing of two very different milieus produce rhythms in lapping waves and tides. Less prosaically, our various academic milieus, which often pride themselves on "control", now intersect directly with chaos. Meter is expressed as dogmatic attempts to accomplish pre-established outcomes, whereas rhythm *is* the expressed incommensurability between predefined goals and our current situation.

Doubtless, the pace and tempo of life has changed during this pandemic. Bridled with shelter-in-place orders, life seems to have slowed to a snail's pace; yet the changes we are experiencing occur at such a velocity that we can scarcely make sense of them. Some may celebrate this relatively slower pace as leisure; others may lament this condition as being forced upon us. Existing literature certainly indicates that we may default to either position (e.g., Foley, 2017; Havitz, 2007; Lamb, 2019; Rojek, 2001). Yet, neither adequately grasps the seismic magnitude and existential nature of this "critical moment." We not only witness trauma on an unimaginable scale—a scale that may come to define a generation—but also the passage of a way of life into an unimaginable future. Instead of focusing on meter, we wonder what might be gained by listening to rhythm during this time? What might rhythm teach us about our world, our place within it, and what may become of life after this initial crisis is abated?

Over the past several semesters, we have challenged ourselves and the students we serve to engage rhythm in this way, by participating in soundwalks. Since its inception in the 1970s, the definition and practice of soundwalking has shifted to embody our mediated world. Currently, "soundwalking can be understood as research and practice that is not about sound but *in* sound, as well as not about walking but *in* walking. Soundwalking is a spatio-temporal, embodied, situated, multi-sensory and mobile practice." (Behrendt, 2019, p. 251). During this critical moment, soundwalking can serve as a channel for listening to the rhythms of COVID-19, becoming a tool, a way to hear, to understand, to cope.

Our first soundwalk occurred as a partnership between Callie and a musicologist on her predominately white university in the southern United States. Students were challenged to attune their ears to voices, both present and absent, and to consider what the rhythms of their campus taught about social justice. The goal was to critically engage historical oppression, the erasure of non-white voices, experiences and belongings. Walking on campus, students were prompted to critically question which paths, steps and movements were privileged in this historically white space. The resulting assignment then challenged students to create their own stop on a soundwalk of their campus,

---

[2]Although a "milieu" may commonly be defined as a social environment, Deleuze and Guattari (1980/2011) inverted the concept to stem from natural environments. They trace the shape of natural milieus as spaces informed by directional vectors and periodic repetitions occurring among various milieu components. For example, a marine milieu is informed, shaped, by the directional vectors of sunlight, weather patterns and various repetitions of activity occurring between aquatic life and geological structures. When such a milieu comes into contact with another milieu (e.g., land, shore or reef) rhythms occur.

[3]For Deleuze and Guattari (1980/2011), chaos is not an unthinkable blur, void or vacuous absence; rather, they conceptualize chaos as a space consisting of directional vectors from which a point of order may spontaneously emerge (see Bogue, 2003, p. 17). Chaos is better conceived as the presence of every possible order existing simultaneously, prior to any actualization as a virtual potentiality (cf, Massumi, 2002).

where rhythms may be experienced. Students turned in recordings of public spaces where resistance to, or reinforcement of, the status quo took place. While visiting Callie's campus and participating in this soundwalk, Joseph was also drawn to the sounds of the natural environment.

Specifically, he recalled a stop on the soundwalk beneath a sycamore tree. He was drawn to the memories of childhood and the unique crunching sound of sycamore leaves typical in late autumn. He began to wonder what rhythms may be expressed during a soundwalk focusing on the natural world over our human, socially constructed world. During the following semester on the campus of his small, private, liberal arts college in the rural Appalachian Mountains of North Georgia, he prompted his students to listen to the rhythms of natural and wild places. Students were invited to experientially engage rhythms, the presence and absence of non-human "voices" and what these may communicate about the world. Ultimately, this was a gesture and positive step toward environmental justice.

Although Brian, working with Callie and Joseph, planned a soundwalk for students in his community recreation course during the spring of 2020, the critical moment of COVID-19 confronted him with unprecedented, previously unheard rhythms. No longer was this assignment merely a pedagogical experience and exploration; rather, (in hindsight) he found himself "flying blind," in a raw emotional state of vulnerability. He worried about student safety, both emotionally and physically, in asking them to stretch their milieus toward intersecting with other people and spaces. Due to COVID-19, the new rhythm in this third soundwalk was expressed as not only a social and environmental challenge, but also a future-oriented task of finding space for connection despite living at a distance. What do our current rhythms sound out in relation to community?

He intended for students to grapple with different ways of engaging their current "shelter-in-place" spaces through modest acts of listening and walking (e.g., how are you coping, are you mindful, are you understanding, are there moments of resistance?). During an online debriefing session, students reported being comforted by the sounds of birds, disturbed by the sound of silence and stirred by the sounds of families playing, arguing and navigating life during the pandemic. Ultimately, this combination resonant sounds suggested the current rhythms we may all be experiencing during this time are taking the form of intensified feelings of anxiety, uncertainty, as well as hope. On one hand, students questioned what this world, now thoroughly in flux, holds for them as they graduate and enter their chosen careers. On the other hand, students seemed to abide in a hope held open for the world, that somehow it may right itself, despite previous generation's mis/steps.

Exhibiting resiliency and trust grounded in something larger, grander than themselves and their individual quandaries, students' comments reminded Brian of Leopold's (1949) *Marshland Elegy*. His lament was written in mourning over whether Life would sustain itself amidst radically unsustainable and unjust practices. Is there any hope to hold for our world amidst despoliation, degradation and exploitation? These students inspired him; they exhibited a faith he lacked. They remembered that they are alive, that the world is full of life. Death, for Brian, was a foregone conclusion.

If we have a message to convey in these few pages, it is the message of these students, which is the same as Strummer's: "Don't forget that you are alive." Rhythm moves in the opposite direction of the beat—the beat down. Rhythm is open; it can generate a productive clash, shaking us from the beat-down of dogmatic tempo, meter and pace (cf, Deleuze & Guattari, 1980/2011). Whether strumming or walking, modest rhythmic actions hold a potential to suspend dogmatic tempo, attuning our bodies to the critical expressions of milieus edging toward something else. Maybe there we can find faith, hope in our world. Consider John Prine, the mail man who wrote beautiful, affective tunes—often with highlighting the clashing differences of everyday living—while walking his route. If we can cease counting steps and begin listening to where and how they land, perhaps we may find spaces worthy of leisure.

While listening our ears may be piqued by repetitive refrains. "What is, is a refrain," according to Stewart (2010): "A refrain is a worlding. Nascent forms quicken, rinding up like the skin of an orange ... . the expressivity of something coming into existence" (pp. 339–340). The future we hear coming into existence is uncertain, unwritten. Yet, we commit to move in the direction of Strummer—rhythmically engaging the changing nature of this world we are humbled to be a part of. Such a move heightens the impetus of Pieper's (1948/1998) thesis. Consider how he asked us to "recall the things that dominate the contemporary working day," and note that "no special effort of the imagination is needed, for we all stand right in the middle of it ... . tensions and burdens—only superficially eased by hastily arranged pauses and diversions: newspapers, movies, cigarettes" (p. 66). We cannot even begin to count the number of movies we watched or cigarettes we smoked, during this pandemic, much less the volume of "news" we consumed. And there is no reason to belabor his point: during the rebuilding of Europe after the Second World War, we needed a spiritually reparative leisure. We needed, and now need, a leisure not based upon tempo or pace, whether metered as slow or quick, *but that suspends the same to arrive upon a critical rhythm.* This is perhaps as important as pain and suffering as a generator of creativity, if not more so.

Ultimately, we only asked our students (and ourselves) to listen to rhythm, to consider what suspension of tempo may mean for us as we move forward. We did not ask them to create the future. That is too much. And as we settle in for the long haul, meaning we do not foresee an end to our "new normal" on the immediate horizon, let us not mistake the disease for the cure (Kleiber, 2000). When we look back over this time, what will we say to our students, to those yet-to-come? Rhythm beckons us to build a future honoring generations-to-come by a "sort of 'dreaming forward,' ... an anticipatory virtue that permeates our lives and activates them .... a powerful motivating force grounded in our collective imagining indeed" (Braidotti, 2010, p. 217). This is the hard part, to catch a rhythm and listen (Lashua & Fox, 2006). The expressivity of our ways of living beckons our engagement.

As we begin to imagine our future and what leisure may hold for us, we wonder whether our discipline will catch the changing rhythms. It is a valuable place to start. Whether strumming, walking and/or listening, "the times they are a-changin'" (Dylan, 1964). We continue to listen to the rhythm of our times, and we ask you to listen as well. What will it speak to us about our current conditions and the world we find ourselves within, as well as the one we endeavor to create for the future?

Listen.

ORCID

Callie S. Schultz (iD) http://orcid.org/0000-0002-6298-8881

References

Behrendt, F. (2019). Soundwalking. In M. Bull (Ed.), *The Routledge companion to sound studies* (pp. 249–257). Routledge.

Bogue, R. (2003). *Deleuze on music, painting, and the arts.* Routledge.

Braidotti, R. (2010). The politics of "life itself" and new ways of dying. In D. Coole & S. Frost (Eds.), *New materialisms: Ontology, agency, and politics.* (pp. 201–218). Duke University Press.

Deleuze, G., & Guattari, F. (2011). *A thousand plateaus: Capitalism and schizophrenia.* (B. Massumi, Trans.). University of Minnesota Press. (Original work published 1980 by Les Editions de Minuit, Paris).

Dylan, B. (1964). The times they are a-changin. [Record]. United States, Columbia.

Foley, C. (2017). The art of wasting time: Sociability, friendship, community and holidays. *Leisure Studies, 36*(1), 1–20. https://doi.org/10.1080/02614367.2015.1055296

Havitz, M. (2007). A host, a guest, and our lifetime relationship: Another hour with grandma Havitz. *Leisure Sciences, 29*(2), 131–141. https://doi.org/10.1080/01490400601160754

Kleiber, D. (2000). The neglect of relaxation. *Journal of Leisure Research, 32*(1), 82–86. https://doi.org/10.1080/00222216.2000.11949891

Kumm, B. E., & Johnson, C. W. (2017). Subversive imagination: Smoothing space for leisure, identity, and politics. In K. Spracklen, B. Lashua, E. Sharpe, & M. B. Swain (Eds.), *Palgrave handbook of leisure theory* (pp. 891–910). Palgrave.

Lamb, D. (2019). Taking it day-by-day: An exploratory study of adult perspectives on slow living in an urban setting. *Annals of Leisure Research, 22*(4), 463–483. https://doi.org/10.1080/11745398.2019.1609366

Lashua, B., & Fox, K. (2006). Rec needs a new rhythm cuz rap is where we're livin. *Leisure Sciences, 28*(3), 267–283. https://doi.org/10.1080/01490400600598129

Leopold, A. (1949). *A sand county Almanac.* Oxford University Press.

Massumi, B. (2002). *Parables for the virtual: Movement, affect, sensation.* Duke University Press.

Pieper, J. (1998). *Leisure, The basis of culture.* St. Augustine's Press. (Original work published 1948).

Rojek, C. (2001). Leisure and life politics. *Leisure Sciences, 23*(2), 115–125. https://doi.org/10.1080/014904001300181701

Stewart, K. (2010). Afterword: Worlding refrains. In M. Gregg & G. J. Seigworth (Eds.), *The affect theory reader* (pp. 339–353). Duke University Press.

Advice for Leisure Studies: Reflections on the Pandemic From a Retired Professor

Diane M. Samdahl

ABSTRACT

The author, a retired leisure studies professor, interweaves stories of her own experience with reflections about the field of leisure studies during early stages of the coronavirus pandemic.

I am old. Or *elderly* as public officials call me, reminding me daily that I am at increased risk of complications from COVID-19. The polite word used to be *senior* which I much preferred. In reality, my age and health are no different than they were a few months ago but the world around me has drastically changed. And, I'll admit, the passing years have given me a welcomed perspective (dare I call it *wisdom*?) that I lacked when I was younger. Before I retired.

Contrary to popular expectations, the biggest benefit that retirement offers right now is security. I realize how privileged I am to have continuing income when so many of my neighbors do not. I cannot be laid off. I will not lose monthly income and health insurance, at least not until the American government undercuts Social Security and Medicare. And though I don't have a pension, my private 403(b) can ride out the declining stock market for a few months. Best of all, I have learned to live frugally. The media wants to label me *at risk* but I feel more secure than most Americans. Some risks are more insidious than others.

I felt most vulnerable when the coronavirus first began spreading in the United States, before we knew very much about it. Early reports described it as a disease that killed the elderly. I'll admit that was a bit unsettling, especially knowing how quickly it could strike. I reexamined my will and updated my advance health care directive. I wrote out instructions for the care of my pets and assembled what I might need if I were taken to the hospital. I thought a lot about mortality. But that fear of becoming victim diminished as the pattern of contagion took shape in the United States, striking hardest in cities a thousand miles away from where I live. Data showed that an increasing number of deaths were among the healthy young adults and that eased the feeling of having a target on my back. Rather than age, reports began to emphasize the risks of preexisting medical conditions and focused on the dangers of crowds and close contact. Nursing homes that housed the frail elderly were definitely at high risk but so were factories and crowded prisons (and we may never know what happened inside the crowded immigrant detention camps). I began to relax as I understood that age alone did not put me at risk; the answers are more complicated. I began to focus instead on what I could control: washing my hands and staying home.

Like everybody else, I was horrified at how quickly the coronavirus ripped apart my world, knowing all the while that the impact on my retired life was minimal compared to the havoc it wreaked on others. The exercise center closed first, cutting me off from the lovely heated pool where I regularly swam. That facility was located in a retirement center and the staff had to ban all outsiders to protect the residents. Then my continuing education classes were canceled; these are special interest topics (e.g., mystery writers of the 1950s) that mostly attract retirees with unquenchable curiosity; I've been taking one or two a semester to keep from becoming a hermit. I wasn't affected much when stores and restaurants closed but the enormity of the pandemic became apparent when community gatherings were banned. The Broadway show *Wicked* was in town; it closed abruptly on Thursday and I held a ticket for Sunday's canceled performance. But what shocked me most was seeing a queue outside the grocery store; a guard with a counter stood at the door, admitting only a few customers at a time. I was relieved when grocers announced that the first hour in the morning (when stores are the cleanest) would be reserved for seniors. Unfortunately, this was 7:00 to 8:00 a.m. at most stores but I found one that didn't open until 10:00 a.m. Now I can sleep late and still be the first to shop, a privilege of my age.

In repeated messages about public safety, officials ask people to check on their elderly neighbors. That makes me uneasy. I suspect I'd be offended if a stranger showed up at my door to see how I was doing, as if I am not capable of getting by on my own, as if they saw me as old. But deep inside, it also bothers a bit that no one has stopped by to ask.

Staying home, alone

"Which is worse," a friend posted on Facebook, "being isolated at home by yourself or being constantly with your family?" Like me, she is retired and lives alone. Those of you who live with others still have daily face-to-face interactions, you have someone to talk to, but those of us who live alone do not. It's a totally different experience when staying home means always being by yourself. I talk to my pets a lot. During the first week of lockdown I took seriously the stay-at-home order and ventured no further than my yard. That total isolation quickly became painful and by the second week I was driving around town just to reassure myself that the world was still there. My car (another privilege) has been an antidote to living alone.

So has my computer. The internet is my lifeline, perhaps better than a roommate. I spend my days researching the news, streaming video and reading e-books from the local library. Most importantly, I reach out to friends through Facebook and other social media, and share virtual happy hour with people in different states. I suspect this aspect of my life is no different than yours.

But I have some friends, also retired, who have never gone online. They don't have Wi-Fi and don't use the data plan on their phones. With libraries now closed and the town shut down, their only diversion is television. It makes me realize that my experience with isolation is quite different than what others may feel. I also have a friend who doesn't drive. Public buses are dangerous right now and are running reduced routes. I want to offer help, to drive her to a grocery store so she can shop for heavy items, but I'm afraid to have her sit next to me in the car. She doesn't keep strict isolation like I do; she visits neighbors and shops several times a week. Though I said earlier that I don't feel vulnerable to COVID-19, my reluctance to drive this friend to the store proves me wrong.

In spite of the ways that social distancing has disrupted our lives, the coronavirus crisis has opened new opportunities. Once or twice a week I find myself thinking about someone I haven't seen in a long time—an old friend or a former student—and reach out by email. The uncertainty of the present makes these old relationships more important. I've begun exploring trails in a nearby nature preserve and discovered a lake I didn't know existed. And there's a growing community spirit: The Little Library in a neighbor's front yard now has canned goods and toiletries in addition to books, free for whoever stops by. I donated bags of leftover Halloween candy to unemployed parents who wanted treats for their children's Easter baskets, and I claimed a handmade face mask from a basket of masks that someone set out on their sidewalk. There are good lessons to learn from this crisis if we are open to them.

But those lessons won't solve the real problem. On the news I see unemployed workers who fear losing their homes and healthcare. I see "essential" workers who risk contracting the virus because they lack facemasks. I see undocumented families who, already living hard lives, will not qualify for unemployment and government stimulus checks. White-collar workers aren't much better off, working from home without the support services their workplace had provided. Our systems of employment, healthcare, childcare, education, housing and food security have all simultaneously failed, illuminating the vulnerable façade that we have been living. The crisis and its solutions are structural; kindness to others might ease the transition but it will not solve the underlying problems.

Reactions in higher education

Against that backdrop, I was appalled to read comments on the Chronicle for Higher Education's Facebook page[1] created as a forum for faculty and staff to discuss impacts of the coronavirus. As campuses moved classes online, that page was filled with expected questions about software, debates about synchronous versus asynchronous classes and concerns about online privacy. But faculty also sought advice for appropriate penalties on late homework, debated whether they should fail students who did not show up for live online classes, and shared a deep concern about monitoring students

---

[1]https://www.facebook.com/groups/higheredandcoronavirus/

during at-home exams (facial recognition? eye tracking software?). I wanted to yell at them, Get your head out of the sand! Take a good look at the world your students have returned to and understand the loss of their dreams and aspirations. Their lives are uprooted, our country is shut down, and you are concerned about cheating on your test?! Let me assure you, those students have more to worry about than your class.

Dear reader, I hope that wasn't you. I also hope you understand my absolute relief at being retired and not having to face the difficult work that you do every day.

You work hard to prepare students for their careers; you've committed yourselves to their well-being and you are still abiding by accreditation standards. None of you signed up for this but you have bravely stepped up to the task: over one weekend, or perhaps over spring break, you moved eight weeks of coursework into an online format (faculty used to be given a semester release to do work like that). Then you moved into an office at home, or perhaps cleaned a corner of your kitchen table to create workspace, and continued to teach. The saints among you reached out to students who needed emotional support, and those who are parents picked up the added task of home-schooling their own children. You are heroes. You've taken multi-tasking to unforesee-able new heights. Like a horse with blinders on, you've stayed focused on the path ahead.

I'm worried about your enslavement to work. Have you allowed yourselves time to mourn for all that's been lost? Do you even *see* how the world will be different once this is over?

After I retired I understood that I'd simply been a cog in the wheel and that my pro-gram, my field, would move on without me, quite likely in a direction I had fought to resist. I saw how foolishly I had believed in my own importance and how I gave too much of myself for the work of the university. And now, in this crisis, I see my col-leagues collectively drinking that same Kool-Aid, sacrificing themselves more and more to work that "has to be done." No, my friends, it does not. Cancel classes, give students a Pass, and take time to collectively grieve. The known world has already collapsed and your frantic efforts will not revive it. And later, once you've gained a better perspective, let's change the social structures that have so painfully failed us.

Advice for leisure studies

When I retired, the most difficult question people asked was "What are you doing now?" I struggled to find an answer they could accept. I felt like I had moved out of the world of *doing*, where time was filled with activity, and existed instead in the realm of *being*. I lived in the moment. I nurtured relationships and fed the birds. I slept late and took naps in the sun. It was hard to explain this without sounding lazy, or maybe I truly had become lazy. I sidestepped their judgment by simply saying, "I'm reading a lot."

The foundational values of our society are tied to a belief in the goodness of work, in the action of being busy. This was a focal point in the graduate classes I taught where we read deGrazia, Dumazedier, Marx, Veblen and others. Collectively, those theorists and social commentators revealed how leisure emerged against the backdrop of indus-trialization. They showed how our work ethic shapes the ways we act and even the language that forms our thoughts. We *are* workers. But my favorite theorist was Josef Pieper (Pieper, 1952) who described a different way of being in the world. Rather than relying on the logical and analytical parts of our brain, Pieper called on us to relax into a richer type of experience. He wanted us to downplay the value of *doing* and replace it with *being*. He called that *leisure* which he equated with living in harmony; living in prayer. I'm not there yet but retirement has brought me closer.

I had intended to end this essay with a call for change. After pointing out systemic failure in our social systems and observing how faculty are running faster and faster on the treadmill, I wanted to anoint you as soldiers in that battle. In an earlier draft of this essay I wrote: "Who are we, the field of leisure studies and services, if we cannot rise above this? We, of all fields, should understand that the answer does not come from working harder within systems that enslave us. Let's fight for a society where everyone has value, not by nature of their employment but by the simple fact of their existence. Let's work toward a culture where everyone can have a rich life fully lived." But that's no longer where my heart is. I'll leave it to younger faculty and students to bear that torch (if you chose to do so) and instead I'll end with a gentler comment.

The crisis brought on by the coronavirus shows us that leisure is important. Even in isolation, people create ways to be together. They've retrieved board games from the back of their closets and play together as a family. In cities where they're allowed to go out, people are taking walks again and rediscovering parks. And from the isolation of homes in different towns, they're laughing together through real-time video chat. It's important that we see this, and that we value the ways that leisure exists independent of the recreation programs and facilities our field provides. We need to ask ourselves how that understanding will change the ways we serve our communities after this crisis is over.

And to my friends working in higher education, this is a surreal moment in history. Don't give your life away to the demands of campus, attempting to cling to normal. Rely on your knowledge of leisure to separate yourself from work and focus only on those tasks you find rewarding. Maybe you most enjoy relationships with students—I hope that's the case. If so, then do that and let everything else slide. In the long run things will be okay, even if you step back from all your effort and simply let yourself *be*.

Reference

Pieper, J. (1952). *Leisure: The basis of culture* (A. Dru, Trans.). Pantheon Books Inc.

Index

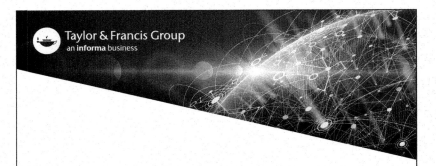